Irish Employment Relations in the New Economy

Edited by

Daryl D'Art
UNIVERSITY OF LIMERICK

and

Thomas Turner
UNIVERSITY OF LIMERICK

BLACKHALL
Publishing

This book was typeset by Gough Typesetting Services for

Blackhall Publishing
27 Carysfort Avenue
Blackrock
Co Dublin
Ireland

e-mail: blackhall@eircom.net
www.blackhallpublishing.com

ISBN: 1 842180 33 9

A catalogue record for this book is available from the British Library.

Printed in Ireland by
ColourBooks Ltd

*In
memory
of my beloved wife
Anne
(1945–1997)*

Contents

SECTION 2

Foreword

The involvement of trade unions in macro-economic policy making is back on the intellectual and political agenda. After falling out of favour under the impact of neo-liberal philosophy and practice, unions are re-emerging as key political actors in national tripartite arrangements, variously described as social pacts (in Spain), concertation (in Italy) and social partnership (in Ireland). The Irish experiment is particularly interesting for a number of reasons: it began in 1987, during the heyday of neo-liberal governments in Britain and the USA, and thus marked a radical departure from the labour relations trajectories mapped out by the Thatcher and Reagan administrations. It has also been associated with a remarkable rate of economic growth, and a correspondingly dramatic fall in unemployment, to the extent that Ireland soon became known as the "Celtic Tiger". Yet, in recent years it has become increasingly clear that there are losers as well as winners in the emerging system of industrial relations. Union density for example has continued to decline whilst the influence exercised by unions at the workplace has failed to match the rhetoric of partnership and involvement. Equally worrying is the persistence of a substantial pool of very low paid jobs.

A comprehensive, detailed and critical analysis of the "new industrial relations" in Ireland is long overdue and this book makes an outstanding contribution to that task. Embracing industrial relations at both national and local level and covering the non-union as well as the unionised sectors, it presents an enormous array of both qualitative and quantitative data in order to assess the character and significance of the Irish experiment in social partnership. Critics of partnership will perhaps take more comfort from the book than advocates, but everybody will find here a wealth of data and analysis to inform serious and wide-ranging debate. This is certain to become the key reference point in debates on the subject for many years to come.

John Kelly,
London School of Economics,
December 2001.

Acknowledgements

We would like to thank all our colleagues in the Department of Personnel and Employment Relations at the University of Limerick for their collegiality and support in the preparation of this book. In particular, Patrick Flood, Patrick Gunnigle and Joseph Wallace for helpful and insightful comments on many of the chapters.

Section 1

Chapter 1

Industrial Relations in the New Economy

Daryl D'Art and Thomas Turner

Ireland's industries would enjoy the full advantages of free trade only if workmen were restrained in their demands for higher wages, compelled to accept new methods of production and persuaded to adopt a more conciliatory attitude towards their employers.

Irish Manufacturers 1779[1]

INTRODUCTION

It may be a feature of the turn of a millennium that utopian, dystopian and millenarian ideas tend to flourish. In the last millennium Christian millenarian movements promised or expected total social change through miraculous means. Contemporary secular variants such as post-industrialism, post-capitalism and post-modernism apparently hold out a similar prospect. However, in their case, knowledge and its associated information technology have replaced divine agency. Indeed, the idea that the global economy is on the eve of or actually engaged in a process of fundamental and radical change is pervasive. All areas of social, economic and political life are expected to undergo a revolutionary transformation constituting a total break with the old order. Nevertheless, some commentators are sceptical regarding the nature, extent and depth of this change. The object of this book is to examine the effect of this change on the nature of Irish employment relations.

In this introductory chapter we briefly describe the "golden era" of managed capitalism which began after 1945, its crisis in the 1980s and the emergence of what many have identified as a new economic order. We consider the post-industrial/post-Fordist/end-of-class interpretations and evaluate the arguments for fundamental change and the arrival of a new economic, social and political order. These arguments provide the context for the contributions in this book which explore many of the critical issues in contemporary employment relations in Ireland.

---

1. Quoted in Boyd (1976: 19).

MANAGED CAPITALISM

In the aftermath of World War II, economists across the political spectrum were almost unanimous in predicting that capitalism would re-enter a massive slump equal to or worse than that of the 1930s (Sutcliffe, 1983). Events were to confound the pessimists: by 1950 capitalism had embarked upon a generation of expansion unequalled in its history. More goods were produced between 1950 and 1975 than in the previous 75 years and, indeed, many more times than in any comparable period in human history (Armstrong et al., 1984: 167).

There were a number of significant features associated with this period (Armstrong et al., 1984). First, a broad political consensus which involved the acceptance of a mixed economy combining a capitalist framework which allowed state enterprise and state management of the economy. The state had a substantial direct involvement in economic activity through the control and management of a number of large commercial and service companies. Secondly, the provision by the state of welfare benefits and the application of Keynesian demand management policies to maintain high levels of employment. During the 1960s an increasing proportion of government income was spent on social welfare and during the 1970s various governments attempted to use Keynesian-type policies to reduce unemployment and stimulate economic activity. Thirdly, employee relations based on a negotiated order which involved recognition and negotiation with trade unions.

However, conditions of labour scarcity strengthened the relative power of union organisation at the workplace and there was a higher incidence of industrial conflict. Increasingly, unions became involved in policy making at government level, most notably, in those countries with bargained corporatist arrangements. One outcome of these arrangements was the promotion by governments and unions of schemes of indirect power-centered employee participation such as worker directors and works councils.

To what extent did Ireland fit this model of industrial society in this period? A review of the evidence and trends would appear to confirm a broad convergence of the Irish experience with the general trends in the industrialised world. Output in Irish manufacturing, for example, increased in the same period by a factor of approximately six (Turner and Morley, 1995: 16). From 1950 to 1970 there were a number of general wage rounds and after 1970 a number of national wage agreements became the dominant means for regulating pay increases tied to the cost of living and productivity increases at firm level. During this period union membership and density increased consistently from 28 per cent in 1945 to 62 per cent by 1980. Trade unions were perceived as legitimate organisations representing the interests of workers. As a consequence, union recognition became less difficult (see Flood and Turner, 1993). At plant level, industrial relations was the chief concern of personnel managers (Gunnigle and Flood, 1995). There were few cases of disputes over union recognition since the prevailing industrial relations climate stressed the legitimacy of collective bargaining as the mode of regulation between employees and employers. Indeed, multi-national companies establishing in Ireland were required by the Industrial Development Authority to recognise a union to represent employees (see Gunnigle at al., this volume, Chapter 10).

Table 1.1: Union Membership and Density in Ireland, 1945–1980

Year	Union Membership	Union Density
1945	172,300	27.7%
1965	358,000	52.4%
1980	527,200	61.8%

Source: Roche and Larraghy, 1989.

This era of stable, managed capitalism between 1954 and 1973 led many to believe that slumps and class antagonisms had been permanently transcended (Dahrendorf, 1959). The various institutions which supported the system appeared as fixed and enduring features of social and economic life. Government direct intervention in the economy and the provision of a welfare system guaranteeing a minimum income needed for subsistence remained generally uncontested throughout the industrialised world. As Crosland (1956: 61) noted, "any government which tampered with the basic framework of the full employment welfare state would meet with a sharp reversal at the polls". By 1970, even a republican president of the United States could announce "we are all Keynesians now" (Green and Sutcliffe, 1987: 339). A minority of economists of a monetarist persuasion who had never accepted the Keynesian orthodoxy of demand management were either marginalised or ignored.

However, the solidity of this compromise was undermined by a number of events which began with the first oil shock of 1973. According to Castells (1996: 19), the Keynesian model, which had brought three decades of "unprecedented economic prosperity", ran into increasing difficulties in the early 1970s. The crisis of the system was manifested in the form of rampant inflation, rising unemployment, falling productivity and profit rates. Governments and firms reacted by engaging in a process of reforming and restructuring the system.

Castells (1996) identified a series of reforms, both at the level of institutions and in the management of firms, undertaken by governments aimed at four main goals: deepening the capitalist logic of profit seeking in capital labour relations; enhancing the productivity of labour and capital; globalising production and markets to seize the most advantageous conditions for profit making everywhere and, lastly, the organisation of state support for competitiveness and productivity gains. Yet, it is arguable to what extent these goals represented a new departure. Capital has always sought to enhance the productivity of labour. Since 1945, at any rate, many governments have actively intervened in the market to support capital with grants, subsidies and favourable tax regimes.

BEYOND INDUSTRIAL SOCIETY: THE POST-INDUSTRIAL THESIS AND THE NEW ECONOMY

Soskice (1999) identifies two critical factors which have impacted on the advanced industrial societies since the 1980s: the liberalisation of external product markets and the development of the microprocessor which, he argues, has resulted in a technological paradigmatic shift. As a consequence of the liberalisation of markets, tariffs, subsidies and other forms of protectionism are no longer practicable or possible; companies are free to locate where they wish and financial and exchange markets are open. In the latter case, the openness of financial markets has seriously curtailed the viability of Keynesian economic policies and exposed a growing number of domestic sectors to international competition. The internationalisation of finance has freed private capital from national ties and allowed it to seek out the most profitable opportunities in the international economy.[2]

Since the 1970s, the development of new production technologies and the electronic revolution in data processing and communications technology are perceived to have brought about fundamental change in production systems and occupational structures. As a consequence of these changes, in particular, the pace of development in information technology, a number of commentators have claimed that a substantial, if not revolutionary, change in the nature of economic and social activity is occurring. A variety of theories under the rubric of post-industrialism have emerged to describe this new society or coming society (Kumar, 1995).

Three perspectives can be identified in the literature on post-industrial society that have featured prominently in the analysis of change in industrial organisations and society. One perspective emphasises the centrality of knowledge and information in the emergence of a new economy. The rapid development of information technology has infused new life into Daniel Bell's (1976) thesis of a new society based on information as the governing principle of economic activity. Castells (1996: 19), for example, argues that the new information technology was "absolutely critical in ensuring the speed and efficiency" of capital restructuring allowing organisations to be adaptable and flexible.

A second perspective emphasises the end of hierarchical Fordist-type production of goods and services. In the post-Fordist scenario information technology and the search for profitability together are perceived to be creating new forms of work organisation and new relations in the workplace. Both of these approaches are premised on fundamental structural changes in the economy as the driving force of change. The post-industrial information thesis posits that the forces of production have changed radically: the production of goods, which was central to industrialised society, is being replaced by the

---

2. According to Kitschelt et al. (1999: 446) this has led to a shift in bargaining power from labour and political parties to private capital.

production of knowledge and information. Post-Fordism stresses that fundamental changes in the relations of production have occurred which significantly alter industrial organisations and the relations between capital and labour.

A third perspective focuses on the political and ideological shifts in the advanced industrial societies since the 1970s. This perspective stresses the emergence of the new right and the end of collective solidarities and social classes. Below we address these perspectives in greater detail.

POST-INDUSTRIAL SOCIETY AND THE INFORMATION REVOLUTION

According to Bell (1976), industrial societies are entering a new phase of their evolution, a post-industrial era. The axial principle or driving force of change is the centrality of theoretical knowledge as a source of innovation and policy making. Theoretical knowledge rather than labour becomes the source of value and growth. Knowledge and information become the means, not only in service but also manufacturing, for adding increased value and in the process become the strategic resource and transforming agent of the post-industrial society (Kumar, 1995). What are the manifestations of this transformation to a post-industrial society? Three predictions or statements can be analytically differentiated (Castells, 1996: Chapter 4).

1. The source of productivity and growth lies in the generation of knowledge that is increasingly extended by information technology to all economic activity.

2. A shift in economic activity from goods to services, a decline in agricultural employment followed by an irreversible decline in manufacturing employment. Ultimately, service jobs would form the overwhelming proportion of employment.

3. Occupations with a high information and knowledge content in their activity would become increasingly important. Managerial, professional and technical jobs would grow faster than any other occupations and would constitute the core of the new social structure. Bell (1973) predicted a general upgrading of the occupational structure with a shift to professional and white-collar work. The majority of the population would be in the middle grouping and a new professional and technical élite would emerge replacing the propertied élite.

The first prediction, that the generation of knowledge is the source of productivity and growth, is open to the criticism that knowledge and technology have in fact been central to industrialised societies throughout the 20th century. Thus, the more rapid extension of knowledge through information technology is merely a maturation of industrial society rather than reflecting a qualitative

or fundamentally new principle. Aside from these observations, it is difficult
to verify at the empirical level the extent of the linkage between the various
concepts. Indeed, it is not clear what evidence would be required to falsify the
premise that knowledge is a new axial principle in post-industrial society.

Both the second and third predictions are more amenable to empirical
scrutiny. There has been a radical shift in economic activity to the service
sector in all of the advanced economies. In Ireland, the services sector has
grown significantly while employment in agricultural and manufacturing has
declined since 1970 (Table 1.2).

Table 1.2: Sectoral Changes in Employment

Year	Agriculture	Industry	Services	Total Labour Force
1951	41%	23%	36%	1,217,000
1970	27%	30%	43%	1,053,000
1991	14%	28%	58%	1,121,000

Source: Labour force survey, CSO.

Similarly, the proportion of managerial, professional and technical occupations
has increased as a proportion of the labour force. Between 1975 and 1996,
excluding agriculture workers, the proportion of professional/technical workers
increased from 14.5 per cent to 20.7 per cent of the labour force (Labour Force
Survey, 1975, 1996). Conversely, labourers and unskilled workers decreased
from 7.5 per cent in 1975 to 3.4 per cent of the labour force by 1996. Similarly,
manual, skilled and semi-skilled producers, makers and repairers decreased
from 28.3 per cent to 22.8 per cent of the labour force.

Is it plausible to extrapolate this trend into a future where low-level, routine
jobs are automated and replaced by new more creative jobs? Information society
theorists argue that these trends are evidence of the rise of a new class of
knowledge worker whose work is characterised by high levels of technical
skill and theoretical knowledge which require long periods of education and
training (Kumar, 1995: 25). However, Kumar (1986, 1995) outlines three
arguments that contest this trend. First, while there is evidence of considerable
upskilling over time there are also examples of deskilling, particularly in skilled
manual occupations. Furthermore, Taylorism and scientific management
remain important methods in industrial and commercial organisations. In
practice firms continuously attempt to simplify and cheapen labour in order to
reduce labour costs and relieve employers' dependency on scarce or skilled
labour.

Secondly, the growth of credentialism – demanding higher qualifications
for the same jobs – and the inflation of job titles (for example plumbers as

heating engineers) can give a misleading impression of the actual growth of the knowledge society.

Thirdly, there is an expectation of the continued growth and expansion of the knowledge worker. However, much of the evidence suggests that the growth in occupations over the last two decades has occurred not in the knowledge area but in the lower tertiary sector of the economy, in the services and retail sectors where the skill and knowledge requirements are not particularly high (Kumar, 1995: 26–27). For example, the tourism sector in Ireland accounted for 43 per cent of the total employment growth during the period 1986 to 1994 and, while some of this employment is of a reasonable quality, Deegan and Dineen (1997:102–103) estimate that about 50 per cent of the total "comprises precarious forms of employment – part-time, seasonal and casual – with limited career paths and prospects for progression".

FROM FORDISM TO POST-FORDISM?

As we have seen, the decade of the 1980s was characterised by intensifying international competition, economic turbulence and instability exacerbated by rapid technological change. Some writer argued that these developments heralded a major change in the production regime and constituted a crisis of Fordism (Piore and Sabel, 1984). Production on Fordist lines used dedicated machinery, moving assembly lines and employed unskilled or semi-skilled workers engaged in fragmented tasks under tight labour discipline. The advantages of mass production in large factories producing a high volume of standardised goods were economies of scale and low unit costs. However, its continuing success depended on the existence of stable mass markets and growing consumer demand for its standardised products. Yet, there were at least two defects inherent in the Fordist system of production. The most obvious was that its method of work organisation seemed to be universally associated with industrial pathologies such as low levels of job satisfaction, casual absenteeism, sabotage, theft and workplace conflict generally (Theobold, 1994: 145). These problems had been the concern of management thinkers since Elton Mayo, though the various remedies applied had at best varying levels of success. A second less obvious defect of the Fordist production system was its inability to respond quickly to changes in demand or to stimulate variable demand (Madry and Kirby, 1996). It was this latter defect according to some commentators that became increasingly evident during the 1980s.

Competition and the supposed increase in consumer demand for high quality customised products led to the fragmentation of mass markets for standardised products. Those firms with sufficient flexibility to engage in small-batch or customised production were consequently less vulnerable while producers of standardised products faced greater competition from low cost economies particularly in the area of labour costs. Indeed, it has been suggested that during the 1970s and 1980s both firms and national economies that were capable of offering more diverse and customised products fared better than the more traditional producers of standardised mass products (Streeck, 1992). According to Piore and Sabel (1984) these developments amounted to a second industrial revolution. With the decline of Fordism a new form of manufacturing organisation was emerging whose novelty would embrace both the methods and relations of production (Piore and Sabel, 1984).

The new technology, particularly computerisation and numerically controlled machine tools allowed for the economic production of small batches of goods directed to specialised sections of the market. It became possible for small firms operating the new tools to make speedy and inexpensive changes in output in response to demand for more variety, individuality and innovation in consumer goods. Flexible technology gives rise to flexible specialisation. Production is customised to highly specific wants and needs, which are in a constant state of flux (Kumar, 1995: 43–44; Abercrombie et al., 1994: 167).

It is predicted that these new methods of production will also affect the relations of production. Flexible specialisation demands skill and flexibility in the workers as much as in the machines (Kumar, 1995: 44). Consequently, the deskilling characteristic of Fordism will be reversed as employees are re-skilled. With more freedom and discretion for employees, jobs are likely to become more satisfying. Furthermore, wages are likely to rise. First, because firms that are flexible enough to engage in small-batch customised production can command higher profit margins. Secondly, it is argued, employers operating a flexible system of production will have to pay more to attract and retain skilled employees, a key ingredient in its success (Abercrombie et al., 1994). The combination of improved pay, greater employee participation and discretion in work will promote an organisational culture of teamwork leading to more harmonious industrial relations and a new mutuality of interests between management and workers. Advocates of flexible specialisation detect in these new managerial initiatives a break with management's past orientation to control and work intensification (Wood, 1989: 14). Piore and Sabel (1984) go so far as to speculate on the revival of a "yeoman democracy" in the west, a form of "collective individualism" that they see as the "political analogue" of the "cooperative competition" that characterised craft production in the 19th century (see also Kumar, 1995: 48).

POST-FORDISM OR NEO-FORDISM?

Critics of the post-Fordist flexible specialisation thesis can be roughly divided into the categories of sceptic and pessimist. According to the sceptics, enthusiasts of flexible specialisation and the second industrial divide over-simplify contemporary reality and history by creating two opposed technological paradigms – mass production and craft production (Abercrombie et al., 1994). This was never the case. Since the industrial revolution small firms and craft production have persisted along side mass production which was never the dominant form of industrial production (Kumar, 1995; Madry and Kirby, 1996).

Indeed, both models have coexisted in many national economies and even within single firms mixes of mass and craft production may occur. Furthermore, flexible manufacturing methods and computer technology are not the exclusive preserve of small firms, but have been adapted by mass producers to manufacture the varied innovative products apparently required by modern markets. Yet, the production for specialised niche markets may simply be special combinations of mass produced parts. For example, some car manufacturers produce special models in low volumes but use standard engines, drive transmissions and chassis components (Abercrombie et al., 1994; Kumar, 1995). Even the growth and development of the giant clothing firm Bennetton, once described as the banner company of post-Fordist practice, renders the theory questionable. Originating in the Emilia Romagna region or Third Italy, it prospered on the basis of flexible specialisation. However, by the 1980s, Bennetton had become a large multinational operation and came to closely resemble the "world car model", the very antithesis of the post-Fordist concept. This development, according to Wood (1989), raises questions not just about Bennetton but about the whole theory based on the opposition of mass production and flexible specialisation. To date, large firms do not seem to have decentralised to the extent suggested by post-Fordist theory. Rather, they remain dominant in the world economy and continue as the chief source of innovative products and processes (Abercrombie et al., 1994; Kumar, 1995).

Sceptics also question the assumption that the application of new technology will necessarily involve up-skilling, autonomy and job satisfaction. This will ultimately depend on a conscious managerial decision to use technology in such a way as to improve low-level jobs. Likewise, the post-Fordist identification of small firms as potential bastions of enlightened managerialism and harmonious working relationships contradicts the historical experience. Many such firms were little better than "sweat shops" with low pay, poor working conditions and little record of innovation (Abercrombie et al., 1994). It is at this point that pessimists take the critique in a more apocalyptic direction. Flexible specialisation as a way of competing against low wage producers will, they assert, principally benefit capital but for labour movements it will mean a return to the worst excesses of industrial capitalism. For if competition between flexible firms is based on cutting costs and wages, this will adversely affect workers in the form of redundancies, labour intensification, inferior contracts, insecure jobs and the erosion of trade union rights. While reskilling or upgrading of jobs may occur, this will be confined, pessimists claim, to a minority of permanent full-time, core workers, excluding the majority on the periphery. Again, the ubiquitous Bennetton is used to support these contentions. In that company, 1,500 workers are employed directly but another 10,000 are largely sub-contractors or home-workers which, pessimists argue, allow the company to avoid direct responsibility for taxes and welfare payments.[3] Additionally, Bennetton makes use of seasonal workers such as

---

3. This organisational set-up seems more redolent of the past than the future. During the

pensioners, students and married women (Madry and Kirby, 1996). Finally, some pessimists warn that even the jobs of core workers may be insecure as some large companies shift wholesale towards the employment of part-time staff. In 1993 the Burton group replaced 1,000 full-time employees with 3,000 part-timers (Madry and Kirby, 1996).

It is difficult to come to any firm conclusion regarding the validity of post-Fordist claims or the counter claims of its critics. This is chiefly because post-Fordist theory is impossible to test, as the various elements are not precisely specified, their interrelationships are vague and so they cannot be measured (Abercrombie et al., 1994). However, a common theme in all variants of the theory is that the post-Fordist workplace will be characterised by multi-skilled employees, decentralised decision making, co-operative rather than hierarchical organisation and democratised decision-making practices for product development and resource allocation (Piore and Sabel, 1984; Lash and Urry, 1987; Lipietz, 1987). Drawing on a study which details the organisation of work and discretion available to employees in seven of the advanced industrial societies, we are able to get a clearer picture of contemporary workplace arrangements and the extent to which they accord with post-Fordist claims (Boreham, 1992).

The study used three categories of control – "autonomy", "production decision making" and "economic decision making" – to encompass different practices of discretion at work. "Autonomy" refers to the extent to which individuals are constrained within the parameters of their own job: for example the degree to which they can control the pace of work. "Production decision making" is the degree of employee involvement or control in decisions to change the product, programmes, procedures or services within the organisation. "Economic decision making" refers to the degree of employee participation in budgetary decisions within the workplace. Evidence of employee autonomy would lay the foundation for the flexibility and deployment of skills required by the post-Fordist organisation. Furthermore, there would have to be some evidence of involvement by low-level employees in production and economic decision making if the post-Fordist organisation of work was to be confirmed (Boreham, 1992). The results summarised in Table 1.3 provide no evidence for the reorganisation of work on post-Fordist lines. The autonomy available to semi-skilled and unskilled workers is extremely limited. For the three lower categories of workers there was almost total exclusion from decision making concerning the organisation of production. Participation in decision making on financial matters concerning production was even more restricted.

The findings in Table 1.3 place the emphasis on continuity rather than change. Indeed, as Boreham points out, his data attest to the continuance for blue-collar employees of the low-trust, low-discretion syndrome identified by

---

1850s the factory operative was not the typical industrial worker, rather they were outnumbered by millions of domestic or out workers (see Thomis, 1974: 89).

Table 1.3: Autonomy and Participation in Decision Making for Different Occupational Levels in Australia, Britain, Canada, Germany, Japan, Sweden and USA*

Occupational Status	% of Employees with High Autonomy	% of Employees with Significant Participation in Production Decision Making	% of Employees with Significant Participation in Economic Decision Making
Managers/Administrators	71	50	48
Professionals	48	25	19
Clerks	29	8	6
Skilled Workers	27	9	5
Semi- and Unskilled Workers	14	4	2

*The mean score for all the countries at each occupational level is reported for each of the three factors in the table.

Source: Adapted from Boreham, 1992.

Fox a quarter of a century ago (Fox, 1974). Furthermore, in interpreting his data, Boreham raises the questions of power, hierarchy, ownership and possible conflicts of interests between capital and labour, topics notably absent from the post-Fordist discourse. For instance, there is a growing body of evidence that the possibility for efficient flexible production through the application of new technology will be enhanced through the adoption of workplace practices described as post-Fordist (Boreham, 1992). Yet, there is little evidence in Boreham's work that management will cede its decision-making prerogatives in the interest of more rational production methods. This is a particularly noteworthy finding for the Irish trade union movement given that some of its prominent spokesmen are apparently convinced that the imperatives of rationality and efficiency will necessarily involve a dilution of managerial prerogative (see Geraghty, 1992). The contrary appears to be the case. However, as Boreham (1992) states, the crucial factor dictating who participates in relatively minor decisions is the location of particular jobs within the organisation's structure of ownership and control. Apparently, in the contemporary workplace it is hierarchy that matters, not the rational application of skill and experience to the methods of production. Production in advanced capitalist societies, Boreham concludes, is largely organised along neo-Fordist lines. Flexible production techniques and organisational forms do not appear to have usurped the Fordist organisation of the labour process and there is little evidence that participative organisational practices have made any significant incursions into traditional managerial prerogatives in the workplace in any of the seven countries studied (Boreham, 1992).[4] Jobs are rarely, if ever, redesigned at the expense of managerial prerogative or control (Fincham and Rhodes, 1988: 168–169). This is borne out by the recent workplace and employee relations survey carried out in Britain in 1999. The evidence indicated that there was comparatively little devolution of authority either from senior management to line management or from management generally to employees. Direct control was the most common mode used to control and monitor the work of individual employees. Retention of control and the minimisation of cost characterised the approach of most employers (Cully et al., 1999: 295).

In the light of the above critiques, post-Fordism as a cohesive theory appears to be substantially weakened. We are left with a series of discrete innovations that fail to add up to a coherent set of changes which would constitute a new regime of accumulation, a second industrial divide. Far from constituting a fundamental break in the order of industrial capitalism, the changes identified as post-Fordist may be merely expressions of the technological dynamism and the constant revolutionising of production inherent in the industrial revolution from the outset (Kumar, 1995).[5] As Schumpeter (1943: 83) remarked, "the fundamental impulse that sets and keeps the capitalist engine in motion comes from the new consumers' goods, the new methods of production or transportation, the new markets, the new forms of industrial organisation that capitalist enterprise creates". [6]

SHIFT IN POLITICS AND THE END OF CLASS THESIS

By the early 1980s the "golden age" of capitalism appeared to be in decline (Kitschelt et al., 1999a). Under the impact of rising unemployment, rampant

---

4. These findings, which do severe if not terminal damage to post-Fordist claims, receive some support from a totally separate international study to assess the effect of national schemes for employee participation carried out by IDE in 1981 and followed up in 1993 (see *Industrial Democracy in Europe* 1981 and 1993).
5. As Edward Mortimer, columnist with the *Financial Times*, observed "Marx and Engels described a world economy more like that of 1998 than of 1848" *Financial Times* 25 March 1998. Quoted in Allen, K. (2000: 189).
6. "The bourgeoisie has through its exploitation of the world market given a cosmopolitan character to production and consumption in every country ... All old established national industries have been destroyed or are daily being destroyed. They are dislodged by new industries, whose introduction becomes a life and death question for all civilised nations, by industries that no longer work up indigenous raw material, but raw material drawn from the remotest zones; industries whose products are consumed, not only at home, but in every quarter of the globe. In place of the old wants, satisfied by the production of the country, we find new wants, requiring for their satisfaction the products of distant lands and climes. In place of the old local national seclusion and self-sufficiency, we have intercourse in every direction, universal inter-dependence of nations."
   Karl Marx and F. Engels (1848: 45) *Manifesto of the Communist Party* Moscow: Progress Publishers.

inflation and a fall in the rate of profits and productivity, the capital labour compromise began to unravel. The economic crisis of the 1970s had served to discredit not only the Keynesian policy of demand management and the maintenance of full employment but also its social democratic practitioners. Milton Friedman and the Chicago school of economists argued that the way out of the crisis was to restore the primacy of the market mechanism (Kuttner, 1999: 31–33). Its working, they claimed, had been progressively impeded by decades of government intervention and rigidities imposed by trade union power (see McCrone et al., 1989). Friedman's monetarism rapidly became the dominant economic orthodoxy of the 1980s. Economic crisis and a revivified economic liberalism espoused and practised by "new right" conservative parties combined to place social democracy on the defensive. In Europe, the political balance of power generally swung against labour. Even some nominally socialist governments pursued conservative economic strategies of retrenchment, control of public expenditure and restructuring of labour markets (Ferner and Hyman 1992). The ideology and practice of these policies were essentially inimical to organised labour. This programme received practical embodiment in the New Right policies of the Republican and Conservative governments in America and Britain during the 1980s. Electoral defeat and demoralisation of social democratic parties left many unions in a vulnerable position – a vulnerability compounded by rising unemployment, declining union membership and legislation designed to reduce the legitimacy of collective bargaining.

These developments have been seen by many as signalling a break-up of the traditionally homogenous and collective experience of employment. They go on to interpret these changes in advanced industrial societies as a "crisis in class politics" or indeed the end of class (Clark and Lipset, 1991; Clarke et al., 1993). The end-of-class thesis is based on a number of structural and lifestyle changes (Esping-Anderson, 1999). These include a shift from manufacturing industry to smaller-scale production units in the service sector, a rise in educational attainment, a decline in people's employment stability over their lifetime, the decline in non-manual occupations and the increase in professional occupations. Beck (1987) argues, for example, that the labour market, through its inter-linked processes of education, mobility and competition, has become the "driving force" behind the individualisation of people's lives. As a result of these changes, the salience of class and its attendant solidarities appear increasingly redundant. The social trends associated with individualisation and detraditionalisation are believed to undermine the conditions associated with collective class actions. Consequently, those formerly identified as working class will be increasingly less inclined to participate in collectively oriented union or political activities based on class identity with an accompanying erosion of solidaristic beliefs in a general union movement.

However, announcements about the end of class have been voiced by many commentators since the early 1950s (see Westergaard, 1972: 85). According to Esping-Andersen (1999: 314), the evidence for the end-of-class thesis "rests on shaky ground". The continued relevance of class has been affirmed by a number of studies (Crompton, 1993; Breen and Whelan, 1996; Wright, 1997). For instance, the end of class thesis holds that increasing levels of education are a "source of class disarticulation" or the erosion of class categories. However, one cross-national study shows that the impact of class background on educational attainment remains as stable as ever (Esping-Andersen, 1999: 303). Thus, a key source of class reproduction appears to have remained largely unchanged.

In Britain, for instance, in the last decade of the 20th century the children of unskilled manual workers had as much chance of getting to university as they had in the first (Beynon and Glavanis, 1999: 3). This also appears to be the case in Ireland. Indeed, the evidence would suggest that increasing levels of education have had a minimal effect on the Irish social class structure. Layte and Whelan (2000: 105) found little evidence of greater equality of opportunity or the emergence of a more meritocratic society. Nor did they find any "diminution in the impact of class origins on educational level" over time. In an analysis of the relationship between social class and education from 1980 to 1997, Smyth and Hannan (2000: 125) observe that there has been "a remarkable persistence of social class inequalities in educational outcomes".

Regarding a possible decline in collective solidarity among workers associated with the changes in the occupational structure and growing service sector employment, the evidence is sparse and inconclusive (Esping-Andersen, 1999). In Ireland, it appears that professional and technical workers are more highly unionised than any other group of workers (Table 1.4). The figures in Table 1.4 also question the assumption that higher levels of education are associated with higher levels of individualism, as levels of union density actually increase with the level of education. These figures would counsel caution regarding the demise of collective solidarities and trade unions.

Three perspectives on post-industrial society, the information revolution, the shift to post-Fordist production systems and the declining salience of class have been reviewed. These have featured prominently in contemporary analyses of change in industrial organisations and society. However, their claims to a total transformation of industrial society must be treated with some caution. Sceptics suggest that the changes identified as characteristic of a post-industrial society express the essence of capitalism rather than its transcendence and that capitalist market principles remain central to economic and political exchanges. On the other hand, it can be argued that sceptics err in over-emphasising continuity and, by implication, a refusal to acknowledge that new things are afoot. Leaving aside the more utopian claims of post-Fordist and information society theorists, it is undeniable that new technology, global competition and the demands for worker flexibility are concretely experienced by many working people. How these global economic imperatives and technological change affect the contemporary work process will be mediated by a country's history, its social relations and industrial relations tradition.

Table 1.4: Unionisation, Education and Occupational Level in Ireland, 1996

	Operatives, Labourers, Transport & Communications	Clerical Workers	Commerce, Insurance & Finance	Service Workers	Professional & Technical Workers
Union Density	46%	45%	20%	33%	53%

	Primary	Junior Certificate	Leaving Certificate	Third Level
Union Density	28%	35%	39%	43%

Source: Labour Force Survey, 1996. Union density is calculated as the number of respondents who indicate membership of a union as a proportion of the estimated number of people at work by industry, occupation and educational level. The overall number of people at work according to the 1996 survey was 1.285 million.

The purpose of these chapters is to assess the effect and extent of these changes in the Irish workplace and on the Irish industrial relations system.

OUTLINE OF THE BOOK

The following chapters consider Irish employee relations in the context of the above discussion. The book is divided into two broad sections. Section 1 deals with firm or micro level employee relations, while section 2 deals with the issues of employee relations in the wider political, economic and legal context.

Section 1

Chapter 2 addresses the nature of the employment relationship in a market economy. It focuses on managerial strategies in managing the contradictory processes of co-operation and conflict that characterises that relationship. It also examines managerial attempts to transcend these conflicts through non-unionism. Finally, it is argued that the traditional method of collective bargaining remains the most effective way to manage the employment relationship in the context of capitalist democracy. Chapter 3 focuses on new forms of work organisation, partnership and direct employee involvement. There is an implicit assumption that the growing diffusion of such new forms of work may have played a major role in Ireland's exceptional economic performance during the 1990s. The chapter draws on a national workplace survey of employee relations to present an assessment of the degree to which new modes of collaborative production have gained ground in Ireland during the 1990s. Chapter 4 addresses some of the industrial relations ramifications of performance-related pay systems using empirical data from both new and longer established firms in the Republic of Ireland. In particular, it examines the implications of such systems for collectivism and solidarity in industrial relations in the context of employer attempts to individualise the employment relationship and exclude union penetration. Chapter 5 explores the management of identity and culture of low waged routine workers in service organisations. New and traditional forms of organisation are compared and the influence of these organisational forms on the outcome of cultural management is described. Chapter 6 seeks to establish whether workforces have become more co-operative in recent times. The demands of the new economy apparently require a flexible and co-operative workforce, a requirement incompatible with traditional adversarial industrial relations. Drawing on a survey of employees in a number of companies in the Irish manufacturing sector, the chapter examines the extent to which changes in the economy and workplace have facilitated a reduction in "them and us" attitudes and an associated weakening of union structure and influence in the workplace.

Section 2

Chapter 7 focuses on the extent to which collectivism and solidarity are still relevant in the context of the trends in industrialised societies since the end of the 1970s. These trends are sometimes claimed to have resulted in the erosion of traditional working class communities. Using a survey of Irish trade union members, the level and types of solidarity among the membership and the implications for the policies and practices of the union leadership are explored. Chapter 8 focuses on the Industrial Relations Act, 1990, as the most important piece of collective labour legislation to be introduced in Ireland since the 1946 Industrial Relations Act that established the Labour Court. Having outlined the main features of the 1990 Act, two main issues arising from it are addressed. First, the implications of the changes to law on trade disputes for the principle of voluntarism are assessed and secondly, a review of the extent to which the institutional provisions have delivered on the objectives established at the time the Act was undertaken. Chapter 9 examines the causes and consequence of the wave of trade union merger activity between 1987 and 1994, which, it is argued, changed the structure of the movement. The chapter outlines the conditions which facilitated this restructuring and the strategies adopted by the union movement. The outcome is an encompassing peak organisation which could potentially lead to a more effective trade union structure and a different strategic approach to representing its members.

Chapter 10 examines trends in declining union recognition. This decline, it is argued, points up a contradiction in Irish Government policy. Formal policy appears to support a strong trade union role in industry. In practice, it appears that new start-up industries actively avoid trade union recognition. Some of the reasons for this phenomenon are explored. Chapter 11 focuses on how union members on the shop floor view the recent national wage agreements. Drawing on a survey of union members the chapter explores their perceptions regarding the outcome of these agreements and how they appear to have affected their union at national and workplace level. A number of emerging difficulties are identified, particularly the tendency for power and influence to shift from the shop floor and national union towards the union centre. The chapter concludes with an evaluation of the response of the Irish Congress of Trade Unions to these emerging difficulties. Chapter 12 examines the economic and social outcomes for the period of social partnership, particularly the recent agreements, in Ireland. The chapter uses a comparative approach to locate Ireland within a European context and assess the outcome for the trade union movement and, more generally, the extent to which the agreements have created a more equitable society. Finally, in Chapter 13, there is a brief summary and conclusion.

REFERENCES

Abercrombie, N., Hill, S. and Turner, B. (1994) *Dictionary of Sociology.* London: Penguin Books.

Allen, K. (2000) *The Celtic Tiger: The Myth of Social Partnership in Ireland.* Manchester: Manchester University Press.

Armstrong, P., Glynn, A. and Harrison, J. (1984) *Capitalism Since World War II. The Making and Breakup of the Great Boom.* London: Fontana.

Beck, U. (1987) "Beyond Status and Class: Will there be an Individualised Class Society?" in Meja, V., Misgeld, D. and Stehr, N. *Modern German Sociology.* New York: Columbia University Press.

Bell, D. (1973) *The Coming of Post-Industrial Society.* New York: Basic Books.

Bell, D. (1976) *The Cultural Contradictions of Capitalism.* London: Heinemann.

Beynon, H. and Glavanis, P. (1999) *Patterns of Social Inequality.* London: Longman.

Boreham, P. (1992) "The Myth of Post-Fordist Management" *Management Decision,* Vol. 30, No. 6.

Boyd, A. (1976) *The Rise of the Irish Trade Unions 1729–1970.* Dublin: Anvil Books.

Breen, R. and Whelan, T. (1996) *Social Mobility and Social Class in Ireland.* Dublin: Gill and Macmillan.

Castells, M. (1996) *The Rise of the Network Society.* Cambridge, Mass.: Blackwell Publishers.

Clark, T. and Lipset, S. (1991) "Are Social Classes Dying?" *International Sociology,* Vol. 4: 297–410.

Clark, T., Lipset, S. and Rempel, M. (1993) "The Declining Political Significance of Class" *International Sociology,* Vol. 3: 293–316.

Crompton, R. (1993) *Class and Stratification: An Introduction to Current Debates.* Cambridge: Polity.

Crosland, A. (1956) *The Future of Socialism*. London: Jonathan Cape.

Cully, M., Woodland, S., O'Reilly, A. and Dix, G. (1999) *Britain at Work as Depicted by the 1998 Employee Relations Survey*. London: Routledge.

Dahrendorf, R. (1959) *Class and Class Conflict in an Industrial Society*. London: Routledge and Kegan Paul.

Deegan, J. and Dineen, D. (1997) *Tourism Policy and Performance: The Irish Experience*. London. International Thomson: Business Press.

Esping-Anderson, G. (1999) "Politics without Class? Postindustrial Cleavages in Europe and America" in Kitschelt, H., Lange, P., Marks, G. and Stephens, J. (eds) *Continuity and Change in Contemporary Capitalism*. Cambridge: Cambridge University Press.

Ferner, A. and Hyman, R. (1992) *Industrial Relations in the New Europe*. Oxford: Blackwell.

Fincham, R. and Rhodes, P. (1988) *The Individual, Work and Organisations*. London: Weidenfeld and Nicholson.

Flood, P. and Turner, T. (1993) "Human Resource Strategy and the Non Union Phenomenon" *Employee Relations*, Vol. 15, No. 6: 54–67.

Fox, A. (1974) *Man Mismanagement*. London: Hutchinson and Co.

Geraghty, D. (1992) *World Class Participation*. The 17th Countess Markievicz Lecture. Dublin

Green, F. and Sutcliffe, B. (1987) *The Profit System: The Economics of Capitalism*. Harmondworth: Penguin Books.

Gunnigle, P. and Flood, P. (1995) *Personnel Management in Ireland*. Dublin: Gill and Macmillan.

IDE (1981) *Industrial Democracy in Europe*. Oxford: Oxford University Press.

IDE (1993) *Industrial Democracy in Europe Revisited*. Oxford: Oxford University Press.

Kitschelt, H., Lange, P., Marks, G. and Stephens, J. (1999) (eds) *Continuity and Change in Contemporary Capitalism*. Cambridge: Cambridge University Press.

Kitschelt, H., Lange, P., Marks, G. and Stephens, J. (1999a) "Introduction" in Kitschelt, H., Lange, P., Marks, G. and Stephens, J. (eds) *Continuity and Change in Contemporary Capitalism*. Cambridge: Cambridge University Press.

Kitschelt, H., Lange, P., Marks, G. and Stephens, J. (1999b) "Convergent and Divergence in Advanced Capitalist Democracies" in Kitschelt, H., Lange, P., Marks, G. and Stephens, J. (eds) *Continuity and Change in Contemporary Capitalism*. Cambridge: Cambridge University Press.

Kumar, K. (1986) *Prophecy and Progress: The Sociology of Industrial and Post-Industrial Society*. Harmondworth: Penguin Books.

Kumar, K. (1995) *From Post-Industrial to Post-Modern Society: New Theories of the Contemporary World*. Cambridge Mass.: Blackwell Publishers.

Kuttner, R. (1999) *Everything for Sale: The Virtues and Limits of Markets*. Chicago: University of Chicago Press.

Lash, S. and Urry, J. (1987) *The End of Organised Capitalism*. Cambridge: Blackwell Polity Press.

Layte, R. and Whelan, C. (2000) "The Rising Tide and Equality of Opportunity: The Changing Class Structure" in Nolan, B., O'Connell, J. and Whelan, C. (eds) *Bust to Boom? The Irish Experience of Growth and Inequality*. Dublin: Institute of Public Administration.

Lipietz, A. (1987) *Miracles and Mirages: The Crisis of Global Fordism*. London: Verso.

Madry, N. and Kirby, M. (1996) *Investigating Work, Unemployment and Leisure*. London: Harper Collins.

McCrone, D., Elliot, B. and Bechhofer, F. (1989) "Corporatism and the New Right" in Scase, R. (ed.) *Industrial Societies: Crisis and Division in Western Capitalism and State Socialism*. London: Unwin.

Nolan, B., O'Connell, J. and Whelan, C. (2000) (eds) *Bust to Boom? The Irish Experience of Growth and Inequality*. Dublin: Institute of Public Administration.

Piore, M. and Sabel, C. (1984) *The Second Industrial Divide: Prospects for Prosperity*. New York: Basic Books.

Roche, W. and Larraghy, J. (1989) "The Trend of Unionisation in the Irish Republic" *Industrial Relations in Ireland: Contemporary Issues and Developments*. Department Industrial Relations, University College Dublin.

Schumpeter, J. (1943) *Capitalism, Socialism and Democracy*. London: George Allen and Unwin.

Smyth, E. and Hannan, D. (2000) "Education and Inequality" in Nolan, B., O'Connell, J. and Whelan, C. (eds) *Bust to Boom? The Irish Experience of Growth and Inequality*. Dublin: Institute of Public Administration.

Soskice, D. (1999) "Divergent Production Regimes: Coordinated and Uncoordinated Market Economies in the 1980's and 1990's" in Kitschelt, H., Lange, P., Marks, G. and Stephens, J. (eds) *Continuity and Change in Contemporary Capitalism*. Cambridge: Cambridge University Press.

Streeck, W. (1992) "Training and the New Industrial Relations: A Strategic Role for Unions?" in Marino Regini (ed.) *The Future of Labour Movements*. London: Sage Publications.

Sutcliffe, B. (1983) *Hard Times The World Economy in Turmoil*. London: Pluto Press.

Theobald, R. (1994) *Understanding Industrial Society: A Sociological Guide*. New York: St. Martins Press.

Thomis, M. I. (1974) *The Town Labourer and the Industrial Revolution*. London: Batsford.

Turner, T. and Morley, M. (1995) *Industrial Relations and the New Order: Case Studies in Conflict and Co-operation*. Dublin: Oak Tree Press.

Westergaard, J. H. (1972) "The Withering Away of Class: A Contemporary Myth" in Blumberg, P. (ed.) *The Impact of Social Class: Selected Readings*. New York: Thomas Y. Cromwell Co.

Wood, S. (1989) "The Transformation of Work" in Wood, S. (ed.) *The Transformation of Work*. London: Unwin Hyman.

Wright, E. (1997) *Class Counts: Comparative Studies in Class Analysis*. Cambridge; New York: Cambridge University Press.

CHAPTER 2

Managing the Employment Relationship in a Market Economy

DARYL D'ART

The appeal to management's right to manage can hardly be considered as very much more than a slogan ... property rights furnish the owner with rights over property not over people. Any right that managers have to manage must in a free society depend on the consent of the managed.

Daniel and McIntosh 1972

INTRODUCTION

Proclaiming the end of something or "endism" seems to be an academic growth industry. The late 1950s and early 1960s were a particularly productive period for endists. Bell's announcement of the "end of ideology" was voguish for a time until exposed by circumstances as an ideology itself (Bell, 1960; Kumar, 1981: 187). Others came forward to proclaim the imminent withering away of the strike (Ross and Hartman, 1960). Again this optimistic prognosis was confounded by events (Giddens, 1989: 497). Another endist product of the period was the gradual withering away of class (Westergaard and Resler, 1975). This is a thesis that is still widely assumed to hold good. Yet, a recent study of social mobility and social class in Ireland provides unambiguous evidence of the continuing significance of social class for life chances (Breen and Whelan, 1996). Even within Human Resource Management (HRM), a supposedly new model of workforce management, stubborn continuities can be detected. Though HRM is dogged by the unresolved problem of definition, its proponents claim it can create mutuality between all organisational stakeholders and so end adversarial relations between employer and employees (Beer and Spector, 1985; Walton, 1985). The "soft" version of HRM proclaims that employees are a unique organisational resource unlike any other and it is only their effort or labour that creates value from all the other resources (Legge, 1989; Brewster and Hegewisch, 1994). A claim that would receive wholehearted assent from proponents of the Marxian labour theory of value. Somewhat confusingly the "hard" version of HRM makes the contrary claim that labour is a commodity just like any of the other organisation's bought-in resources and as a consequence should be obtained as cheaply as possible and used accordingly

(Brewster and Hegewisch, 1994). Of course it was this treatment of labour as a commodity that brought into being trade unions and labour movements and inspired the Marxian critique of capitalism. Nevertheless "endism" remains irrepressible. Witness the startling announcement of the "end of history" (Fukuyama, 1992). This has been characterised as a reassertion of the end of ideology thesis in the context of the 1990s (Goodwin, 1997: 26). Finally, there are the most ambitious endists of all, the post-modernists, who, apparently, proclaim the end of everything.

This chapter takes issue with such a prognosis and emphasises the enduring and continuing aspect of industrial or employee relations in a market economy. Even in the supposedly new post-Fordist, post-industrialist or post-capitalist economies, labour management conflict seems more or less to be an endemic feature of industrial and commercial organisations. The term "industrial relations" Miliband (1973: 73) describes as "the consecrated euphemism for the permanent conflict, now acute, now subdued, between capital and labour". This remains so, it will be argued, because of the contradictory forces of conflict and co-operation that characterise the employment relationship in a market system. Of course, the argument rests on the assumption that even in the supposedly new economic order, the essential nature of the employment relationship remains unchanged. It has been suggested that the growth in self-employment and the shift from contracts of, to contracts for service erodes capitalism and its employment relationship (Hodgson, 1999: 167). This is not convincing for a number of reasons. First, it is questionable if there has been a significant growth in self-employment.[1] Secondly, Hodgson (1999: 168) concedes some truth to the argument that changes in the legal forms of contracts are surface phenomena leaving the underlying relationship between bosses and workers unaltered. Indeed, a survey by Gallie et al. (1998: 314) casts considerable doubt on claims for a change in the nature of the employment relationship. Finally, the principal aim of Hodgson's work is not so much to engage with present reality but "to raise the possibility of a more developed utopian discourse" (Hodgson, 1999: 4). Consequently, once speculation regarding unknowable futures is left aside, the essential nature of the employment relationship in the market system appears to remain unchanged in its fundamentals.

The argument in this chapter is developed in three main sections. First, the traditional view of the employment relationship and the forces of conflict and co-operation are outlined. Secondly, the historical and contemporary innovations in the management of the employment relationship are examined. Thirdly, it is argued that recognition and negotiation with trade unions through

---

1. For example, in Ireland between 1985 and 1999, the proportion defined as employees increased from 78.3% to 82% of the employed labour force. Conversely, the proportion defined as employers and self-employed declined from 21.1% to 17.8%. However, while the proportion of employers and self-employed increased in industry and services, the number of self-employed in the agricultural sector declined dramatically.

collective bargaining remains the most effective and practical method of managing the employment relationship in the context of capitalist democracy.

THE EMPLOYMENT RELATIONSHIP

The employment relationship in labour process theory is generally understood as a dynamic equilibrium between the contending forces or processes of conflict and co-operation (Friedman, 1977, 1990; Salaman, 1979; Thompson, 1989). As illustrated in Figure 2.1 below, there are a number of elements or forces affecting the relationship.

Figure 2.1: Model of Dynamic Tension in the Employment Relationship

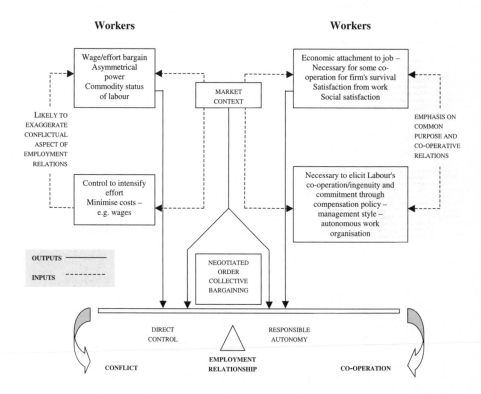

Sources of Conflict in the Employment Relationship

The Wage Bargain

Employers and potential employees meet in the labour market as buyers and sellers of labour power (Offe, 1985: 14). Inevitably there is a conflict of interest between the buyers and sellers of labour as the parties to the wage bargain.

What is good for one is frequently a cost for the other (Edwards and Scullion, 1982: 3). Yet, a mutually satisfactory bargain can be concluded based on pragmatic acceptance of the existing labour market context and the relative power balance between the parties. This can only be a temporary accommodation. Signals from the market impinging on employer/employees or shifts in the relative power balance caused by labour shortage/surplus will likely require readjustment of the initial wage bargain, thus bringing the underlying conflicting interests, if not conflict, to the fore (Watson, 1980: 62–67).

The Effort Bargain

Apart from the wage bargain another potential source of conflict is the effort bargain or how much effort is to be expended by the employee in return for a wage. It is not the purchase of labour power but its use that creates value for the employer. Even after its purchase, labour power, unlike other factors of production, remains a potential not a realised asset (Storey, 1980: 57). As a purchaser or investor in the commodity of labour the employer attempts to maximise the economic returns by making the level of effort – physical, intellectual or emotional – as great as possible. Yet, no labour contract can specify precisely in advance of the work being carried out exactly what should be done and the amount of effort to be expended (Edwards, 1986: 32). Even if this could be done it might prove counterproductive. As Offe (1985: 23–24) points out, it is precisely the limited autonomy left to the worker which makes the utilisation of "living" labour power attractive to the employer. Thus, the labour contract may be well adapted to the shifting requirements of a changing technology but fail to clarify the day-to-day expectations of labour and management. This means that it contributes little to the requirements of a stable social system (Gouldner, 1954 quoted in Cressey, et al. 1985: 138).

The case of the unskilled worker illustrates this lacuna in the employment contract. Generally, the tasks of such workers have a very low discretionary content (Jacques, 1996: 88). However, their ability to disrupt production by strict adherence to employer rules (working to rule) has been demonstrated on numerous occasions. Thus, endemic imprecision in the labour contract or "the central indeterminacy of labour potential" provides a rich soil in which bargaining and conflict around different interpretations can flourish (Thompson, 1989: 242). Indeed, managerial and employee judgement of what constitutes a fair day's work may rarely coincide (Eldridge, 1973: 27; Salamon, 1987: 48).

Asymmetrical Power and Managerial Legitimacy

Organisations are essentially structures of power and control (Salaman, 1979: 109; Marchington, 1982: 94). Contrary to popular perception, there is a real and substantial imbalance of power in industrial and commercial organisations and its distribution between management and worker is fundamentally unequal (Hawkins, 1981: 229; Hill, 1981). Subordinates at the base of the enterprise hierarchy experience most directly the exercise of managerial power and control in the pursuit of economic success and competitive effectiveness (Hawkins, 1981). A differential distribution of power, a relationship of domination and subordination will tend to nurture opposing or conflicting interests between those in possession and those excluded from power (Hill, 1981: 12; Brannen, 1983: 13; Thompson, 1989: 245; Wheeler, 1989). Indeed, unionisation can be seen as an attempt to offset the superior market power of the employer in the bargaining relationship and the subordinate control position of the worker in the enterprise (Giddens, 1973: 205). Of course, unionism does not usually imply outright rejection by subordinate employees of managerial authority or legitimacy in the exercise of its power but more a qualified acceptance. Meanwhile, the problematic nature of managerial legitimacy remains a potential source of conflict between the parties to the employment relationship.

The Duality of the Labour Commodity

Organisations have many machine-like aspects and are often run as if they are machines (Morgan, 1986). Raw materials or commodities are bought in, processed and the resultant outputs of goods or services are sold for a profit in the market. One of the bought-in commodities is labour power. A unique characteristic of the labour commodity is its embodiment in people. This duality can be simultaneously a source of creativity and difficulty. While human effort or intellect is the central means of goal achievement in organisations this can compromise the reliability of a person as a machine. First, because human beings are not automatons and while they may sell their labour power they cannot alienate their minds or their will (Friedman, 1977: 94). Secondly, in work organisations people are used as means towards ends rather than as ends in themselves. Yet, in western democratic cultures people tend to be assertive, questioning, self-considering citizens who may have ends of their own which may not necessarily coincide with those of their employer (Watson, 1986: 23; Thompson, 1989: 242–243). The tension between the use of labour as a commodity or factor of production and its human essence is potentially another point of conflict in the employment relationship. As Hobsbawm (1994: 414) observes, "human beings are not efficiently designed for a capitalist system of production".

The Dynamics of the Employment Relationship

An exclusive focus on the above features would characterise the employment relationship in purely conflictual terms – management control versus worker resistance. Yet strikes, official or unofficial, the most dramatic manifestations of such conflict, are comparatively rare events in the history of most organisations (Hyman, 1972). This relatively successful maintenance of order and stability cannot be solely ascribed to managerial coercion or bamboozlement and supported by a socially induced false consciousness in their subordinates (Fox, 1974: 15–26). A contributory factor is to be found in the complex paradoxical nature of the employment relationship that comprises elements of conflict and co-operation, dissent and accommodation (Blyton and Turnbull, 1994: 31).

For instance, while managers pursue the object of control they must simultaneously attempt to engage and mobilise worker consent, creativity and co-operative power (Edwards, 1995: 15; Thompson, 1989). Employees similarly experience the pull of contending forces. A number of studies of employee attitudes indicate how extensive the view is that management and workers have conflicting interests (Ramsay, 1975; Whelan, 1982; D'Art and Turner, 1999). Even the introduction of the so-called "new industrial relations" techniques have failed to eradicate "them and us" attitudes (Kelly and Kelly, 1991). The persistence of these attitudes might be expected to issue in outright opposition or guerrilla actions by workers against management. Yet, a countervailing force or check to such opposition is the worker's experience of economic interdependence with the employer (Cressey et al., 1985). If the firm is to survive and employment maintained, goods must be produced or services provided. This necessarily requires some measure of co-operation between the managerial agents of the employer and employees (Hill, 1981: 3). That co-operation, grudging or otherwise, is forthcoming can be partly explained by the importance attached in modern societies to having a job. Paid employment, even if dull and unpleasant, tends to be a structuring element in people's lives and a source of social contact and personal identity (Giddens, 1989: 505). Indeed, in many instances employees may find intrinsic satisfaction in the work itself.

The above interplay of antagonism and co-operation creates a dynamic tension in the employment relationship. While conflicts over the effort or wage bargain prompt worker resistance, their material interest in the firm's survival counsels restraint if not co-operation. Equally, management's pursuit of productivity and efficiency through the exercise of control may prove counterproductive without eliciting some measure of consent from subordinates. Consequently, management and workers are locked into a relationship that is one of both structured antagonism and calculative co-operation (Edwards, 1986: 77). According to Watson (1986: 63), enterprises are in essence "a highly fragile set of co-operative arrangements tentatively agreed by individuals and groups who have a variety of social, political and economic interests". An important aspect of the managerial task is to minimise the potentially disruptive effect of these conflicting interests on organisational effectiveness.

MANAGING THE EMPLOYMENT RELATIONSHIP

The history of labour management can be viewed as a search for a formula or strategy that attempts to align employer and employee interests and reduce or negate the conflictual elements in the employment relationship and also end employee ambiguity regarding management's right to manage. Since the late 19th century, employers and their agents have seen such equivocation as a constraint, inhibiting rapid and effective responses to market pressures. There began a search for a philosopher's stone that would transmute the base metal of conditional consent into the gold of unstinting employee commitment. Indeed, modern management is an activity very much concerned with establishing its legitimacy and especially justifying its authority over the managed (Bendix, 1963: 1; Child, 1969: 22–23; Watson, 1986: 173). The history of personnel techniques such as profit sharing, co-partnership, paternalism, human relations, the job enrichment of neo-human relations, employee involvement, organisation development all record that search for a solid foundation securing managerial legitimacy in exercising power and stabilising capital/labour relations (Fox, 1971: 47; Anthony, 1986: 171; Reed, 1989: 46).

To date the success of such initiatives has been, at best, uneven. It has not been a systematic search displaying an ordered chronological progression. Management, according to Reed (1989), is a process shot through with inconsistency, incrementalism, contradiction, conflict and uncertainty. In Mintzberg's famous phrase, management work is characterised by brevity, variety and fragmentation (quoted in Buckingham and Lawerence, 1985: 40).

This incrementalism and fragmentation is reflected in managerial attempts to deal with the conflictual elements in the employment relationship (Pollert, 1996: 205). There is a familiar pattern. A particular employee relations strategy might be partially taken up (for example scientific management) overlaid with a new approach (human relations) or later abandoned and then in different circumstances revived. Joint consultation and collective bargaining are cases in point. Joint consultation, popular with management during the 1940s and 1950s, fell into disuse in the following decades and was revived in the 1980s as employee involvement. In Britain during the 1960s few managers apparently dissented when the Donovan Commission claimed that collective bargaining is the best method of conducting industrial relations (Donovan, 1968). Since 1980, dissent and dissenters have grown in volume and numbers (Flood and Turner, 1993; Beaumount, 1995).

Management's adoption or discontinuance of a particular employee relations' strategy seems to be principally determined by competitive conditions in the firms product market, surplus or scarcity in the labour market and the balance of political forces in the wider society. This is illustrated in Table 2.1.

Table 2.1: Managerial Strategies and the Employment Relationship

Employee Relations Strategy	Period	Method	Elements of Employment Relationship Addressed	Context
Despotic Control	Early stages of industrialisation – Examples of both still extant	Coercion – Intensification of effort – Lengthening of the working day – Downward pressure on wages	The wage/effort bargain – Conflict ignored or suppressed	Frenetically competitive product market – wild fluctuations in demand for labour which is generally oversupplied Nascent union movement weak – impermanent government favours employer interest
Paternalism		Inspired by altruism/noblesse oblige Concern for employee material/ spiritual welfare – shortened working day – good working conditions – profit sharing etc.	Attempt to move beyond cash nexus to more diffuse relationship based on mutual obligation/ responsibility	
Direct Control or scientific management and variants (Unitarist)	1900 –	Separation of conception from execution – job fragmentation – structured – timed – directed by management – increased management control – minimal worker discretion	Individual wage/effort bargain – consent predicated on employer/ employee co-operation to maximise output so more to share – productivisim appeals to some union leaders – resistance by rank and file	Increasing scale and technical complexity of industry intensifies problem of control by traditional methods – growing power of organised labour – government less openly partisan
Human Relations (Unitarist)	1930s –	Communication/ subordinate-centred participative supervision – manipulation of employees' supposed social needs to engender labour/management co-operation	Emphasis on group dynamics – social and human aspects of employment relationship	Wall Street crash – depression Capitalism/*laissez-faire* / businessmen temporarily discredited – government favourable to labour – New Deal

Table 2.1: Managerial Strategies and the Employment Relationship (*cont/d*)

Employee Relations Strategy	Period	Method	Elements of Employment Relationship Addressed	Context
Regulation Strategy or negotiated order (Pluralist)	1945 –	Recognition and negotiation with trade unions – conflict institutionalised through procedural mechanisms	Continual renegotiation/ adjustment of terms of wage/ effort bargain	Steady growth in consumer demand – Keynesian policy of full employment – enhanced power and legitimacy of labour – culminating in bargained corporatism – Governments mostly Social Democratic responsive and sympathetic to labour
Neo-Human Relations	1950s –	Reunite conception with execution in shop floor work to counter low trust and worker alienation generated by Taylorism	Focus on humanity/creativity of labour – capable of initiative, responsibility, co-operation given intrinsically satisfying work	Increasing resistance of labour to fragmented work and managerial control – supposed crisis or decline in worker motivation
Responsible Autonomy or HRM/HR practice	1980s –	An amalgam of elements of paternalism, human and neo-human relations – high wages, participation, enriched jobs, autonomous workgroups or teams	Wage/effort bargain – commodity status of labour – asymmetrical power – emphasis co-operative aspect of employment relationship. Conflict partly addressed, partly obscured	Keynesian policy crisis – deregulation – increased international competition, globalisation of capital, high unemployment, decline union power/numbers. Rise of new right – government hostile/unsympathetic to labour

Table 2.1 illustrates that there is little novel in the techniques employed by contemporary labour management strategy, whether it be labelled HRM, responsible autonomy or world-class manufacturing.

Old Techniques in a New Context

So can contemporary strategy be dismissed as a mere rehash of formerly less than successful techniques? Two considerations substantially qualify such a conclusion. First, and most importantly, the changed social, economic and political context in which these techniques are being reapplied (Roche and Gunnigle, 1995). Recognition and negotiation with trade unions, a characteristic of the regulation strategy in the management of employees (see Table 2.1), has come under increasing strain. Neo-economic liberalism, individualism and general deregulation espoused and practiced by the New Right presents a formidable ideological and material challenge to trade unions and collective bargaining (see Legge, 1995: 80–84). Indeed, the overall decline in strike activity would suggest that trade union room for manoeuvre, even of a defensive kind, has been severely circumscribed. Furthermore, high levels of unemployment may have strengthened workers attachment to jobs threatened by intensified international competition and mobile capital. As Rose (1985: 140) observes, "economic stress encourages a closer calculative compliance with work discipline". The conciliatory line adopted by some trade union leaders may have unwittingly compounded these pressures (see Kelly, 1996). This is illustrated by the advise to members to co-operate or seek accommodation with management bent on the installation of HRM or new forms of work (ICTU, 1993; Beaumont, 1995: 88–94). One optimistic official sees in these developments "the possibility for a growing convergence of interest between progressive employers and progressive trade unions in the modern enterprise" (Geraghty, 1992: 6). Finally, at the political level, former advocates of collectivist/interventionist solutions have fallen silent, possibly fearful of associations with the failed regimes of the Soviet Union and Eastern Europe. These are favourable circumstances for the implementation of current labour management strategy.

Secondly, though the techniques now being applied have past exemplars there is a significant difference. Previous applications were narrowly focused on one, or at most two, conflictual aspects of the employment relationship. Taylorism, for instance, sought to resolve labour management conflict centred on the wage/effort bargain with the formula "a fair day's work for a fair day's pay". However, the commitment model of HRM aspires to synergistically combine a number of old techniques, retitled as human resource practices, into a more comprehensive labour-management strategy addressing all aspects of the employment relationship (see Table 2.1). It attempts to mitigate the conflictual aspects of the relationship while coincidentally emphasising its co-operative aspects. Conflict around the wage bargain is minimised by pay above the norm or through profit and gain sharing schemes. Performance-related pay is a less benign version. By individualising the wage bargain it may neutralise the deployment of collective power in disputes concerning levels of remuneration (Gunnigle et al., 1998). Job enrichment and team working apparently increasing worker autonomy, responsibility and control in job performance renders the effort bargain less visibly conflictual. Quality circles, consultation, a participative management style and minimal status differentiation are used to increase employee commitment and managerial legitimacy. The commodity status of labour is denied by relative employment security and claims to treat the employee as a valuable resource rather than as a cost to be minimised (Friedman, 1990: 179; Storey, 1992: 26). Finally, attempts to structure meaning through unitarist cultural management combines to heavily emphasise the co-operative elements in the employment relationship (Anthony, 1994: 24, 36, 106). This ideological apparatus is underpinned by continual reference to competitive market conditions and consequently the vital necessity for worker flexibility and co-operation in the firm's struggle for survival against competitors (Friedman, 1977: 6; Keenoy and Anthony, 1992: 240–241; Turner and Morley, 1995: 8–10).

However, the extent and thoroughness to which the above commitment/ responsible autonomy model of HRM is being applied remains questionable. Much of the discussion concerning the nature of HRM rests on statements of "espoused" policy rather than rigorous examination of enacted practices (Legge, 1995: 60). In Britain it seems the prescriptions advocated by HRM literature are a long way from being realised (Purcell, 1992: 80). According to Storey (1992: 116) their application has been "patchy." Even large companies are likely to exhibit "an odd hybrid of HRM practices" (Sisson, 1994: 42). Studies of companies using "new management techniques" such as multi-tasking, team working, quality initiatives, communications briefings, underline the partial and contradictory character of such policies. All note the persistence of tightly regulated work routines, the limits of worker involvement, and the continuing importance of the politics of workplace industrial relations (Elger, 1999: 140–141). Writing in 1985 Walton (1985: 84), admitted "that only a small fraction of companies in the US were managed by a comprehensive commitment model of HRM" but he confidently predicted "an accelerated rate of transformation". Little has occurred in the interim to justify such an optimistic prognosis. Five years latter Guest (1990) noted that the impact of HRM in the US had been minimal in all but a small handful of cases. Ireland exhibits a similar pattern (see Roche and Turner, 1997). This partial and piecemeal application of HRM techniques exemplifies the history of management thought and practice.

There is the possibility that in a minority of firms a comprehensive commitment/responsible autonomy model of HRM is consistently and rigorously applied. In that event there may be a good prospect of transcending the conflicting interests integral to the employment relationship. Yet the Achilles Heel of all such schemes emphasising the mutuality of labour management interests is the market context in which they operate. As Anthony

(1986: 35) remarks, "capitalists are driven to seek a co-operative relationship with labour in a market context that limits the potential for achieving that co-operation". The potential for co-operation is limited because managerial conduct is driven by an inevitable economic logic that can only be resisted at the cost of organisational destruction (Reed, 1989: 18).

PROFIT, THE EMPLOYMENT RELATIONSHIP AND THE MARKET CONTEXT

Undoubtedly, the configuration or shape of modern capitalism has radically altered when compared with its 19th century counterpart. These alterations are manifest in the growth of the welfare state, public ownership and increasing state intervention. Furthermore, the divorce of the firm's ownership from its administration has been one of the major structural changes in industry associated with the rise of management (Hill, 1981: 71). These developments, according to Scott (1979: 143), do not constitute any alteration in the basic nature of capitalism, which is still dominated by the priorities, mechanisms and structures of the search for profit. Indeed, the expectation that the separation of the firm's ownership from its control would allow managers to pursue more socially responsible policies do not appear to have been realised. There is little to suggest that the goals of top-level managers are different from those of capitalists in general (Hill, 1981: 74). Apparently, the entrepreneurial and managerial strata have converged rather than moved apart (Nichols, 1969: 142; Nichols, 1980). It is mistaken, Salaman (1981: 245) claims, to view the professionals and experts employed within large corporations as being ultimately concerned with anything but the efficient achievement of the overall goal of profitability. This is hardly surprising given that the purpose of managerial organisation is defined in terms of economic success and competitive effectiveness (Anthony, 1986: 161). So for management the pursuit of profit remains an undiminished guiding force and the underlying principle defining rational action (Storey, 1980: 77; Farnham, 1993: 5). Or as Weber (1958: 17) observes, "capitalism is identical with the pursuit of profit, and forever renewed profit, by means of continuous, rational, capitalistic enterprise".

Given the primacy of profit making it is inevitable that employee interests or needs will be of secondary importance. As Drucker (1951: 81) remarks, "the main function and purpose of the enterprise is the production of goods, not the governance of men and its governmental authority over men must always be subordinated to its economic performance". Or as a contemporary practitioner of HRM warns "it is very easy to forget when endeavouring to develop people and to care for them and even to love them that the needs of the business must come first" (quoted in Legge, 1989: 33). Indeed, Armstrong (1989: 164–165) argues that HRM, far from promoting a strategic treatment of human resources, is likely to subordinate it still further to budgetary controls (see also Dawson, 1989: 11). It follows, therefore, that by the very nature of its profit seeking function, "management must sometimes act against the interests of work people as they see them, and this is incompatible with the concept of a common purpose" (Fox, 1966: 5).

The suggestion that such an outcome is inevitable may seem to overstate the constraints of profit making on managerial action in employee relations. Indeed, the scope for management action in this area is likely to vary with the firm's market situation and its particular business strategy. Managers in firms with a high degree of monopoly power or producing high quality innovative products for niche markets will likely have greater room for manoeuvre (Flood and Turner, 1993). Such firms tend to install the commitment/responsible autonomy model of HRM which operates to obscure the conflictual aspect of the employment relationship and the commodity status of labour. Yet, this model of workforce management is inherently unstable as it is ultimately subject to the vagaries of the market over which management may have little or no control. This is illustrated by the problems that faced computer companies when simultaneously confronted by recession and growing market maturity. Companies such as IBM and Hewlett Packard were caught between their very public commitment to no redundancy and the need for fewer people and different skills. Their difficulty was to secure a lower headcount while appearing to maintain their pledge of no redundancy. It was resolved, to the satisfaction of management at any rate, by the use of "dubious masking strategies" such as compulsory unpaid leave and early retirement incentives (see Legge, 1989: 39).

Again the destabilising effect of the market on the employment relationship is evident in a study of six companies, one of which was a multinational, operating in the industrial and service sectors (Cressey et al., 1985). In all these companies management had attempted to generate employee commitment and co-operation through the use of various human relations devices such as profit sharing, consultative committees and a participative management style. While these initiatives had varying levels of success in establishing a consensus, this was sustained, Cressey (1985: 153) claims, by situations of stability or growth in the particular firm's market. With the onset of recession, consensus in the companies quickly crumbled (Cressey et al., 1985: 153). In the multinational firm, recession forced the abandonment of human relations ideology and practice. It was replaced by a tougher form of management intervention which simply asserted that certain decisions were necessary and not open to question. As management control changed into a coercive form of power the legitimacy of the company's position in relation to its employees was undermined (Cressey et al., 1985: 131; see also Waddington and Whitson, 1996: 174).

Finally, the disruptive effect of the market at a macro level is illustrated by the case of Japan. During the 1980s some American commentators identified Japanese personnel practice as a source of competitive advantage and urged its adoption by western business (Ouchi, 1981; Peters and

Waterman, 1982). Essentially the components of Japanese personnel practice are lifetime or long-term employment, seniority-based wages and enterprise unionism. These are not universally applicable but confined to core employees in the major industrial firms making up about one third of the workforce (Dalzell et al., 1997). However, during the 1990s, a maturing economy and increasing international competition have forced modifications on the minority practice of lifetime employment. Apparently the modifications introduced so far are aimed more at reducing costs than at the abandonment of the long-term employment principle (Befu and Cernosia, 1990; Dalzell et. al., 1997: 163). According to the chairman of the Bank of Japan "the lifetime employment system will not disappear immediately but it will become very weak" (quoted in Eaton, 2000: 31). Difficulties at IBM and Hewlett Packard have already been cited as illustrating the destabilising effect of the market on commitment/responsible autonomy models of workforce management. It is ironic, therefore, that these were among the companies singled out by Ouchi (1981: 219, 225) as coming closest to implementing Japanese personnel practice.

The above examples suggest that a slack or deteriorating market for the firm's goods or services may force management to revert to a direct control strategy, intensify work, reduce wages or shed labour. All or any of these actions can be easily justified as a perfectly logical response to market imperatives and as necessary for firm survival. Nevertheless, their impact, particularly labour shedding, will likely undermine the ethos of co-operation and mutuality and bring into sharp focus the commodity status of labour and previously obscured conflicting interests (see Friedman, 1977: 101–102). As Hyman (1987: 42) observes, in a market system employees are "required to be both dependable and disposable". Consequently, the threadbare rhetoric of "tough love" will likely be an insufficient restraint and then, Sisyphus like, the stone of co-operation and commitment will roll to the bottom of the hill.

In summary, the employment relationship is a dynamic equilibrium between the contending forces or processes of conflict and co-operation. The particular employee relation's strategy adopted by management may serve to tip the balance in favour of one or other of these forces. For instance a direct control strategy or Taylorist organisation of production seems to be universally associated with the industrial pathologies of poor job satisfaction, casual absenteeism, sabotage, theft and workplace conflict generally (Theobald, 1994: 145). Alternatively, the responsible autonomy/commitment model of workforce management will likely shift the balance towards co-operation. Yet, as already noted, this can only be a precarious and temporary equilibrium as long as it remains exposed and vulnerable to the vagaries of the market. The interplay of these forces of conflict, co-operation and the market are illustrated above (see Figure 2.1).

It could be argued that proponents of sophisticated unitarism and its HRM variants have an unreal and fundamentally flawed conception of the employment relationship in a market system. They apparently ignore that remunerative power, the dominant form of power deployed in industrial and commercial organisation, will mainly elicit a calculative involvement of low intensity from subordinates (Anthony, 1994: 23). Attempts to transcend this relationship, a characteristic of market organisations, by substituting normative power and concomitant moral involvement from subordinates will create what has been described as an "incongruent compliance structure" (Etzioni, 1961). If successful, such an arrangement will be short lived because of its inherent instability. Pressure on the firm for efficiency and survival will more than likely force a reversion to a congruent compliance structure of remunerative power and calculative involvement (Etzioni, 1961; Anthony, 1994: 23–24). Yet, these observations may fall well short of the mark. It is no good carping, Keenoy and Anthony (1992: 239) remark, about the differences between image and reality if it is the business of HRM to shift perceptions of that reality or to "manage meaning". "Once it was deemed sufficient," they continue, "to redesign the organisation so as to make it fit human capacity and understanding: now it is better to redesign human understanding to fit the organisation's purpose" (Keenoy and Anthony, 1992: 239). Apart altogether from the dubious morality and totalitarian tinge of such a project, two factors militate against its success. First, the intelligence of subordinates and their capacity for resistance or covert rejection may create difficulties (see Reed, 1992: 280–281; McKinlay and Taylor, 1996; Noon and Blyton, 1997: 206–209; Ackroyd and Thompson, 1999: 155–162). Secondly, the cloudy and obscurantist rhetoric of HRM remains continually vulnerable to exposure by market operations (Sisson, 1994: 15). Marx and Engels long ago noted the effect of the market and its cash nexus relationships or calculative involvement on ideological constructions. "It has drowned," they observed, "the most heavenly ecstasies of religious fervour, of chivalrous enthusiasm, of philistine sentimentalism, in the icy water of egotistical calculation" (Marx and Engels, 1965: 43). In that event the constructing of "realities" or the "management of meaning" may prove a futile and even counterproductive exercise (Keenoy and Anthony, 1992: 244). Those employees who survive the unemployment or "downsizing" required by "tough love" may be a distrustful, sullen and cynically resentful group. The employees who allowed their "realities" or "meanings" to be managed may see themselves as victims of a cruel confidence trick.

COLLECTIVE BARGAINING AND THE EMPLOYMENT RELATIONSHIP

It is a truism that the prospect for success of any management action or strategy will likely improve when grounded in a realistic assessment of the context in which it is to operate. This would equally apply to management action in employee relations. It can be argued that a prerequisite for the effective management of employees is an accurate and authentic comprehension of the nature of the employment relationship. As already outlined, the employment relationship is characterised by conflicting and co-operative interests. Contemporary managerial attempts to escape this complexity through sophisticated unitarism or simple coercion may turn out to be cul-de-sacs (see Hyman, 1980: 313; Scott, 1994; Flood and Toner, 1997). In contemporary management thinking, Torrington (1998: 27) observes, "nothing is more important than to latch onto the latest fashionable idea to change the world, which is much more agreeable than confronting the real problems of working life".

The effective management of the employment relationship would apparently require a recognition and engagement with its complexities and contradictions and be sufficiently flexible to negotiate and renegotiate the maintenance of order and co-operation. Such a method, involving the recognition and negotiation with trade unions through collective bargaining, has been in existence since the 19th century. Trade unions and collective bargaining are not, as is sometimes implied, abnormal distortions alien to the market economy but its very creation and arose out of the worker's daily experience of its operation (Burkitt and Bowers, 1979; Taylor, 1989). The trade unions were both an expression of divergent interests aggravated by the employment relationship of the cash nexus and an attempt to modify market forces and the absolutism of employers. Eventually, collective bargaining as a method of managing discontent in a sensitive and flexible manner came to be regarded by most experts as being without parallel (Keenoy 1985: 106). The Donovan report (1968: 50) claimed that it was the best method of conducting industrial relations. These sentiments are echoed in a submission by the Engineering Employers Federation to a 1992 House of Commons select committee on the future of trade unions. Trade unions, they believed, could continue to develop a constructive relationship with employers and formal procedures for the resolution of individual and collective grievances contributed to the maintenance of orderly industrial relations (quoted in Taylor, 1994: 26). This facility of collective bargaining to maintain or restore order by creating and recreating new equilibriums is illustrated in Figure 2.1. Collective bargaining therefore is a flexible and adaptable set of arrangements that can accommodate to the highly diverse needs and changing circumstances of individual workplaces and their markets (Beaumount, 1995). Ireland provides a concrete example of this ductility where, under the impact of intensifying international competition, there has been a shift from adversarialism towards co-operation and the Irish Congress of Trade Unions has advised members to co-operate with new managerial initiatives designed to improve competitiveness (ICTU 1993; see also Wallace, 1999). Yet, even greater claims have been made for the utility of collective bargaining. According to Harbison (1954), it is inseparable from private enterprise and provides one of the most important bulwarks for its preservation. Through the process of collective bargaining, he argues, unions organise and direct the discontents of labour in such a way as to bolster rather than upset the system of capitalist democracy (Harbison, 1954). For radical critics the ability of collective bargaining to facilitate non-revolutionary change and marginal improvements, though important for employees, only serves to legitimise the domination of the capitalist class and their managerial agents (see Anderson, 1967; Hyman, 1973).

Collective Bargaining and Trade Unions: Anachronisms?

At the beginning of the 21st century, to advance an argument for collective bargaining as an effective method of managing the employment relationship may appear redundant. Furthermore, such an argument is apparently weakened by association with the "old" as against the supposedly "new" models of workforce management (see Dunn, 1990, 1991; Keenoy, 1991). It is undeniable that sizeable falls in union membership and a corresponding decline in the role and influence of collective bargaining have been recorded in many countries (Beaumount, 1995). Recession, unemployment, structural transformation involving a shift from manufacturing to service, growth in white-collar employment, the expansion of micro-electronic-based consumer and capital goods industries, increasing social differentiation and individualisation have all been identified as factors in this decline (Ferner and Hyman, 1992: xix; Zoll, 1996). The sometimes less than successful responses by trade unions to these formidable challenges apparently raise questions regarding the continuing relevance of these organisations and collective bargaining. Yet, before concluding that worker collectivities are anachronisms, unfortunate victims of socio-economic development and change, the political and ideological context in which this occurred must be considered.

The economic crises of the 1970s served to discredit not only the Keynesian policy of demand management and the maintenance of full employment but also its social democratic practitioners. Milton Friedman and the Chicago school of economists argued that the way out of the crisis was to restore the primacy of the market mechanism. Its working, they claimed, had been progressively impeded by decades of government intervention and rigidities imposed by trade union power (see McCrone et al., 1989). Friedman's monetarism rapidly became the dominant economic orthodoxy of the 1980s. Economic crisis and a revivified economic liberalism espoused and practised by "new right" conservative parties combined to place social democracy on the defensive. In Europe the political balance of power generally swung against labour. Even some nominally socialist governments pursued conservative economic strategies of retrenchment, control of public expenditure and restructuring of labour markets (Ferner and Hyman, 1992). At enterprise level, new right ideology in the guise of HRM laid a heavy emphasis on individualism, the common interests of employer and employee and by implication the redundancy of collective representation. The ideology and practice of these policies, essentially inimical to organised labour, received their fullest and unrestricted expression at both a political and enterprise level under Prime Minister Thatcher in Britain and President Reagan in the US.

Structural transformation, political change and managerial action have all been identified as factors contributing to union decline. However, the relative weight or importance of these factors in contributing to this outcome has implications for the argument in this chapter. Trade unions and collective bargaining, it was argued, retain a contemporary relevance. Yet, this argument is substantially weakened if structural factors, such as shifts in the demographic, industrial and occupational composition of the workforce, are the major elements in union decline. This would suggest that union representation is unnecessary and irrelevant for the growing number of employees in the new sectors of the economy and workplaces. Far from retaining a contemporary relevance, trade unions would seem likely to wither away.

A different conclusion can be drawn if employer opposition and a hostile state are the major elements in union decline. In this case, union decline might be chiefly due to suppressing the exercise of employee choice with regard to union membership. This might constitute a challenge to the existence of trade unions, but not their relevance. An indication of the relative importance of political, managerial and structural factors in union decline can be gained by examining their effect in the US.

Trade Unions in the US: A Natural Death or Homicide?

Among the industrialised nations the US furnishes one of the more dramatic examples of trade union decline. In 1955 approximately 36 per cent of private sector workers were organised in unions. By 1975 this figure had fallen to 28 per cent (Freeman and Medoff, 1984: 222). Beyond that time the decline became precipitous and by 1995 a little over 10 per cent of private sector workers were union members (Miller, 1997: 238). An analysis of data produced by the National Labour Relations Board (NLRB) found that shifts in the demographic, industrial and occupational composition of the workforce accounted for only 20 per cent of the decline in union density since the mid 1970s (quoted in Kochan and Weinstein, 1994: 487). Indeed, Freeman and Medoff (1984: 227) dismiss the technocratic or structural change hypothesis as the major explanation of union decline as erroneous. First, in Canada, which experienced the same structural changes and where many of the same unions and firms operate, the percentage of unionised workers has increased. Secondly, it does not allow for factors such as union organisational activity or management opposition to affect unionisation (Freeman and Medoff, 1984: 227).[2] They

---

2. The National Labour Relations Act, 1935, conferred on American workers the right to join a trade union and bargain collectively with the employer through representatives of their own choosing. To ensure employees could exercise these rights, the Act

estimate that from 25 per cent to 50 per cent of the decline in union election successes can be attributed to rising management opposition (Freeman and Medoff, 1984: 237). Yet this estimate may err on the side of caution.

There is a long history of opposition by American employers to trade unions (Lewin, 1987). Indeed, the US has had the bloodiest and most violent labour history of any industrial nation in the world (Taft and Ross, 1969: 270). Since the end of the 1970s, many commentators have noted increasing management opposition to trade unions and collective bargaining (Lewin, 1987; Wheeler, 1987; Lawler, 1990). For instance, two surveys on the management of labour relations interviewed corporate executives in several hundred of the largest firms in the US. These firms varied considerably regarding the degree of unionisation. Respondents were asked whether the firm attached greater priority to achieving the best bargain in contract negotiations or forestalling unionisation. In the 1978 survey, over 30 per cent of the unionised firms identified their priority as "keeping the company as non-union as possible". This had risen to 50 per cent in the 1983 survey (quoted in Lawler, 1990: 69–70). Apparently, this hostility has continued to intensify. Writing over a decade later, Miller (1997: 250) noted that employer resistance to union organising campaigns is now extreme and intense.

In short, it has become increasingly common for employers to actively campaign to persuade employees not to join unions. Attorneys or labour management consultants who specialise in defeating union-organising drives can assist employers in this endeavour. In 1979 American industry was estimated to spend more than 100 million dollars annually in fees for such consultants (*Economist*, 1979). By the late 1980s, consultant activity was at unprecedented levels (Lawler, 1990: 83). Some forms of consultant activity, though technically legal, may involve serious breaches of professional ethics, while many of the tactics they employ are incompatible with public policy (Lawler, 1990: 117). A final expedient is to sack workers who express a wish or exhibit a propensity to join a union. Though illegal, this may be the most effective intervention. In the early 1980s, one in twenty workers who favoured a union got fired (Freeman and Medoff, 1984: 232). Such illegal activity appears to be on the increase. Data from the Commission on the Future of Worker-Management Relations show that the incidence of illegal firing

established a National Labour Relations Board. Its principal functions are to determine through secret ballot election the free democratic choice of employees whether they wish to be represented by a union and to prevent unlawful acts or unfair labour practices by employers interfering with that right (Quinn Mills, 1978: 308–309). Initially employers were required to remain outside the election process. However, the enactment by a Republican-dominated Congress of the Taft Hartley Act 1947 provided that the expression of any view, argument or opinion in printed, graphic or visual form did not constitute an unfair labour practice by employers. Threats of reprisal, promise of benefits, coercion or intimidation by employers still remained illegal. Nevertheless the so-called "free speech" provision had the effect of putting employers back into the matter of union organisation, usually in opposition (Quinn Mills, 1978: 320).

increased from 1 in every 25 elections and 1 in every 600 union supporters in the early 1950s to 1 in every 4 elections and 1 in every 48 union supporters by the end of the 1980s (quoted in Kochan and Weinstein, 1994: 486). In 1997 the NLRB formally charged employers with committing "unfair labour practices" in 12,000 cases (Palast, 1998). There can be little doubt of the negative effect of management intervention on the outcome of a union election (see Table 6.4, Fossum, 1995: 163). It has been estimated that a campaign combining both legal and illegal approaches reduces union victories to 4 per cent, or one union win in every 25 elections (Fossum, 1995: 167). It is noteworthy that the unions primarily affected by consultant activity are those attempting to organise workers in the growth sectors of the economy such as the service sector (Lawler, 1990: 97). This further points up the inadequacy of the structural change hypothesis as the major explanation for union decline. Finally, a majority of scholars ascribe the increase in union avoidance and rising number of unfair labour practices to a rational choice or response by employers to the cost of unionisation as measured against the non-union wage differential (see Lawler, 1990: Chapter 4). Nevertheless, it has been suggested that anti-unionism on management's part is less a reaction to the costs associated with collective bargaining and more an emotional response prompted by a fear of lost power and status (Lawler, 1990: 77).

Since 1981 under the Reagan and Bush administrations the state has served as an auxiliary in the employers' war of attrition against trade unions. Appointees of the Regan and Bush administrations to key political positions in the state regulatory agencies dealing with employee management relations were at best unsympathetic to labour. The chairman of the NLRB, a Reagan appointee, claimed that "collective bargaining frequently means labour monopoly, the destruction of individual freedom and the destruction of the market place as the mechanism for determining the value of labour" (quoted in Barbash, 1985: 12). Under this regime there was a drastic change in the interpretation and enforcement of labour law (Kovach, 1992). In some instances, federal agencies used their rule-making powers to modify existing occupational health, safety and labour laws, while in other cases chose not to enforce the law (Barbash, 1985). Judgements from previous administrations considered favourable to labour were reversed (Kovach, 1992). Finally, there were substantial reductions in the budgets of the agencies administering labour law. This served to create a backlog of cases that had a twofold effect. It tended to discourage the filing of charges, while of those actually filed a smaller percentage could be heard and, if necessary, prosecuted (Kovach, 1992). According to Kovach (1992), these developments weaken the position of organised labour and in turn make unions less attractive to potential members. The political factor, he concludes, is equally important as structural change in explaining union decline (Kovach, 1992: 9). Yet, when factors such as the unprecedented intensity of legal and illegal management opposition and the hostile political climate for labour are considered in combination, then the structural change explanation for union decline is relegated to one of secondary importance. Thus, the claim that union decline is primarily due to its redundancy and irrelevance for employees in the new economic order is difficult to sustain.

Employee Perceptions and Union Relevance

Given the prevailing anti-union employer stance and a sometimes hostile state, the decline in private sector unionism in the US is hardly surprising. Outside its ranks, American labour appears to have few allies. History and the culture of individualism among the general public and mass media seems to have fostered an unfavourable attitude to organised labour (see Bok and Dunlop, 1970: 22; Jacoby, 1991). Apparently, the outlook for private sector unionism is extremely bleak. Yet, a recent attitude survey (1999) conducted by Hart Associates for the American Federation of Labour and the Congress of Industrial Organisations (AFL/CIO) questions such a pessimistic prognosis. Among the population generally, negative attitudes towards unions have declined from one out of every three Americans to one out of every four since 1997. In the six years since 1993 there has been an eleven point drop in negative attitudes from 34 to 23 per cent. A majority of those polled (52 per cent) believed it would be good for the country if more workers had union representation. When Americans who are not members of a union were asked how they would vote if a union election were held in their workplace tomorrow, 43 per cent said they would definitely or probably vote for a union. This percentage has increased by nearly half in the past fifteen years, while the percentage of those who say they would vote against a union has dropped dramatically. Among non-union, non-supervisory young adults between 18 and 34, negative attitudes towards unions are lower than among all other age brackets. The majority of young workers (54 per cent) not in a union report they would definitely or probably vote for one. As this figure represents a 6 per cent increase on the 1997 figure it would seem to suggest that young workers are increasingly likely to vote for union representation. Finally, a majority of American workers (69 per cent) were of the opinion that employees were more successful in getting problems resolved with their employer when they bring these problems as a group rather than individuals (Hart Research Associates Inc., 1999)

In the context of the active aggression of anti-union employers, along with an unfavourable cultural and political climate for collectivism, these findings are remarkable. Despite powerful forces promoting a contrary view, a belief in the utility, necessity and effectiveness of collective representation persists among the workers surveyed. Assuming a rational basis for this conviction then its likely origin is to be found in the daily experience of these workers in the operation of the employment relationship in a market system. Trade unions and collective bargaining, far from being anachronisms, appear to retain an immediate and contemporary relevance.

Non-unionism: An Effective Alternative?

The opposition of American employers or their managerial agents to trade unionism may be exceptional but only in regard to its extent and intensity. Ideally the generality of managers would probably prefer to manage without unions. Certainly contemporary circumstances in sapping the strength of organised labour have served to advance non-unionism as an increasingly feasible proposition (see Flood and Toner, 1996). Short of simple coercion, can non-unionism be effective in managing employees and so transcend the power imbalance and conflicting interests, characteristics of the employment relationship, that trade unions both express and temporarily resolve? The main perceived advantage for management in avoiding trade unions has been the ability to pay lower wages than unionised competitors and the ability to make potentially unpopular decisions without facing an organised challenge from the workforce (Flood and Toner, 1996: 154). Additional reasons for management opposition to unions have been reported by Toner (1987). For instance, some of the managers interviewed claimed that unions promote an adversarial industrial relations climate, provide a platform for troublemakers and inhibit individual rewards (Toner, 1987). Yet, even a cursory examination of some of the stated reasons for opposition would show that they owe more to ideological prejudice than rational analysis. Union representation of employees does not introduce conflict but merely reflects the conflict that already exists (see Fox, 1966; Daniel and McIntosh, 1972: 115). Indeed, management action can be an important determinant in tipping the balance in favour of conflict or co-operation. As for the agitator thesis, this has been comprehensively dismissed by Fox (1966). In the absence of genuine conflicts of interest the gospel of discontent is likely to fall on stony ground. Anyway, those regarded by management as agitators may be perceived by employees as their democratically elected representative acting in their collective interest. The claim of Toner's managerial respondents that unions inhibit individual rewards would seem to be more substantial. Generally, trade unions oppose individual reward systems or individual bargaining because it strikes at the heart of collectivism (see Gunnigle et al., 1998). However, this opposition may be more pragmatic than ideological. Given the conflicts of interest and the gross disparity in power between the parties, individual bargaining will most likely favour the employer (Crouch, 1982: 45). In any case, management's own arrangement of operations within the enterprise promotes the development of a collective basis to the employment relationship (see Salamon, 1987: 53). For instance, HRM simultaneously attempts to promote individualism through performance-related pay and collectivism through team working. The value in rehearsing these old truisms allows one to make an a priori assumption regarding the effectiveness of non-unionism. Short of simple coercion, the prospect held out by non-unionism of an absolute freedom to manage seems likely to prove illusory. The conflicts of interest in the employment relationship have an endemic potential to generate worker resistance. Admittedly, in the absence of independent collective representation of employees, these conflicts may be less overt (see Pollert, 1996: 206). Yet, to anticipate and deal effectively with covert conflict may require a greater expenditure of managerial time, vigilance and money. Consequently, the freedom to manage will remain circumscribed.

The above argument is supported by a number of studies of non-union firms. One study of large non-union firms found that they were unable to take advantage of union absence to impose less favourable pay and conditions. Rather, wage rates and conditions were marginally better in the non-union firms than in their unionised counterparts (Flood and Toner, 1996: 168). Furthermore, the necessity of dealing with so-called "trivial grievances" could not be avoided by the non-union firm. Indeed, the monitoring of grievances seemed to be a constant worry for the managers of these firms (Flood and Toner, 1996: 172). It is not certain, they conclude, that non-union status ensures significantly greater flexibility than union status (Flood and Toner, 1996: 179). For these large high-wage firms, managing without unions was a far cry from the supposed freedom that union avoidance might be expected to confer (Flood and Toner, 1996: 180). These findings are echoed in a study of British industrial relations in non-union firms in the high technology sector (McLoughlin and Gourlay, 1994; McLoughlin, 1996). In three workforces, whose technical and professional composition might have been expected to underpin a low propensity to unionise, it was found that at least three out of every ten employees showed a propensity to join a union (McLoughlin, 1996: 316). Even in the high-tech sector, non-union employers do not appear to have found a universally applicable solution to the problems of managing without unions. Managing without unions, McLoughlin (1996: 317) concludes, could conceivably turn out to be more trouble than managing with them.

Finally, evidence from three company case studies suggests that a non-union approach to managing the employment relationship may not be a stable or productive course in the long run (Scott, 1994: 152). Summarising the results of his case studies, Scott concludes that they illustrate a simple point: a genuine consensus about the goals of an organisation cannot be created by denying that there are differences of interest between workers and management. Rather workers' morale and willingness to co-operate with management depends not only upon their being kept well informed of management decisions but also upon their being able to analyse, challenge and influence those decisions, without fear of being seen as disloyal or disruptive by management (Scott, 1994: 157–158). This necessarily involves a pluralist approach to industrial relations or the recognition and negotiation with independent trade unions. The evidence from Scott's case studies suggests that where management devoted attention to making this approach work it yielded substantial flexibility and a considerable measure of co-operation (Scott, 1994: 157). This pluralist or "old fashioned" approach to managing change proved more effective than the strategies of sophisticated unitarism or union marginalisation implemented in the other two companies.

The case studies in question highlight a paradox of non-unionism. It apparently holds out the promise of freedom from the checks and balances imposed by collectivism on the exercise of managerial discretion and power. While the non-union firms in these studies may have escaped the internal check of collectivism, they remained in the shadow of the external unionised environment which influenced or at least provided a benchmark for their employee relations policy, procedures and wages. How many large non-union companies would continue to invest in their high wage, high commitment strategies in the absence of unions is, Flood and Toner (1996: 180) remark, an empirical question. Yet, if an external union presence renders non-unionism a pyrrhic victory, then its absence should allow employers to adopt a less costly employee relations strategy. After all, the ability to pay lower wages and manage without challenge is the very *raison d'être* of non-unionism. Consequently, it seems logical to argue that many of these non-union companies would abandon their high-wage, high-commitment strategies once the external check of collectivism were removed. Yet, this argument is somewhat academic in a number of respects. The examples cited of large non-union companies and their relatively benign employee relations' policies are probably atypical. Among the generality of non-union companies they would appear to be the exception rather than the rule (Blyton and Turnbull, 1994: 223–249). Secondly, the autocratic benevolence practiced by some large non-union firms is not historically unique. Even in the early period of industrialisation, there was always a tiny minority of employers who, motivated by Christian, humanitarian or paternalist sentiment, pursued relatively similar policies (Fitton and Wadsworth, 1958). Nevertheless, their existence did not prevent the rise of trade unions. Finally, another atypical aspect of the large contemporary non-union firm is its market situation. Usually capital intensive, they occupy a temporarily favourable or commanding position in the market (see Flood and Turner, 1993). In such circumstances management in these firms may have greater discretion to pursue more benevolent employee relations policies. These firms could be said to operate in the airy uplands of the capitalist market. In small firms operating in the fiercely competitive undergrowth, non-unionism manifests a more malign aspect.

Since 1980, successive Conservative governments in Britain have sought in various way to systematically weaken the power of unions and workers in relation to employers (Crouch, 1991). In this hostile political climate for organised labour, non-unionism has apparently flourished. Typically, these non-union firms seem to be small and recently established in the service sector (Beaumount, 1995: 63). The British Workplace Industrial Relations Survey (WIRS) provides a fairly detailed picture of employee relations in the non-union sector (Millward et al., 1992). From this picture an inference can be drawn as to the future shape of employee relations in the private sector if the trend away from unionisation were to continue (Millward et al., 1992: 363).

The WIRS reported that employee relations in the non-union sector were seen by management as good or very good. Certainly, strikes were unheard of and indicators of dissatisfaction such as absenteeism were no worse than the unionised sector. However, labour turnover was high and there was a higher rate of injuries at work. In the absence of unions, pay levels were unilaterally determined by management. Commercial and financial considerations were the dominant criteria in pay determination. As a result, lower-paid employees were more common and differentials between the highest and lowest paid earners in the non-union firms tended to be relatively wide. Nevertheless, labour flexibility was higher in the non-union sector with a greater use of freelance and temporary contract workers. Managers were less constrained in the way they organised work, as opposition from employees to changes in working methods were rare. This quiescence may be explained by the high rate of dismissal, which was nearly twice as frequent per employee as in the union sector. There seemed to be a scarcity of employee voice mechanisms. In a quarter of the non-union firms surveyed there was no procedure for employees to use if they had a grievance while in another quarter there was no procedure for employees to raise health and safety issues. Another fifth of these firms had no procedures for dealing with discipline and dismissal. It is little wonder that in these workplaces, morale was identified by managers as one of the most important employee relations issues (Millward et al., 1992: 363–364).

Overall, the non-union industrial and commercial firms surveyed by Millward et al. had relatively few formal mechanisms through which employees could contribute to the operation of their workplace in a broader context beyond that of their specific job. Nor were they likely to have opportunities to air grievances or resolve problems in ways that were systematic and designed to ensure fairness of treatment. Apparently, no alternative model of employee representation had emerged as a substitute for trade union representation (Millward et al., 1992: 365). Indeed the "representation gap" that existed in 1990 was even bigger by 1998 (Cully et al., 1999: 297). A situation described by Beaumount (1995: 105) as "an institutional vacuum".[3] Going on the evidence provided by the surveys cited, the freedom to manage conferred by non-unionism does not appear to result in an improvement but in deterioration in the management of employee relations. This outcome lends substance to the old claim that a union presence

---

3. A solution for the problematic absence of employee voice and representation in the non-union firm has been proposed by Sparrow and Marchington (1998). They suggest that the key task for HR practitioners and HR academics "is to find ways of ensuring that proper notice is taken of the employee contribution to organisations, and that short-term financial solutions are not allowed to dominate management decisions" (Sparrow and Marchington, 1998: 313). This may be a less than effective solution as it fails to offer any source of independent representation for employees and appears to be administratively unworkable.

helps management to manage better.[4] Even in the non-union firms managerial freedom of action remains subject to the constraints of the market. These constraints are likely to be particularly pressing on those firms operating in a fiercely competitive market. Undoubtedly, the supposed freedom allowed by non-unionism to respond to these pressures without a challenge from or reference to employees may retain a superficial attractiveness for many managers. It was precisely the pursuit of such a strategy in the early period of industrialisation that brought trade unions and collective bargaining into being in the first instance. They continue to feature in the contemporary landscape because the conflicts of interest and disparity of power that characterise the employment relationship in a market system persist. Recognition and negotiation with trade unions is not only a pragmatic and practical response to managing the contradictions and conflicts that characterise the employment relationship but, as already noted, it also has a long history of proven effectiveness.

COLLECTIVE BARGAINING AND DEMOCRACY

It can be argued that trade unions, acting as a counterweight to the overweening power of capital, may help to preserve a modicum of democratic accountability in capitalist democracies. A truly democratic society would seem to require some extension of democratic procedures, processes and control to the economic arena (Bullock, 1977: 20–25). For instance, when confronted with the inevitability of universal suffrage, John Stuart Mill was concerned as to how the newly enfranchised working classes might participate in the state. He suggested that the educative effect of participation at local level and in the workplace would prepare workers for involvement in the wider political arena (Pateman, 1970: 38). Since that time, employee participation has achieved its most concrete form through collective bargaining. Indeed, it eventually came to be regarded as the most effective means through which employees could influence organisational decision making (Gunnigle, 1999: 7). Collective bargaining, it was claimed, is an integral part of the democratisation of work (Schuller, 1985: 5).

In many European countries during the 1960s, within a context of full employment and social democratic hegemony, collective bargaining came to be seen as a relatively restricted form of participation. Collective bargaining, it was argued, whilst preserving the union's independence from management, presented no challenge to management's ultimate authority but indeed accepted and underwrote it (Brannen, 1983: 27). A wide range of managerial

---

4. Union density was found by Cully et al. (1999: 111) to relate to the spread of high commitment management practices; the more practices there were in place in recognised workplaces the greater the union density. They found a positive relationship between recognised unions and the spread of these practices (Cully et al., 1999: 133).

decisions, such as investment, location, closures, mergers or take-overs which had important consequences for employees were largely beyond the control or influence of trade unions and collective bargaining (Bullock, 1977: 24). This appeared at odds with the citizen's right in a democracy to choose a government for the wider society while within the enterprise the influence or control exercised by the employee citizen was severely curtailed. Consequently, worker participation became a "democratic imperative". This meant that "those who will be substantially affected by decisions made by social and political institutions must be involved in the making of those decisions" (Bulletin of EC, 1972; Bullock, 1977: 25). Out of these concerns came proposals for industrial democracy or worker representatives on company boards. These elected representatives were to extend worker influence on managerial decisions that were beyond the reach of collective bargaining and trade unions. Such proposals attempted to balance economic interests in maintaining efficient production against social concern for employees as industrial citizens who, under hierarchical management authority, enjoyed only restricted rights in the workplace (Hyman and Mason, 1995: 15). They were also manifestations of social democratic reformism and its sensitivity to the potential deprivations that accompany unregulated market operations (Hyman and Mason, 1995: 29).

The various attempts during the 1970s to promote schemes of participation inspired by democratic principles encountered sustained and ultimately successful employer opposition (see Leat, 1998: 272–316). In contemporary market-driven economies, Hyman and Mason argue (1995: 8), industrial democracy is a term with little currency and as a set of ideas and practice has largely disintegrated to be replaced by the managerial initiative of employee involvement. These schemes are primarily designed to serve managerial and commercial objectives rather than that of employee interests (Hyman and Mason, 1995: 193). Employees are increasingly left with management inspired and controlled involvement as their main or sole source of information, communication and action. In an increasingly individualised and deregulated labour market with global competition acting as the prime motor for management practice, it seems likely that the bulk of employees will be left with few resources either to query or contest the direction taken by management control, despite the rhetoric of empowerment, involvement and a host of other metaphors raised to disguise the workers' growing occupational impoverishment (Hyman and Mason, 1995: 193).

However, these pessimistic prognostications are only likely to be fully realised in the absence of collective bargaining and trade unions. In industrial and commercial organisations, hierarchy defines many employees as subordinates, inferiors in responsibility, authority, status and value to the enterprise. Indeed, "it is difficult to conceive of any practicable business organisation where this is not the case" (Daniel and McIntosh, 1972: 111). This locates the employee in a position of dependence on the good will, discretion and patronage of his or her superiors in a whole range of areas affecting a job and career. Such a context is not conducive to an atmosphere in which ideas and criticisms that may implicitly challenge superiors can be freely expressed (Daniel and McIntosh, 1972: 111). Autocratic rule, no matter how benevolent, flatly contradicts the classic democratic ideals of participation, free expression and egalitarianism. It seems more likely that the voice of those at the bottom of the hierarchy will be more freely expressed and more effectively heard when backed by a framework independent of the power, status and reward system of the organisation. By the deployment of their collective strength, trade unions compensate employees for the power they cannot have within the formal hierarchy (Daniel and McIntosh, 1972: 112). As the Donovan report remarked, "collective bargaining is the most effective means of giving workers the right to representation in decisions affecting their working lives – a right which is or should be the prerequisite of every worker in a democratic society" (Donovan, 1968: 54). Trade unions, therefore, not only emphasise the human value of the labour commodity in a market system but in imposing a check on the exercise of power both express and foster democratic values and culture.

CONCLUSION

The employment relationship is characterised by conflicting and co-operative interests, asymmetrical power relations and the dualism of the labour commodity, and operates within a dynamic market context. This continuously and variously operates to advance or retard the predominance of these variables. The effective management of the employment relationship requires a recognition and engagement with its complexities and contradictions and must be sufficiently flexible to negotiate and re-negotiate the maintenance of order and co-operation. Such a method, involving the recognition and negotiation with trade unions through collective bargaining, has been in existence since the 19th century. Trade unions were both an expression of divergent interests and an attempt to modify market forces and the absolutism of employers. Eventually, collective bargaining, as a method of managing discontent in a sensitive and flexible manner, came to be regarded by many as being without parallel (Keenoy, 1985: 106; Donovan, 1968). Nevertheless, trade unions and collective bargaining constitute a check, though of a limited kind, on management freedom of action. As a result, their acceptance by the generality of managers has probably owed more to pragmatism than enthusiasm.

Union decline during the 1980s was interpreted by some commentators as indicative of their decreasing relevance in the new economic and social order. Yet, far from being a natural evolutionary development, this decline was primarily due to unemployment, a revivified economic liberalism, a corresponding ideological crisis in European social democracy, accompanied in some cases by increasingly hostile state and managerial action directed against trade unions. Nevertheless, these facts were not allowed to stand in the way of a good news story: the coming managerial liberation from the incubus of worker collectivities. However, many studies show that the promised freedoms of non-unionism, in either its benign or coercive forms, is questionable. Indeed, in some non-union companies management's freedom to manage appeared to be under greater constraint than that of their counterparts in unionised firms. The lack-lustre performance of non-unionism may be explained by its failure to engage directly with the enduring contradictions and complexities that characterise the employment relationship. Rather, it deals with these complexities through evasion, suppression and cultural manipulation – strategies that remain continually vulnerable to exposure or challenge. Yet, non-unionism is hardly a novel approach to managing the employment relationship. Its contemporary variants are still beset by the old contradictions and conflicts. There is little evidence here of a paradigm shift in the nature of the employment relationship. In contrast to non-unionism, the strength of collective bargaining is its proven ability to deal effectively with the endemic instability that characterises the employment relationship in a market context. Trade unions and collective bargaining function to create and recreate new equilibriums in that relationship.

Apart from the pragmatic argument for collective bargaining and trade unions there is the ideological argument that has a particular appeal for democrats. The exercise of absolute power, the absence of accountability and countervailing checks and balances, are foreign to any democratic polity. In essence, this is the situation in the non-union firm. Thus, the non-union firm appears as an anomaly, an autocratic enclave within democratic society. The starkness of this anomaly is reduced by the operation of trade unions and collective bargaining within the enterprise. At the micro level of the enterprise, trade unions express the ongoing tensions and conflicts between democratic humanistic values and market values. Clashes between these values have dogged market economies since the advent of universal suffrage.

REFERENCES

Ackroyd, S. and Thompson, P. (1999) *Organisational Misbehaviour*. London. Sage Publications.

Anderson, P. (1967) "The Limits and Possibilities of Trade Union Action" in Blackburn, R. and Cockburn, A. (eds) *The Incompatibles: Trade Union Militancy and the Consensus*. Harmondsworth: Penguin Books.

Anthony, P. (1994) *Managing Culture*. Buckingham: Open University Press.

Anthony, P. D. (1986) *The Foundations of Management*. London: Tavistock Publications.

Armstrong, P. (1989) "Limits and Possibilities for HRM in an Age of Management Accountancy" in Storey, J. (ed.) *New Perspectives on Human Resource Management*. London: Routledge.

Barbash, J. (1985) "Do we really want Labour on the Ropes?" *Harvard Business Review,* July–August: 10–15.

Beaumont, P. (1995) *The Future of Employment Relations.* London: Sage Publications.

Beer, M. and Spector, B. (1985) (eds) *Readings in Human Resource Management.* New York: Free Press.

Befu, H. and Cernosia, C. (1990) "Demise of 'Permanent Employment' in Japan" *Human Resource Management,* Fall, Vol. 29, No. 3: 231–250.

Bell, D. (1960) *The End of Ideology.* New York: Free Press.

Bendix, R. (1963) *Work and Authority in Industry.* New York: Harper and Row.

Blyton, P. and Turnbull, P. (1994) *The Dynamics of Employee Relations.* London: Macmillan.

Bok, D. C. and Dunlop, J. T. (1970) *Labour and the American Community.* New York: Simon Schuster.

Brannen, P. (1983) *Authority and Participation in Industry.* London: Batsford.

Breen, R. and Whelan, C. (1996) *Social Mobility and Social Class in Ireland.* Dublin: Gill and Macmillan.

Brewster, C. and Hegewisch, A. (1994) *Policy and Practice in European Human Resource Management: The Price Waterhouse Cranfield Survey.* London: Routledge.

Buckingham, J. and Lawrence, P. (1985) "The Real Work of Managers" in Lawrence, P. and Elliot, K. (eds) *Introducing Management.* London: Penguin Business.

Bullock Report. *Report of the Committee of Inquiry on Industrial Democracy.* (1977). London: HMSO.

Burkitt, B. and Bowers, D. (1979) *Trade Unions and the Economy.* London: Macmillan.

Child, J. (1969) *British Management Thought.* London: Allen and Unwin.

Cressey, P., Eldridge, J. and MacInnes, J. (1985) *Just Managing: Authority and Democracy in Industry.* Milton Keynes: Open University Press.

Crouch, C. (1982) *Trade Unions: The Logic of Collective Action.* Glasgow: Fontana.

Crouch, C. (1991) "United Kingdom: The Rejection of Compromise" in Baglioni, G. and Crouch, C. (eds) *European Industrial Relations The Challenge of Flexibility.* London: Sage Publications.

Cully, M., Woodland, S., O'Reilly, A. and Dix, G. (1999) *Britain at Work: As Depicted by the 1998 Workplace Employee Relations Survey.* London: Routledge.

D'Art, D. (1992) *Economic Democracy and Financial Participation: A Comparative Study.* London: Routledge.

D'Art, D. and Turner, T. (1999) "An Attitudinal Revolution in Irish Industrial Relations: The End of 'Them and Us'?" *British Journal of Industrial Relations,* Vol. 37, No. 1.

Dalzell, T., Wallace, J. and Delany, B. (1997) "The Westernisation of Japanese

Personnel Management" in Wallace, J., Dalzell, T. and Delany, B. (eds) *Continuity and Change in the Employment Relationship*. Vol. 1 of the Official Proceedings of the Fifth IIRA European Regional Industrial Relations Congress. Dublin: Oak Tree Press.

Daniel, W. W. and McIntosh, N. (1972) *The Right to Manage?* London: Macdonald and Jane's. 3rd Impression.

Dawson, C. (1989) "The Moving Frontiers of Personnel Management: Human Resource Management or Human Resource Accounting" *Personnel Review*, Vol. 18, No. 3: 3–12.

Donovan Report. *Royal Commission on Trade Unions and Employers' Associations 1965–1968*. (1968) London: HMSO.

Drucker, P. (1951) *The New Society: The Anatomy of the Industrial Order*. London: Heinemann.

Dunn, S. (1990) "Root Metaphor in the Old and New Industrial Relations" *British Journal of Industrial Relations*, Vol. 28: 1 March.

Dunn, S. (1991) "Root Metaphor in Industrial Relations: A Reply to Tom Keenoy" *British Journal of Industrial Relations*, Vol. 29: 2 June.

Eaton, J. (2000) *Comparative Industrial Relations: An Introduction*. Cambridge: Polity Press.

Edwards, P. (1995) "The Employment Relationship" in Edwards, P. (ed.) *Industrial Relations: Theory and Practice in Britain*. Oxford: Blackwell.

Edwards, P. K. (1986) *Conflict at Work: A Materialist Analysis of Workplace Relations*. London: Blackwell.

Edwards, P. K. and Scullion, H. (1982) *The Social Organisation of Industrial Conflict*. Oxford. Oxford University Press.

Eldridge, J. E. T. (1973) *Sociology and Industrial Life*. London: Nelson's University Paperbacks.

Elger, T. (1999) "Manufacturing Myths and Miracles: Work Reorganisation in British Manufacturing since 1979" in Beynon, H. and Glavanis, P. (eds) *Patterns of Social Inequality*. London: Longman.

Etzioni, A. (1961) *A Comparative Analysis of Complex Organisations: On Power, Involvement and their Correlates*. New York: Free Press.

Farnham, D. (1993) *Employee Relations*. London: Institute of Personnel Management.

Ferner, A. and Hyman, R. (1992) *Industrial Relations in the New Europe*. Oxford: Blackwell.

Fitton, R. S. and Wadsworth, A. P. (1958) *The Strutts and the Arkwrights: A Study of the Early Factory System*. Manchester: Manchester University Press.

Flood, P. and Toner, B. (1996) "Managing without Unions: A Pyrrhic Victory?" in Flood, P. C., Gannon, M. J. and Paauwe, J. (eds) *Managing without Traditional Methods*. Addison-Wesley: University Press Cambridge.

Flood, P. and Toner, B. (1997) "Large Non-Union Companies: How do they Avoid a Catch-22?" in D'Art, D. and Turner, T. (eds) *Collectivism and Individualism: Trends and Prospects*. Vol. 7 of the Official Proceedings of the Fifth IIRA European Regional Industrial Relations Congress. Dublin: Oak Tree Press.

Flood, P. and Turner, T. (1993) "Human Resource Strategy and the Non-Union Phenomenon" *Employee Relations*, Vol. 15, No. 6.

Fossum, J. A. (1995) *Labour Relations: Development – Structure – Process*. (6th edition) Chicago: Irwin.

Fox, A. (1966) *Industrial Sociology and Industrial Relations*. Research Papers No. 3. London: HMSO.

Fox, A. (1971) *A Sociology of Work in Industry*. London: Collier-Macmillan.

Fox, A. (1974) *Man Mismanagement*. London: Huthchinson.

Freeman, R. B. and Medoff, J. L. (1984) *What do Unions do?* New York: Basic Books.

Friedman, A. (1977) *Industry and Labour: Class Struggle at Work and Monopoly Capitalism*. London: Macmillan.

Friedman, A. (1990) "Managerial Strategies, Activities, Techniques and Technology: Towards a Complex Theory of the Labour Process" in Knight, D. and Wilmott, H. (eds) *Labour Process Theory*. London: Macmillan.

Fukuyama, F. (1992) *The End of History and the Last Man*. London: Hamish Hamilton.

Gallie, D., White, M., Cheng, Y. and Tomlinson, M. (1998) *Restructuring the Employment Relationship*. Oxford: Clarendon Press.

Geraghty, D. (1992) *World Class Participation*. The 17th Countess Markievicz Memorial Lecture. Dublin.

Giddens, A. (1973) *The Class Structure of the Advanced Societies*. London: Hutchinson.

Giddens, A. (1989) *Sociology*. Oxford: Basil Blackwell. Polity Press.

Goodwin, B. (1997) *Using Political Ideas*. (4th edition) New York: John Wiley and Sons.

Gouldner, A. (1954) *Wildcat Strike*. Harper: Torch Books.

Guest, D. (1990) "Human Resource Management and the American Dream" *Journal of Management Studies*, Vol. 27: 4 July.

Gunnigle, P. (1999) *Involvement, Participation and Partnership: A Review of the Debate and Some Reflections on the Irish Context*. The 24th Countess Markievecz Memorial Lecture, Dublin.

Gunnigle, P., Turner, T. and D'Art, D. (1998) "Counterpoising Collectivism: Performance Related Pay and Industrial Relations in Greenfield Sites" *British Journal of Industrial Relations*, Vol. 36, No. 4: 565–579, December.

Harbison, F. H. (1954) "Collective Bargaining and American Capitalism" in Kornhauser, A., Dubin, R. and Ross, A. M. (eds) *Industrial Conflict*. New York: McGraw Hill.

Hart Research Associates (1999) *Americans' Views on Key National Issues*. Survey conducted on behalf of the AFL-CIO Washington DC. http://www.aflcio.org/labor99/am_attitude.htm

Hawkins, K. (1981) *Trade Unions*. London: Hutchinson.

Hill, S. (1981) *Competition and Control at Work*. London: Heinmann.

Hobsbawm, E. (1994) *Age of Extremes: The Short Twentieth Century 1914–1991*. London: Michael Joseph.

Hodgson, G. (1999) *Economics and Utopia*. London: Routledge.

Hyman, J. and Mason, B. (1995) *Managing Employee Involvement and Participation*. London: Sage Publications.

Hyman, R. (1972) *Strikes*. Glasgow: Fontana.

Hyman, R. (1973) *Marxism and the Sociology of Trade Unions*. London: Pluto Press.

Hyman, R. (1980) "Trade Unions, Control and Resistance" in Esland, G. and Salaman, G. (eds) *The Politics of Work and Occupations*. Milton Keynes: Open University Press.

Hyman, R. (1987) "Strategy or Structure? Capital, Labour and Control" *Work, Employment and Society*, Vol. 1, No. 1: March.

Jacoby, S. M. (1991) "American Exceptionalism Revisited: The Importance of Management" in Jacoby, S. M. (ed.) *Masters to Managers: Historical and Comparative Perspectives on American Employers*. New York: Columbia University Press.

Jacques, R. (1996) *Manufacturing the Employee: Management Knowledge from the 19th to 21st Centuries*. Cambridge: Sage Publications.

Keenoy, T. and Anthony, P. (1992) "HRM: Metaphor, Meaning and Morality" in Blyton, P. and Turnbull, P. (eds) *Reassessing Human Resource Management*. London: Sage Publications.

Keenoy, T. (1985) *Invitation to Industrial Relations*. Oxford: Blackwell.

Keenoy, T. (1991) "The Roots of Metaphor in the Old and the New Industrial Relations" *British Journal of Industrial Relations*, Vol. 29: 2 June.

Kelly, J. (1996) "Union Militancy and Social Partnership" in Ackers, P., Smith, C. and Smith, P. (eds) *The New Workplace and Trade Unionism*. London: Routledge.

Kelly, J. and Kelly, C. (1991) "'Them and Us' Social Psychology and the New Industrial Relations" *British Journal of Industrial Relations*, Vol. 29, No. 1.

Kochan, T. and Weinstein, M. (1994) "Recent Developments in US Industrial Relations" *British Journal of Industrial Relations*, Vol. 32: 4 December.

Kovach, K. A. (1992) *Labour Relations: A Diagnostic Approach*. New York: University Press of America.

Kumar, K. (1981) *Prophecy and Progress: The Sociology of Industrial and Post Industrial Society*. Middlesex: Penguin Books.

Lawler, J. J. (1990) *Unionisation and Deunionisation: Strategy, Tactics and Outcomes*. Columbia: University of South Carolina Press.

Leat, M. (1998) *Human Resource Issues of the European Union*. London: Pitman.

Legge, K. (1989) "Human Resource Management: A Critical Analysis" in Storey, J. (ed.) *New Perspectives on Human Resource Management*. London: Routledge.

Legge, K. (1995) *Human Resource Management: Rhetorics and Realities*.

London: Macmillan Business.

Lewin, D. (1987) "Industrial Relations as a Strategic Variable" in Kleiner, M., Block, N. and Marchington, M. (1982) *Managing Industrial Relations*. Oxford: McGraw Hill.

Marx, K. and Engels, F. (1965) *Manifesto of the Communist Party*. Moscow: Progress Publishers.

Mathewson, S. B. (1969) *Restriction of Output Among Unorganised Workers*. Southern Illinois University Press.

McCrone, D. Elliot, B. and Bechhofer, F. (1989) "Corporatism and the New Right" in Scase, R. (ed.) *Industrial Societies: Crisis and Division in Western Capitalism and State Socialism*. London: Unwin.

McKinaly, A. and Taylor, P. (1996) "Power, Surveillance and Resistance: Inside the Factory of the Future" in Ackers, P., Smith, C. and Smith, P. (eds) *The New Workplace and Trade Unionism*. London: Routledge.

McLoughlin, I. (1996) "Inside the Non-Union Firm" in Ackers, P., Smith, C. and Smith, P. (eds) *The New Workplace and Trade Unionism*. London: Routledge.

McLoughlin, I. and Gourlay, S. (1994) *Enterprise Without Unions: Industrial Relations in the Non-Union Firm*. Philadelphia: Open University Press.

Miliband, R. (1973) *The State in Capitalist Society*. London: Quartet Books.

Miller, R. (1997) "The American Labour Movement in Transition" in Mortimer, D., Leece, P. and Morris, R. (eds) *Readings in Contemporary Employment Relations*. Centre for Employment Relations: University of Western Sydney.

Millward, N., Stevens, M., Smart, D. and Hawes, W. (1992) *Workplace Industrial Relations in Transition*. Aldershot: Dartmouth Publishing Company.

Morgan, G. (1986) *Images of Organisation*. London: Sage Publications.

New Forms of Work Organisations: Options for Unions (1993) Irish Congress of Trade Unions. Dublin.

Nichols, T. (1969) *Ownership, Control and Ideology*. London: Allen and Unwin.

Nichols,T. (1980) "Management: Ideology and Practice" in Esland, G. and Salaman, G. (eds) *The Politics of Work and Occupations*. Milton Keynes: Open University Press.

Noon, M. and Blyton, P. (1997) *The Realities of Work*. London: Macmillan Business.

Offe, C. (1985) *Disorganised Capitalism: Contemporary Transformations of Work and Politics*. Cambridge: Polity Press.

Ouchi, W. (1981) *Theory Z: How American Business can meet the Japanese Challenge*. Reading, Mass.: Addison, Wesley.

Palast, G. (1998) "Workers Win the Battle – but Bosses Win the War". *Observer*, 13 September.

Pateman, C. (1970) *Participation and Democratic Theory*. Cambridge: Cambridge University Press.

Peters, T. and Waterman, R. (1982) *In Search of Excellence*. New York: Harper and Row.

Pfeffer, J. (1981) *Power in Organisations*. Marshfield, MA: Pitman.

Pollert, A. (1996) "Team Work on the Assembly Line: Contradictions and the Dynamics of Union Resilience" in Ackers, P., Smith, C. and Smith, P. (eds) *The New Workplace and Trade Unionism*. London: Routledge.

Proposal for a Fifth Directive to Co-ordinate Laws of Member States. (1972) Bulletin of the European Communities, Supplement 10/72.

Purcell, J. (1992) "The Impact of Corporate Strategy on Human Resource Management" in Salaman, G. (ed.) *Human Resource Strategies*. London: Sage Publications.

Quinn Mills, D. (1978) *Labour Management Relations*. New York: McGraw Hill.

Ramsay, H. (1975) "Firms and Football Teams" *British Journal of Industrial Relations*, Vol. 13, No. 3.

Reed, M. I. (1989) *The Sociology of Management*. London: Harvester Wheatsheaf.

Reed, M. I. (1992) *The Sociology of Organisations, Themes, Perspectives and Prospects*. London: Harvester Wheatsheaf.

Roche, W. and Gunnigle, P. (1995) "Competition and the New Industrial Relations Agenda" in Gunnigle, P. and Roche, W. (eds) *New Challenges to Irish Industrial Relations*. Dublin: Oak Tree Press in association with the Labour Relations Commission.

Roche, W. and Turner, T. (1997) "The Diffusion of the Commitment Model in the Republic of Ireland" *Review of Employment Topics*, Vol. 5, No. 1: 108–151.

Roomkin, M. and Salsburg, S. (eds) *Human Resources and the Performance of the Firm*. Industrial Relations Research Association: University of Wisconsin.

Rose, M. (1985) *Reworking the Work Ethic*. London: Batsford.

Ross, A. and Hartman, P. (1960) *Changing Patterns of Industrial Conflict*. New York: Wiley.

Salaman, G. (1979) *Work Organisations: Resistance and Control*. New York: Longmans.

Salaman, G. (1981) *Class and the Corporation*. Glasgow: Fontana Paperbacks.

Salamon, M. (1987) *Industrial Relations: Theory and Practice*. London: Prentice Hall.

Schuller, T. (1985) *Democracy at Work*. Oxford University Press.

Scott, A. (1994) *Willing Slaves? British Workers under Human Resource Management*. Cambridge: Cambridge University Press.

Scott, J. (1979) *Corporations, Classes and Capitalism*. New York: St. Martin's Press.

Sisson, K. (1994) "Personnel Management: Paradigms, Practices and Prospects" in Sisson, K. (ed.) *Personnel Management: A Comprehensive Guide to Theory and Practice in Britain*. Oxford: Blackwell Business.

Sparrow, P. and Marchington, M. (1998) "Re-engaging the HRM Function: Rebuilding Work, Trust and Voice" in Sparrow, P. and Marchington, M. (eds) *Human Resource Management: The New Agenda*. London: Pitman.

Storey, J. (1980) *The Challenge to Management Control*. London: Kogan Page.

Storey, J. (1992) *Developments in the Management of Human Resources*. Oxford: Blackwell Business.

Taft, P. and Ross, P. (1969) "American Labour Violence: Its Causes, Character and Outcome" in Graham, H. D. and Gurr, T. R. (eds) *Violence in America: Historical and Comparative Perspectives*. Report to the National Commission on the causes and prevention of violence, June 1969. New York: Signet Books.

Taylor, A. J. (1989) *Trade Unions and Politics*. London: Macmillan.

Taylor, R. (1994) *The Future of Trade Unions*. London: Andre Deutsch.

Theobald, R. (1994) *Understanding Industrial Society: A Sociological Guide*. New York: St Martin's Press.

Thompson, P. (1989) *The Nature of Work: An Introduction to Debates on the Labour Process*. (2nd edition) London: Macmillan.

Toner, B. (1987) Union or Non-Union: Employee Relations Strategies in the Republic of Ireland. Unpublished Ph.D, London School of Economics.

Torrington, D. (1998) "Crisis and Opportunity in HRM" in Sparrow, P. and Marchington, M. (eds) *Human Resource Management: The New Agenda*. London: Pitman.

Turner, T. and Morley, M. (1995) *Industrial Relations and the New Order*. Dublin: Oak Tree Press.

Waddington, J. and Whitson, C. (1996) "Empowerment Versus Intensification: Union Perspectives of Change at the Workplace" in Ackers, P., Smith, C. and Smith, P. (eds) *The New Workplace and Trade Unionism*. London: Routledge.

Wallace, J. (1999) *Investigating Employment Pacts: Collective Agreements Dealing with the Relationship between Employment and Competitiveness*. Report to the European Foundation for the Improvement of Working and Living Conditions (unpublished).

Walton, R. E. (1985) "From Control to Commitment in the Workplace" *Harvard Business Review*, March/April: 77–84.

Watson, T. J. (1980) *Sociology, Work and Industry*. London: Routledge and Kegan Paul.

Watson, T. J. (1986) *Management, Organisation and Employment Strategy*. London: Routledge.

Weber, M. (1958) *The Protestant Ethic and the Spirit of Capitalism*. New York: Charles Scribner and Sons.

Westergaard, J. and Resler, H. (1975) *Class in a Capitalist Society: A Study of Contemporary Britain*. London: Heinemann.

Wheeler, H. (1987) "Management-Labour Relations in the USA" in Bamber, G. J. and Lansbury, R. D. (eds) *International and Comparative Industrial Relations*. London: Unwin.

Wheeler, H. N. (1989) "Social Dominance and Industrial Relations" in Barbash, J. and Barbash, K. (eds) *Theories and Concepts in Comparative Industrial Relations*. University of South Carolina Press.

Whelan, C. (1982) *Worker Priorities, Trust in Management and Prospects for Worker Participation*. Paper No. 111, Dublin: Economic and Social Research Institute.

Zoll, R. (1996) "Modernisation, Trade Unions and Solidarity" in Leisink, P., Van Leemput, J. and Vilrokx, J. (eds) *The Challenge to Trade Unions in Europe*. Cheltenham: Edward Elgar.

CHAPTER 3

"Collaborative Production" and the Irish Boom: Work Organisation, Partnership and Direct Involvement in Irish Workplaces

WILLIAM K. ROCHE AND JOHN F. GEARY

INTRODUCTION

The 1990s witnessed a radical change in the fortunes of the Irish economy. Ireland has moved from being one of the low-performing economies of Europe to being hailed as the "Celtic Tiger", registering rates of economic and employment growth far ahead of OECD countries and attracting levels of foreign direct investment envied by competitors. Spectacular and unexpected economic success has brought in its train a literature seeking to interpret the Irish story. A number of themes recur in this literature: the role of a plentiful supply of well-educated labour; the increasing irrelevance of peripheral location for industries based on information technology; the benign effects of neo-corporatist concertation on cost competitiveness and employer-union accommodation; and, somewhat more prosaically, the advantages accruing from Ireland's prodigious success in garnering EU structural funds.

But figuring prominently also in this literature is an "upbeat" account of both the ways in which the productive base of the economy has been changing and the potential for further change as new forms of work organisation and new approaches to industrial relations and human resource management gain ground. Ireland is often now represented as a place where innovative approaches to work organisation, based on teamwork and flexible forms of work organisation, are common; where various forms of direct employee involvement are extensive; and where "partnership" arrangements between management and unions at workplace and enterprise levels are becoming more common and face a generally positive climate. These themes have received emphasis in a series of documents issued by public agencies and by trade union and employer federations. They also inform a number of important social-scientific and research-based accounts of the features and prospects of the "Celtic Tiger" (Sabel, 1996; McCartney and Teague, 1997; Sweeney, 1997; Tansey, 1998).

The Irish literature on workplace transformation has strong affinities with the recent UK literature on various forms of voluntary enterprise and workplace partnership (Guest and Peccei, 1997; IPA, 1997; Ackers and Payne, 1998; Coupar and Stevens, 1998; Department of Trade and Industry, 1998; Marchington, 1998). More generally, the themes of the Irish literature reflect an important strand of macro-level industrial relations commentary over the past decade. A range of writers have argued that economies competing on the basis of diversified, flexible and quality-focused product strategies faced the challenge of developing forms of employee and union involvement and joint governance variously described as "collaborative production", "partnership", "mutual gains" and a "new productivist covenant between capital and labour" (Piore and Sabel, 1984; Kochan and Osterman, 1994; Rogers and Streeck, 1995).

This chapter seeks to contribute to the literature on voluntary forms of partnership and employee involvement by examining and interpreting empirical data on the incidence, nature and context of both new forms of work organisation and of union-inclusive and employee-inclusive modes of handling change in Irish workplaces during the 1990s.

"COLLABORATIVE PRODUCTION" AND THE IRISH BOOM

Three social-scientific studies to be discussed below stand out as paradigmatic of the positive view of the penetration and prospects of collaborative production in Ireland. In the first of these, a wide-ranging review conducted for the OECD, Charles Sabel (1996: Chapter 2) seeks to contest what he believes to be the "official view" of recent Irish economic development, claiming that it fails to comprehend the degree to which enterprises were adopting the types of "decentralised production" principles and strategies best suited to a post-Taylorist economy. While Sabel's analysis is admittedly rather tentative regarding both the extent to which the "new collaborative production" had actually diffused across the Irish economy and the implications for labour markets and industrial relations, he suggests that it was safe to assume that its "impact is substantial" and that "a great deal" has changed "in the direction of the new methods" (Sabel, 1996: 29).[1] While noting also that unions were frequently marginal to new developments in production systems, Sabel urges on Irish commentators a new interpretation of workplace change based on a proper appreciation of the penetration and prospects of collaborative production – both within and between enterprises – in the new Irish economic order.

A second optimistic analysis of workplace innovation in Ireland is provided by McCartney and Teague's (1997) research on new forms of work organisation and their human resource underpinnings in the food/drink/tobacco, electronics

---

1. It should be noted here that statements made in respect of change by Sabel draw for their evidence from case studies and cross-sectional surveys: change in practice cannot, therefore, be inferred from levels of innovation.

and banking and finance sectors. While representing an apparent change of perspective from Teague's earlier pessimism regarding the nature of workplace change in Ireland under the regime of tripartite national bargaining (see Teague, 1995), McCartney and Teague (1997: 196) report that "it is clear that the vast majority of Irish firms are experimenting with workplace reorganisation", comprising such discrete initiatives as job rotation, quality circles, total quality management and team working. The extent to which new approaches to work organisation have taken hold, they argue, reflects the strategic decisions of Irish firms to move out of low value-added, cost-competitive commodity markets into more quality-sensitive export markets (1997: 384).

A table comparing the incidence of high performance work organisation in Irish establishments with Osterman's (1994) estimates for US establishments appears to suggest that new forms of work organisation, with the exception of team working, are *more* pervasive in Ireland than in the US. These innovations, they find, are also likely to be associated with complementary bundles of human resource practices (1997: 391–396). McCartney and Teague conclude that workplace change can be seen as a "neo-Schumpeterian" response to Ireland's economic openness and that "[A]ll in all, the evidence is that important, and in some cases, far-reaching changes are occurring to ground-level employee relations in Ireland. As a result, the improved economic performance currently being enjoyed by the country has solid corporate foundations" (McCartney and Teague, 1997: 396).

These highly optimistic accounts of Irish economic transformation are discordant with findings emerging from a growing international literature pointing to the limited penetration of workplace innovation and associated modes of industrial relations across Europe, the United States and Australia (see Locke et al., 1995; Regini, 1995; Ichniowski, et al., 1996; Sisson, 1997). If employment in Ireland is indeed changing in the manner and at the pace suggested by writers such as Sabel and McCartney and Teague, Ireland represents a quite exceptional case – an "outlier" in the international economic order.

But the optimistic scenario is discordant too with the views and findings of other Irish researchers – as Sabel indeed openly admits. A number of Irish commentators have stressed the partial, piecemeal and fragile character of innovation in work organisation, human resource management and industrial relations across much of Irish industry; the uneven and far from widespread diffusion of new practices; and the uncertain prospects of innovation based on partnership with unions in the face of substantial barriers and not uncommonly deep resistance by employers (Roche and Kochan, 1996; Geary, 1999; Roche, 1998; Gunnigle, 1998; Roche and Turner, 1998; McGovern, 1998).

While some of this corpus deals with general aspects of change in industrial relations and human resource management, the studies that explicitly address partnership and new forms of work organisation sound a sombre note. Turner and Morley (1995: 205–206) fail to find compelling evidence of a general shift towards a "distinctly new industrial relations" in their case studies of seventeen manufacturing plants. Gunnigle (1998), reflecting on the case study and exploratory data available, wonders if enterprise partnership amounts more to "rhetoric than reality". D'Art and Turner's analysis of the attitudes of members of a general union towards workplace partnership concluded that, in their eyes, it was of very limited significance (as cited in Gunnigle, 1999: 18–20).

The evidence so far adduced in favour of the optimistic position is far from compelling. Sabel's arguments are substantiated empirically by means of a small number of paradigmatic case studies, a small-scale survey of Q-mark companies and a highly contestable reading of Irish research evidence assembled for the OECD (see Roche and Kochan, 1996). To test Sabel's arguments it will be necessary to estimate the degree to which "collaborative production" has taken root in Irish workplaces, both in respect of its diffusion and the extent to which it has penetrated management decision-making processes; that is, whether in fact it has now reached "critical mass". Its future prospects in each of these respects will also need to be examined. It needs to be acknowledged, though, that the data reported here do not allow us to say by how much "collaborative production" has grown from a baseline of say five or ten years ago, but this is say arguably less relevant than its current level of penetration and future prospects, which we have measured.

McCartney and Teague follow Osterman (1994) closely in using the incidence of a range of discrete aspects of work reorganisation as an index of change and innovation. A well-understood problem with this approach is that it fails to delve behind terms such as "team working", "quality circles" and "job rotation", which are used to describe diverse substantive practices, which depart from traditional work arrangement to greater or lesser degrees (Appelbaum and Batt, 1994; Geary, 1999). While Osterman (1994) interprets his data as providing evidence of substantial change and innovation in US workplaces, a wide-ranging review of all relevant US research evidence to date reaches a more pessimistic conclusion concerning the depth and penetration of innovation in work organisation, industrial relations and human resource practices (Appelbaum and Batt, 1994; Ichniowski et al., 1996).

McCartney and Teague's research is based on three sectors, two of which, electronics and banking and finance, are likely everywhere to be closer to leading-edge change than most other sectors. It is, therefore, inappropriate to compare data from these sectors with Osterman's estimates of high performance work practices across US establishments in all non-agricultural industries (excluding non-profit organisations), and thereby to imply that Ireland is abreast or ahead of the US in the penetration of innovative approaches to work organisation. This may be the case, or it may not, but McCartney and Teague's research cannot settle the issue. Nor do data on the sectors chosen provide a sound or valid basis on which to claim that "most Irish establishments are actively reorganising work arrangements", or to advance related claims regarding the extent of industrial relations transformation (McCartney and

Teague, 1997: 381).[2] The critical issue here then is to obtain better estimates of new forms of work organisation – given McCartney and Teague's skewed sample – and, more importantly, to investigate as far as possible what these "labels" mean through further examination of their practical consequences for work organisation.

In short, McCartney and Teague appear willing to accept uncritically results based on a methodology excessively reliant on the simple enumeration of practices which may mask significantly different approaches to work organisation and to generalise to the Irish economy results which are also derived from a sample in all probability characterised by a triple skew: first towards sectors in which change is likely to be more pronounced, second towards larger establishments in which again change is likely to be more pronounced and finally towards multinationals which by common reckoning are in the vanguard of innovation in work organisation, human resource management and industrial relations (see note 2).

In the third study to be considered, a stimulating short article, Robert McKersie (1996: 12) speculates that the Irish case, with its strong trade unions and high level of investment by leading multinational companies, represented an ideal locale in which to test the premise that "strategic partnerships, coupled with modern human resource systems" could be the basis for a new and successful model of industrial relations. Such a proposition assumes that "strategic partnerships" and "modern human resource systems" are generally compatible bedfellows in the Irish case. The reality is considerably more complex. A significant number of multinational companies located in Ireland, particularly the plants of major US electronics firms, use modern human resource systems to pursue union substitution as vigorously as in their home base – a point which McKersie concedes (see McGovern, 1989; Gunnigle, 1995). Others support partnership but resist instituting the kind of structures commonly thought to support "strategic partnerships" in plants and workplaces. Others still promote the idea of partnership but at the same time seek to contain union influence in the workplace. Some it is true support strategic partnership and joint decision making of the kind McKersie supposes might become the basis of a common pattern in Ireland. But these remain very much a minority.

---

2. Questions must also be posed about the provenance of McCartney and Teague's sample and about the confidence with which the results can be generalised even *within* the sectors chosen. While the 102 establishments in the sample are said to be representative of the chosen sectors in respect of size and age, to have cut the size threshold at 50 employees incurs a significant size bias. Most branches of financial service companies, for example, employ far fewer employees and would thus seem to fall outside the scope of the survey. Further, no details are provided as to the representativeness of the sample with respect to the incidence of indigenous companies and multinationals. Based on data that are provided, 57 per cent of the sample is comprised of non-Irish establishments and the sample of Irish establishments is also likely to contain a number of Irish multinationals. The apparent skew towards multinational establishments is clearly significant with respect to the provenance of the research results and their generalisability, especially beyond the sectors studied.

At a more institutional level, fear of provoking capital flight by multinational companies has dissuaded Irish governments from adopting legislative measures in support of collaborative production (see Roche, 1998).

The evidence relevant to testing McKersie's position concerns just how far management-union partnerships have diffused and, in particular, whether such arrangements have allowed for employees and their representatives to influence issues of a more "strategic" nature, as well as what the future prospects look like.

THE UCD WORKPLACE SURVEY

In 1996–1997 a research team at the Graduate School of Business at University College Dublin undertook the largest and most detailed survey conducted to date of management practices in establishments in Ireland. The study, *Irish Management Practice in the Changing Marketplace*, examined a range of areas, including industrial relations, human resource management (HRM) and work organisation, manufacturing/services management and buyer-supplier relations. The survey, a postal survey, covered workplaces in all areas of the private sector, with the sole exception of the construction industry, and also included commercial public ("semi-state") companies.

Workplaces in which separate managers were responsible for industrial relations/human resources and operations/services management received two questionnaires. A questionnaire covering industrial relations and HRM issues and containing a set of basic questions on work organisation was sent to the designated human resource/industrial relations manager.[3] Another questionnaire covering operations/services and incorporating more detailed questions on work organisation was sent to the designated production or operations manager. Workplaces where one manager was responsible for both areas (and often other areas besides) received a composite but shorter version of both questionnaires.[4]

The results reported below on basic features of work organisation and on the incidence and focus of partnership and direct employee involvement are based on the combined responses of human resource/industrial relations managers *and* managers with a general brief covering human resource, operations and often other areas. This will be referred to in the text and at the

---

3. The target respondent for the IR-HRM survey was the designated human resource managers with responsibility for the area at workplace level. In the great majority of cases the relevant managers were located at workplace level but, in some cases, for example in financial services companies, they were located at higher levels (regional/ national) in the enterprise.

4. In the questionnaires completed by designated production managers and the managers with a general brief, questions relating to work organisation or industrial relations and human resource management were confined to practices pertaining to the largest occupational group in the establishment.

foot of relevant tables as the *IR-HRM Survey*, as most respondents were, in fact, IR-HRM specialists. Data on more detailed aspects of work organisation provided by production/operations specialists will also be presented and text and tables will identify these data as deriving from the *Production/Operations Management Survey*.

The survey fieldwork was administered by the Survey Unit of the Economic and Social Research Institute (ESRI), Dublin, in conjunction with the authors.[5] No reliable population list of Irish workplaces exists. Consequently a two-stage sampling strategy was followed. Stage 1 involved drawing a sample of enterprises from the enterprise population file maintained by the ESRI. The population for stage 1 comprised all enterprises in the sectors included employing more than twenty persons. Stage 2 involved inspecting the sample of enterprises to distinguish single- and multi-establishment enterprises. For 39 per cent of firms, the enterprise and the workplace were not synonymous. All multi-establishment enterprises in the sample were then "decomposed" into their constituent workplaces using a range of sources and business directories and, in many cases, following detailed discussions with managers in the enterprises concerned. The multi-site sample companies were then resampled and the selected workplaces were added to the single-establishment sample.

A disproportionate stratified probability sampling procedure was employed. As is standard in workplace surveys such as the UK and Australian workplace industrial relations surveys, a proportionately higher number of larger enterprises were selected at stage 1. The overall survey response rate was 36 per cent – very much higher than common for postal surveys. The total effective samples of 450 workplaces, in the case of the *IR-HRM Survey*, and 273 workplaces, in the case of the *Production/Operations Management Survey*, were then reweighted to restore the numbers of cases in each size stratum to their proportions in the survey population. The data analysis reported on here was carried out in respect of the reweighted samples. The resulting reweighted samples are well representative of workplaces in the survey population and provide a reliable basis for statistical generalisation (see Table 3.1).

5. It is important to note that over half of the survey fieldwork was completed before unions, employers and government concluded a national agreement in early 1997 containing proposals on the adoption of partnership and employee involvement in enterprises. A systematic examination of the most reliable source of ongoing developments in Irish industrial relations, the weekly periodical, *Industrial Relations News*, reveals that no widespread trend towards the adoption of partnership and employee involvement has been evident since the agreement was signed.

**Table 3.1: Sample Representativeness – Population and Sample
Distributions by Company Size and Sector**

Number of Employees	Population %	Target Sample %	Effective Sample %	Reweighted Sample %
20 – 49	54	20	31	53
50 – 99	21	30	25	23
100 – 249	15	30	26	15
250 – 499	5	10	10	6
500 plus	5	10	8	4
Sector				
Services	56	55	51	53
Manufacturing	44	45	49	47
Total N	4,062	1,328	450	927

NEW APPROACHES TO WORK ORGANISATION

In examining new approaches to work organisation we draw on a number of indicators, some of which were examined by McCartney and Teague (1997) (for example TQM, quality circles (QCs) and teamwork). In addition, we provide estimates of the incidence of two other indicators of employee involvement: periodic or *ad hoc* task forces, and joint consultative committees (JCCs) and works councils (WCs). Both would normally be seen to constitute forms of consultative participation, with the difference being that the former is often regarded as a feature permitting employees *direct* involvement (as opposed to indirect representative participation) in the resolution of workplace problems. The latter, on the other hand, are more usually seen as an older, *indirect* avenue for consulting with employees and often as an accompaniment to collective bargaining (see Marchington and Armstrong, 1986).[6]

The incidence of these practices is detailed in Table 3.2 and their distribution compared with the findings of McCartney and Teague (1997). In respect of TQM, respondents were asked if their organisation operated a Quality Improvement Process with the rider that it need not have constituted a full-scale TQM programme. Notwithstanding this, the diffusion of TQM is surprisingly high and quite similar to the level found by McCartney and Teague.

6. Although it should be noted that, in recent years, works councils attracted renewed attention in Ireland, particularly from trade unions, and would have been seen very much as a desired form of employee voice within workplaces in negotiations in the run-up to *Programme 2000*.

Table 3.2: The Incidence of Collaborative Work Organisation and Employee Involvement Practices

	% of Workplaces[i]
TQM[ii]	71.1 (68.7)[v]
Team work[iii]	59.0 (27.5)
Quality circles	15.0 (44.1)
Ad hoc task forces[iv]	45.5
Joint consultative committees/works councils	12.7

N (unweighted) = 450. The data reported here are in respect of workplaces' largest occupational group.

Notes
i. The percentages reported in this and all subsequent tables derive from the reweighted samples.
ii. The data on the TQM item are drawn from a question asked only of IR/HRM managers (N unweighted = 329).
iii. Teamwork was defined as instances where: employees work in formally designated teams, where the group is responsible for managing working arrangements.
iv. *Ad hoc* task forces were defined as initiatives which: involve employees in the resolution of production or business problems through periodic/*ad hoc* task forces.
v. McCartney and Teague's (1997) results are in parentheses.

Source: IR/HRM Survey.

But in respect of the other two innovations – teamwork and QCs – the difference between the two sets of findings is stark. Teamwork was found in 59 per cent of workplaces in the UCD study but in only 27.5 per cent of establishments in McCartney and Teague's study. The difference in the distribution of QCs was in the opposite direction with a far greater incidence reported in McCartney and Teague than the UCD survey.

The incidence of *ad hoc* task forces is surprisingly widespread but, in comparison, the distribution of JCCS/WCs is significantly less so. This finding is consistent with other results from our study which we report on below: that is, direct forms of employee involvement would seem to be gaining ground on representative mechanisms of participation which, arguably, provide employees with a more significant say in organisational decision making.

The Depth and Penetration of New Forms of Work Organisation

Thus far, the findings from the UCD survey confirm that experimentation with collaborative work organisation and employee involvement strategies in

Ireland is impressive. But while the data reported on in Table 3.2 are certainly useful in estimating the *incidence* of collaborative work practices, it is limited as an indicator of the *depth* and *scope* of change. For this we have to go beyond mere estimates of diffusion. To say that a workplace has team working, for instance, says little or nothing about its nature or implications for work organisation. To overcome this handicap we asked some detailed questions about the form of team working in the production/operations management questionnaire. We report on these data in this section, as well as using evidence from the recent EPOC study, which examined various elements of direct participation in ten European countries.[7] The incidence and depth of change in Ireland can, therefore, be compared with other European economies.

The UCD workplace survey found that team working was present in 57 per cent of workplaces. This figure, which is derived from the *Production/ Operations Management Survey*, is remarkably similar to the one from the combined *IR-HRM and Production/Operations Management Surveys* (see Table 3.2). The EPOC survey found that in the area of "consultative participation", "temporary groups", such as project groups or task forces, were present in 36 per cent of firms and "permanent groups", such as QCs, were used in 28 per cent of enterprises. This compared with a ten-country average of 31 per cent and 30 per cent respectively. "Delegative participation" organised around team structures was found in 42 per cent of organisations. This is above the average score of 36 per cent in the study as a whole coming third

---

7. A highly innovative study, the EPOC survey was conducted in 1996 under the auspices of the European Foundation. The main objective of the study was to examine the nature and extent of "direct participation" (DP). "DP" was seen to constitute two forms: (1) *consulatative participation* – management encourages employees to make their views known on work-related matters but reserves the right to take action or not; (2) *delegative participation* – management grants employees increased discretion and responsibility to organise their work without the requirement to refer back (for further details, see Geary and Sisson, 1994). Like the UCD survey, the EPOC survey was not just concerned with measuring incidence, but also took into account coverage, scope and penetration of "DP". It was a cross-national survey with the same instrument being used in ten European countries. We can thus reliably compare the extent of workplace innovation in Ireland with the other countries surveyed. The workplace general manager was invited to complete the questionnaire or to give it to a colleague who might have been better placed to respond to the questions asked. The size threshold for the larger countries was 50 employees but was lowered to 20 employees in small and medium-sized countries (including Ireland). For the larger countries (France, Germany, Italy, UK, Spain) the gross sample was 5,000 workplaces; for medium (Denmark, the Netherlands and Sweden) and smaller countries (Ireland and Portugal) it was 2,500 and 1,000 respectively. Over 32,000 workplaces in the private sector and public services were surveyed. An overall response rate of 17.8 per cent was achieved. In Ireland, the survey achieved a response rate of nearly 39 per cent, 382 organisations in all. The findings were reweighted to make adjustments for any distortions in the size and industrial sector of companies. All questions were asked in respect of the firm's largest occupational group. The only major shortcoming of the study was that, while it was designed to survey practice at the level of the workplace, in respect of Ireland at least no such population listing was available. The enterprise was thus the unit of analysis.

behind Sweden (56 per cent) and the Netherlands (48 per cent). From these estimates it would seem that direct participation is practised in about a third of Irish workplaces.

When coverage is taken into account, that is whether the participation initiative involved more than 50 per cent of the largest occupational group, the figures for Ireland compare favourably with other European countries. They are (the average ten-country score is given in brackets): temporary group consultation 73 per cent (48 per cent); permanent group consultation 71 per cent (48 per cent) and group delegation (team working) 58 per cent (47 per cent). Where participation is practised in Ireland, well over half and in some cases nearly two-thirds of enterprises involve more than half of the largest occupational group.

Taken on their own, these findings would suggest that new work practices are quite widely practised in Ireland and, in comparison to most other countries where similar research has been conducted, Ireland would rank amongst those countries at the top of any "league table" that one might develop. At this point, which is the point at which most previous Irish studies to date have stopped, the notion of Irish exceptionality can at least be countenanced. But the thesis of Ireland as an "advanced" or even exceptional case is quickly called into question when one digs a little deeper through the data. First, data from the UCD *Production/Operations Management Survey* reveal that employers' experimentation with team working is a relatively recent phenomenon, with only 19 per cent of workplaces having introduced it three or more years ago. It can only be safely assumed, then, that team working is only firmly embedded in a fifth of Irish workplaces; elsewhere, its introduction is too recent to make any firm claims as to its durability or permanence.

Secondly, there is the issue of the level of discretion permitted to employees under these new working arrangements. In workplaces using teams, respondents were asked whether management or team members played the leading role in deciding on a range of issues. The results are listed in Table 3.3.

The Organisation of Work

One might normally associate the use of team working with managerial efforts to reorganise the structure of work and, as part of that, to grant employees autonomy to manage work allocation, scheduling and pace. In respect of the first of these two items, less than half of the workplaces surveyed permitted team members to play the leading role, and in only 53 per cent of cases was control over pace of work vested in team members. While it would seem that responsibility for the organisation of work has moved from management to teams in some workplaces, in the majority of cases control continues to reside with management.

Table 3.3: Levels of Autonomy Permitted to Team Members

	% of Workplaces where Team Members Play the Leading Role
The Organisation of Work	
Allocation of work	41
Scheduling of work	47
Pace of work	5
Quality Management and Continuous Improvement	
Dealing with customers and suppliers outside this establishment	33
Addressing/resolving problems with employees from other teams	36
Responsibility for the quality of work	71
Making suggestions for improving work processes	90
Management of Attendance and Working Time	
Control of absence/attendance	32
Control of time keeping	51
Control of Team Boundaries and Team Composition	
Selection of team members	15
Selection of the team leader	24

N (unweighted) = 273

Source: Production/Operations Management Survey.

Quality Management and Continuous Improvement

Working in teams is often seen to provide employees with a means for identifying problems and empowering them to make suggestions and resolve difficulties. There is considerable evidence to show that teams have been given significant levels of autonomy in this field, particularly in regard to making suggestions for improving work processes (90 per cent) and responsibility for the quality of work (71 per cent). But the evidence would suggest that significantly less discretion is permitted to teams in dealing with problems which are shared by, or arise between, a number of teams. In only a third of cases were employees said to be given control in this area. Similarly, in only a third of workplaces did teams exercise a significant say in dealings with external customers.

The Management of Attendance and Working Time

Arguably this dimension of team working and the items listed under the next head represent a critical litmus test of the level of autonomy management has been prepared to permit to employees. Where management are prepared to grant employees a say in defining and policing acceptable standards of time keeping and attendance this might be reasonably taken as a significant departure from traditional practice. Interestingly, in over half of companies team members controlled the management of time keeping. Control of attendance rested with employees in about a third of workplaces. From this evidence the management of discipline around two key aspects of work – the time one comes to work and attendance at work – is vested in work teams in a surprisingly high number of workplaces.

Control of Team Boundaries and Team Composition

Employees were given very little discretion over the selection of team members and team leaders; control rested very firmly with management. In only 15 per cent of cases were employees allowed to select team members and in a little under a quarter of workplaces were teams in a position to choose their own team leader.

Another finding that merits attention is that team working was associated with a reduction in the number of supervisors in 45 per cent of workplaces, an indication perhaps that employees were acquiring tasks and responsibilities once performed by their immediate superiors. That 47 per cent of respondents reported that there was no such reduction does illustrate, though, that in many Irish workplaces teams operate *alongside* traditional hierarchical relations. The continued presence of supervisors and the limited discretion permitted to team members in most instances would suggest that conventional forms of authority relations continue to persist in most Irish organisations, *even* where team working has been introduced.

It would seem, though, that the "new workplace order" contains many elements, some of which a priori might not have been expected, especially in regard to the management of attendance and time keeping. Yet alongside this management would seem to exercise more control in other areas, such as the organisation of work, where it might not have been anticipated.

One of the most novel features of the EPOC survey was its attempt to measure the intensity of team working. Two indicators were used. The first was the "scope" of team working which measured the number of rights of employees to make decisions on how they performed their work without reference to immediate management in areas such as scheduling and allocation of work. The second was the degree of autonomy permitted to employees to choose their own team members and to decide which issues the group might address. Where high levels of discretion are granted to employees this form of team working would approximate closely with what has often been referred to as "semi-autonomous work groups". Of those Irish enterprises using team working only 17 per cent were found to have a high level of intensity of group delegation; most (51 per cent) had a medium level and a third had a low level of intensity.

In yet another attempt to distinguish between forms of team working, the EPOC team made a distinction between two forms: the first a "Scandinavian" model; the second a "Toyota" or lean production model. The former permits more autonomy to team members; team members come from a variety of skill groupings and there is considerable emphasis on training. The "Toyota" or lean production model, in contrast, places strict limits on teams' autonomy and employees' skills are largely of a generalist or routine kind. This distinction proved to be very illuminating in accounting for the different economic effects of team working. Organisations which used teams that came close to the Scandinavian model were considerably more likely to report improvements in organisational performance along indicators such as reductions in costs and through-put times, improvements in quality and, most strikingly, in increases in total output. They were also more likely to indicate a decrease in sickness and absenteeism levels and reductions in the number of employees and managers employed.

In Ireland, the more advanced Scandinavian model was a very rare occurrence. It would seem then that while team working is as widely diffused in Ireland as elsewhere in Europe, it is predominantly of a form that comes close to the Toyota model. Only 0.3 per cent of Irish companies have adopted the Scandinavian model, which compares with a ten-country average of 1.4 per cent and, not surprisingly, a high of 4.6 per cent in Sweden.

In summary then, it can be claimed that work reorganisation is well advanced in only a minority of Irish workplaces. Change of a kind is evident in more workplaces but any claim that Ireland is equal to, or ahead of, other countries is clearly found to be wanting, especially when one probes more deeply behind the distribution of practices.

PARTNERSHIP, EMPLOYEE INVOLVEMENT AND CHANGE IN IRISH WORKPLACES

In examining partnership and direct employee involvement as modes of "collaborative production" it was decided to consider directly the extent to which management sought to handle workplace change in either of these ways as alternatives to more established or traditional modes of handling change, such as simply exercising "managerial prerogative" or engaging in conventional adversarial collective bargaining with unions. While structures for partnership and forms of employee involvement are of course important issues, what matters most in considering employers' behaviour is the extent to which postures towards working with unions and employees have changed to embrace partnership or direct employee involvement where significant issues are at stake (see Marchington, 1998). Moreover, relatively little is known about the types of structures and arrangements put in place to give expression to partnership with trade unions, as will be discussed below.

In respect of workplace change, a list of twelve items was presented to respondents, eight of which were concerned with *operational issues*, such as changes to pay levels, working practices and so on, with the remainder focusing on issues of a more *strategic* nature, such as introducing new products and services, formulating business targets and formulating plans with respect to mergers/acquisitions and divestments. Respondents were asked to indicate whether they had introduced changes in any of these areas over the five years preceding the survey and, where they had done so, to indicate from a list of four possible approaches to managing or handling change which approach had been adopted. The four approaches to handling workplace change were:

1. "determined solely by management"

2. "decided through traditional collective bargaining with trade union(s) or on the basis of custom and practice"

3. "decided by involving trade unions to solve problems or seek consensus on a partnership basis"

4. "decided by management with the direct involvement of employees".

It is important to note that we were keen to identify the *predominant* approach used by establishments in introducing workplace change. As such, respondents were asked to specify only one of the four approaches outlined above for each relevant dimension of workplace change.[8] To take account of the possibility that postures towards change could have varied across categories of employees *within* an establishment, respondents were asked to identify their predominant approach in the case of the largest occupational group.

The wording used to describe what may count as the two modes of "collaborative production" requires some comment. In defining "partnership" with unions we decided against precise delimitation in terms of, for example, structural arrangements or bundles of practices, both for the reasons outlined above and fearing that such an approach would fail to capture possibly miscellaneous instances where the management of workplace change was being conducted with the active involvement of unions but outside the traditional collective bargaining arena. The definition adopted thus provides for a large number of possible scenarios where workplace partnership arrangements might

---

8. To have permitted respondents to chose more than one option would not only have made it very difficult to provide estimates of, say, the presence of workplace partnership or collective bargaining in Ireland but it would also have led to confusing and possibly contradictory results. For instance in the pilot study, where respondents were permitted to specify more than one option, a number of respondents ticked both the management prerogative and collective bargaining boxes. For these reasons, respondents were asked to specify which approach had predominated in their handling of each of the change items.

be in use. This approach seemed advisable since virtually nothing was known about the incidence of partnership in Ireland and scarcely more about the forms and arrangements through which it was given expression by management and unions. But with this broad definition we were careful to lay stress on involving unions "to solve problems or seek consensus on a partnership basis". By providing this definition of a partnership approach we were making a clear distinction between the adversarialism and arms-length postures often associated with collective bargaining arrangements and efforts by employers and trade unions in recent years to move towards "win-win" forms of exchange. The option of looking at a very narrow form of workplace partnership would run the risk of excluding many firms, which are adopting workplace partnership arrangements, but perhaps of a "softer" or "looser" kind than works councils or other structural mechanisms. Thus, while our definition and approach critically allows for an examination of the types of issues around which partnership has come into play, it says nothing of the *degree* of influence exercised by trade unions over such issues. By identifying and focusing upon terms such as "consensus" and "involving trade unions to solve problems" it has the benefit of capturing a large number of scenarios where employers and unions may be trying to develop new partnership arrangements and to use them for handling workplace change.

Our use of the term "direct employee involvement" was similarly deliberately phrased to capture all those instances where employers may be seeking to introduce change through the direct participation of employees. Thus, it is again a broad definition which was designed to capture initiatives as diverse as team working arrangements, quality circles, total quality management programmes, briefing groups, task forces and individual face-to-face consultations. We cannot obviously deduce from the data on how change was handled the types of channels or processes established to give employees a role in management decisions; whether they were formal or informal; whether employees were permitted to exercise a veto over management's proposals, or whether involvement initiatives were simply designed to communicate and inform employees of proposed changes.

Before turning to the data on the incidence of partnership, involvement and more traditional modes of handling change, it is noteworthy that the level and scope of workplace change in Ireland in the 1990s is indeed very significant (Tables 3.4 and 3.5). While it is obviously difficult to estimate the *depth* of change from these data, the level of workplace change and the range of issues addressed appear very significant. Evidently workplaces in the "Celtic Tiger" economy are indeed highly dynamic. The issue is the extent to which widespread change and restructuring in Ireland has been handled through various modes of "collaborative production" or whether "traditional" and more exclusionary forms of employee relations remain strongly embedded. It will be helpful to consider the results separately for unionised and non-union workplaces.

Unionised Workplaces

Table 3.4 details how workplace change was introduced in unionised companies. Partnership with unions was most widely used to handle changes to working practices (20 per cent), changes in payment systems (17 per cent) and changes in working time arrangements (16 per cent). Overall the incidence of partnership as a mode of productive collaboration was clearly very modest in unionised companies. At most one in five establishments have resorted to partnership to respond to change but, more commonly, the numbers favouring partnership as a means of handling change issues were much lower. Partnership emerges as a strategy confined primarily to changes in operational areas and was rarely used as a means of handling change in more strategic areas.

The introduction of change through the direct involvement of employees was found to be considerably more widespread than the use of partnership arrangements. Its use was striking in the introduction of a number of changes in both operational and strategic areas: hardly surprisingly in the *introduction* of initiatives to involve employees (46 per cent) but also in such areas as changes in working practices (41 per cent), identifying ways of realising targets (40 per cent), changes in working time arrangements (38 per cent) and the introduction of new products and services (29 per cent).

Management preference for direct employee involvement over partnership with trade unions can fairly readily be explained. Direct involvement represents involvement very much on management's terms: through such measures as QCs, objective setting and appraisal, briefing and communication, feedback and consultation measures and so on. These types of practices have a long vintage in the management literature and their operation is well understood. If they fail to function as expected they can be rescinded or simply allowed to atrophy. Partnership, on the other hand, involves giving unions access to areas of decision making from which in the past they were excluded, and in this way underlining or strengthening the legitimacy and scope of union "voice". Models for successful partnership are much less familiar in the professional management canon. Partnership may commonly be seen to carry significant risks: the "capture" of management decision making by unchanged adversarial union postures bargaining, for example, or the possible slowing up of decision making, the dilution of management authority. Should partnership arrangements not work out as management hoped they might, they cannot be so easily rescinded or ignored, being subject to collective agreements or accords with trade unions.

In the light of arguments concerning the depth and penetration of collaborative production in Irish establishments, what bears emphasis is that management prerogative or unilateral decision making was the most common approach to the handling of workplace change in the 1990s. In respect of seven of the twelve change areas examined, Irish employers were more likely to decide unilaterally on how change was to be effected than to adopt either mode of collaborative production, or to engage unions at arms-length through

Table 3.4: Approaches to the Handling of Workplace Change in Unionised Workplaces

	Workplaces Affected by Change Issue %	No. of Workplaces Affected (unweighted)	Approach to the Handling of Change			
			Management Prerogative %	Collective Bargaining %	Partnership with Union(s) %	Direct Employee Involvement %
Operational Issues						
Changing pay levels	80	228	17	62	11	10
Changes in payment systems	59	155	21	40	18	22
Introduction of new plant and technology	78	228	48	13	11	27
Changes in working time arrangements	64	176	8	38	16	38
Changes in working practices (e.g. multi-skilling, work re-organisation, teamworking)	67	197	13	25	20	41
Changes in numbers employed	86	240	65	13	14	8
Introduction of initiatives to involve employees (e.g. quality circles, suggestion schemes, team briefing)	58	167	26	14	14	46
Revision of promotional structures and criteria	41	121	77	8	11	5
Strategic Issues						
Introduction of new products/product range/services	76	219	62	2	8	29
Setting business targets for this workplace	78	229	71	3	3	23
Identifying ways of realising targets for this workplace	76	223	47	4	8	41
Formulating plans with respect to mergers/acquisitions/divestments	39	112	92	1	2	6

Source: IR-HRM Survey.

collective bargaining. Not surprisingly, the use of management prerogative was most common in those areas of decision making which are of a strategic nature. However, decisions were also commonly made unilaterally in the case of more operational matters such as the revision of promotional structures and criteria (77 per cent), changes in numbers employed (65 per cent), the introduction of new plant and technology (48 per cent) and even the introduction of initiatives to involve employees (26 per cent).

When the two more "traditional" modes of handling change, managerial prerogative and collective bargaining, are combined, it emerges clearly that they predominate over collaborative production across a range of operational areas, often to a quite marked degree, and particularly so when it comes to strategic aspects of running establishments. In all but three of the twelve areas of change examined "exclusionary" ways of responding to change were much more commonly adopted than modes of collaborative production.

In summary, the data for unionised workplaces demonstrate quite clearly that employers in the main have continued to regulate the workplace through unilateral managerial control and collective bargaining. Workplace partnership had never been used to introduce change in more than a fifth of workplaces. In most instances, a little more than one in ten employers used it and it was rarely if ever adopted in strategic areas of management decision making. In place of representative forms of employee participation, management would seem to be showing a clear preference for introducing change through mechanisms which allow for the direct involvement of employees but, more commonly, to exclude any forms of employee participation and to maintain management's freedom and right to manage as they might see fit.

Non-union Workplaces

In non-union workplaces, the management of change obviously did not allow for two of our options – collective bargaining and workplace partnership. Respondents were confined to choosing from two alternatives: management prerogative and direct employee involvement (see Table 3.5). Direct employee involvement was particularly apparent in the introduction of changes in working time (80 per cent), working practices (62 per cent), not surprisingly, in the introduction of initiatives to involve employees (66 per cent) and in identifying ways of achieving targets (62 per cent). In the case of the remainder of the change areas, however, employers were less likely to use direct employee involvement than to introduce change through management prerogative. A surprising result, though, is the absence of any neat division between those items where direct employee involvement and management prerogative were practised. One might have assumed that the latter would have been much more pronounced in areas of strategic decision making than in operational matters. This is not supported by the data. While use of managerial prerogative, for example, was virtually universal in respect of formulating plans for mergers, acquisitions and divestments, decisions were also commonly made unilaterally

Table 3.5: Approaches to the Handling of Workplace Change in Non-Union Workplaces

	Workplaces Affected by Change Issue %	No. of Workplaces Affected (unweighted)	Approach to the Handling of Change	
			Management Prerogative %	Direct Employee Management %
Operational Issues				
Changing pay levels	89	142	62	38
Changes in payment systems	53	84	51	49
Introduction of new plant and technology	72	117	52	48
Changes in working time arrangements	61	103	20	80
Changes in working practices (e.g. multi-skilling, work re-organisation, team working)	61	100	32	68
Introduction of initiatives to involve employees (e.g. quality circles, suggestion schemes, team briefing)	70	113	33	67
Changes in numbers employed	92	150	81	19
Revision of promotional structures and criteria	49	85	76	24
Strategic Issues				
Introduction of new products/product ranges/services	84	135	56	44
Setting business targets for this workplace	83	135	68	32
Identifying ways of realising targets for this workplace	83	130	38	62
Formulating plans with respect to mergers/acquisitions/divestments	47	82	97	3

Source: IR-HRM Survey.

in respect of changes in numbers employed, revising promotional structures and criteria and changing pay levels.

In summary, the incidence of direct employee involvement in handling change is indeed significant in non-union Irish workplaces. But in eight out of twelve areas of change, and in all areas of strategic change, other than identifying ways of realising workplace targets, most non-union establishments relied mainly on managerial prerogative, and often by a wide margin over collaborative production.

Managers' Future Intentions

In a cross-sectional survey such as this it is only possible to identify the degree of diffusion of given practices in one period of time. In an attempt to overcome this constraint and in order to measure the likely future for workplace partnership and direct employee involvement, as well as the likely durability of current arrangements, we sought to examine employers' commitment to adopting these approaches when responding to workplace change in the future. Using, then, the same four approaches to those outlined in the previous question, we asked how managers would be likely to handle change over the next five years, assuming that they were faced with a range of change imperatives. The survey retained five change items which are operational in nature, and which affect different dimensions of the wage-effort bargain – change in pay levels and payment systems, the introduction of new technology, working practices and working time arrangements, and making significant reductions in numbers employed. One area of strategic decision making was maintained – developing new business targets. This number of items was considered sufficient to estimate the likely future penetration of partnership and involvement approaches based on current declared postures.

Starting with unionised workplaces, a number of the findings in Table 3.6 deserve comment. First, employers would seem to be indicating a clear preference to rely less on collective bargaining in the near future as a means for handling workplace change and to rely more both on partnership with unions and on direct employee involvement – both roughly in equal measure. Interestingly, direct employee involvement recorded the highest score for three of the change items listed (changes in payment systems, 31 per cent; introduction of new technology and new working practices, 50 per cent; changes in working time, 45 per cent). In respect of the other means for handling change, not surprisingly collective bargaining was cited most often for changing pay levels; management prerogative for developing new business targets; and, finally, workplace partnership for making significant reductions in numbers employed.

Secondly, management prerogative is as likely to remain as entrenched over the next five years as is currently the case, except for when it comes to handling change in two areas: introducing job losses and developing new business targets.

Table 3.6: Intentions as to the Handling of Workplace Change in the Future in Unionised Workplaces

	Workplaces Affected by Change Issue %	No. of Workplaces Affected (unweighted)	Approach to the Handling of Change	
			Management Prerogative %	Direct Employee Management %
Operational Issues				
Changes in pay levels	16	41	22	21
Changes in payment systems	18	24	27	31
Introduction of new technology and new working practices	16	12	22	50
Changes in working time arrangements	7	21	27	45
Making significant reductions in numbers employed	28	24	28	20
Strategic Issues				
Developing new business targets for the workplace	46	7	9	38

N (unweighted) = 282

Source: IR-HRM Survey.

Table 3.7: Intentions as to the Handling of Workplace Change in the Future in Non-Union Workplaces

	Approach to the Handling of Change	
	Management Prerogative %	Direct Employee Involvement %
Operational Issues		
Changes in pay levels	52	42
Changes in payment systems	44	54
Introduction of new technology and new working practices	23	77
Changes in working time arrangements	16	84
Making significant reductions in numbers employed	61	39
Strategic Issues		
Developing new business targets for the workplace	56	43

N (unweighted) = 163

Source: IR-HRM Survey.

Thirdly, the areas in which employers see workplace partnership to be of particular benefit were areas close to the wage-effort bargain: changes in payment systems, working time arrangements and managing job loses. Close on a third of respondents indicated that they would favour partnership if they were to introduce change in these areas. The proportion of respondents who reported that they would resort to a partnership approach in the case of developing new business targets is still modest at 9 per cent.

While the intended use of partnership arrangements across both operational and strategic aspects of change would seem to be significantly higher than at present, partnership nevertheless seems likely to be favoured for handling operational challenges in no more than about one in four workplaces and the prospects of partnership embracing strategic decision making appear little brighter than at present. It is clear that the incidence of direct employee involvement is also likely to increase significantly, with substantially higher proportions of workplaces likely to involve employees directly in both operational and strategic decision making. Overall, higher proportions of establishments still intend to rely on unilateral decision making or collective bargaining, rather than collaborative production, to handle change in three of the six areas examined in the assessment of future intentions.

While the range of approaches available to non-union employers is again more confined, a broadly similar pattern was evident in the non-union sector. In comparing the results in Table 3.5 with those in Table 3.7, intentions to rely to an increased extent on direct employee involvement are particularly marked when managers countenance having to make significant numbers of employees redundant and, to a lesser extent, were they have to face further technological change, changes in payment systems, changes in working practices and development of new business targets for the workplace. Notwithstanding this, however, in non-union companies the use of management prerogative looks set to prevail over direct employee involvement in areas such as changes in pay levels, making significant reductions in numbers employed and in developing new business targets.

Accounting for the Uptake of Collaborative Production

Up to now the data presented have focused on the general incidence and prospects of various modes of collaborative production in unionised and non-union workplaces. This section examines whether collaborative approaches to the handling of change are related in any consistent manner to a series of workplace characteristics. These comprise sector (comparing advanced manufacturing, financial and professional services and other service industries with traditional manufacturing), size (greater than 100 employees), US ownership and whether a workplace was a new or "greenfield" site (defined as in operation at that location for no more than ten years). The analysis uses logistic regressions to estimate the effects of these variables on the odds that workplaces show a preference for collaborative production in the handling of change issues. Separate estimates are presented for workplaces where unions are recognised and for non-union workplaces. In the case of unionised workplaces partnership and direct employee involvement are combined to provide an overall indicator of an employer preference for a collaborative approach rather than an "exclusionary" approach to handling change. It needs to be borne in mind that the incidence of collaborative approaches, as a whole, to particular *strategic* change issues is so low that the issue of accounting for variability becomes almost redundant.

The results presented in Table 3.8 show some influences having an impact on specific areas of collaborative production. For example, US-owned workplaces are considerably more likely to adopt "task-based" forms of collaborative management, as indexed by a higher incidence of such techniques as work teams, TQM and *ad hoc* task forces in all workplaces, as well as QCs in unionised workplaces (see Geary and Roche, 2001). Non-union workplaces undertaking advanced manufacturing or delivering financial and professional services are also more likely to have adopted various task-based forms of collaborative production. But the overriding result to emerge from Table 3.8 is the lack of any consistent pattern in the incidence of modes of collaborative production in respect of the variables examined. In other words, thus far in its history at any rate, the adoption of collaborative production appears largely random with respect to its sectoral penetration, relationship to workplace size, US ownership and with respect to whether workplaces have commenced operations over the past decade. Surprisingly perhaps, no consistent preference for collaborative production as a mode of handling change is apparent in the relatively more highly skilled advanced manufacturing and financial and professional services sectors, nor in newer greenfield workplaces, commonly thought to be in the vanguard of new approaches to work organisation and employment relations. Nor do the often-cited US unionised and non-union exemplars of various types of collaborative arrangements represent anything like a generalised distinctive US effect.

These findings in turn raise the question of how collaborative production has emerged in some workplaces but not in others. Here, we feel it is important to distinguish between partnership involving trade unions and direct employee involvement. The case study evidence suggests that partnership is most likely to emerge in uncommon sets of circumstances, involving such combinations of factors as commercial or impending crisis, actual or imminent reorganisation of businesses, a broadly positive pre-existing employment relations climate, powerful and visionary senior human resource executives and influential and pioneering union officials (see Roche and Turner, 1998). It is common enough perhaps to find one or several such factors in play but less common to find a range of them in combination. The dynamic driving direct employee involvement may be the mirror image of that driving partnership with unions. The various techniques and approaches associated with direct involvement are much better known in the professional management literature and they have been well tried and tested in workplaces nationally and internationally.

Table 3.8: Examining Possible Influences on the Adoption of Collaborative Production[i]

	Unionised Workplaces: Odds Ratios[ii]							Non-Union Workplaces: Odds Ratios[ii]						
	"New" work-places	Advanced manufact-uring	Financial and professional services	Other services	US-owned workplaces	>100 employees	Ns (un-weighted)	"New" Work-places	Advanced Manufac-turing	Financial and professional services	Other services	US-owned workplaces	>100 employees	Ns (un-weighted)
Work Organisation:														
Formally designated work teams	1.7	1.1	2.3	1.1	2.7*	0.6*	228	0.6*	7.5**	7.3**	2.7**	3.1**	1.2	121
Total quality management	2.5	1.5	1.4	0.2	C	1.5	188	1.1	0.9	0.7	1.0	10.8**	4.5*	88
Quality circles	0.7	0.3	2.0	1.8	8.8**	0.6	212	0.9	6.5**	12.5**	5.5**	1.3	2.4*	115
Ad hoc task forces	1.2	0.7	0.8	1.1	2.4*	1.8*	222	0.7	1.6	32.3**	1.1	14.4**	1.5	119
Joint consultative committees	0.3*	0.7	5.1	1.6	1.6	6.4**	214	0.2**	1.5	0.0	0.4	2.7	2.7	116
Operational Issues:														
Change in pay levels	1.1	1.8	0.8	0.8	0.3	0.6	202	0.4**	0.9	0.6	0.5**	0.1**	0.8	118
Change in pay systems	0.3**	1.1	0.3*	0.9	0.5	0.9	138	0.2**	2.2	0.2*	1.0	0.5	0.6	69
Change in technology	1.2	1.3	0.7	1.1	0.7	0.7	201	0.6	1.3	8.9**	2.4**	0.5	1.5	99
Change in working time	1.5	2.1	0.5	0.9	0.6	0.4**	157	1.0	C	0.3*	1.7	0.8	1.3	85
Change in work organisation	0.5*	0.9	0.2**	0.6	0.9	0.6*	173	0.9	2.1	0.9	1.7	1.3	1.8	81
Changes in numbers employed	3.7**	0.7	0.2*	0.3**	0.9	0.8	212	0.4*	3.9**	0.0	2.5**	0.5	1.2	122
Introduction of involvement programmes	1.5	1.4	0.5	0.6	0.5*	0.8	150	2.4*	0.9	0.4	1.0	8.6**	0.8	90
Changes in promotional arrangements	0.1	9.6**	1.5	2.1	0.6	2.1	111	0.5	4.2*	0.0	1.6	2.4	2.1	69
Strategic Issues:														
New products/services	1.8	0.9	0.6	0.9	1.2	0.6	195	0.5	1.2	17.6**	3.1**	0.6	1.5	107
Setting business targets	0.9	1.5	0.9	1.3	0.9	0.6	203	1.2	1.5	0.4	1.0	0.8	0.6	112
Identifying ways of realising targets	0.4**	1.2	1.5	2.0**	1.0	1.2	198	0.7	2.1	5.5**	2.3**	0.8	1.9	107
Plans with respect to mergers, acquisitions and divestments	7.9**	1.0	0.0	0.2	2.0	2.0	101	1.0	0.0	0.0	0.0	0.0	0.0	63

i   With the exception of the Total Quality Management item, all items measure the use of collaborative production as the main mode of handling change with respect to the largest category of the workforce.

ii   Independent variables are specified as outlined in the text. In the case of the sectoral variable, the reference category is traditional manufacturing.

c   Odds ratio is improbably large and has a large standard error.

*   Significant at the 0.05 level.

**   Significant at the 0.01 level.

Source: IR-HRM Survey.

As such, workplaces judging that the business environment warranted organisational innovation – however, they may otherwise differ with respect to external and internal forces – may have been predisposed to adopt forms of direct employee involvement. In consequence, no clear-cut pattern with respect to sector, scale or other major distinguishing features of workplaces, need be expected.

THE INSTITUTIONAL CONTEXT OF INNOVATION: IRELAND IN COMPARATIVE PERSPECTIVE

It will be helpful to present a general summary of the pattern of the findings before considering the Irish case in comparative context. The overall incidence of new forms of work organisation in Irish workplaces is indeed impressive, but closer analysis reveals that the changes which have occurred permit employees limited discretion and narrowly circumscribed decision-making authority. The incidence of partnership with trade unions is very modest indeed and only in exceptional cases are unions involved in strategic decision making. Partnership is most common in areas close to the wage-effort bargain and, thus, likely to be subject to union influence. Direct employee involvement is common in unionised establishments and employers show a clear preference for this mode of collaborative production over partnership with unions. The findings indicate that unilateral management decision making remains the most common approach to handling change in unionised workplaces and that management prerogative and collective bargaining combined by far predominate over collaborative production. In non-union workplaces, while the incidence of direct employee involvement is again significant, unilateral management decision making is predominant. Managers' future intentions point to the further diffusion of collaborative production and, in particular, of direct employee involvement. But management prerogative looks set to remain entrenched in the handling of about half the issues examined.

We would argue that the pattern of findings for Ireland revealed in this study indicate that Ireland has much in common with larger Western economies. Studies generally report a significant incidence of experimentation with new forms of work organisation and new approaches to management-union and management-employee dialogue and collaboration (Appelbaum and Batt, 1994; Locke et al., 1995; Regini, 1995; Sisson, 1997). It is also common to report management intentions to rely to greater degrees on new forms of collaboration in the future. But these studies also emphasise that the pattern of change nearly everywhere is piecemeal and fragmented, with strong areas of continuity and inertia even in workplaces experimenting with new modes of collaborative production.

The detailed findings for Ireland and the picture of recent change emerging from the comparative literature indicate that Ireland cannot be viewed in any sense as being in the vanguard of workplace change along collaborative lines.

Thus, our findings support the conclusions of pre-existing "sober" accounts of workplace change in Ireland by showing the limited penetration and depth of partnership and new forms of work organisation. Nor does the Irish case present itself as an "ideal locale" for the emergence of partnership. Nor can the argument reasonably be sustained that the transformation and performance of the "Celtic Tiger" economy of the 1990s can be attributed to any decisive degree to collaborative production (see Sabel, 1996: Chapter 2; McCartney and Teague, 1997: 381–382, 396). As emerges from the data reported in this study, change and dynamism are indeed widespread in Irish establishments but they are more likely to have been driven through by unilateral management decision making than by collaborative production in any of its various forms.

The comparative literature on recent change in industrial relations systems and human resource management, can also be used to develop a framework for understanding the forces assisting and retarding change in Irish workplaces and for "locating" Ireland analytically against other national cases in the 1990s. Locke et al. (1995) propose six major sets of factors to account for cross-country differences in levels of diffusion of new forms of work organisation and associated patterns of employment relations:

1. pre-existing patterns of work organisation

2. state postures towards innovation

3. the "climate" of industrial relations

4. the priority accorded to human resources in firm governance

5. the competitive postures of firms

6. prevailing bargaining levels and arrangements.

The study implies that a broad distinction can be made with respect to levels of innovation between "Anglo-American" systems and "Continental-Japanese" systems. The latter are viewed, on balance, as having been more receptive to changes favouring collaborative production in their attempts to adjust to the new international economic order. This framework can be used to portray the Irish pattern of adjustment to intensified competition.

Pre-existing Patterns of Work Organisation

In terms of work reorganisation, Ireland's "starting point" is a Taylorist tradition of job specialisation, overlain in unionised companies by a tradition of control linked to employment and skill protection.

Innovation and the State

Government support for innovation in Ireland can best be portrayed as a positive but largely non-interventionist and "hortatory" posture. The National Centre for Partnership, established under the national tripartite agreement, *Programme 2000*, operates as a voluntary catalyst for partnership and employee involvement.

The Industrial Relations Climate

The climate of industrial relations has historically been adversarial but in recent years the Irish trade union movement has strategically reoriented its policy to favour partnership and new forms of work organisation. The continuing decline in density being experienced by Irish unions has bolstered their support for partnership in the workplace. The postures and policies of employers are more ambiguous. The Irish Business and Employers' Confederation (IBEC) has a declared policy of favouring partnership and employee involvement but it is clear that sharp divergences of view exist among its membership on the desirability of partnership with unions. IBEC might also be disposed to weigh in the balance its support for partnership against the advantages that might be seen to accrue to employers generally from a continuing decline in union organisation. As such, a national-level consensus between the "social partners" that partnership and involvement should be fostered translates far from easily or directly into strong backing for "collaborative production" at workplace level. IBEC, The Irish Congress of Trade Unions and state agencies have collaborated on several change programmes aimed at fostering partnership and involvement but these have directly involved only small numbers of companies and the prospects of the wider diffusion of the models developed remain uncertain.

Corporate Governance and Human Resources

The status of human resource issues in corporate governance in Ireland is not in general highly pronounced. Worker directors have been elected to the boards of commercial state-owned companies since the 1970s but Ireland possesses no works council system mandated by legislation or collective bargaining. In a study of all "greenfield" sites established in manufacturing and internationally traded services over the period 1987–1992, Gunnigle and Morley (1998) found that only one in five was characterised by high levels of strategic integration of human resource management into competitive strategy. In their composite measure of strategic integration, the lowest-scoring dimension of all was the degree to which industrial relations considerations impacted on broader business policy decisions. In the UCD workplace survey, a somewhat more positive picture emerged. Just over one in three managers claimed that human resource concerns influence the "choice and implementation of business strategy"; approximately the same proportion of managers suggested, however, that human resource concerns had little influence on business strategy. Overall, therefore, the non-existence of institutional systems for worker or union involvement, mandated by law or collective bargaining, and the pattern of survey evidence reflect a reality in which the large majority of enterprises and their establishments are neither constrained nor disposed to assign priority to human resource issues in the governance of the firm or the workplace.

The Competitive Postures of Firms

While "national" competitive strategy, as outlined in a range of policy documents by public agencies, favours competing on the basis of quality, innovation and skill, in reality, considerable variation exists in firms' competitive postures both across and within industrial sectors. In the key electronics and pharmaceuticals sectors, dominated by multinational companies, competitive postures are commonly – though by no means universally – focused on quality and innovation in addition to price. Attempts by public agencies to persuade companies in these sectors to invest significantly in research and development in their Irish plants have met with limited success. Much of the work done in Ireland involves routine production or routine fabrication and software localisation in the electronics sector (see McGovern, 1998). In the important Irish food industry, national policy also calls for product innovation and higher levels of penetration of "upstream" consumer export markets, particularly in Europe. While the sector harbours areas of significant product innovation, based on biotechnology and proactive marketing, it remains heavily wedded to basic food processing and distribution. Key service industries such as tourism remain reliant on relatively low-wage employment and high levels of part-time and seasonal employment. Large areas of retailing and "blue-collar" services are also characterised by similar employment practices, as very often are small indigenous companies (see Roche, 1998). Financial services companies have been in the vanguard of quality and innovation-focused strategies as the industry experienced more intense competition following on from deregulation. In the publicly-owned utilities, EU-led deregulation and growing commercialisation have resulted in a range of competitive responses: some companies seeking to drive down costs as a major priority; others seeking to compete on the basis of quality.

National policy aspirations aside, it would be invalid to describe the economy as dominated in employment terms by sectors and firms strongly wedded to competitive postures emphasising quality, innovation and customisation.[9] Ireland's "voluntary" system of industrial relations is of particular relevance to the competitive postures adopted by firms and associated employment practices. Firms are free to choose any combination of employment practices or any employment model within very wide parameters.

---

9. A question in the workplace survey asked establishments to indicate whether they produced products or services wholly or mainly customised to the requirements of different markets or customers. In all, 40 per cent of the sample responded that this was their product strategy.

Over the past decade, the scope available to companies to craft their employment relations as they choose has increased significantly. The State and its agencies have felt constrained to move away from a long-standing policy of encouraging incoming multinationals and indigenous companies to concede union recognition and support collective bargaining. In the FDI sector, in particular, there has been a strong growth in the incidence of multinational companies committed to policies of "union substitution", sometimes backed by "soft" human resource practices, but sometimes also backed by "union suppression" and relying on fear and anxiety to discourage unionisation – the two postures, of course, are by no means mutually exclusive (McGovern, 1989; Gunnigle, 1995). In consequence, Ireland now possesses a highly fragmented industrial relations system (Roche, 1998). Different employment models coexist side-by-side and no compelling constraints exist to push firms in general towards quality and innovation-focused competitive postures, supported by collaborative employment relations, as they seek to respond to more intense international competition.

Bargaining Levels and Arrangements

Growing fragmentation also has a bearing on the role of national-level tripartite bargaining in the diffusion of new forms of work organisation, partnership and employee involvement. Locke et al. (1995: 368) argue that strong national or industry-level bargaining arrangements can provide a "supportive institutional umbrella" for labour-management co-operation and innovation in specific enterprises and workplaces. As outlined above, even after a decade of neo-corporatist concertation and the inclusion in the current national agreement of proposals akin to a framework agreement on workplace innovation, deadlock, stalemate and ambivalence characterise the activities of the social partners at workplace level much more than active collaboration to promote productivity coalitions.

When Ireland is thus located in comparative and analytical context, its adjustment to international competition emerges, on the whole, as strongly characterised still by responses of Anglo-American systems, which have shown themselves to be less receptive or permeable to innovation and collaborative production than many Continental European systems. The Irish case further appears to share with Anglo-American systems a tendency for much innovation to be piecemeal and fragmentary (see Roche and Kochan, 1996).[10] Systematic programmes of innovation, in the minority of establishments where they occur, also tend to be more heavily skewed towards modes of collaborative production offering low and tightly circumscribed degrees of "voice" to employees and unions (Appelbaum and Batt, 1994; Geary, 1999).

---

10. Though here the evidence for Continental European systems may not be all that different (see for example Regini, 1995: Chapter 7; Sisson, 1997).

CONCLUSION

Some recent social-scientific writing on Ireland has assigned great importance to various forms of collaborative production, sometimes even suggesting that their growing diffusion might have played a major role in Ireland's exceptional economic performance during the 1990s. This chapter has questioned the degree to which new modes of collaborative production have gained ground in Ireland during the 1990s. While collaborative production is undoubtedly significant, exclusionary forms of decision making are shown to have dominated the postures of establishments towards the handling of change. Suggestions of "transformation", actual or imminent, realised through various forms of collaborative production, are rejected and change in Ireland is shown to have much in common with other economies, particularly those characterised by "Anglo-American" institutional systems. Thus, our work, drawing on the first Irish workplace survey, gives substance to the sober reflections of a number of previous commentators whose work on partnership has of necessity drawn largely or exclusively on case study evidence or exploratory survey work (Turner and Morley, 1995; Gunnigle, 1997).

More generally, the Irish case adds to the weight of evidence against "functionalist" modes of macro-theorising which propose a direct correspondence between changing forms of competition and resulting forms of employment relations in industrial economies. Various "post-Fordist" models of economic organisation depend on such a postulate. These models fail to comprehend the extent to which firms in advanced economies may continue to eschew collaborative production and rely on traditional exclusionary management practices to engender the levels of dynamism they require (see Cappelli et al., 1997). The forces shaping "trajectories" of adjustment and response to new patterns of competition across nations – engendering that is, "path dependency" in the way change occurs – are also relegated to "residual categories" in macro-paradigms of changing economic forms. Different "historical starting points" and institutional patterns become at most mediating influences that add local detail and coloration to economic responses. The writers on Ireland, whose work we examined here, showed little concern with institutional forces, their effects on the diffusion of collaborative production or their impact on the prospects of wider diffusion in the future. Nor do such models, with their focus on all-encompassing "transformations", appreciate the extent to which firms within national boundaries appear capable of a diversity of responses to new competitive forces or that the range of responses and associated employment models may be widening in advanced industrial societies. If national institutions continue to be "hollowed out" by competitive forces, the consequence is likely to be a greater diversity of competitive postures and employment models within nations rather than the dominance of any one "post-Fordist" economic form, supported by collaborative production (see Darbishire and Katz, 1997; Roche, 1998).

Rejecting arguments that advanced economies adjust "organically" to competitive forces through product strategies favouring collaborative production, a number of writers have argued that the institutionalisation of collaborative production is predicated on supportive institutional systems (Streeck, 1992; Appelbaum and Batt, 1994; Kochan and Osterman, 1994; Pfeffer, 1994). A failure to take adequate account of institutional forces, combined with an inadequate empirical base, limits the validity of the stream of "upbeat" writings on collaborative production and the Irish boom.

REFERENCES

Ackers, P. and Payne, J. (1998) "British Trade Unions and Social Partnership: Rhetoric Reality and Strategy" *The International Journal of Human Resource Management*, Vol. 9, No. 3: 529–550.

Appelbaum, E. and Batt, R. (1994) *The New American Workplace: Transforming Work Systems in the United States*. Ithaca, N.Y.: Cornell University Press.

Cappelli, P., Bassi, L., Katz, H., Knoke, D., Osterman, P. and Useem, M. (1997) *Change at Work*. Oxford: Oxford University Press.

Coupar, W. and Stevens, B. (1998) "Towards a New Model of Industrial Partnership: Beyond the HRM versus Industrial Relations Argument" in P. Sparrow and M. Marchington (eds) *Human Resource Management: The New Agenda*. London: Financial Times/Pitman Publishing.

Darbishire, O. and Katz, H. (1997) *Converging Divergences: Worldwide Changes in Employment Relations*. Working Paper, School of Industrial and Labor Relations, Cornell University.

Department of Trade and Industry (1998) *Fairness at Work*. London: HMSO, Cm 3968.

Geary, J. F. (1999) "The New Workplace: Change at Work in Ireland" *The International Journal of Human Resource Management*, Vol. 10, No. 5: 870–890.

Geary, J. F. and Roche, W. K. (forthcoming) "Multinationals and Human Resource Practices in Ireland: A Rejection of the 'New Conformance Thesis'" *The International Journal of Human Resource Management*.

Geary, J. F. and Sisson, K. (1994) *Conceptualising Direct Participation in Organisational Change*. Luxembourg: Office for Official Publications of the European Communities.

Guest, D. and Peccei, R. (1997) *The Partnership Company: Benchmarks for the Future*. London: IPA.

Gunnigle, P. (1995) "Collectivism and the Management of Industrial Relations in Greenfield Sites" *Human Resource Management Journal*, Vol. 5, No. 3: 24–40.

Gunnigle, P. (1997) "More Rhetoric than Reality: Enterprise Level Industrial Relations Partnership in Ireland" *The Economic and Social Review*, Vol.

28, No. 4: 179–200.

Gunnigle, P. (1999) "Involvement, Participation and Partnership: A Review of the Debate and Some Reflections on the Irish Context". The 24th Countess Markeivicz Lecture. Dublin.

Gunnigle, P. and Morley, M. (1998) "Strategic Integration and the Management of Industrial Relations in Greenfield Sites" in Skinner, D., Mabey, C. and Clark, T. (eds) *Experiencing Human Resource Management: The Inside Story*, London: Sage Publications.

Ichniowski, C., Kochan, T., Levine, D., Olson, C. and Strauss, G. (1996) "What Works at Work?" *Industrial Relations*, Vol. 35, No. 3: 299–333.

IPA (1997) *Towards Industrial Partnership: New Ways of Working in British Companies*. London: IPA.

Kochan, T. and Osterman, P. (1994) *The Mutual Gains Enterprise: Forging a Winning Partnership Among Labor, Management and Government*, Boston Mass.: Harvard Business School Press.

Locke, R., Kochan, T. and Piore, M. (1995) (eds) *Employment Relations in a Changing World Economy*. Cambridge: The MIT Press.

Marchington, M. (1998) "Partnership in Context: Towards a European Model" in Sparrow, P. and Marchington, M. (eds) *Human Resource Management: The New Agenda*. London: Financial Times/Pitman Publishing.

Marchington, M. and Armstrong, P. (1986) "The Nature of the New Joint Consultation" *Industrial Relations Journal*, Vol. 17, No. 2: 158–70.

McCartney, J. and Teague, P. (1997) "Workplace Innovations in the Republic of Ireland" *The Economic and Social Review*, Vol. 28, No. 4: 381–399.

McGovern, P. (1989) "Union Recognition and Union Avoidance in the 1980s" in T. Murphy (ed.) *Industrial Relations in Ireland*. Dublin: Department of Industrial Relations, University College Dublin.

McGovern, P. (1998) *HRM, Technical Workers and the Multinational Company*. London: Routledge and LSE.

McKersie, R. (1996) "Labour-Management Partnerships: U.S. Evidence and Implications for Ireland" *Irish Business and Administrative Research*, Vol. 17: 1–13.

Osterman, P. (1994) "How Common is Workplace Transformation and How can we Explain who Adopts it?" *Industrial and Labor Relations Review*, Vol. 47, No. 1: 173–87.

Pfeffer, J. (1994) *Competitive Advantage through People: Unleashing the Power of the Work Force*. Boston, Mass.: Harvard Business School Press.

Piore, M. and Sabel, C. (1984) *The Second Industrial Divide*. New York: Basic Books.

Regini, M. (1995) *Uncertain Boundaries: The Social and Political Construction of European Economies*. Cambridge: Cambridge University Press.

Roche, W. K. (1998) "Between Regime Fragmentation and Realignment: Irish Industrial Relations in the 1990s" *Industrial Relations Journal*, Vol. 29, No. 2: 112–125.

Roche, W. K. and Kochan, T. (1996) *Strategies for Extending Social Partnership to Enterprise and Workplace Levels in Ireland*. Report prepared for the National Economic and Social Council, Dublin.

Roche, W. K. and Turner, T. (1998) "Human Resource Management and Industrial Relations: Substitution Dualism and Partnership" in Roche, W. K., Monks K. and Walsh J. (eds) *Human Resource Strategies: Policy and Practice in Ireland*. Dublin: Oak Tree Press.

Roche, W. K., Geary, J. F., Brannick, T., Aahmore, J. and Fahy, M. (1998) *Partnership and Involvement in Irish Workplaces*. Report presented to the National Centre for Partnership, Department of An Taoiseach, Dublin, Centre for Employment Relations and Organisational Performance, University College Dublin.

Rogers, J. and Streeck, W. (1995) (eds) *Works Councils: Consultation, Representation and Co-operation in Industrial Relations*. Chicago: University of Chicago Press.

Sabel, C. (1996) *Ireland: Local Partnerships and Social Innovation*. Paris: Organisation for Economic Co-operation and Development.

Sisson, K. (1997) (ed.) *Towards New Forms of Work Organisation – Can Europe Realise its Innovative Potential? An Interim Report of the Results of the EPOC Questionnaire Survey of Direct Employee Participation in Europe*. Luxembourg: European Foundation/Office for the Official Publication of the European Communities.

Streeck, W. (1992) "National Diversity, Regime Competition and Institutional Deadlock: Problems in Forming a European Industrial Relations System" *Journal of Public Policy*, Vol. 12, No. 4: 301–30.

Sweeney, P. (1997) *The Celtic Tiger: Ireland's Economic Miracle Explained*. Dublin: Oak Tree Press.

Tansey, P. (1998) *Ireland at Work: Economic Growth and the Labour Market, 1987–1997*. Dublin: Oak Tree Press.

Teague, P. (1995) "Pay Determination in the Republic of Ireland: Towards Social Corporatism?" *British Journal of Industrial Relations*, Vol. 33, No. 2: 253–274.

Turner, T. and Morley, M. (1995) *Industrial Relations and the New Order: Case Studies in Conflict and Co-operation*. Dublin: Oak Tree Press.

Chapter 4

Counterposing Collectivism: Performance-Related Pay and Industrial Relations in Greenfield Sites[1]

Patrick Gunnigle, Thomas Turner and Daryl D'Art

INTRODUCTION

This chapter considers some of the industrial relations ramifications of performance-related pay (PRP). It particularly focuses on the use of PRP systems based on performance appraisal and, specifically, the implications of such systems for collectivism and individualism as dimensions of management approaches to industrial relations. Using a database of all "large" greenfield sites established in Ireland over a five year period, the evidence indicates extensive use of PRP systems based on appraisal, particularly among non-union companies. We conclude that the diffusion of such systems is indicative of increasing employer attempts to individualise the employment relationship and exclude union penetration.

Collectivism and Individualism in Industrial Relations

A number of commentators have identified changes in the extent and nature of collective employee representation as a critical dimension of contemporary changes in industrial relations (Kochan et al., 1986; Salamon, 1992). Collectivism in industrial relations incorporates the extent to which management acknowledges the right of employees to collective representation and the involvement of the collective in influencing management decision making (Purcell, 1987; Sisson, 1994; Storey and Sisson, 1994). Collectivism is, therefore, primarily concerned with the role of trade unions in industrial relations. The Republic of Ireland is characterised by comparatively high levels of trade union density. Currently, approximately 39 per cent of the Irish workforce (45 per cent of employees) are trade union members.

    A pervasive theme in the literature is the contention that firms locating at greenfield sites are likely to adopt an increasingly individualist focus in

1. This chapter was first published in the *British Journal of Industrial Relations*, Vol. 36, 4: 565–579, and is reprinted with their permission.

industrial relations and pursue some key features of human resource management (HRM) such as flexible working, enhanced quality initiatives and employee involvement (Beaumont, 1985; Beaumont and Townley, 1985; Kochan et al., 1986; Guest, 1989; Guest and Hoque, 1994). Indeed, some commentators have identified a greenfield site as a requisite condition for the adoption of an individualist management focus in industrial relations (see Blyton and Turnbull, 1994).

The extent of collectivism in industrial relations may be accurately gauged through measures of trade union penetration (density and recognition) and reliance on collective bargaining. However, finding acceptable indicators of management attempts to individualise the employment relationship is an altogether more complex task. Apart from Purcell's (1987) and Storey and Bacon's (1993) attempts to explore key dimensions of individualist management approaches or "styles" in industrial relations, it remains quite an amorphous concept. It is variously suggested that increased individualism is associated with a comprehensive employee development emphasis, (individual) performance-related pay, a focus on management–individual as opposed to management–trade union interactions (particularly "direct" communications) and initiatives designed to facilitate higher levels of individual employee involvement and autonomy at work (see Beer, 1984; Beaumont, 1985; Guest, 1987; Purcell, 1987; Hannaway, 1987, 1992; Storey, 1992; Bacon and Storey, 1993; Storey and Bacon 1993; Storey and Sisson, 1994). However, many of these areas present difficulties in constructing valid measures of the extent of an individualist management orientation in industrial relations. Performance-related pay (PRP) may be one exception in this respect. Pay determination has traditionally been a critical focus of industrial relations interactions. In particular, trade unions have sought to ensure that decisions on pay rates and, particularly, on pay increases are subject to collective bargaining. However, some forms of PRP, particularly those based on performance appraisal, reflect an essentially individualist orientation which excludes or severely limits trade union involvement.

PERFORMANCE-RELATED PAY AND THE INDIVIDUALISATION OF INDUSTRIAL RELATIONS

Collective bargaining is the primary means of determining levels of pay increases in Ireland. The level of such bargaining has tended to oscillate between national and enterprise level. Since 1987 the main focus of pay bargaining has been at national level, involving the negotiation of centralised agreements between employers, trade unions and government. At enterprise level, the past decade has seen considerable debate on the nature of pay systems. This debate has tended to focus on two aspects: first, the ability of organisations to ensure that basic pay levels reflect market conditions (particularly the external labour market) and secondly, the introduction of merit/performance-related payment systems. The Irish research evidence does not point to any discernible pattern. There is some evidence of increased utilisation of PRP systems (Brewster and Hegewisch, 1994; Gunnigle et al., 1994). However, this same evidence finds quite a traditional picture in the application of such systems, with merit or performance-related pay being largely confined to managerial and professional categories.

Individuals at higher levels in the organisational hierarchy have traditionally received individual pay packages, reflecting their predominantly non-union status and their ability to impact more directly on organisational performance. Thus, a much more significant indicator of the development of a more individualist approach to industrial relations is the degree to which companies utilise individual performance-related pay (PRP) systems for non-managerial/professional grades (see Foulkes, 1980, 1981; Kochan et al., 1986).

As noted above, a critical manifestation of higher levels of individualism is the adoption of performance-related pay systems linked to formal appraisals of individual performance (Rollinson, 1993; Roche and Turner, 1994). The incidence of performance-related pay based on formal performance appraisals for *all* employee grades, particularly non-managerial/professional categories, is seen as a stronger indicator of individualist (as opposed to collectivist) management approaches to industrial relations than PRP alone (Foulkes, 1980; Kochan et al., 1986; Purcell, 1987; Blyton and Turnbull, 1992; Storey, 1992; Sisson, 1994). The use of PRP systems based on performance appraisal is an important innovation since the use of PRP systems among manual/operative grades is nothing new (see Clegg, 1979; Mooney, 1980). Traditionally, most PRP systems (for example measured day work) were based on quantitative evaluations of employee performance and were normally the subject of collective bargaining. As such, quantitative PRP systems were very much integral to the collectivist industrial relations tradition (Mooney, 1980; Grafton, 1988; Roche, 1992; also see Armstrong and Murliss, 1994). In contrast, performance appraisal is essentially an individualist management tool (Beer et al., 1984) and may be used to either replace collective bargaining or reduce its significance in pay determination.

Concepts and Methodology

Trade union presence, as measured by trade union recognition and trade union density, is used as the key indicator of "collectivism" in industrial relations. *Performance-related pay* (PRP), as measured by the utilisation of PRP systems which are linked to formal appraisals of employee performance, is used as the key indicator of the extent of individualisation of the employment relationship. Of course a number of other measures considered indicative of collectivism and individualism are available. In another paper the authors tested some of these measures (Gunnigle et al., 1997) and concluded that trade union presence and PRP provided the most robust indicators.

To explore the role of PRP systems and their industrial relations impact, we consider findings from a study of all greenfield site firms established in the manufacturing and internationally traded services sectors in the Republic of Ireland in the period 1987–1992. The study population amounted to some 53 firms.[2] The study excluded firms with less than 100 employees. The research was conducted using a methodologically pluralist approach involving: qualitative semi-structured interviews with senior managers in all of the sites; statistical analysis of a questionnaire-based survey completed by the senior manager responsible for personnel/HR in each site; and presentation of research findings to HRM/IR "expert" panels. Information on the industrial relations strategies and practices of "greenfield" companies is a useful barometer of change in industrial relations. Greenfield companies are less constrained by established practice and thus possess greater scope to choose what they feel are "appropriate" industrial relations approaches and to establish polices and practices which will develop and reinforce their chosen approach.

Research Hypotheses

A key aspect of the individualism and industrial relations debate is the impact on trade unions (Guest, 1987, 1995). Of particular interest is the extent to which individualist HRM polices and approaches may co-exist alongside "traditional" industrial relations or, alternatively, whether such approaches effectively replace or severely diminish the role of trade unions and collective bargaining. In this debate, two bodies of literature are significant. First, the "non-union" literature is based on the premise that individualism counterpoises collectivism (see Foulkes, 1980, 1981; Purcell, 1987). Thus, it might be expected that companies with individualist policies will seek to avoid trade union recognition and collective bargaining. Drawing on this literature base we might argue that the extent of utilisation of PRP systems tied to appraisals of individual employee performance will be negatively associated with trade union presence (also see Beer et al., 1984; Kochan et al., 1986; Guest, 1990; McLoughlin and Gourlay, 1992; Beaumont and Harris, 1994). A second and contrasting literature source is that based on what is termed "dualism" (Purcell, 1987; Storey, 1992; Brewster, 1993, 1994). This suggests that individualism need not necessarily counterpoise collectivism and that firms may concurrently utilise collectivist and individualist approaches. In relation to PRP, this line of reasoning suggests that not only should we expect no relationship (the null hypothesis) but, more significantly, that the extent of utilisation of PRP systems tied to appraisals of individual employee performance will be positively associated with trade union presence. It is further argued that dualist approaches are appropriate where there is a strong tradition of collective employee representation (see Roche and Turner, 1994; Roche and Kochan, 1996). In

---

2. Greenfield sites were defined as "locations where an organisation establishes a new facility in a start-up mode incorporating design of plant and recruitment of a new workforce".

the Irish context, therefore, it might plausibly be argued that experimentation with PRP will occur alongside collectivist structures incorporating a significant union presence.

A range of factors have been advanced to explain variations in management approaches to industrial relations, such as size, technology, labour costs, market performance and sector (Beaumont, 1985; Kochan et al., 1986; Beaumont and Harris, 1994; Turner, 1994; Storey and Sisson, 1994). A factor considered particularly influential in explaining variations in industrial relations is company ownership (Beaumont, 1985). This is based on the rationale that revealed managerial preferences in industrial relations will most significantly be exposed in greenfield sites and that the actual approaches chosen will closely reflect underlying managerial values associated with country of ownership (Beaumont, 1985; Beaumont and Townley, 1985; Poole, 1986; Whitaker, 1986; Guest and Rosenthal, 1992; Rollinson, 1993). Since managerial opposition to pluralism, and particularly unionisation, is characteristic of the value system of American managers, whereas industrial relations "styles" which emphasise individualism and performance-based rewards are very much in line with this value system (Bendix, 1956; Kochan et al., 1986), it can be predicted that the extent of utilisation of PRP systems tied to appraisals of individual employee performance will be positively associated with US ownership.

FINDINGS: PERFORMANCE-RELATED PAY IN GREENFIELD SITES

Table 4.1 summarises the study findings on the level of utilisation of PRP in greenfield sites. It indicates that PRP is most commonly used among managerial/professional grades: 39 (74 per cent) of the 53 greenfield companies used PRP for management/professional grades, while 32 (60 per cent) did so for hourly paid/manual employees.

Table 4.1: Performance-Related Pay and Performance Appraisal
(N = 53)

PRP		Performance Appraisal Used to Decide PRP	
Management/ Professional	*Manual/ Hourly*	*Management/ Professional*	*Manual/ Hourly*
39 (74%)	32 (60%)	37 (70%)	22 (42%)

Source: Greenfield site study.

Only in the indigenous companies was PRP more common among manual/ hourly grades. The case-study investigations revealed that this apparent discrepancy was explained by the fact that five of the eight indigenous companies who used PRP among its manual grades adopted traditional quantitative measures of employee performance. Three of the companies operated in the clothing industry and used measured day-work systems, while the other two companies operated in the food processing sector and used a PRP system which was based on quantitative measures of employee output. Such "conventional" quantitative PRP systems do not generally challenge collectivist industrial relations traditions and indeed are integral to union–management agreements in the clothing and food sectors.

Rather, the novel dimension in PRP systems, as outlined above, is the extent to which they are based on formal appraisals of individual employee performance *and* extend to all employee grades. Twenty-two (42 per cent) of the greenfield companies studied based their PRP decisions on formal appraisals of individual employee performance among all employee grades. The incidence of PRP based on formal appraisals of individual employee performance among non-managerial/professional grades was strongly linked to trade union recognition and company ownership (Table 4.2).

Table 4.2: Unionisation, Ownership and the Use of Performance Appraisal to Assess PRP (N = 53)

Union Status	Performance Appraisal to Decide PRP	USA	Irish	Ownership European	Asian	Total
Union	Used	0	1	0	0	1 (4%)
	Not Used	4	8	8	4	24 (96%)
Non-Union	Used	18	1	0	2	21 (75%)
	Not Used	5	1	0	1	7 (25%)
Total		27	11	8	7	53

Source: Greenfield site study.

Table 4.2 indicates that almost all the firms (21 out of 22) which used performance appraisal to aid PRP decisions were non-union and twenty were foreign-owned, of which eighteen were from the USA. These findings are quite clear-cut. It is non-union companies, emanating from the more individualist US corporate culture, which predominantly utilise PRP systems linked to formal employee appraisals.

In examining the relative impact of ownership and union status, we find union status is the primary factor in explaining the use of PRP with performance appraisal. Among the non-union US companies only five did not use this system. When all of the non-union companies are included, 21 use this system while seven do not. Conversely, only one unionised (Irish) company used PRP based on performance appraisal, indicating the dominant effect of union status.[3] Union status is more highly correlated with the use of PRP with performance appraisal (p = 0.72***) than US ownership (p = 0.52***).[4]

These findings point to a significant negative relationship between PRP and trade union presence. It is clear that PRP systems linked to performance appraisal are most likely to be employed where there is no union presence. Collectivism is weakest in the US firms and strongest in the European firms. In particular, it is clear that PRP clearly counterpoises collectivism and, thus, our findings provide little evidence of "dualist" approaches or styles (Purcell, 1987; Storey, 1989). The higher the levels of union recognition the lower the usage of PRP with appraisal. Indeed, it appears that the trend indicates increasing polarisation between collectivist and individualist approaches. Greenfield companies appear to be choosing one *or* the other approach rather than any combination of both. This is not to say that PRP based on performance appraisal cannot be accommodated in unionised establishments. Indeed, one can find considerable evidence of firms where such PRP systems are subject to joint regulation through collective bargaining (see Heery, 1997a, 1997b). However, our findings do not support this trend but rather point to union exclusion in firms operating PRP schemes based on performance appraisal.

Greenfield Versus "Brownfield" Companies

Roche (1990) has argued that, traditionally, management approaches to industrial relations in Ireland have been based on a willingness to accept collective bargaining. However, while levels of union density in Ireland have held up comparatively well, there is conclusive evidence of a severe erosion in levels of trade union recognition and density in newly established firms (Gunnigle, 1995; Hourihan, 1996). It appears that in greenfield sites, companies are adopting patterns of industrial relations management which exclude trade unions and incorporate a greater individualist orientation. The use of performance-related pay systems based on formal appraisals of individual performance among non-managerial/white-collar grades emerges as an integral component of these management approaches.

To evaluate the extent to which patterns of utilisation of PRP systems in the greenfield companies differ from longer established ("brownfield") companies we draw on the Price Waterhouse Cranfield (PWC) survey of 160

3. Multivariate analysis using a logistic regression equation was used to confirm this finding. A number of control variables were included (such as labour costs, level of competition, size, manufacturing sector) to check for other possible causal factors. The only two variables with any significant impact on the use of PRP were union recognition and US ownership. Because of multi-collinearity problems with these two variables they were run in separate equations. When both variables were included simultaneously, recognition was significant and masked the effects of ownership.
4. *significant at 0.05; **significant at 0.01; = significant at 0.001.

private sector companies employing more than 100 employees.[5] This study was carried out in 1992, the last year for which data on greenfield sites are available and, therefore, should provide a relatively accurate comparison between older established companies and greenfield sites. However, two caveats need to be highlighted which limit the usefulness of comparison between the greenfield and brownfield data sets. First, there is the possibility that a few of the greenfield sites are included in the PWC survey, thus reducing potential differences between the two samples. A second and more significant problem is that only performance-related pay *without* performance appraisal is measured in the PWC survey. Thus, the PWC data set provide information on the use of PRP only and does not provide any insights on the use of appraisal to aid PRP decisions. While the potential errors in using PRP only have been pointed out, nevertheless it should be noted that those companies in the greenfield study who used PRP systems were also more likely to combine the use of PRP systems with performance appraisal. The correlation between firms using PRP and those using PRP with performance appraisal was $p=0.82$*** for white-collar workers and $p=0.68$*** for manual workers, indicating a strong and significant relationship. Consequently, a comparison of greenfield and brownfield sites using PRP alone should give a relatively reliable indication of trends, subject to the "health warnings" above.

Table 4.3: The Use of PPR in Greenfield and Established Companies for White-Collar and Manual Workers

Ownership	Greenfield Sites using PRP			Established Sites using PRP		
	Mgt/White-Collar	*Manual/Hourly*	N	*Mgt/White-Collar*	*Manual/Hourly*	N
US	93%	70%	27	75%	22%	46
Asian	71%	29%	11	50%	25%	4
Irish	36%	73%*	8	27%	12%	50
Europe	62%	38%	7	61%	11%	28
Overall Mean	**74%**	**60%**	**53**	**52%**	**16%**	**128**

* The use of traditional quantitative performance-related pay systems for manual workers which are the subject of collective bargaining has already been noted and most likely accounts for the high figure of 73% reported here for Irish companies.

Source: Greenfield site study and PWC survey.

5. These data are drawn from The Price Waterhouse Cranfield Study of Human Resource Management in eighteen European Countries. In Ireland the 1992 study was based on a postal survey distributed to *Top 1500* trading and non-trading organisations. This survey achieved a response rate of 23%. For more information see Brewster and Hegewisch 1994; Gunnigle et al. 1994.

As Table 4.3 indicates more of the greenfield companies use PRP for management and white-collar grades than established companies, 74 per cent and 52 per cent respectively. Similarly, the use of PRP for manual employees is significantly different with 60 per cent of greenfield companies using PRP compared to 16 per cent of the established companies. In particular, there is a large difference between US greenfield companies and established companies, 70 per cent compared to 22 per cent. There are also considerable differences in the extent of union recognition: 79 per cent of established companies recognised unions compared to 47 per cent of greenfield companies (Table 4.4). In general, in the established companies, the lower the level of utilisation of PRP among manual/hourly employees, the higher the level of union recognition.

Table 4.4: PRP and Union Recognition in Greenfield and Established Companies

Ownership	Greenfield Sites			Established Sites		
	PRP for Manual Workers	*Union(s) Recognised*	N	*PRP for Manual Workers*	*Union(s) Recognised*	N
US	70%	15%	27	22%	70%	46
Asian	29%	57%	11	25%	100%	4
Irish	73%	82%	8	12%	80%	50
Europe	38%	100%	7	11%	89%	28
Overall Mean	**60%**	**47%**	**53**	**16%**	**79%**	**128**

Source: Greenfield site study and PWC survey.

These findings suggest quite a contrasting picture between pay practices in greenfield and brownfield companies in Ireland. The PWC data indicate that, while a substantial proportion of brownfield companies operated PRP schemes for managerial and professional employees, the figures decrease quite rapidly as one descends the organisational hierarchy (see Brewster and Hegewisch, 1994; Turner, 1994). While the traditional practice of differentiating between manual/hourly and managerial/professional employees in the application of PRP is still very much in evidence in brownfield organisations, this is certainly not the case in greenfield companies. Among established companies, union presence is also the critical factor explaining the existence of PRP for manual employees. This is also true for the 46 brownfield US companies in the PWC survey. A majority (32) are unionised while only fourteen are non-union. However, PRP is much more prevalent in the non-union companies. Seven of the fourteen non-union companies used PRP for manual grades while only three of the 32 unionised companies used PRP for manual employees.

This evidence suggests that managements in greenfield companies are placing a major emphasis on individual PRP systems as part of their overall approach to industrial relations. The most obvious explanatory factors here are trade union recognition and ownership. In both the brownfield and greenfield data sets, PRP systems were most common in non-union companies, particularly those of US ownership (also see Turner, 1994). In the greenfield sector, the proportion of non-union and US-owned companies is considerably higher as a proportion of the total study population.

CONCLUSION

The findings outlined in this chapter point to a high take up of performance-related pay systems based on appraisals in non-union greenfield companies. As noted earlier, the crucial innovation in PRP systems is the use of appraisal as the key means of determining PRP increases *and* the application of such systems among non-managerial/white-collar grades. Traditionally, PRP systems for manual/hourly grades were based on quantitative criteria. Such schemes were normally covered by collective bargaining arrangements and were thus integral to pluralist industrial relations traditions (Mooney, 1980; Grafton, 1988; Roche, 1992; see also Armstrong and Murliss, 1994). This is not the case with PRP systems based on performance appraisal. Rather such systems are essentially an individualist management tool with important implications for industrial relations. By linking performance appraisals to incremental pay decisions, managements in greenfield sites are posing an explicit challenge to collectivism in industrial relations. The collectivist tradition implies that incremental pay decisions are achieved through collective bargaining and, once agreed, apply "across the board" to all relevant employee categories. In contrast, PRP decisions based on performance appraisal are normally the subject of a management (only) review of individual employee performance. Consequently, incremental pay decisions are made by management rather than through collective bargaining and vary according to individual appraisals rather than applying equally to all through a collective agreement. Thus, individualism replaces collectivism at two critical junctures: first, the process of appraisal is individualist rather than collectivist (individual appraisal rather than collective bargaining); and secondly, the outcome takes the form of varying PRP decisions among individual employees rather than a fixed amount which applies equally to all employees.

Some commentators take issue with this counterpoising hypothesis, suggesting that PRP does not necessarily have negative implications for collectivism and specifically trade unions (Heery, 1992, 1997a, 1997b). This argument is based on the contention that PRP systems may be subject to joint regulation via collective bargaining (also see Guest, 1987, 1989; Purcell, 1987;

Casey et al., 1992; Storey, 1992; Roche and Turner, 1994). Indeed, Heery (1997a) points out that PRP systems may often be subject to joint management-union regulation via collective bargaining. While one can point to examples of such joint regulation in Ireland and the UK, our evidence from Irish greenfield sites does not support this argument. Using measures of trade union presence and PRP we find a polarisation of approaches. In the greenfield firms studied, PRP based on appraisal was essentially a non-union phenomenon while companies with union recognition tended, by and large, not to use PRP based on appraisals.

The evidence identifies company ownership and trade union recognition as the major factors impacting on the adoption of PRP systems based on appraisal. Such systems were predominantly used in non-union and US-owned companies and were largely absent in unionised companies.

The findings also point to quite a contrasting picture between pay practices in greenfield and brownfield companies. While the traditional practice of differentiating between manual/hourly and managerial/professional employees in the application of PRP is still very much in evidence in brownfield organisations, this is certainly not the case in greenfield companies.

The contrast between brownfield and greenfield companies in the levels of utilisation of PRP systems among non-managerial/professional grades may be explained in a number of ways. The conventional explanation for differentiating between "white-collar" and "blue-collar" employees in the application of PRP schemes is the perceived difficulty in disaggregating the impact of the individual employee's performance on overall company performance at lower levels in the organisational hierarchy (Armstrong and Murliss, 1994). A second, more compelling explanation relates to the collectivist tradition in Irish industrial relations. Within this tradition, which is noticeably weaker in greenfield sites, trade unions have generally opposed PRP systems which incorporate assessments of individual employee performance (see Murray, 1984; Grafton, 1988; Roche and Turner, 1994). Rather, Irish trade unions have indicated their explicit preference for standard pay increases achieved through collective bargaining (see Roche, 1994). This is hardly surprising since trade union collectivism originated primarily as a pragmatic response by workers to individualised workplace relations, the disparity in power and divergent economic interests between employers as buyers and employees as sellers of their labour in a market system (Taylor, 1989). Consequently, workers embraced trade unions as an instrument with which to exert some influence on wage determination and check the exercise of arbitrary employer power. In pursuit of these objectives, solidarity, that is a community of feeling, interest and action, remains a prerequisite for effective trade unionism. Systems of PRP, irrespective of the motivation for their establishment tend to corrode the essence of collectivism and solidarity. Their tendency is to dissolve the collectivity into a number of discrete, isolated and sometimes powerless individuals. This is particularly the case with workers whose skills are over-supplied in the labour market. The determination of pay on an individual basis substantially reduces or removes what many union members have long regarded as a primary function and justification for a trade union presence. Indeed, the experience of some British unions with PRP has been one of a substantial erosion of the union position in pay determination and difficulty in maintaining their role as bargaining agent (Heery, 1997a). Alternatively, there is some evidence to suggest that the introduction of PRP has stimulated a demand for union representation (see Heery, 1997b). Moreover, from the perspective of employees with a large measure of autonomy in their work and possessing scarce skills that command premium rates PRP may appear, in the short term at any rate, an equitable and stimulating reward system. In conclusion, the issue of PRP systems based on appraisal and their compatibility or otherwise with collectivism raises a range of complex issues and requires more longitudinal data to inform the debate.

REFERENCES

Armstrong, M. (1995) *A Handbook of Personnel Management Practice*. London: Kogan Page.

Armstrong, M. and Murliss, H. (1994) *Reward Management: A Handbook of Remuneration Strategy and Practice*. London: Kogan Page in association with the Institute of Personnel Management.

Bacon, N. and Storey, J. (1993) "Individualization of the Employment Relationship and the Implications for Trade Unions" *Employee Relations*, Vol. 15, No. 1: 5–17.

Beaumont, P. B. (1985) "New Plant Work Practices" *Personnel Review*, Vol. 14, No. 5: 15–19.

Beaumont, P. B. (1986) "Management Opposition to Union Organisation: Researching the Indicators" *Employee Relations*, Vol. 8, No. 5: 31–38.

Beaumont, P. B. (1992) "The US Human Resource Management Literature: A Review" in Salaman, G. (ed.) *Human Resource Strategies*. London: Open University/Sage Publications.

Beaumont, P. B. and Harris, R. I. D. (1994) "Opposition to Unions in the Non-Union Sector in Britain" *International Journal of Human Resource Management*, Vol. 5, No. 2: 457–471.

Beaumont, P. B. and Townley, B. (1985) "Greenfield Sites, New Plants and Work Practices" in Hammond, V. (ed.) *Current Research in Management*. London: Frances Pinter.

Beer, M., Spector, B., Lawrence, P., Mills, Q. and Walton, R. (1984) *Human Resource Management: A General Manager's Perspective*. New York: The Free Press.

Bendix, R. (1956) *Work and Authority in Industry*. New York: John Wiley.

Blyton, P. and Turnbull, P. (1992) *Reassessing Human Resource Management*. London: Sage Publications.

Blyton, P. and Turnbull, P. (1994) *The Dynamics of Employee Relations*.

London: Macmillan.

Brewster, C. (1993) "Developing a 'European' Model of Human Resource Management" *International Journal of Human Resource Management*, Vol. 4, No. 4: 765–784.

Brewster, C. (1994) "HRM: The European Dimension" in Storey, J. (ed.) *Human Resource Management: A Critical Text*. London: Routledge.

Brewster, C. and Hegewisch, A. (1994) *Policy and Practice in European Human Resource Management: The Price Waterhouse Cranfield Survey*. London: Routledge.

Casey, B., Lakey, J. and White, M. (1992) *"Payment Systems: A Look at Current Practice"* Research Series, No. 5, Department of Employment. London: Policy Studies Institute.

Clegg, H. A. (1979) *The Changing System of Industrial Relations in Great Britain*. Oxford: Blackwell.

Daly, A. (1989) *Pay and Benefits in Irish Industry*, Mimeo. Dublin: Irish Business and Employers' Confederation.

Foulkes, F. (1980) *Personnel Policies in Large Non-Union Companies*. Englewood Cliffs N. J.: Prentice-Hall.

Foulkes, F. K. (1981) "How Top Non-Union Companies Manage Employees" *Harvard Business Review*, September–October: 90–96.

Grafton, D. (1988) "Performance Related Pay: Securing Employee Trust" *Industrial Relations News*, Vol. 44: 11–12.

Guest, D. (1987) "Human Resource Management and Industrial Relations" *Journal of Management Studies*, Vol. 24, No. 5: 503–521.

Guest, D. (1989) "Human Resource Management: Its Implications for Industrial Relations and Trade Unions" in Storey, J. (ed.) *New Perspectives on Human Resource Management*. London: Routledge.

Guest, D. (1990) "Human Resource Management and the American Dream" *Journal of Management Studies*, Vol. 27, No. 4: 503–523.

Guest, D. (1995) "Human Resource Management, Trade Unions and Industrial Relations" in Storey, J. (ed.) *Human Resource Management: A Critical Text*. London: Routledge.

Guest, D. and Hoque, K. (1994) "Employee Relations in Non-Union Greenfield Sites: The Good, the Bad and the Ugly" *Human Resource Management Journal*, Vol. 5, No. 1: 1–14.

Guest, D. and Rosenthal, P. (1992) *Industrial Relations in Greenfield Sites*, Mimeo. Centre of Economic Performance, London School of Economics.

Gunnigle, P. (1995) "Collectivism and the Management of Industrial Relations in Greenfield Sites" *Human Resource Management Journal*, Vol. 5, No. 3: 24–40.

Gunnigle, P., Flood, P., Morley, M. and Turner, T. (1994) *Continuity and Change in Irish Employee Relations*. Dublin: Oak Tree Press.

Gunnigle, P., Morley, M. and Turner, T. (1996) *Individualism and the Management of Industrial Relations*. Paper presented at the First *Irish Academy of Management* Conference, University College Cork, September.

Hannaway, C. (1987) "New Style Collective Agreements: An Irish Approach" *Industrial Relations News*, Vol. 13: 16–22.

Hannaway, C. (1992) "Why Irish Eyes are Smiling" *Personnel Management*, May: 38–42.

Heery, E. (1997a) "Performance-Related Pay and Trade Union De-Recognition" *Employee Relations*, Vol. 19, No. 3: 208–221.

Heery, E. (1997b) "Performance-Related Pay and Trade Union Membership" *Employee Relations*, Vol. 19, No. 5: 430–442.

Heery, E. (1992) *Divided We Fall? Trade Unions and Performance Related Pay*. Paper presented to London School of Economics/Trade Union Congress Seminar: London School of Economics, 19 March.

Hillery, B. (1994) "The Institutions of Industrial Relations" in Murphy, T. V. and Roche, W. K. (eds) *Irish Industrial Relations in Practice*. Dublin: Oak Tree Press.

Hourihan, F. (1996) "Non-Union Policies on the Increase Among New Overseas Firms" *Industrial Relations News*, Vol. 4: 17–23.

Kochan, T. A., Katz, H. C. and McKersie, R. B. (1986) *The Transformation of American Industrial Relations*. New York: Basic Books.

McLoughlin, I. and Gourlay, S. (1992) "Enterprise Without Unions: The Management of Employee Relations in Non-Union Firms" *Journal of Management Studies*, Vol. 29, No. 5: 669–691.

Mooney, P. (1980) *An Inquiry into Wage Payment Systems in Ireland*. Dublin: Economic and Social Research Institute/European Institute for the Improvement of Living and Working Conditions.

Murray, S. (1984) *Industrial Relations in Irish Private Sector Manufacturing Industry*. Dublin: Industrial Development Authority.

Poole, M. (1986) "Managerial Strategies and Styles in Industrial Relations: A Comparative Analysis" *Journal of General Management*, Vol. 12, No. 1: 40–53.

Purcell, J. (1987) "Mapping Management Styles in Employee Relations" *Journal of Management Studies*, Vol. 24, No. 5: 533–548.

Roche, W. K. (1990) *Industrial Relations Research in Ireland and the Trade Union Interest*. Paper presented to the Irish Congress of Trades Unions Conference on Joint Research between Trade Unions, Universities, Third Level Colleges and Research Institutes, Dublin.

Roche, W. K. (1992) "The Liberal Theory of Industrialism and the Development of Industrial Relations in Ireland" in Golthorpe, J. H. and Whelan, C. T. (eds) *The Development of Industrial Society in Ireland*. Oxford: Oxford University Press.

Roche, W. K. (1994) "The Trend of Unionisation" in Murphy T. V. and Roche, W. K. (eds) *Irish Industrial Relations in Practice*. Oak Tree Press: Dublin.

Roche, W. K. and Kochan, T. A. (1997) "Strategies for Extending Social Partnership to Enterprise and Workplace Levels in Ireland" Report Prepared for the National Economic and Social Council (Draft), Dublin: July.

Roche, W. K. and Turner, T. (1994) "Testing Alternative Models of Human Resource Policy Effects on Trade Union Recognition in the Republic of Ireland" *International Journal of Human Resource Management*, Vol. 5, No. 3: 721–753.

Rollinson, D. (1993) *Understanding Employee Relations: A Behavioural Approach*. Wokingham: Addison-Wesley.

Salamon, M. (1992) *Industrial Relations: Theory and Practice*. Hemel Hempstead: Prentice Hall.

Sisson, K. (1994) *Personnel Management: A Comprehensive Guide to Theory and Practice in Britain*. Oxford: Blackwell.

Storey, J. (1989) (ed.) *New Perspectives on Human Resource Management*. London: Routledge.

Storey, J. (1992) *Developments in the Management of Human Resources*. Oxford: Basil Blackwell.

Storey, J. and Bacon, N. (1993) "Individualism and Collectivism: Into the 1990s" *International Journal of Human Resource Management*, Vol. 4, No. 3: 665–683.

Storey, J. and Sisson, K. (1994) *Managing Human Resources and Industrial Relations*. Buckingham: Open University Press.

Taylor, A. J. (1989) *Trade Unions and Politics: A Comparative Introduction*. London: Macmillan.

Turner, T. (1994) "Unionisation and Human Resource Management in Irish Companies" *Industrial Relations Journal*, Vol. 25, No. 1: 39–51.

Whitaker, A. (1986) "Managerial Strategy and Industrial relations: A Case Study of Plant Relocation" *Journal of Management Studies*, Vol. 23, No. 6: 657–678.

CHAPTER 5

The Part-Time Soul: Identity Management and Organisational Structure in the Old Service Sector

ROLAND TORMEY

INTRODUCTION

Advocates of post-Fordist or "post-modern" understandings of organisations have in recent years focused on a number of changes which organisations were supposedly undergoing. These writers argue that the new workplace is now quite different from the workplace of even a few years ago. They speak in terms of a paradigm shift from Fordism to post-Fordism or from modernity to post-modernity. In his review of writings on post-modernity and work, for example, Andy Hargreaves identifies seven different themes which are key to the post-modern project: flexible economies; globalisation; the death of certainties; the moving mosaic as an organisational form; the self and identity; safe simulation; and compression of time and space (1994: 47). Similar lists of changes evident in post-Fordism exist (see Turner and D'Art, this volume, Chapter 1). This chapter looks at a number of these processes that are supposedly underway and explores their possible contradictions. In particular, the possibility of successfully managing culture in flexible environments is examined. The evidence appears to indicate that in numerically flexible, low-paying jobs, cultural and identity management (concerned with the self and identity) is only modestly successful. However, it is more successful in organisations that have traditionally clear and hierarchical bureaucracy rather than new organisational forms. The management of culture and identity, thought of as amongst the most post-modern of ideas, seems to be tied directly to the symbol of Fordism and bureaucracy.

Yet, this chapter is not an attack on post-modernism. While it argues that the contemporary workplace is not post-modern, it does so using a theoretical framework which is known as post-modernist (or more specifically post-structuralist). In this sense, it is worth distinguishing between post-modernity – a description of a post-modern world – and post-modernism – a post-modern description of the world. Insofar as the world of work is not found to be post-modern, it can be argued that there is no need to use different ways of looking at that world. The next section briefly outlines something of the post-structuralist understanding of identity research indicating how it differs from modernist conceptions. In the following section the methodology used in this study is described, and the final section presents data from a number of case studies.

IDENTITY MANAGEMENT

One of the central concerns of personnel management is managing the identity or culture of the workforce. In the past this was articulated in terms of producing compliant workers through the management of rewards. In recent years the focus has moved towards producing committed workers through managing the culture of the workforce. This is most evident in the shift in the literature from personnel management to human resources management (HRM). In her reviews of the normative literature on HRM, Legge (1989, 1995) identifies that among the common elements in otherwise disparate definitions of HRM are the promotion of commitment and the fostering of a willingness in employees to act flexibly (1995: 66).

This focus on the management of culture has given rise to a host of studies designed to measure the extent to which cultural management has been effective. Such studies often use surveys to measure whether management and staff are divided into a "them and us" (that is two mutually exclusive groups experiencing some degree of antagonism) (for example D'Art and Turner, 1999). They are "modernist" insofar as they are based on the idea of "scientific" social research and based on what sociologists would call a functionalist conception of identity. In his review of such studies, Guest identifies that this approach can be problematic, insofar as most of these studies are based on surveys and as such are "correlational and therefore can do no more than offer hypotheses about cause and effect relationships" (1992: 118). The studies may tell you something about who is committed and who is not, but they tell you little about why.

A second methodological problem arises because of the way in which workplace identity is measured. Anthropologists sometimes distinguish between an "etic" and an "emic" mode of analysis (Silverman, 1993: 24; Vidich and Lyman, 1994: 26). An etic analysis involves working from an objective position: creating a yardstick which is thought of as objective and applying this to all situations. This is what much of the literature does in measuring organisational culture. A series of issues are identified by the researcher, questions based on them are constructed by the researcher and the staff are then surveyed. The problem here is that it assumes that the issues and questions raised by the researcher meaningfully approximate the issues and questions which are of concern to the staff. The alternative is an emic mode of analysis. This involves using the frame of reference of the researched subject, identifying what they see as important and using this as a yardstick. This is likely to be a more valuable approach precisely since identity is a subjective construct. It is "a symbolic meaning system, a way for a 'people' to organise social reality" (Tovey et al., 1989: 9). Rather than using a predefined list of characteristics which are thought to be important in assigning identity, the issues which become symbolic in defining identity are chosen and their meanings constructed by the group in interaction with other groups. While researchers may survey "trust" in management or "commitment to the organisation's goals", other issues may be in much sharper focus for the staff: uniforms, management style and interaction or even the food in the canteen.

This emic or subjective conception of identity gives rise to a third difficulty with existing studies: their strict dichotomisation of the world into an "us" and "them". Identities rarely show such clean breaks. Although identity tends to be defined in opposition to other groups, it is rarely fixed and unchanging. The same can be said of workplace identity. If you listen carefully to the way in which people talk about their work, you will hear a range of groups described as "us", depending on the circumstances. The "us" might be the company, "them" the competition: "In this company we do it like this, they do it differently in other companies." The "us" might be the staff, "them" the management: "They are never there when you need one, and we have to carry the can." Identity, in this formulation, is clearly a more flexible, contingent and active concept than that utilised by the mainstream of IR researchers. As Cohen (1978: 359) puts it, "... identities of members and categorisations by others are more or less fluid, more or less multiple, forming nesting hierarchies of we/they dichotomizations".

The alternative to the etic analysis, based on survey research and strict dichotomies of identity, is an emic analysis based on in-depth interviews, the identification and use of criteria of definition and measurement which are identified as important by the staff and using the more fluid post-structuralist definition of identity described above.

BUREAUCRACY, MOVING MOSAICS AND IDENTITY MANAGEMENT

Fluid organisational forms are frequently noted in the literature on the new workplace. Kanter, for example, describes the post-modern organisation as being a "moving mosaic", where clarity, order and hierarchy are replaced by multiple pathways rather than a chain of command (Kanter et al., 1992: 12–13). Likewise, Toffler identifies the new management structure as lacking the clarity of the old ("shifting see-through panels, one behind the other, overlapping, interconnected, the colours and shapes continually blending, contrasting, changing" (Toffler, 1990: 53)). As Turner and D'Art have noted in the introduction to this volume, other writers have also noted a shift towards greater teamwork, less hierarchy and less rigidity in organisational forms. Such organisational forms are to be understood as the opposite of the classic symbol of modernity and Fordism: the bureaucracy.

Accounts of bureaucracy tend to start with Weber, whose account is "neither accepted nor rejected, but ... put to use" in most modern work on the subject (Coser and Rosenberg, 1976: 252). According to Weber (1968) the ideal type of a bureaucracy can be understood as having a number of features including a formal hierarchy, different ranks, the application of rules according to the book and promotion according to clear criteria such as merit or seniority.

This model has been embedded in the labour process debate by Edwards (1979) who argued that in the modern world, managers do not act on their own behalf (exercising personal control) but operate "the rule book". When they exercise the rules in a dehumanised way, removing from "official business love, hatred, and all purely personal, irrational, and emotional elements which escape calculation" (Weber, 1968: 975), they do not themselves have to take responsibility for their action. It becomes reified – the responsibility of no one but the gods. This account has been challenged because of its lack of a role for the resistant worker – (Thompson, 1982; and many contributions in Jermier et al., 1994). The post-structuralist writer Michel Foucault develops on the idea of the bureaucracy in a way which attempts to balance the claims of both organisation and organised, structure and agency. Foucault claims (1977) that there are discrete practices of discipline which come to be used at different historical periods which operate on a person's subjectivity and their body to constrain them in certain ways, ideally producing docile bodies. In other words, techniques of discipline act to manage the culture and identity of the person. The modern variant of these techniques of discipline fixes meanings, it "arrests or regulates movements; it clears up confusion; it dissipates compact groupings of individuals wandering about the country in unpredictable ways; it establishes calculated distributions" and is enforced using a variety of techniques, most notably those of total and detailed surveillance (Foucault, 1977: 219). Discipline is exercised, not through "the brilliance of those who exercise it" (the sort of personalised control also noted by Edwards (1979) and other labour process contributors) but through the formation of a body of knowledge about its subjects. This happens through "hierarchical surveillance, continuous registration, perpetual assessment and classification" through "anonymous instruments of power" (Foucault, 1977: 220).

Foucault argues that disciplinary practices are directed at the subjectivity, the sense of self of the individual, and have already been internalised by people via the operation of disciplining institutions (school, medicine, employment). Disciplinary practices work by diminishing the political force of the subject and increasing the "capacity" of the subject, their ability to become something – something which is directed towards the "normal":

> In short, it dissociates power from the body; on one hand, it turns into an "aptitude" a "capacity", which it seeks to increase; on the other hand, it reverses the course of energy, the power that might result from it, and turns it into a relation of strict subjugation (Foucault, 1977: 138).

In the firm, the person's capacity to be that which the firm wants them to be is to be developed through the techniques of discipline. Not only is obedience obtained through techniques of discipline, the person is actually made into the sort of person they are required to be. The techniques of discipline do not target the person's obedience. They target the person's soul.

However, as Knights and Vurdubakis (1994) show, Foucault does not treat his subjects as cultural dopes, trapped within techniques of discipline that they cannot escape: "[they] are a presence within, rather than simply bearers of discursive relations. They are active in both positioning themselves within such relations and in committing themselves to particular subject positions" (Knights and Vurdubakis, 1994: 184). Disciplinary practices are totalising in their tendency but not total in their effects. The disciplined can work within the capacities and language, which is made available by the techniques of discipline, and re-articulate it in different ways. They are resistant within discipline, not to it.

Foucault's model of disciplinary practices differs from Weber's model of bureaucracy in a number of key respects. Foucault sees the effects of disciplinary practices, not in the eradication of love, hatred and other purely personal motives (which Weber sees as the goal of bureaucracy) but in their harnessing in a project of docility which the disciplined subject is to undertake. Nor does he argue that these processes will, like the iron cage of bureaucracy, continue to close in on the subjectivity and eventually remove it. He argues that the actor remains active in the construction of subjectivities within power relations. However, there are a number of key similarities. The pyramidal-organisational form, the clarity of instruction and of criteria of selection and promotion, for example, are common to both. Essentially, Foucault's disciplinary procedures can be seen articulated clearly in bureaucratically organised firms even if their ends are not those that Weber imagined they were.

The suggestion then, arising from Foucault, is that the most successful disciplinary practices will be those which are found in particular forms of bureaucratic organisations; organisations which prioritise clarity, fixity of meaning, surveillance, self-surveillance and training. They will be hierarchical organisations which are clear as to what constitutes "right" or "normal" action in order to enable them to measure and check behavioural action against it. They are organisations which consistently make clear to people what is expected of them in order that they can live up to it. They are organisations which enable people to live up to this ideal by providing them with training in how to do so and an opportunity to do so. Foucault is not suggesting that such organisations are necessarily totally successful in the construction of docile, obedient bodies. He is arguing that these practices have been developed as more successful than other ones. These practices are clearly not of the "moving mosaic" organisational form, where clarity, order and hierarchy are removed. Crucially, in terms of the question at which this research is addressed, Foucault's model suggests that flexibility in the shape of a moving mosaic organisational form will be incompatible with the generation of docile bodies insofar as it moves away from the aspects of bureaucratic techniques outlined here.

METHODOLOGY

A detailed description of the methodology for this study is found in Tormey (1999, Chapter 3). This research is based on three case studies of large retail organisations in Ireland. A case study is defined by Hakim (1987: 61) as follows:

> Case studies take as their subject one or more *selected* examples of a social entity – such as communities, social groups, organisations, events, life histories, families, work teams, roles or relationships – that are studied using a variety of data collection techniques. [Italics in original]

Case studies are best understood as being like individual experiments. For Hakim, (1987: 64) the experimental logic of case studies can often be best served by choosing a number of cases which are thought to cover the range of situations, starting with the extremes. Sudman (1976: 26) notes that the confidence in the general significance and robustness of research findings increases with the number of sites. He also claims that the single largest gain occurs when the number of sites is increased from one to two. Yin (1994: 45), in developing this, borrows and adapts the conceptual usage of another term common to survey research – replication (1994: 45).

Table 5.1: An Analytical Model of the Case Studies Chosen

Small Irish-Owned Store Super Store	**Large Irish-Owned Store** Home Store
	Large Foreign-Owned Store Quality Store

In this study I have used three case studies. They have been chosen to allow comparison of different contexts. The case studies chosen ensure that contingency factors such as size and other factors such as national origin of the company could be taken into account. Surveys were carried out in two of the stores. Staff and management were interviewed in all three. Forty-three staff and management were interviewed overall. I also had ongoing discussions with a number of key informants in each case study store.

The case studies chosen here are not intended to be representative of Irish industry or even of the retail trade. The case studies are designed to be generalised to the theoretical level rather than generalised to the empirical level (Yin, 1994).

Throughout this chapter I use the term "I" to refer to myself. This style may be unfamiliar to some readers. The more traditional form, which involves referring to oneself in the third person or not at all, is derived from the belief that "scientific" research is objective and that the researcher is not an active participant. In fact, the "I" is not unfamiliar in sociology, even if it still offends some of those who make claims to objectivity which cannot be sustained. William Foote Whyte (1955) was using the "I" as far back as 1943. As Devault has noted, "Social scientists have become increasingly aware ... that writing is not a transparent medium with which researchers simply convey 'truths' discovered in the field, but itself constructs and controls meaning and interpretation" (1990: 110). Likewise Warren (1988: 7) notes that, "the myth of the ethnographer as any person, without gender, personality and historical location, who would objectively (or at the very least intersubjectively) produce the same findings as any other person has been increasingly challenged".

In reality any research involves the researcher. Even in modernist, "scientific" research, surveys have to be constructed by someone and administered by someone else. Questions are framed and benchmarks for measurement identified. Since the research is always a product of the researcher, of me, I will use the term "I" in order to denote this.

Why Retail?

While much of this sort of research tends to focus on successful management of culture in specific, tightly defined environments in relatively small employment sectors (for example banking and computer services) this study is based on experiences in a very large employment sector. The retail trade in Ireland accounted for 139,900 workers in 1995, 11.34 per cent of the total number of people at work and more people than worked in the agriculture, forestry and fishing sector. It is almost twice the size of the insurance, finance and business services sector. The distribution sector as a whole makes up 14.98 per cent of those at work in Ireland (CSO, 1996a: Table 13). The distribution sector is also very often the site of a person's first job. This means that the working life in retail will have a formative effect on many more people than are currently employed there. Though it is rarely thought of as a "sexy" industry to research, it tells us far more about the "new workplace" than significantly smaller, sexier sectors.

The retail trade is also a perfect testing ground for the post-modernist organisational model, since competitive success is thought to be predicated on the management of identity and service culture, and the workforce is highly numerically flexible.

Using the categories employed by the Central Statistics Office Labour Force Survey, we can see that retail has a very high density of part-time work. Retail has the second highest proportion of the workforce made up of flexible (that is part-time, occasional part-time and occasional full-time) workers, with 6.3 regular full-time workers for every flexible worker. The category which has a higher rate is the catch-all non-category called Other, which has a ratio of 3.9:1 (CSO, 1996b unpublished). In the supermarket sector, there are more part-time workers than full-time. There is also evidence from the international literature that management in retail do attempt to manage the identity and the service culture of the workplace (Ogbonna, 1990, 1992; Ogbonna and Wilkinson, 1990; Pollert, 1995; du Gay, 1996). As Rosenthal et al. (1997: 481) have noted:

> Products, technology and price are vulnerable to emulation by competitors. Thus many companies choose now to differentiate themselves on something which they assume is less easy to copy: quality of customer service. The role of the *deliverers* of the service – those employees with direct customer contact – is thought to be critical in the quality management and applied business literature.

In the retail trade, then, two of the prongs of the post-Fordist, post-modern revolution are to be found. Management of identity is critical, while flexibility is widespread and regarded as essential. The retail sector is, therefore, an excellent test of possible contradictions between different components of the post-Fordist model.

Description of the Case Studies

In all cases the management of identity and culture was tied to the creation of a version of a unitary culture. The purpose of the exercise was that the mobilisation of specific cultural resources would allow the staff to see themselves as on the same side as the management. In other words, the project of management was to do away with "them and us" and replace it with "us" by using specific ideas (or language) which could constitute an "us". Such concepts included notions of service, family and the enterprising individual.

Super Store

Super Store was a supermarket employing less than 50 people. It was a low-paying highly flexible working environment, largely populated by young people. As in the other two stores, the management had set out to create a unitary culture with a particular type of service concept – what Pollert (1995: 653) has identified as the "Anglo-US unqualified retail service model" – which is based on obtaining high-quality service without substantial upskilling. This meant the staff should act according to certain behavioural indicators (smiling at a certain time, welcoming, checking, processing, bagging, thanking and so on) and also accept changes in working practices to open longer and more flexible hours. They were also supposed to identify themselves with the "family" of the store, an ill-defined concept.

The store did not have what could be described as a strong or unitary culture. There were some networks of staff in which there was a sense of opposition to management. Some staff, essentially the permanent staff, also distinguished between their sense of team working and service and a sense of common identity with management. For example, in talking about their sense of service some staff used it to define themselves in opposition to management. Management was trying to develop a service ethos in the store and was succeeding reasonably well, yet this became a stick with which to beat the management. The very discourse which management were trying to mobilise became mobilised against them. This shows the way in which subjects become active within the discourses made available by techniques of discipline. One staff member put it most clearly when she said, "at first we used to think he actually cared about the shop but now it only seems to be about money". While these staff were clear about their own investment in service and teamwork, the management were regarded as not being part of the team.

As for the contingent staff, their job was not an important part of their lives. They were largely students gaining some experience and some pocket money. They tended to be more accepting and happy with their situation in work. However their relative contentment was less important to the company than their more dissatisfied permanent part-time and full-time colleagues.

In describing their relationship with management, all staff used words such as rudeness and unprofessionalism, particularly in describing the owner of the store, who was frequently on site. There was also a lack of clarity in the organisational structure. As one staff member indicated, "With so many people to tell them what to do, they didn't know who to take the main order from. One person would tell them one thing, someone else would tell them to do another".

The term which best describes the culture of the workplace was uncertainty. Employees did not know basic information about their own contracts, such as scales of pay and the length of the probation period. Nor did they know the rules of conduct – what was allowed and what was not allowed. In fact, it seemed that rules were negotiated in interaction rather than clearly articulated in advance. Overall, the uncertainty and continual negotiation in the company was suggestive of a moving mosaic organisational form. Staff could be shifted from area to area, from designation to designation, and they did not have an overall picture of the company and their place in it. However, this lack of formality had been accompanied by what the staff experienced as a personalised dictatorial management style which was not conducive to building a unitary culture.

Home Store

Home Store was a branch of a large retail company. It employed about 600 staff. While the pay was slightly above average for the sector, the part-time employees were required to be highly flexible and the company did not have benefits such as pension provisions, sick pay an so on – the sort of things taken for granted in many other working environments. The employees here were more mixed in age and marital status than in Super Store. Here the staff were also expected to adhere to the service ethic. Staff were also asked to identify with and actualise themselves through being good at serving customers.

As in Super Store there was a range of different groups who displayed different types of relationships with the management. On one hand there was the permanent staff who displayed a high degree of commitment to service and to "doing their job well". As in Super Store, this service ethic became mobilised in opposition to management who were seen to conspire with short-term part-time staff in exploiting this commitment. One full-timer noted:

> It's probably our own fault at the end of the day because we allow them to do that. We are so dominant in our own departments. We take on so much, and I have to say, I have never seen it in other stores that you take so much pride in what you do.

While the part-time staff did not display the same level of commitment to service, their relationship with management was characterised by a lack of reciprocity. Managers were spoken of as unprofessional, rude and always taking and never giving. While one could have friendly relationships with managers, they could not be depended upon. When a strike was called over issues which the part-time flexible staff felt did not affect them, they nonetheless joined the union in their droves and went on the picket line.

Overall, like Super Store, this store was characterised by a high degree of uncertainty. There was a lack of clarity about the organisational structure of the company, about employee's basic rights and terms and conditions. Instead, stories and myths developed through telling and retelling in small group networks. There was a substantial degree of *ad hoc* management of human resources. Compared to Super Store, the lack of immediacy of the real source of power (the owners) took some of the venom out of interpersonal relationships between management and staff. But overall, the store was similar to Super Store in many respects, despite the difference in scale of the operation.

Quality Store

Quality Store was actually two stores of a large multinational retailer frequently cited in the literature as a good example of HRM style management. The two stores between them had about 420 staff. Both were situated near each other in a town-centre location. Here the staff were reasonably well paid for the retail sector and could also avail of a number of benefits ranging from a staff canteen through to doctors and chiropodists. Although the store did have some student labour, most of the floor staff were non-student women who had graduated from post-primary schooling. Here the management of culture project was also engaged in trying to create a service ethos much like that in the other two stores. Here the management of identity project was more than simply the imagination of self as server, it was an attempt to create enterprising individuals who would actualise themselves through making the goals of the company their goals and sharing in the company's profitability, what du Gay (1996: 181) calls *homo economicus*, though *feminina economica* might be more appropriate in this case.

Different groups of staff were also evident here. Although most of the full-time staff seemed to have a reasonably strong relationship with management, a small group of long-serving staff had understood the introduction of part-time work as a betrayal of the service ethos of the company. They spoke about the loss of a career structure and of a training regime. They saw this as part of a deskilling of the job. Most of the other employees, however, showed a more positive attitude to management than was evident in the other stores. However, there was still some ambiguity in their relationship with the management. For example, the supervisory category of staff operated as a *de facto* line management role. Unlike the other staff, supervisors were not unionised. However, when the company tried to redesignate the supervisory category as departmental management, some supervisors felt that their position was in fact being threatened:

> Once that was said – BANG! Fury! "What's going to happen to my job? If I don't make it up to this I'm going to come down to this. I've got a mortgage on my house on top of everything else ... ". I think people felt ladled to the whims of a constantly changing management team ... They were trying to manoeuvre on certain issues and we had very little back up ... They said "Right, here's your new job description and that's it". So we said "Right. We best join some sort of association – a union".

Overall then, Quality Store was far more harmonious in management–staff relations than the other two locations. It was characterised by a high level of bureaucratisation: the company did not approximate a moving mosaic. Training was structured, communication was generally clear. There was an institutional framework for staff's voice to be heard. While staff may not agree with the management on everything, the management position was at least understood and could be articulated by staff. While this does not make a unitary culture, it is the most successful of the stores at sharing a vision between management and staff.

THE MANAGEMENT OF CULTURE IN THE CASE STUDIES

The case studies turned out to be far from the ideal, in most respects. No case study can be said to show a unitary culture, for example. In all three cases staff and management were in conflict. Management and staff did not tell the same stories or experience the same events in the same way. However, one case – Quality Store – had been far more successful than the other two in creating something of a unitary culture. Even if staff did not share the stories and experiences of management they could at least see things from a manager's point of view. The staff did not do this in the other two stores. Also, management here was regarded as consisting of professionals working as part of a team. In the other two case studies the professionalism of management was questioned.

In the three case studies the comparative unity of the culture depended on a number of factors. These were: differences in material preferences[1] between management and staff over pay, working hours and the deployment of staff; the tendency for flexible working practices to fragment the workforce; the level of bureaucracy and clarity in the organisation of the stores; and interaction between management and staff. The first two factors tended to fragment culture of the workplace, the third and fourth could either work to fragment or unify the culture.

Material Preferences

In all three case studies the different material preferences of staff and managers helped to divide them. It was clear in all three case studies that management and staff were not necessarily on the same side when it came to the distribution of resources. In Super Store this was articulated through questions over the owner's lack of commitment to service and his emphasis on his personal profit. There was a feeling that he was under-staffing the store for short-term gain. In Home Store, the same question of material preferences arose. As in Super Store, full-time and long-term staff felt that the store was understaffed. They also questioned the lack of pay for increased responsibility in recent years. The lack of a pension scheme, adequate provision for sick leave and so on were all cited by staff, and indeed were the basis for a major industrial dispute which closed the shop during the course of the case study. The material differences of work conditions affected short-term workers less, though the same idea had taken root among them too. They argued, for example, that such things as a nylon uniform demonstrated that the company was only interested in doing things on the cheap. In Quality Store too there was a realisation that the material preferences of management were not the same as the preferences of the employees. For both part-time and full-time workers the deployment of part-time work was questioned since it affects their working practices. The effect of the growth in part-time work on service was questioned by some. Mostly there was a recognition that while the quality of work and remuneration in Quality Store is good, this had partially got to do with union representation in the store.

---

1. I use the term "preferences" instead of the more familiar term "interests" since I do not wish to imply that I as a researcher can impute real or objective interests to people (see Hindess, 1989; Clegg, 1989).

These material limits may represent the necessary limits of the culture (Bourdieu and Passeron, 1977; Nash, 1990). It may be that management and staff are forced to accept differences in their material preferences simply by virtue of the fact that they work in commercial businesses. The necessity for profit puts a premium on material issues, and highlights the material and instrumentalist aspect of the relationship between staff and management/ ownership. While the relationship is not only instrumental, it may be that its instrumentalism is indissoluble as long as profit remains the ultimate goal of the company.

Fragmentation of Staff due to Working Hours

In all three cases there was fragmentation of the workforce due to the fact that many staff were in work for comparatively short periods of time. This fragmentation was aided by differences of age and orientations to work by the staff. Studies of work have often indicated that the Taylorist separation of work tasks into different work areas can develop workplace sub-cultures (see for example, Benyon, 1984). As symbolic interactionists have long shown, common characteristics, proximity and subsequent interaction is a crucial factor in the development of a common set of values, understandings and knowledge base (Fine and Kleinmna, 1983). As the above data suggest, in all three case studies there were notably different sub-groups. Groups tended to be formed by people with similar hours, working in similar areas, though sometimes pre-existing friendships caused links across these groups. Stories tended to circulate within these groups. Within a group a number of people would tell a similar story, but outside the group either no-one would have heard it or would tell it very differently with a different outcome and moral. This was slightly less pronounced in Quality Store than in the other two.

Bureaucracy and Clarity in the Stores

The stores were organised quite differently in relation to this measure. Quality Store was highly bureaucratic. Everything went by the book, there were no grey areas, everyone knew the rules and, by and large, everyone stuck to the rules. One of the staff described the store as an ant colony. This type of organisation happened at two levels: management were trained according to clear and measurable criteria and they were continually assessed according to clear criteria. In Foucault's terms, their capacity to manage had been developed as they became subject to techniques of discipline. They then applied these same techniques through the use of various clear means of communication, through training and continuous assessment according to clear measurable criteria. The story was quite different in the other stores.

In Home Store there was far less clarity. Staff did not know the basics of the hierarchy of the store. They were unclear about the positions of some of those they had daily dealings with. They did not know how many people worked for the company (estimates ranged from 2,000 to 7,000). A sizeable percentage of those interviewed did not know the reasons for the strike they were on. Staff's relationship with their managers was characterised by a degree of informality which opened up for negotiation the meanings of any given interaction (Goffman, 1959). Rather than bringing clear conceptual resources to any interaction (who was in charge, what they could ask you to do, how they would respond to refusal and so on), the meaning tended to end up being worked out in interaction. This lack of clarity was also found at management level. While the management of culture was promoted, the only area in which management was subject to the sort of techniques of clarity, surveillance and discipline as is found in Quality Store is in relation to profits. One manager went so far as to say that the only thing that head office cared about was:

> ... the results. You could be the hardest man causing problems with the staff, handling the staff with bad manners but if you are still getting results you will be tolerated. It was notorious in the early days – Home Store had a very bad name, and we did have some pigs of managers. That is the only way I could describe them. Ignorant. Treated staff very badly.

Only financial mismanagement would earn a rebuke. Super Store also operated on a far less bureaucratic manner than Quality Store. In fact, management did not even have the same level of clarity and surveillance in relation to commercial or financial issues as Home Store did. As a consequence the fragmentation of the staff was augmented and increased by a lack of clarity about any number of issues. Staff were unclear as to the length of a their probation period, one staff member did not know that she had been recently promoted (she saw it simply as a re-deployment), others did not know the basis on which you could be fired or if the company was unionised. Again, this left a great deal of space in which the staff could negotiate meanings with the management. Staff with resources (being well liked or having long service) tended to do better in these interactions. Sometimes other resources could be brought to bear as this story told by one of the staff shows:

> This one lad got sacked and he was put back two days later. He was there about two years ago and one of the managers told him to do something or told him he was meant to be in [on another day] and the young lad said "I wasn't". And the manager said "You'll get out there and f***ing do it", and this lad says "No I f***ing won't", and because he'd cursed back the manager said "You used bad language at me. You're fired". Like, he'd [i.e. the manager] cursed first! There was about six lads that heard it, and his Da was on the phone the next day threatening [them with] solicitors and everything. He had his job back within an hour with an apology and everything. But if they can get away with it they will.

Interaction between Staff and Management

The presentation of self adopted by the management when dealing with the staff was another important factor in determining the strength of the culture. The way in which the managers presented themselves, their consistency, their willingness to work according to clear rules or principles and their willingness to be reciprocal in their interactions with staff came up on a number of occasions and was important in the manager's capacity to generate the types of culture required. In Super Store, managers were thought of as inconsistent, operating according to their own personal whims and were not thought to be reciprocal. Staff could be required to give up free time in order to work at short notice and those who refused could have their hours cut without explanation. Nor did the staff feel that the management's actions portrayed many signs of being interested in service to customers. In Home Store too, management was said to be subject to whims, inconsistent and were not reciprocal in their interactions with staff. As one staff member said, it was not so much "you scratch my back and I scratch yours as you scratch my back and then you scratch my a***". Here too, the management was deemed not to have a service orientation. In Quality Store, as I have already said, the management was not seen as being subject to whims. They operated the rule book and there was no space which lacked clarity:

> I worked for Home Store and two other supermarkets. I worked everywhere and you just see a total change in attitude here. Everything is so well done and so well organised. I'm two years here and I still feel that great feeling of it's so well organised.

Of course issues did arise such as the lack of consultation about the new uniform (which was felt to be too short and unflattering for heavier people). Occasionally managers were felt to be inconsistent (one manager closed the store during World Cup matches in 1990, so when his successor did not do the same in 1994 the staff attributed it to jealousy since England – the manager was English – had not qualified for that competition). But even in relation to such issues the strength of the communication between management and staff ensured that staff were at least aware of the management rationale.

The central point here again is that the clear, reciprocal and bureaucratic nature of Quality Store prevented exactly this sort of feeling of inconsistency and lack of professionalism. This clarity and bureaucracy did not simply derive from organisational structures but from interpersonal interaction between management and staff. Managers were not going to give contradictory instructions since the chain of command was clear. There was no space in which to negotiate meanings so there was no space for inconsistency. Management actions were going to be clear because communication systems were part of the management's training and managers were assessed on it. Their presentation of self was itself regulated by the techniques of discipline operating within the store.

SUMMARY

No store was successful at generating a unitary culture. However, in Quality Store the staff at least were aware of the management's view of any given situation. They did not necessarily agree with it but at least they had it as an option. While the service culture was to be developed in all stores and while it existed in all stores to some extent (particularly among long-term and older staff), in Super Store and Home Store it became a tool of opposition to the managers. The staff were interested in service; the managers were not. In this context, the management's interest in fostering service was either taken to be a sham or taken as a suggestion that the management were trying to blame the staff for their own mismanagement. However, in all cases the staff's orientations to work also played a role in determining how successful the creation of a service ethic was. Those for whom it was not a "real job" were unlikely to develop a strong service ethos.

CONCLUSION

Quality Store, which was more successful in creating a unitary culture, achieved its (limited) success partially due to its bureaucratic organisation. Its managers presented themselves as part of a bureaucracy. They were consistent in their interaction with staff and they followed the company hierarchy. In Weber's terms, they applied the rule book "without regard for persons" (Gerth and Mills, 1970: 215). Part of this consistency was visible in the coherent way in which they used training and communications to support the highly organised bureaucratic culture which they wished to create. While they were unable to address the way in which the staff experienced a difference in material interests between themselves and management, they did at least manage to create a culture in which management had legitimacy and in which the management rationale for action was one of the possible rationales the staff were aware of. Agreeing with management was at least an option in Quality Store.

It appears clear that the disassembling of bureaucracy and the management of culture do not go hand in hand. In this very tight product market, where competitive pressures are clear and evident and where flexibility is at a premium, the capacity to even partially manage culture is dependent on a high degree of bureaucracy. The post-Fordist management of identity is predicated on the management structure that is the symbol of Fordism: bureaucracy.

It is also clear that in order to develop such a detailed understanding of the construction of identities in the workplace, we need to use concepts more fluid and elastic than the "them" and "us" of mainstream research. The Supervisors in Quality Store were both "them" and "us", management and staff. The managers in Home Store were not really the "them" (since "they" were the owners of the company), but nor were they the "us". Staff sometimes sympathised with their plight but did not regard them as some of their own.

Full-time workers in Home Store and Super Store were clearly a group which were committed to the stated goals of the company; however, they remained separate from the management since they questioned the management and the company's commitment to these same goals.

Likewise, standard measures of "organisational commitment", "employee trust" or "them and us" based on surveys are unlikely to get at the full complexity of identities. The meaningful symbols of identity are so historically specific (in one store it was the World Cup of 1994 and short jackets, in another it was nylon uniforms and a lack of reciprocity, in another it was rudeness and arbitrariness), that it is difficult to see how any survey could be constructed which might actually address the symbols which are meaningful for different groups of staff. In short, while the workplace might stay the same, our ways of researching it may need to change.

REFERENCES

Benyon, H. (1984) *Working For Ford*. Harmondsworth: Penguin.

Bourdieu, P. and Passerson, J. (1977) *Reproduction in Education, Society and Culture*. London: Sage Publications.

Clegg, S. R. (1989) *Frameworks of Power*. London: Sage Publications.

Cohen, R. (1978) "Ethnicity – Problem and Focus in Anthropology" *Annual Review of Anthropology*, Vol. 7: 379–403.

Coser, L. A. and Rosenberg, B. (1976) (eds) *Sociological Theory: A Book of Readings*. (4th edition) New York: Macmillan.

CSO (1996a) *Labour Force Survey 1995*. Dublin: Stationery Office.

CSO (1996b) *Unpublished Labour Force Data*. Cork: Central Statistics Office.

D'Art, D. and Turner, T. (1999) "An Attitudinal Revolution in Irish Industrial Relations: The End of 'Them and Us?'" *British Journal of Industrial Relations*, Vol. 37, No. 1: 101–116.

Devault, M. L. (1990) "Talking and Listening from a Women's Standpoint: Feminist Strategies for Interviewing and Analysis" *Social Problems*, Vol. 37: 96 –116.

Edwards, R. (1979) *Contested Terrain: The Transformation of the Workplace in the Twentieth Century*. London: Heinemann.

Fine, G. and Kleinmna, S. (1983) "Network and Meaning: An Interactionist Approach to Structure" *Symbolic Interaction*, Vol. 6, No. 1: 97–110.

Foucault, M. (1977) *Discipline and Punish: The Birth of the Prison*. Harmondsworth: Penguin.

du Gay, P. (1996) *Consumption and Identity at Work*. London: Sage Publications.

Gerth, H. H. and Mills, C. W. (1970) *From Max Weber*. London: Routledge and Kegan Paul.

Goffman, E. (1959) *The Presentation of Self in Everyday Life*. Harmondsworth: Penguin.

Guest, D. (1992) "Employee Commitment and Control" in Hartley, J. F. and Stephenson, G. M. (eds) *Employment Relations*. Oxford: Blackwell.

Hakim, C. (1987) *Research Design, Strategies and Choices in the Design of Social Research*. London: Routledge.

Hargreaves, A. (1994) *Changing Teachers, Changing Times: Teachers' Work and Culture in The Post-Modern Age*. London: Cassell.

Hindess, B. (1989) "Classes, Collectives and Corporate Actors" in Clegg, S. (ed.) *Organisational Theory and Class Analysis, New Approaches and New Issues*. Berlin: De Gruyter.

Jermier, J. M., Knights, D. and Nord, W. R. (1994) (eds) *Resistance and Power in Organizations*. London: Routledge.

Kanter, R. M., Stein, B. A. and Jick, T. D. (1992) *The Challenge of Organisational Change*. New York: The Free Press

Knights, D. and Vurdubakis, T. (1994) "Foucault, Power, Resistance and All That" in Jermier, J. M., Knights, D. and Nord, W. R. (eds) *Resistance and Power in Organizations*. London: Routledge.

Legge, K. (1989) "Human Resources Management: A Critical Analysis" in Storey, J. (ed.) *New Perspectives on Human Resources Management*. London: Routledge.

Legge, K. (1995) *Human Resources Management, Rhetorics and Realities*. Basingstoke, Hampshire: Macmillan.

Nash, R. (1990) "Bourdieu on Education and Social and Cultural Reproduction" *British Journal of Sociology of Education*, Vol. 11, No. 4: 431–448.

Ogbonna, E. (1990) *Organisational Culture and Strategy in the UK Supermarket Industry*. Cardiff: PhD Thesis, Cardiff Business School.

Ogbonna, E. (1992) "Organisational Culture and HRM" in Blyton, P. and Turnbull, P. (eds) *Reassessing Human Resource Management*. London: Sage Publications.

Ogbonna, E. and B. Wilkinson (1990) "Corporate Strategy and Corporate Culture: The View from the Checkout" *Personnel Review*, Vol. 19, No. 4: 9–15.

Pollert, A. (1995) "Women's Employment and Service Sector Transformation in Central Eastern Europe: Case Studies in Retail in the Czech Republic" *Work, Employment and Society*, Vol. 9, No. 4: 629–655.

Rosenthal, P., Hill, S. and Peccei, R. (1997) "Checking out Service: Evaluating Excellence, HRM and TQM in Retailing" *Work, Employment and Society*, Vol. 11, No. 3: 481–503.

Silverman, D. (1993) *Interpreting Qualitative Data, Methods for Analysing Talk, Text, and Interaction*. London: Sage Publications.

Sudman, S. (1976) *Applied Sampling*. London: Academic Press.

Thompson, P. (1982) *The Nature of Work: An Introduction to Debates on the Labour Process*. Basingstoke, Hampshire: Macmillan.

Toffler, A. (1990) *Powershift*. New York: Bantham Books.

Tormey, R. (1999) *The Part-Time Soul: Case Studies in the Management of*

Culture and Flexibility in Irish Retail. Dublin: Unpublished PhD Dissertation, Department of Sociology, Trinity College.

Tovey, H., Hannan, D. and Abramson, H. (1989) *Cad Chuig and Gaeilge? Language and Identity in Ireland Today*. Dublin: Bord an Gaeilge.

Vidich, A. J. and Lyman, S. M. (1994) "Qualitative Methods: Their History in Sociology and Anthropology" in Denzin, N. K. and Lincon, Y. S. (eds) *Handbook of Qualitative Research*. London: Sage Publications.

Warren, C. A. B. (1988) *Gender Issues in Field Research*. London: Sage Publications.

Weber, M. (1968) *Economy and Society* New York: Bedminster Press.

Whyte, W. F. (1955) *Street Corner Society: The Social Structure of an Italian Slum*. Chicago: University of Chicago Press.

Yin, R. K. (1994) *Case Study Research Design and Methods*. London: Sage Publications.

Chapter 6

An Attitudinal Revolution in Irish Industrial Relations: The End of "Them" and "Us"?

Daryl D'Art and Thomas Turner[1]

INTRODUCTION

Since 1980, western economies have entered a period of turbulence and change characterised by the extension of free markets, intensified international competition and the re-emergence of mass unemployment. According to Piore and Sabel (1984) the development of new technologies and the fragmentation of mass markets heralds a new industrial revolution and a major restructuring of capitalism. A firm's survival in such an environment demands the development of new structures and policies centring on product quality, productivity and labour flexibility. These imperatives pose a fundamental challenge to the continuance of traditional industrial relations conduct and practice. Apparently the response of workers and their unions has been co-operative and conciliatory, presaging a new departure in employer/employee relations.

This chapter examines to what extent a decade of national agreements between employers and unions, an increasingly co-operative union leadership and the decline in overt indices of conflict at firm level are associated with low levels of a "them and us" divide. The optimistic perspective would assume these changes are associated with reduced "them and us" attitudes. Consequently, the main hypothesis to be tested is that there remains no significant employee perception of a "them and us" divide. Alternatively, the pessimistic view assumes the persistence of "them and us" attitudes. Drawing on Kelly and Kelly's (1991) conditions for attitudinal change, it can be suggested that the acceptance by employees of a superordinate goal, such as the survival of the firm in a competitive market, leads to attitudinal change. A second hypothesis can be stated as follows: the acceptance by employees of a superordinate goal will be negatively associated with a "them and us" divide. A further condition for variance in attitudes is the presence of co-operative initiatives with management. Consequently, a third hypothesis is that the

---

1. This chapter was published in the *British Journal of Industrial Relations*, Vol. 37, No. 1:101–117, and is reprinted with their permission.

participation of employees in co-operative initiatives is associated with reduced "them and us" attitudes.

THE DECLINE OF ADVERSARIALISM?

Since 1987, the negotiation of continuous social pacts between the trade unions, employers and government in Ireland indicate a high degree of social consensus in industrial relations at national level. At firm level, the Irish Congress of Trade Unions has advised members to co-operate with new managerial initiatives designed to improve competitiveness (ICTU, 1993). Furthermore, there has been a general decline in all of the indices measuring strike activity (Brannick et al., 1997). One interpretation of these trends would be to view them as heralding the decline of adversarialism in Irish industrial relations. Technological developments and increased international competition are perceived to have forced the abandonment of Fordist mass production systems and supporting institutions (Piore and Sabel, 1984). This apparent break with Fordism has facilitated managerial adoption of responsible autonomy strategies involving increased employee discretion. A new identity of interest is created and management is no longer identified by workers as "opponents" but rather as allies in the competitive struggle for markets (Basset, 1986). This new identity of interest has the potential to create both an institutional and ideological crisis for workplace trade unionism (Terry, 1989). With worker acceptance and commitment to the logic of the enterprise and a management agenda, the old conflicts traditionally associated with the employment relationship are less evident, while union membership and collective bargaining appear increasingly irrelevant.

Alternatively, a less sanguine interpretation would suggest that high levels of unemployment and the fear of job loss increases worker attachment to firms threatened by intensifying international competition. This creates a "new realism" among workers and brings an "acceptance or even the active pursuit of production organisation which sustains the firm's market position" (Hyman, 1989: 196). These difficult circumstances for trade unions are compounded by a reassertion of managerial prerogative. A number of studies in Britain based on the Workplace Industrial Relations Survey have emphasised increased management control and the exclusion or marginalisation of trade unions in the workplace (Kessler and Bayliss, 1992; Smith and Morton, 1994). Although there is no direct research evidence similar to the workplace survey available in Ireland, anecdotal evidence from union officials, activists and members suggests that unions have become weaker and the capacity of organised labour to shape working practices on the shopfloor has declined sharply in the 1980s and 1990s. Furthermore, research on the establishment of companies setting up in the commercial and trading sectors since the mid 1980s indicates that many of these companies are remaining non-union (Gunnigle, 1995; Hourihan, 1996). Thus, the crisis for trade unions arises not from members' internalisation of managerial values but rather from declining union effectiveness. As a consequence of trade union weakness, members may have little alternative but to go along as conscripts rather than volunteers with the management project.

Scott (1994: 4) has identified two contrasting interpretations of these changes which he describes as the "new industrial account" and the "traditional account". For convenience we have labelled these interpretations of changes in industrial relations as the optimistic and pessimistic view. The object of this chapter is to evaluate the validity of these opposing interpretations using an employee attitude survey. We attempt to assess the extent to which workers identify with management or, alternatively, whether traditional adversarial attitudes have persisted. The measure used is the extent to which employees perceive that management and workers are on different sides, that is, the existence of a "them and us" divide.

"THEM AND US" ATTITUDES

According to Kelly and Kelly (1991: 26) "them and us" attitudes, involve both the perception of a clear division between management and workers, a feeling of identification with one of these groups and a belief that the groups have conflicting interests. Such attitudes or a predisposition to evaluate other individuals or groups in a certain way is principally determined by membership of a particular socio-economic group or class (see Keenoy, 1995). Members of the working class or lower socio-economic groups are likely to be distrustful of high status groups or individuals, particularly when they occupy positions of authority (Hoggart, 1967: 62). Indeed, Whelan noted that class-related attitudes of Irish manual workers were indicative of strikingly low levels of trust in management (Whelan, 1982: 2). This is all the more surprising given the official ideology of populist nationalism which promotes a view of Irish society as essentially classless (Breen and Whelan, 1996). It is likely, therefore, that members of lower socio-economic groups, even before they enter the workplace, will be predisposed to adopt a "them and us" attitude. This nascent attitude tends to be confirmed in organisations characterised by a power-centred hierarchical structure in which those at its lower reaches perform highly prescribed fragmented work. These conditions create a structure and climate which tends to foster "them and us" attitudes (see for example Fox, 1974).

Conditions for Attitudinal Change

However, attitudes formed by early socialisation may be later modified by education, age or, more importantly, experience. Kelly and Kelly (1991: 26) identify three possible routes to attitudinal change. First, increased personal contact between members of two social groups who are in conflict has the potential to shift inter-group attitudes. Group members may learn their stereotype perceptions of each other are inaccurate and may find they share common opinions and beliefs. Secondly, the introduction of a common or superordinate goal into a situation of inter-group conflict will serve to unite the warring parties in its pursuit. A good example of such a goal would be an acceptance by employees that their co-operation is essential for firm survival in an internationally competitive market. A third possible route to restructuring worker attitudes identifies employee participation in co-operative initiatives with management.

The optimistic view suggests that the conditions which serve to produce and reinforce "them and us" attitudes are no longer operative. First, with regard to social class, some utopian proponents would suggest that in post-modern western societies, class stratification, at the root of "them and us" attitudes, is being dissolved (Kumar, 1995). This is a suggestion that may owe more to wishful thinking than accurate observation. Yet there is little evidence that affluence alone automatically alters working class perceptions (see for example, Hamilton et al., 1993). Admittedly there has been considerable fragmentation of solidarity in old working class communities and the development of more privatised attitudes to work. However, as Giddens (1989: 224) claims, "them and us" imagery has not disappeared but is an outlook that persists in many working class neighbourhoods (see also Breen and Whelan, 1996: 167–182). Secondly, it is argued that organisational hierarchies are being compressed resulting in a devolution of power and increased autonomy for shopfloor employees (Walton, 1985; Scott, 1994). The conditions which have given rise to and reinforce a "them and us" divide are no longer present and consequently, "them and us" attitudes become dissonant and erode. The optimistic interpretation thus assumes that there has been a corresponding change not only in behaviour but also in attitudes. This is a problematic assumption. It is possible for employee behaviour to change and "them and us" attitudes to persist. The work of Mowday, Porter and Steers (1982: 31) on employee commitment provides a useful distinction between behavioural commitment and attitudinal commitment. Attitudinal commitment, going beyond mere behavioural expediency, is the extent to which the individual internalises, identifies and believes in the attitude adopted. In the organisational context, this involves employees identifying with and internalising managerial goals. Such internalisation or attitudinal commitment would at the very least substantially reduce if not eradicate adversarial attitudes. Indeed for employees to simultaneously hold "them and us" attitudes and identify with managerial goals would be incompatible or incongruent. Thus, the optimist assumption of an automatic association between behavioural and attitudinal commitment implies the absence of "them and us" attitudes.

In the case of behavioural commitment, individual behaviour which conforms to managerial norms, results from the employees' desire for job security, income maintenance and career progression rather than an internalised commitment to the organisation. Behavioural commitment is, we would argue, a calculative exchange between the employee and the organisation (see Etzioni,

1961). Consequently, changes in behaviour are essentially calculative and are not necessarily accompanied by attitudinal change. This would be an outcome close to the pessimistic interpretation. For pessimists, behavioural commitment by workers is a pragmatic accommodation to high unemployment, insecurity, competitive markets and decreased union effectiveness. The persistence of "them and us" attitudes would lend support to this interpretation.

Data and Description of Variables

In the following sections the hypotheses outlined are assessed using qualitative and quantitative data from a survey of 402 employees in nine unionised Irish manufacturing plants (see Appendix for details of plants and survey). The existence of a conflict of interest between workers and management is commonly measured by the extent to which workers adopt a "them and us" attitude towards management. Respondents in the survey were asked to indicate, on a range from "strongly agree" to "strongly disagree", whether they believe management and workers to be on opposite sides or on the same side. This question has been regularly used in employee surveys to test for the presence of "them and us" attitudes (for comprehensive reviews see Ramsay, 1975). The extent of "them and us" attitudes are evaluated using the above question (hypothesis 1).

The existence of superordinate goals are measured here by the extent to which workers perceive that they are in competition with other companies who produce similar products (hypothesis 2). A second, though weaker, indication of the existence of superordinate goals is measured by the importance which workers attach to their firm in terms of their life interests. Co-operative behaviour and initiatives are measured at two levels: in terms of work experience for individual employees and relations between union and management. Work experience is measured by the degree to which employees perceive increased autonomy in work. An important element in forming employee attitudes in an organisation is the extent to which management closely monitor employee behaviour (Fox, 1974). Employee perception of increased discretion in the performance of their work is predicted to reduce "them and us" attitudes (hypothesis 3). We interpret co-operative behaviour and initiatives to include the policies and procedures governing union management relations. Union management relations are measured by the level of satisfaction with grievance procedures and the presence of a cohesive union organisation (hypothesis 3). We would argue that in the latter case, the presence of a well-organised shop steward committee is partly dependent on management recognition of the legitimacy of unions to represent workers. Union organisation is measured by the presence of a formal shop steward committee. The cohesion of union organisation is evaluated and categorised by the regularity of committee meetings and the cohesion or unity of the committee. Companies are categorised as either having: a disorganised committee (no regular meetings and a lack of unity); a loosely organised committee (irregular

Table 6.1: Variable Means and Description

Dependent Variable	Description	Mean	SD	N
Them and us	Measures whether respondents believe that workers and management are on the same side: 1=strongly disagree; 2=disagree; 3=no opinion; 4=agree; 5=strongly agree.	2.5	1.2	400
Independent Variables				
Superordinate Goals				
Firm survival	Measures whether respondents believe that they are in competition with similar type companies: scored as above.	3.5	1.1	355
Priority of firm	Ranks priority of firm in worker's life interests from 1=highest priority to 5=lowest priority.*	3.5	1.2	394
Co-operative Behaviour				
More discretion in work	Measures whether respondents have more freedom in deciding how to do work than previously: 1=yes; 0=no.	49%		329
IR procedures	Satisfaction with grievance procedures: 1=yes; 0=no.	74%		380
Cohesive union organisation	1=disorganised committee; 2=loosely organised; 3=high level of organisation.			9 (firms)
Individual Characteristics				
Age	Scored as follows: 1=15 – 25 years; 2=26 – 35; 3=36 – 45; 4=46 – 55; 5=56+.	2.6	1.0	399
Occupation	1=unskilled; 2=skilled; 3=clerical; 4=supervisory; 5=tech/admin; 5=professional.	2.1		402
Gender	1=male; 0=female.	64%		390
Take-home pay	Satisfaction with take-home pay: 1=satisfied; 2=no opinion; 3=dissatisfied.	2.38	0.9	398
Economic Circumstances				
Employment	Measures the trend in employment numbers over the past ten years: 1=employment increased; 2=moderate decrease; 3=large decrease.	1.8	0.6	9 (firms)**

*Respondents were asked to rank in order of priority the following: immediate family; friends; the firm they work in; their church/religious beliefs; and social/leisure life.

**Each respondent in the survey is scored according to the employment trend in his or her firm. Thus, 30% of respondents were in firms where employment increased; 60% where employment decreased moderately and 10% in firms where employment decreased substantially. The variable "union cohesion" is scored in a similar manner.

meetings but high degree of cohesion); or a highly organised committee (cohesive with regular meetings). These categories are based on comprehensive interviews with senior shop stewards in each firm (see Turner and Morley, 1995, Chapter 2). While hypothesis 1 is concerned with the extent of "them and us" attitudes, hypotheses 2 and 3 examine the factors which are associated with variations in these attitudes within the sample.

A number of variables measuring individual characteristics which possibly influence individual attitudes are also included. It is possible that worker attitudes towards management become more entrenched over time and older workers, particularly those at the bottom of the organisational hierarchy, may be more likely to perceive management negatively. Age of respondents is used to test for this possibility. Additionally, gender and occupation may be significant. In particular, occupation as a proxy for hierarchical position can be expected to influence the prevalence of "them and us" attitudes. Finally, satisfaction or dissatisfaction with take-home pay may affect workers attitudes towards management. These individual characteristics are used essentially as controls in order to assess the impact of superordinate goals and co-operative behaviour on "them and us" attitudes. To control for firm specific circumstances a variable measuring recent trends in employment numbers over the previous three years is also used (see Table 6.1 for variable descriptions and means for all variables discussed in this section).

EXISTENCE OF "THEM AND US" ATTITUDES

Our results indicate that a majority of the employees surveyed (56 per cent) disagreed with the statement that workers and managers are on the same side

Table 6.2: Employee Perceptions of Management

Question	Response	Profess-ionals	White Collar	Skilled	Un-Skilled	All
Manage-ment and workers are on the same side?	Agree	16 (52%)*	21 (25%)	20 (29%)	63 (29%)	120 (30%)
	No Opinion	4 (13%)	12 (14%)	9 (13%)	30 (14%)	55 (14%)
	Disagree	11 (36%)	53 (62%)	40 (58%)	121 (57%)	225 (56%)
	Total	31 (100%)	86 (100%)	69 (100%)	214 (100%)	400 (100%)

*Percentages in parentheses.

Source: Employee Survey, 1994.

while 30 per cent agreed with the statement (Table 6.2). If we exclude those with no opinion the majority increases to 65 per cent.

At the very least these results point to the existence of a substantial level of "them and us" attitudes. In the absence of longitudinal data, it is not possible to say whether these responses represent a decline or intensification of respondents' attitudes in the companies surveyed. However, in the late 1970s, a survey of employee attitudes in the Dublin region concluded that Irish workers displayed extremely high levels of distrust in management with only 39 per cent agreeing that management and workers were on the same side (Whelan 1982: 39–40). Thus, there is a marked similarity between our results and those of Whelan. It would appear that the results provide scant support for the optimist case that there is no longer a significant employee perception of a "them and us" divide (hypothesis 1). On the contrary, our evidence demonstrates the existence of high levels of "them and us" attitudes.

Factors Affecting Variations in "Them and Us" Attitudes

Two routes have been identified, superordinate goals and co-operative behaviour, both of which have the potential to reduce the prevalence of "them and us" attitudes among workers. Below we test these relationships using multivariate analysis. The method specified here assumes that variations in "them and us" attitudes are caused by the independent variables described in the previous section. While there is a possibility that causality is in the reverse direction, with variations in the independent variables being caused by variations in "them and us" attitudes, we would argue that it is more plausible to accept the former assumption. In the first instance the "them and us" attitudes of subordinate employees are largely determined by social class prior to organisational entry. Secondly, experience in the workplace can confirm or challenge these attitudes.

Equations 1, 2 and 3 in Table 6.3 regress the team question on the various independent variables described earlier. Equation 1 tests for the effect of the variables measuring superordinate and co-operative behaviour on "them and us" attitudes while omitting individual characteristics and firm specific circumstances. The perception by respondents that they are in competition with other firms making similar products (firm survival) is significantly associated with lower levels of "them and us" attitudes and provides some confirmation for hypothesis 2. Indeed, firm survival has the largest impact in equation 1. The priority accorded the firm in terms of life interests is not significant. Both levels of co-operative behaviour, task autonomy and union measures are significantly related to "them and us" attitudes. At the task level, employees who believe they are being given more discretion in organising and carrying out work tasks are less likely to hold "them and us" attitudes. This result is encouraging for advocates of work reorganisation where autonomy is an important element in restructuring relations between

Table 6.3: Determinants of Variations in "Them and Us" Attitudes[+]

Independent Variables	Dependent Variable "Management and workers are on the same side" 1=strongly disagree to 5=strongly agree. (standardised Beta coefficients reported)		
	1	**2**	**3**
Superordinate Goals			
Firm survival	0.33***	0.34***	0.34***
Priority of firm	- 0.05	- 0.06	-0.1*
Co-operative Behaviour **(a) Task level**			
More discretion in work	0.12**	0.13**	0.1*
(b) Firm level			
IR procedures	0.3**	0.32***	0.29***
Cohesive union organisation	0.11*	0.11*	0.08
Individual Characteristics			
Age		- 0.06	- 0.03
Gender		0.04	0.07
Occupation		0.06	0.05
Satisfaction with take home pay		- 0.07	- 0.05
Firm Circumstances			
Employment trends			-0.13**
R2 (adjusted)	0.33	0.35	0.35
F ratio	46***	49***	41***
N	372	362	362
DW	1.75	1.75	1.8

Significance levels: * < .05   ** < .01   *** < .001

[+] Stepwise regression: beta coefficients reported.

management and employees. However, this should not be viewed in isolation from the union measures. Satisfaction with grievance procedures has the second strongest impact after firm survival. Respondents who are satisfied with established procedures for dealing with grievances are less likely to hold "them and us" attitudes. A cohesive union organisation is also associated with reduced "them and us" attitudes, but this measure is a firm level measure and needs to be treated with some caution (see discussion below). The results on co-operative behaviour in equation 1 support hypothesis 3. In equation 2 the variables measuring individual characteristics are also included.

While the results for superordinate goals and co-operative behaviour remain significant it is somewhat surprising that variables such as occupational level and satisfaction with pay do not attain significance. Table 6.4 shows the

Table 6.4: Occupational Level and Satisfaction with Pay by Attitudes Towards Management

"On the same side" *1=strongly disagree to 5=strongly agree*			
Occupation	**Mean**	**SD**	**N**
Unskilled	2.5	1.2	214
Skilled	2.5	1.2	69
Clerical	2.3	0.9	34
Tech/Admin	2.4	1.2	45
Supervisory	3.0	1.1	7
Professional	3.2	0.9	31
Overall Mean	2.55	1.2	400
Take-Home Pay*			
Satisfied	2.8	1.2	114
Dissatisfied	2.4	1.2	265

* Excludes respondents with no opinion.

Source: Employee survey, 1994.

mean scores of "them and us" attitudes categorised by occupation and satisfaction with pay.

As Table 6.4 indicates, there is a considerable difference between the professional and supervisory levels and other levels as predicted but the numbers in the former categories are too small (9 per cent of the sample) to have a significant effect on "them and us" attitudes. There is also a significant difference between those satisfied with take-home pay and those dissatisfied. However, there is a significant if low correlation between take-home pay and the measures firm survival and satisfaction with grievance procedures (R=0.15, P>0.01; and R=0.14, P>0.01 respectively) which may account for the lack of significance of take-home pay in equation 2.

In equation 3 both individual characteristics and firm employment trends are included. The pattern of results is again similar, with firm survival and satisfaction with grievance procedures having the largest effect on variations in "them and us" attitudes. The priority accorded to the firm is significant, indicating that those respondents who rank the firm higher in terms of their life interests are more likely to agree that management and workers are on the same side. This relationship is, however, relatively weak and may only become significant because of the inclusion of the employment measure. Union cohesion and organisation may also be related to the employment measure as it fails to reach significance. But the effects of the measures, employment trends and union cohesion must be treated with caution since these are firm level measures and there are only nine firms in the survey. Although there is a discernible relationship between the two, the numbers involved are such as to make any conclusions extremely tentative and are more suggestive than explanatory.

The relationship between union cohesion and "them and us" attitudes is, nevertheless, revealing if only indicative. Ranking the companies in ascending order from the company with the highest proportion of respondents agreeing that management and workers are on the same side, Table 6.5 indicates that, aside from company 2, companies high on union organisation and cohesion tend to have a higher proportion of workers agreeing that management and workers are on the same side. Likewise, the proportion of respondents concerned with firm survival in a competitive market follows a similar pattern.

The results in Table 6.5 could be interpreted as evidence of dual

Table 6.5: Employee Attitudes, Union Organisation and Firm Survival

Company	% Agreeing Management and Workers on Same Side	% Agreeing they are in Competition with Others	Organisation of a Shop Steward Committee
1	60	94	High on organisation and cohesion
2	58	64	Low on organisation and cohesion
3	46	78	High on organisation and cohesion
4	43	80	High on organisation and cohesion
5	41	77	Low on organisation, high on cohesion
6	39	76	Low on organisation, high on cohesion
7	32	70	Low on organisation, high on cohesion
8	24	71	Disorganised and low on cohesion
9	8	54	Disorganised and low on cohesion

Source: Employee survey, 1994 and interviews with shop stewards (see Turner and Morley, 1995).

commitment. Dual commitment has been described as a situation where employees are simultaneously committed to the organisation and the union which represents them (Savery and Soutar, 1997). However, as Angle and Perry (1986) observe, there is no agreed definition of commitment. Guest and Dewe (1991: 78), for example, argue that "the desire to maintain membership of an organisation is, logically, a consequence of identity with the organisation". This, we would argue, is not necessarily so. For instance low discretion employees with few marketable skills confronted by a glutted labour market may well value organisational membership against the alternative of unemployment. Such economically coercive or calculative involvement is unlikely to promote employee internalisation of the firm's goals and values. Indeed, employee identity or commitment to the firm in such circumstances has been characterised as an incongruent compliance structure (Etzioni, 1961). Co-operation in industrial and commercial organisations, Sable (1993) argues, results from a continuous calculation of self-interest.

Consequently, we do not interpret Table 6.5 as evidence of dual commitment in the sense that it involves the internalisation of managerial goals, but rather as an outcome of a calculative exchange process. Collective bargaining institutionalises this exchange process where an effective union may ensure a more equitable bargain. This is considered further below.

CONCLUSION

Three hypotheses were examined. First, that there remains no significant employee perception of a "them and us" divide among employees in Irish firms. Secondly, that acceptance by employees of a superordinate goal will be negatively associated with a "them and us" divide. Thirdly, that the participation of employees in co-operative initiatives is associated with reduced "them and us" attitudes. The responses from the employees across the nine firms surveyed does not support hypothesis 1 – that there was no significant perception of a "them and us" divide. However, both the second and third hypotheses received significant support in explaining variations in the intensity of "them and us" attitudes. Variation in "them and us" attitudes is significantly related to employee awareness of the need for firm survival, greater discretion in work, satisfaction with industrial relations procedures and a cohesive union organisation. The presence of a strong and cohesive union organisation is associated with relatively lower levels of a "them and us" divide. This finding appears somewhat paradoxical since a common perception is that trade unions sharpen the divide between workers and employers. In a review of the UK literature on "them and us" attitudes and new industrial relations initiatives, Kelly and Kelly (1991) concluded that while employees had positive attitudes towards co-operative initiatives, it did not generalise to reduce "them and us" attitudes. They attributed the failure of the initiatives to bring about an attitudinal change to four causes: employees' lack of choice over participating in the initiative; a lack of trust between workers and management; an inequality of status and outcomes; and a lack of institutional support from top management. We would argue that, where firms are unionised, the presence of a cohesive and functioning union organisation at firm level has the potential to address a number of these problems. Unions are more effective than individual employees in seeking improvements and safeguards for their members' working conditions and ensuring that management are aware of the preferences of their members when new work arrangements are introduced. Generally, unions insist that workers participate in the development of new arrangements. For example, the Irish Congress of Trade Unions has produced a number of reports advocating union involvement in new working arrangements and encouraging affiliated unions to become involved in new initiatives (ICTU, 1991, 1993). Unions act as a check against arbitrary management decisions and actions, thus ensuring adherence to jointly agreed procedures. In addition, collective bargaining allows for workers to participate in and negotiate for a share in the surplus of the firm *vis-à-vis* employers, shareholders and senior management. As a result, unions can increase worker morale and confidence in dealings with management (Freeman and Medoff, 1984).

A secondary finding of this chapter is that a strong union presence in the firms surveyed tends to be associated with lower levels of "them and us" attitudes. These firms, we would argue, are effectively utilising the potential benefits of trade unions. However, this conclusion requires qualification given the small number of firms involved. While this finding could benefit from further research it is concurrent with an extensive, if controversial, literature which argues that unions can have beneficial effects on a firm's industrial relations and economic performance. Williamson (1975: 73), for example, argues that trade unions can reduce opportunistic bargaining on the part of individual employees and encourage "consummate rather than perfunctory cooperation". Similarly, Freeman and Medoff (1979, 1984) have argued that unions can ensure that workers' preferences concerning pay and working conditions are voiced leading to lower labour turnover, lower training costs, lower accidents and better worker morale.

Intensified competition, high unemployment, rapid technological and organisational change have become characteristic features of many western economies since 1980. In responding to these conditions, employees in the companies surveyed have apparently become more conciliatory and co-operative as indicated by continuous social pacts at national level, partnership initiatives at firm level and a decline in all measures of overt conflict. Yet, despite these changes, the old adversarial attitudes have apparently persisted. A plausible explanation for this paradox may lie in the enduring and dualistic nature of the employment relationship where the elements of antagonism and co-operation co-exist. While workers may co-operate with management in pursuit of mutual survival the antagonism integral to the capital labour relationship remains. The persistence, however muted, of "them and us" attitudes is one manifestation of that antagonism. Thirty years ago Fox (1966: 9) argued that:

> ... to regard high morale and high (organised) conflict as opposite poles of a dichotomy is a dangerous fallacy. In an industry which by its very nature throws up a considerable number of disputed issues, their compromise or reconciliation through institutionalised forms of conflict may indeed be a condition of high morale, or of the positive attachment of the members of sub-groups to the activities of the organisation.

Thus, it can be argued that the presence of an effective union gives some assurance of a future equitable outcome. The greater likelihood of equitable outcomes can diminish the intensity of "them and us" attitudes.

APPENDIX

The data analysed here come from a study undertaken by the Department of Personnel and Employment Relations, University of Limerick in 1994/95 on behalf of the Department of Enterprise and Employment. Altogether twelve unionised companies were chosen for the study on the basis of their industrial relations record. The companies were equally divided between those with good industrial relations and those with a poor record in this area as measured by the frequency of third party intervention. The study included a survey of 402 employees in nine of these companies in the manufacturing sector. Survey access was denied by three of the companies, all with a poor industrial relations record. The size of survey conducted and the manner in which it was carried out varied across the nine companies (see Table 6A). For logistical and practical reasons, it was not possible to conduct a proper random survey in all of the companies. Thus, the small sample size in some of the companies and the way in which the questionnaires were distributed could possibly bias results in these instances (see Table 6A).

Table 6A: Summary of Company Characteristics

Company	Sector	Size	Owner-ship	Establbi-shed	Number Surveyed	Type of Survey**
1	Chemical	Medium	US	1970s	33	Random
2	Chemical	Medium	US	1970s	42	Convenient
3	Textiles	Medium	US	1970s	15	Convenient
4	Food & Drink	Large	British	1930s	31	Random
5	Food & Drink	Medium	British	1950s	40	Convenient
6	Food & Drink	Large	Irish	*	106	Random
7	Food & Drink	Medium	Irish	*	41	Convenient
8	Engineering	Medium	US	1960s	18	Random
9	Engineering	Large	US	1980s	76	Random

*Both of these companies changed from Cooperatives to Public Limited Companies in the 1980s.

**Convenience sampling usually involved the distribution of questionnaires through a combination of the personnel manager and the senior shop steward. All questionnaires were provided with an addressed envelope for mailing directly to the authors. Apart from one engineering firm the companies have been established for at least 20 years and in each company all of the manual employees are unionised. As such, the companies are representative of medium/large companies in the manufacturing sector. Two companies are Irish and the remainder are subsidiaries of multinational companies.

REFERENCES

Angle, H. and Perry, J. (1986) "Dual Commitment and Labour-Management Relationship Climates" *Academy of Management Journal*, Vol. 29, No. 1: 31–50.

Basset, P. (1986) *Strike Free*. London: Macmillan.

Brannick, T., Doyle, L. and Kelly, A. (1997) "Industrial Conflict" in Murphy, T. and Roche, W. K. (eds) *Irish Industrial Relations in Practice*. Dublin: Oak Tree Press.

Breen, R. and Whelan, T. (1996) *Social Mobility and Social Class in Ireland*. Dublin: Gill and Macmillan.

Etzioni, A. (1961) *The Comparative Analysis of Complex Organisations*. Glencoe: Free Press.

Fox, A. (1966) *Industrial Sociology and Industrial Relations*. Research Papers 3, London: HMSO.

Fox, A. (1974) *Beyond Contract: Work, Power and Trust Relations*. London: Faber and Faber.

Freeman, R. B. and Medoff, J. L. (1979) "The Two Faces of Unionism" *Public Interest*, Vol. 57: 69–93, (Fall).

Freeman, R. B. and Medoff, J. L. (1984) *What Do Unions Do?* New York: Basic Books.

Giddens, A. (1989) *Sociology*. Cambridge: Polity Press.

Goldthorpe, J. H., Lockwood, P., Beckhoffer, F. and Platt, J. (1968). *The Affluent Worker: Industrial Attitudes and Behaviour*. Cambridge: University Press.

Guest, D. and Dewe, P. (1991) "Company or Trade Union: Which Wins Workers Allegiance?" *British Journal of Industrial Relations*, Vol. 29, No. 1: 74–96.

Gunnigle, P. (1995) "Collectivism and the Management of Industrial Relations in Greenfield Sites" *Human Resource Management Journal*, Vol. 5, No. 3: 24–40.

Gunnigle, P., Flood, P., Morley, M. and Turner, T. (1994) *Continuity and Change in Irish Employee Relations*. Dublin: Oak Tree Press.

Hamilton, M. and Hirszowicz, M. (1993) *Class and Inequality – Comparitive Perspectives*. London: Harvester Wheatsheaf.

Hoggart R. (1967) *The Uses of Literacy*. London: Chatto and Windus.

Hourihan, F. (1996) "Non Union Policies on the Increase Among New Overseas Firms" *Industrial Relations News*, Vol. 4: 17–23, 25 January.

Hyman, R. (1989) "Dualism and Division in Labour Strategies" in Hyman, R. (ed.) *The Political Economy of Industrial Relations*. London: Macmillan.

Irish Congress of Trade Unions (1993) *New Forms of Work Organisation: Options for Unions*. Dublin.

Irish Congress of Trade Unions (with the Federation of Irish Employers) (1991) *Joint Declaration on Employee Involvement in the Private Sector*. Dublin.

Keenoy, T. (1985) *Invitation to Industrial Relations*. Oxford: Blackwell.

Kelly, J. and Kelly, C. (1991) "'Them and Us': Social Psychology and 'The New Industrial Relations'" *British Journal of Industrial Relations*, Vol. 29: 24–48.

Kessler, S. and Bayliss, F. (1992) *Contemporary British Industrial Relations*. Basingstoke: Macmillan.

Kochan, T., Katz, H. and McKersie, R. (1986) *The Transformation of American Industrial Relations*. New York: Basic Books.

Kumar, K. (1995) *From Post-Industrial to Post-Modern Society: New Theories of the Contemporary World*. Oxford: Blackwell.

Mowday, R. T., Porter, L. W. and Steers, R. M. (1982) *Employee-Organization Linkages: The Psychology of Commitment, Absenteeism and Turnover*. San Diego: Academic Press Inc.

Piore, M. and Sabel, C. (1984) *The Second Industrial Divide: Prospects for Prosperity*. New York: Basic Books.

Ramsay, H. (1975) "Firms and Football Teams" *British Journal of Industrial Relations*, Vol. 13, No. 3: 396–400.

Sabel, C. (1993) "Studied Trust: Building New Forms of Co-operation in a Volatile Economy" *Human Relations*, Vol. 46, No. 9: 1133–1170.

Savery, L. K. and Soutar, G. K. (1997) "Employee commitment to Organisations and Unions: 'Some Preliminary Australian Evidence'" in Mortimer, D., Leece, P. and Morris, R. (eds) *Readings in Contemporary*

Employment Relations. University of Western Sydney, Australia.

Scott, A. (1994). *Willing Slaves? British Workers Under Human Resource Management*. Cambridge University Press.

Smith, P. and Morton, G. (1994) "Union Exclusion in Britain – Next Steps" *Industrial Relations Journal*, Vol. 25, No. 1: 3–14.

Terry, M. (1989) "Recontextualising Shopfloor Industrial Relations" in Tailby, S. and Whitson, C. (eds) *Manufacturing Change: Industrial Relations and Restructuring*. Oxford: Blackwell.

Turner, T. and Morley, M. (1995) *Industrial Relations and the New Order*. Dublin: Oak Tree Press.

Walton, R. E. (1985) "From Control to Commitment in the Workplace" *Harvard Business Review*, March/April: 77–84.

Wedderburn, D. and Crampton, R. (1972) *Worker's Attitudes and Technology*. Cambridge: Cambridge University Press.

Whelan, C. (1982) *Worker Priorities, Trust in Management and Prospects for Workers Participation*. Paper No. 111, Dublin: Economic and Social Research Institute.

Williamson, O. E. (1975) *Markets, Hierarchies: Analysis and Anti-Trust Implications*. Glencoe: Free Press.

SECTION 2

CHAPTER 7

The Decline of Worker Solidarity and the End of Collectivism?

DARYL D'ART AND THOMAS TURNER

INTRODUCTION

Developments in industrial society since the end of the 1970s such as the erosion and fracturing of traditional working class communities, increasing individualisation, the growth of service sector employment, new forms of work arrangements and declining union membership apparently question the continuing relevance of collectivism and solidarity. These developments have been seen by many as signaling a breakup of the traditionally homogenous and collective experience of employment. Changes in the advanced industrial societies have been interpreted as a "crisis in class politics" or indeed, the end of class (Clark and Lipset, 1991; Clarke et al., 1993). Consequently, it is argued that the salience of class and its attendant solidarities are increasingly redundant. The social trends associated with individualisation and detraditionalisation are believed to undermine the conditions associated with collective class actions. The logic of this argument suggests that those formerly identified as working class will be increasingly less inclined to participate in collectively oriented union or political activities based on class identity, with an accompanying erosion of solidaristic beliefs in a general union movement. In the context of these predictions, this chapter examines the existing strength of solidarity based on a survey of members in an Irish general union. The focus of this chapter is not on the process of class fragmentation but its supposed effects on worker solidarity.

THE DEVELOPMENT OF WORKER SOLIDARITY

The origins of worker solidarity can be found in the industrial revolution and the factory system. Gathering formerly scattered groups of workers within single enterprises threw into sharp relief the widening social gulf and changed relations between masters and men (Thompson, 1967). There emerged a pattern of employer/employee relations that has become characteristic of western industrial society. According to Fox (1974), it was a pattern marked by increasingly impersonal and narrowly contractual attitudes and behaviour, by mutual distrust and grudging calculation and by the decay of whatever diffuse bonds of obligation that might have mitigated the harshness of employer/ employee power relations in earlier times. Relations between the parties had been reduced to the cash nexus and, as the Webbs (1894) noted, one-time semi-independent workers now occupied the position of permanent wage earners.

The ideology of industrial capitalism held that all individuals were politically and economically equal and, therefore, relations between master and man should be conducted on an individual basis (Taylor, 1989: 1). Workers embraced collectivism or trade unions as an instrument with which to exert some influence on wage determination and check the exercise of absolute and arbitrary employer power. Historically, worker collectivities have experienced varying levels of accommodation or opposition from the dominant groups. Despite this ebb and flow, solidarity, that is a community of feeling, interest and action, remains a prerequisite for effective collectivism (Poole, 1984: 184; Kelly and Breinlinger, 1996). As Salaman (1998: 76) notes, "the power and ability of employees collectivity to further the individual's interests rests largely on its internal fraternalism or solidarity, that is, the extent to which the individual members are prepared to subordinate personal aspirations to the collective needs, goals and decisions of the group".

This location of solidarity and collectivism at the level of a group is a useful corrective to those who tend to assume an automatic connection between solidarity and a revolutionary political class consciousness and action (see Fantasia, 1989). Of course solidarity can have such a focus but it can also support the pursuit of narrow sectional interests (see Lockwood, 1966: 137). For instance, some 19th century Chartist leaders complained that trade unions pursued sectional aims at the expense of the whole movement (Stevenson, 1991). Examining the internal relations of the trade union world in the mid 1870s, the Webbs (1894: 342) noted that it was dominated by a narrow particularism and broken up into struggling groups each preoccupied with its separate concerns which frequently ran counter to the policy or aims of the rest. Similarly, Clarkson (1970: 164), reviewing Irish trade unions in the latter half of the 19th century, remarked, "they were prepared to accept the station in life to which God had called them, thankful that He had not assigned to them the role of general labourers". Particularism, he concluded, was the "order of the day". However, by the end of the 19th century in both Britain and Ireland, it was the rise of unskilled unions, assisted and sometimes led by socialists, that fostered a notion of solidarity that transcended the particular group. Some of the leaders of unskilled unionism went on to campaign for the establishment of a distinct political party to defend and promote the claims of labour at a political level. With the rise of labour parties in these islands the concept of solidarity broadened to potentially include the work group, the union, political and class solidarity.

Yet, this gradual broadening of the concept of solidarity may be peculiar to Britain given it was the first country to industrialise. According to Visser

(1995), the later the industrial revolution arrived, the more rapidly it evolved and the more worker's social struggle to gain better living and working conditions was accompanied by political struggle. In Europe, the period between 1900 and 1913 saw the rise of what Streek (1993) describes as the industrial–political trade union model. Industrial unions and their peak organisations were set up as the industrial arm of socialist or catholic political parties (Visser, 1995: 43). The development of the Swedish labour movement is an example where, from the beginning, the primary focus for solidarity was the class, party and trade union rather than a particular group. On its formation in 1889, the Swedish Social Democratic party saw its main task as fostering the growth of a socialist trade union movement. A decade later the Swedish Trade Union Confederation was established. While this involved the formal separation of the industrial and political wings of the labour movement, nevertheless, socialist ideology remained very influential (Tilton, 1979). Indeed, it was instrumental in encouraging the union congress of 1912 to adopt the principal of industrial unionism in preference to the particularism of craft unionism. Up to the 1970s at any rate, the idea of a united labour movement whose political and industrial struggles were completely interdependent, was to remain deeply embedded in the ideology of the party and unions at all levels (Elvander, 1974).

THE DECLINE OF WORKER SOLIDARITY?

The high point of worker solidarity is often associated with the period of trade union struggle for recognition in the late 19th century and early 20th century in industrialised societies. Industrial society in this period was characterised by large mass-production factories, cohesive working class communities, a deep divide between rich and poor, and antagonistic relations between capital and labour, which all provided rich grounds for the development of worker solidarity, revolutionary ideas and political parties. If we use the numbers in trade unions and the numbers voting for social democratic parties as proxy measures of worker solidarity, the high water mark of this period was the 1960s and 1970s. However, even at this time the characteristics associated with industrialised society were undergoing substantial change. The old "smoke stack industries" were disappearing and with them the traditional community of workers which lived nearby. The numbers employed in industry declined while the numbers working in the service sector increased dramatically. This was reflected in changes in the occupational structure of labour markets as the number of manual/blue-collar workers declined and white-collar work expanded. This created a substantial middle class, reducing the sharp division between capital and labour prevalent in previous periods. In addition to the above economic and occupational changes, the declining role of associations in the labour market is attributed to shifts in the industrial and occupational structure of advanced economies, namely the rise of the service sector. These industrial and occupational changes, it is argued, have fostered the diffusion of individual orientations at the expense of traditional forms of class related solidarity (Lash and Urry, 1987; Valkenburg, 1996; Zoll, 1996).

These changes have initiated a considerable debate on the consequences for class formation and class solidarities. It is argued by commentators such as Beck, Giddens and Lasch that processes of individualisation, detraditionalisation and class fragmentation are occurring in modern industrialised societies. Beck (1987) argues, for example, that we are no longer witnessing the history of the formation of class solidarities. Instead, changes in the labour market, through its inter-linked processes of education, mobility and competition, have become the "driving force" behind the individualisation of peoples lives.

DEFINING SOLIDARITY

Solidarity can be defined as a community of interests, feelings and actions (see Bild and Madsen, 1997: 1; Poole, 1984: 183). A community of interests refers to the existence of similar material conditions and a realisation that these interests can be best advanced through collective means. Solidarity, however, only arises when workers not only realise that there is a community of interests but have a strong sense of identity, attachment and allegiance which leads to solidaristic actions such as the protection of weaker members and the honouring of strike pickets. Given the rather amorphous meaning of solidarity, Bild and Madsen (1997) suggest that two fundamental questions need to be addressed to give greater clarity to the concept. First, solidarity with whom? Identity and allegiance can vary from "real" to "imagined" communities. A real community includes a worker's immediate work group and the collectivity in the same organisation. Solidarity with imagined communities goes beyond the worker's immediate experience to embrace national union movements and political parties.

From this distinction between real and imagined community, three levels of worker solidarity or three types of interest have been identified (see Lockwood, 1966; Bild and Madsen, 1997). The first level is the real community at the workplace which Bild and Madsen label the "workers' collective". At this level of solidarity, workers refer to themselves as "we" in relation to the "others". Often the "we" and "others" represent workers and management where workers create an informal and spontaneous shield of solidarity against the continuous demands of the company.

The second level of solidarity identified by Bild and Madsen (1997) is that of wage-earner solidarity. Here solidarity arises out of the common interests of wage earners in the labour market. The traditional expression of this level of solidarity is the trade union. In Lockwood's (1966) typology this would represent what he calls "immediate" and "instrumental interests". Immediate interests are matters such as salaries, hours, holidays, promotion and superannuation within the firm, while instrumental interests are matters common to all unions of employees, such as the legal status of trade unions, recognition, strike action, negotiation machinery and political representation (Lockwood, 1966: 195–96).

The third form of solidarity is based on workers' interests in the political system and is described by Bild and Madsen (1997) as political solidarity. Political solidarity emerges out of workers' critical conceptions of existing social class arrangements and the distribution of wealth between these classes. It is particularly manifested in a general support for a universal welfare system and electoral support for social democratic parties. This level is described by Lockwood as one of "ideological interests", which imply wider interests of a political kind based on the principles and assumptions arising out the connection between the trade union movement and the Labour Party (Lockwood, 1966: 196). Lockwood's more general description of ideological interests or political solidarity may reflect the looser connection between trade unions and the Labour Party in Britain compared to their Scandinavian counterparts.

The second fundamental question concerns solidarity in pursuit of what kind of interests. Bild and Madsen (1997) distinguish between defensive and offensive forms of wage-earner solidarity. Defensive solidarity is orientated towards minimising competition between wage earners within an organisation with outcomes such as employment security and standardised wages and conditions of work. Offensive forms of solidarity may include strikes for higher wages, but is more aptly associated with attempts to change the existing social structure in favour of wage earners and essentially takes a political form. Table 7.1 below illustrates these various categories.

Table 7.1: Levels of Solidarity

Levels of Solidarity	Defensive Solidarity	Offensive Solidarity
Group Solidarity	• Strong "them and us" feeling • Protective shield against authority	• Use of custom and practice • Informal group control • Job control
Wage Earner/Union Solidarity	• Instrumental interests • A curb on arbitrary management action	• Perception of the union as a means of achieving a higher standard of living
Political Solidarity	• Critical of existing wealth distribution • Non-acceptance of the legitimacy of existing distribution of wealth	• Critical of existing social structures • Support for social democratic parties and fundamental reform of existing structures

Solidarity, Age and Occupational Status

Although much of the debate on the relevance of social solidarity in contemporary society necessarily requires a historical perspective, it is possible, nonetheless, to address some of the issues in a cross-sectional survey. The above debate suggests a number of propositions that can be tested based on the acceptance of the class fragmentation argument and its consequent effect on solidarity. A number of factors can be identified which may influence levels of worker solidarity: historical trends, class and union identity and the characteristics of organisations. In the absence of longitudinal data we use age as a proxy for change over time. It could be argued that the young workers in our sample are possibly not representative of young workers generally and are a self-selecting group with a relatively high degree of solidarity consciousness. However, this is unlikely to be the case as the companies surveyed are almost entirely unionised, particularly at shopfloor level. Furthermore, new employees tend as a matter of course to join the union. If classes are fragmenting and solidarities are weakening, it can be expected that younger workers will display significantly lower levels of solidarity than older workers.

Hypothesis 1: *It can be predicted that younger workers will have lower levels of solidarity than older workers.*
Traditionally, employees at the higher reaches of the organisational hierarchy are less likely to be unionised if not unfavourably disposed towards the collectivism which trade unionism represents. Even those in higher-level occupations who are unionised are likely to have lower levels of solidarity. The assumption is sometimes made that manual trade unionists are committed proletarian collectivists in contrast to their white-collar counterparts who supposedly espouse an individualist and instrumental attitude to trade unionism (Hyman and Price, 1983). A workers' position in the social stratification system is assumed to produce a certain picture or social image of industry and the wider society. These different social images are classified into two basic types – a class ideology and a status ideology. The class ideology which most manual workers are believed to possess is favourable to unionism, while the status ideology supposedly possessed by white-collar employees would be less supportive of unionism or collectivism (Bain et al., 1973). Thus, we could expect blue-collar workers to exhibit higher levels of group, wage earner and political solidarity than their white-collar counterparts. In general, decreasing levels of solidarity are likely at the higher reaches of the organisational hierarchy.

Hypothesis 2: *Routine white-collar workers will have lower levels of solidarity than blue-collar semi and unskilled workers. More generally, higher occupational levels will be associated with lower levels of solidarity*
There has been a strong historical tendency for women's work to be viewed

as relatively short term and marginal to the labour force, thus discouraging the adoption of collectivist responses to the issues of pay and conditions (Lockwood, 1966; Hyman and Price, 1983). Solidarity has tended to be seen as a predominantly male, working class attribute. While, on the one hand, it can be predicted that females will have lower levels of solidarity than males, alternatively there is compelling evidence from a number of studies that, where there are differences in attitudes towards unionisation, these are a result of structural factors such as union availability and size of establishment and are not inherent to gender (Hartley, 1992: 169). Thus, the relationship between gender and solidarity is best treated as an empirical test.

Union Activism and Class Identity

The extent to which union members identify with their union is an important indicator of their participation in union activities (see Nicholson, 1981; Flood et al., 1996). In this chapter union orientation is used to measure members' degree of identification with the union (Nicholson et al., 1981). Union orientation comprises five categories denoting increasing levels of psychological involvement in union affairs: first, those who are reluctant members; secondly, card carriers who are indifferent to the trade union; thirdly, members who are active only on special issues; fourthly, apolitical stalwarts who are active trade unionists but non-political; and finally, ideological activists who are politically/ideologically committed to the union movement and its wider aims. This measure incorporates the degree of participation in union activities, commitment to the principles of trade unionism and wider political commitments or ideological beliefs. Flood et al. (1996) in their study of members of an Irish general union found union orientation to be strongly predictive of both internal participation (canvassing for the union, raising grievances, attending meetings) and external participation (attending and voting at section and union AGMs). It is plausible, therefore, to argue that a member's union orientation will also be related to the three levels of solidarity.

Hypothesis 3: *The extent to which union members identify with the union will be associated with higher levels of solidarity.*
As noted above, a worker's position in the social stratification system is assumed to produce a certain picture or social image of industry and the wider society. Indeed, members of lower-socio economic groups, even before they enter the workplace, will be predisposed to adopt a "them and us" attitude (Hoggart, 1967). In addition, Bain et al. (1973) note that stratification variables are also relevant to the study of union character and that the social imagery of union leaders and shop stewards may well be a determinant of a union behaviour. This being the case, workers who identify themselves as belonging to the working class are more likely to have higher levels of solidarity.

Hypothesis 4: *Workers who explicitly identify themselves as working class are more likely to be higher on all three levels of solidarity.*

In addition, it is possible that managerial policies and the general industrial relations climate in a particular firm may affect levels of solidarity. To control for the influence of variations in organisational climate and possible effects on worker solidarity two factors, employee commitment to the organisation and the frequency of disputes, are used to measure the nature of the relationship between employer and union members. Commitment is measured by feelings of loyalty towards the organisation, the willingness to make extra efforts and the propensity to remain in the organisation.

In unionised firms where there is a high frequency of disputes between workers and management it is likely that the union will have a higher profile since shop stewards will be engaged with management on a more regular basis. The frequent threat or use of industrial action is one indicator of a militant trade union (Kelly, 1996). According to Kelly (1996: 81), a militant union is one that stresses conflicts of interests between workers and employers and generally "promotes a corresponding adversarial ideology". Thus, a high frequency of disputes is likely to reinforce "them and us" attitudes and levels of wage earner solidarity. The above relationships of the determinants of solidarity are illustrated in Figure 7.1.

Figure 7.1: Firm Level Determinants of Solidarity

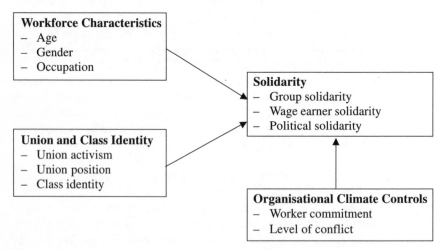

Data and Measures

The data in this chapter is based on a survey of members of a general union in Ireland carried out in 1998. Support for the project was provided by the general union. A total of 2,080 members were surveyed in 43 companies. Union members were randomly selected using the membership list for each company provided by the trade union. The questionnaires were addressed to the selected members and distributed to the companies either directly by the authors or through relevant union officers. Each questionnaire included an envelope addressed to the authors for the completed questionnaire. A total of 605 completed questionnaires were returned, giving a response rate of 29 per cent[1] of the sample surveyed. Such a return rate is acceptable for a postal survey. The majority of respondents, 64 per cent, worked in the private sector and the remainder, 34 per cent, in the public sector. In all, 78 per cent worked in the manufacturing sector and 22 per cent in services. In the following sections, using questions from the survey, we address the various levels of solidarity. Table 7A in the Appendix indicates the dependent measures, means and standard deviation for the three levels of solidarity used in this chapter. We have divided the independent variables into three groups: demographic or workforce composition measures; organisational process measures; and union/ class related measures. These are outlined in Table 7B in the Appendix. Finally, Table 7C in the Appendix is a correlation matrix of all the variables.

RESULTS

Below, using the data from the survey, we first examine the three levels of solidarity: group, wage earner and political; secondly, using multivariate analysis, the trends and causal relationships between solidarity and the various changes are addressed.

Group Solidarity at the Workplace

The measure of group solidarity can be gauged from the strength of a "them and us" feeling among workers. A large majority of the members surveyed (74 per cent) believed that workers and management were on opposite sides in their company. Only 19 per cent disagreed with the statement. In addition, 79 per cent of respondents agreed with the statement that there is a strong sense of "them and us" between workers and management in their firm (Table 7.2).

Wage Earner Solidarity

Four measures from the survey – union solidarity, instrumental solidarity, offensive wage-earner solidarity and offensive union solidarity – are used to gauge levels of wage-earner solidarity. A substantial majority of members

---

1. It has been suggested to the authors that there is a possibility that union members who returned questionnaires may have a higher degree of union involvement than the sample as a whole, thus leading to biased responses. However, 34% of respondents were either reluctant union members or had no interest in union activities and 33% did not get involved most of the time with the union but were only active on special issues. Thus, there is no evidence of high union involvement among the majority of respondents.

Table 7.2: Group, Wage Earner and Political Solidarity

	Disagree/ Strongly	No View	Agree/ Strongly	Total
1. Group Solidarity in the Workplace				
I feel that workers and management are on opposite sides in my firm	19%	7%	74%	100%
There is a strong sense of "them and us" between workers and management in this firm	12%	9%	79%	100%
2. Wage Earner Solidarity				
A union is not necessary in this company because management treat workers fairly	87%	7%	6%	100%
If there was no union in this firm management would take greater advantage of the workforce (*union solidarity*)	5%	5%	90%	100%
Improvements in terms and conditions at work will only be achieved through trade union action (*offensive wage earner solidarity*)	20%	4%	76%	100%
It is only through trade union activity that higher standards of living are achieved (*offensive union solidarity*)	25%	12%	63%	100%
3. Political Solidarity				
Everybody in Irish society is fairly rewarded for the contribution they make	83%	6%	11%	100%
The unequal distribution of wealth in Ireland is a fair result given the contribution made by each particular class	69%	13%	19%	100%
The poor are largely to blame for their poverty	83%	8%	9%	100%
It is very important to reduce the gap between rich and poor	4%	4%	93%	100%

surveyed, 87 per cent, disagreed or strongly disagreed with the statement that unions were unnecessary because management treated workers fairly in their company. Indeed, 90 per cent of members believed that without a union presence management would take greater advantage of the workforce. Only 5 per cent of members surveyed believed management would not take advantage. The results indicate a strong sense of solidarity with their trade union.

We can distinguish between defensive wage earner solidarity at workplace or company level and offensive wage earner solidarity. In the first case firm level solidarity or instrumental solidarity is measured by members' perceptions of who best represents their interests and offensive wage earner solidarity by whether the union is perceived as the best means for improving terms and conditions of employment. A majority of respondents indicated that the union best represents their interests on pay, job security, pensions and working conditions. However, there was a significant minority who believed otherwise.

Table 7.3: Instrumental Solidarity

Who best represents your interests in the following areas?	**Union**	**Management**	**Nobody**	**Yourself**
Pay Issues	76%	2%	6%	17%
Job Security	68%	7%	8%	17%
Pensions	62%	10%	10%	18%
Working Conditions	66%	4%	5%	24%

A majority of respondents believed that the union best represented their interests in all areas, ranging from a high of 76 per cent for pay issues to 62 per cent on pension matters. In terms of offensive wage earner solidarity, 76 per cent believed that improvements in terms and conditions of employment can only be improved by trade union action in their workplace. Offensive union solidarity is measured by the extent to which union members believe that trade union activity can achieve higher standards of living for workers. Commitment to the trade union movement as the only means of achieving higher standards of living is also supported by a majority (63 per cent) of those surveyed.

The evidence from Tables 7.2 and 7.3 indicates high levels of defensive and offensive wage-earner solidarity at company level. The importance of union action in promoting the interests of union members and in providing an alternative voice to workers is supported by a majority of the union members surveyed.

Political Solidarity

Four questions are used to assess the level of defensive political solidarity among the union members surveyed (Table 7.2). The first two questions evaluate members' perceptions of how fairly wealth is distributed in Ireland, while the remaining questions are concerned with the gap between rich and poor. A large majority of members (83 per cent) disagreed with the statement that people in Irish society are fairly rewarded for the contribution they make. Likewise, a substantial majority (69 per cent) did not believe that the unequal distribution of wealth was a fair result given the contribution of each particular class. While 83 per cent of respondents disagreed with the statement that the poor were to blame for their poverty, 93 per cent of union members believed it was very important to reduce the gap between rich and poor. These results reveal a substantial level of defensive political solidarity among respondents.

DETERMINANTS OF WORKER SOLIDARITY

A number of hypotheses were suggested based on the trends emerging from the class fragmentation debate. These hypotheses are tested using multivariate analysis (Table 7.4).

Compositional Effects

It was argued that if classes are fragmenting over time then a decline in solidarity among younger workers could be expected. However, there is little evidence that this is the case. Age has a significant effect on only two measures – union solidarity and defensive political solidarity – and the effect is not in the direction predicted. Indeed, younger workers are more likely to believe a union is necessary in their company and that, without a union, management would take greater advantage of workers (equation 2). In addition, older workers are associated with lower levels of defensive political solidarity. Thus, not only is hypothesis 1 (that older workers have higher levels of solidarity than younger workers) not confirmed but it appears that in some instances younger workers have higher levels of solidarity.

There is no significant association between gender and any of the measures of solidarity, indicating that females' levels of solidarity are as high as their male counterparts. The position of union members in the occupational hierarchy has a significant effect on a member's level of solidarity. Union members in higher occupational levels in the hierarchy have significantly lower levels of solidarity on all measures, providing support for the latter part of hypothesis 2 that higher occupations will be associated with lower levels of solidarity. Given the traditional association of blue-collar workers with trade unionism, it was suggested that white-collar workers would have lower levels of solidarity than blue-collar workers. To test this hypothesis, only unskilled and semi-skilled employees were compared to routine white-collar employees. Separate equations were run using this manual white-collar divide. In Table 7.4 only the results for the latter variable and not the full equations are reported. There is no significant difference between both groups in relation to levels of group

Table 7.4: The Determinants of Worker Solidarity

	Group Solidarity		Wage Earner Solidarity		Political Solidarity	
	1. Group Solidarity+	2. Union Solidarity	3. Instrumental Solidarity+	4. Offensive Wage Earner Solidarity	5. Offensive Union Solidarity	6. Defensive Political Solidarity+
Step 1: Workforce Profile						
Age	Ns	-0.1*	Ns	Ns	0.11**	Ns
Gender	Ns	Ns	Ns	Ns	Ns	Ns
Occupation	-0.09*	-0.16***	-0.15***	-0.17***	-0.16***	-0.16***
Manual v White-Collar Routine	Ns	0.12*	0.13*	0.12*	Ns	Ns
R^2 (Added)	0.037	0.04	0.17	0.028	0.044	0.02
Step 2: Organisation Controls						
Commitment	-0.31***	-0.14**	0.15***	Ns	Ns	Ns
Conflict	-0.22***	-0.12**	Ns	Ns	Ns	Ns
R^2 (Added)	0.164	0.025	0.034	/	0.002	/
Step 3: Union/Class						
Activism	0.13**	0.16***	0.31***	0.19***	0.26***	0.15***
Union Position	Ns	Ns	Ns	Ns	Ns	Ns
Class Identity	Ns	Ns	0.09*	Ns	0.1*	Ns
R^2 (Added)	0.011	0.033	0.096	0.047	0.082	0.014
F	17***	7.7***	11.6***	5.6***	9.9***	3.1***
R^2 (adjusted)	0.212	0.102	0.147	0.071	0.128	0.034
N	535	536	555	545	550	526
DW	1.9	1.9	1.9	1.9	1.8	2.1

Ns = not significant

Significance levels: * < .05   ** < .01 *** < .001

+The group solidarity variable is composed of two questions measuring "them and us" attitudes, alpha = (see Table 7B). Defensive union solidarity is composed of two questions, "a union is not necessary" and "with no union management would take advantage", alpha = (see Table 7B). Instrumental solidarity is composed of four questions on whether the union best represent interests in pay issues, job security, pensions and working conditions, alpha = (see Table 7B). Defensive political solidarity is composed of four questions on wealth and inequality in Irish society, alpha = (see Table 7B).

and political solidarity (equations 1 and 5 to 6). However, white-collar workers are significantly lower on all the measures of wage earner solidarity (equations 2 to 4). This provides partial support for the first section of hypothesis 2 that routine white-collar workers will have lower levels of solidarity than blue-collar semi/unskilled workers.

Union Activism and Class Identity

The extent to which members identify or are active in their union (activism) is significantly and positively associated with all the measures of solidarity but is particularly strong for wage-earner and political levels of solidarity. This confirms hypothesis 3 – that union activism or orientation will be associated with higher levels of solidarity. While union members who identify themselves as working class are positively and significantly associated with increased instrumental and offensive union solidarity (equations 3 and 6), the beta coefficients are relatively low and are significant only at the 5 per cent level. Thus, there is no evidence that those who explicitly identify themselves as working class are more likely to be higher on all three levels of solidarity (hypothesis 4), though there is a relatively weak relationship between identifying with the working class and increased instrumental and offensive union solidarity.

Turning to the organisational control measures, employee commitment as measured by the extent to which employees feel part of the company, make extra efforts on the company's behalf and remain with the company was negatively associated with "them and us" attitudes and the necessity for a union to protect workers. However, higher levels of commitment are positively associated with instrumental solidarity, that is, the extent to which members feel the union represents their interests on issues such as pay and working conditions (equation 3). Finally, as equations 1 and 2 indicate, organisations experiencing higher levels of conflict are more likely to have higher levels of solidarity particularly at the group and wage-earner levels.

SUMMARY

In the compositional group, hierarchical position (occupation) affects all three levels of solidarity. However, using the distinction between unskilled/semi-skilled and routine white-collar workers, the predominant effect is the positive association of the former group with wage-earner solidarity. Organisational controls, measured here by levels of commitment and conflict, mostly affect levels of group solidarity and defensive union solidarity. Lastly, the extent to which union members identify with their union has a positive effect on all three levels of solidarity, while class identity has a minimal impact. We can evaluate the relative impact of the compositional, organisational controls and union/class measures on each of the levels of solidarity by comparing the additional variance (see the added R^2 in Table 7.4) added in each step of the equations in Table 7.4. Organisational controls explain more of the variance in levels of group solidarity than any other factors. The variance in wage-earner solidarity is predominantly explained by union activism which also explains more of the variance in levels of political solidarity.

CONCLUSION

There are a number of difficulties regarding the interpretation of our results. First, solidarity is an abstract concept and can only be measured indirectly through a survey instrument. The measures we have used as indicators of the level and strength solidarity are, therefore, indirect and exploratory and based on the work of Bild and Madsen (1997). At the group level, the intensity of solidarity is measured by the extent of members' perceptions of a "them and us" divide. Wage-earner level solidarity is measured by the degree to which members regard a union as necessary in their workplace, as the best representative and means of advancing their interests. Lastly, political solidarity is measured by members' perceptions of inequality and the fairness of the distribution of rewards in society. This latter indicator is relatively weak as it fails to measure or identify attachment to a labour or social democratic political party. Nevertheless, the former two indicators of solidarity we consider to be sufficiently robust.

Secondly, as it is a single union survey caution must be exercised in applying the findings generally to members in other unions. Moreover, the paucity of evidence on solidarity in other unions creates further difficulties in applying the results to a wider community. On our measures of solidarity at group, union and political level, the evidence from the survey of the Amalgamated Transport and General Workers Union would suggest a high level of solidarity across the three levels. For example, 79 per cent of respondents registered a strong sense of "them and us" between workers and management, up to 90 per cent of respondents believed a union was essential in their firm, 76 per cent believed that improvements in work could be achieved through trade union action and 83 per cent did not believe that the rewards in Irish society are fairly distributed according to contribution.

However, a common denominator in studies of trade unions has been the level of union activism. In our survey, there is a strong correlation between the three levels of solidarity and union activism. If, as we have already suggested, levels of solidarity are high among ATGWU members surveyed, it would follow that higher levels of activism could be expected. Indeed, there is evidence that the level of activism in the ATGWU is higher than that recorded in similar surveys using similar measures (Table 7.5). The mean for union activism in the ATGWU is substantially higher than that found in a number of previous surveys using a similar measure of activism (Nicholson et al., 1981; Fosh and Cohen, 1990; Flood, 1991) of union activism studies.

Table 7.5: Union Activism in Four Surveys

Union activism is scored from 1=reluctant members to 5=ideological activists	ATGWU Survey (1998)	Flood (1991)	Nicholson et al. (1981)	Fosh & Cohen (1990)
Mean of Union Activism	2.98	2.57	2.46	2.44
Standard Deviation	1.2	1.19	0.98	0.99
N	588	706	2019	70

Source

Flood, P. (1991) "Membership Involvement and Union Attachment: An opinion survey of the Irish Transport and General Workers Union", *Irish Business and Administrative Research*, Vol. 12: 67–78.

Nicholson N., Blyton P. and Ursell G. (1981) *The Dynamics of White Collar Trade Unionism*, Academic Press. Nicholson et al. surveyed a branch of the National and Local Government Officers Association (a white-collar union). Survey respondents were composed of 20% senior grades, 33% middle grades and 47% lower grades.

The data in Fosh P. and Cohen S. (1990), "Local Trade Unionists in Action: Patterns of Union Democracy" is from a survey of car assembly workers. Their paper is in P. Fosh and E. Heery (1990) *Trade Unions and their Members: Studies in Union Democracy and Organisation*, London: Macmillan.

A possible explanation for the higher levels of activism in the ATGWU may lie in the nature of this general union's leadership style. For example, a study of state sector unions in the UK identified union leadership style as an important factor in the development of active forms of workplace unionism (Fairbrother, 1996: 111–112). In a study of white-collar workers in Australia and Britain, Deery and Walsh (1997) found that increasing levels of effectiveness, efficiency and performance of a union could enhance an individual's collectivist orientations. The ATGWU has consistently taken a comparatively militant stance regarding social partnership or national wage agreements. It has been suggested that ideologies of partnership, such as those sponsored by the ICTU at national and firm level can weaken the perception of conflicting interests, the legitimacy of conflict and so erode both the willingness and capacity of members to resist or challenge the employer's demands (Marchington, 1982; Kelly, 1996). Furthermore, reliance on employer sponsorship and co-operation with consultative and advisory institutions can weaken or inhibit the growth of workplace union organisation and of any capacity to mobilise the union's membership for action against the employer (Kelly, 1996: 101). The critical though pragmatic position adopted by the leadership of the ATGWU regarding national partnership may have prevented such developments within the union and account for the higher levels of membership activism. If classes are fragmenting, though this is debatable (see Esping-Anderson, 1999), the evidence from our survey provides little support for its supposed corrosive effect on worker solidarity.

Multivariate analysis was used to test for the consequences of the supposed class fragmentation and increased individualism on worker solidarity. The characteristics associated with the change from an industrial society to a post-Fordist or post-industrial society such as the disappearance of the old smoke stack and mass production industries, the switch from the production of goods to the production of knowledge as the core driving principle of the economy and the accompanying shift to the service sector employment are held to undermine traditional worker and union solidarities. In particular, it was predicted that if such changes were undermining solidarity it would be most evident in the attitudes and perceptions of younger workers who are free of the experience and memories of harsher exploitative working conditions and the prevailing adversarial industrial relations of the time. Metaphors such as the "Frontier of Control", "them and us", "digging in" and "wage offensive" were apt descriptions of the old industrial relations but inappropriate to the new economy (see Dunn, 1990). However, the results here do not support any change in solidarity between young and older workers. Perceptions of a "them and us" divide between management and workers were equally strong in younger workers compared to older workers. Indeed, younger workers reported higher levels of union solidarity measured by the necessity of a union to protect workers from arbitrary management actions.

The dramatic shift towards the service sector and the expansion of white-collar work is also a factor held to foster the diffusion of individualism at the expense of traditional class solidarities. It was predicted that unskilled and semi-skilled blue-collar workers would exhibit higher levels of group, wage earner and political solidarity than routine white-collar workers. There was partial support for this position as blue-collar workers had significantly higher levels of wage earner solidarity, but there was no difference between the two groups regarding levels of group and political solidarity.

The extent to which members identify or are active in their union (activism) is significantly and positively associated with all the measures of solidarity, but is particularly strong for wage-earner and political levels of solidarity. Thus, the extent of member activism is one indicator of the trend in the strength of worker solidarity. This evidence from the ATGWU cautions any generalisation concerning a decline in worker solidarity.

Finally, it can be argued that solidarity is an active construct and not simply a passive historical outcome. The high levels of solidarity evident in the ATGWU may be partly determined by workers experience inside the firm, but is also due to the nature of the union structure and leadership policies. Consequently, it can be argued that members' solidarity is not just a function of impersonal socio-economic factors such as those associated with increasing individualisation and structural change. Worker solidarity is a process arising from a recognition of the common and conflicting interests that characterise the employment relationship. A crucial factor in the development of solidarity is the perceived legitimacy of workplace opposition that can be promoted or retarded by the policy and practice of particular unions.

APPENDIX

Table 7A: Description of Dependent Variables

	Mean	SD	N
1. Group Solidarity I feel that workers and management are on opposite sides in my firm.	3.76	1.06	571
There is a strong sense of "them and us" between workers and management in this firm. (Both are scored 1=strongly disagree to 5=strongly agree.)	3.96	0.99	572
2. Wage Earner Solidarity **(a) Union solidarity** A union is not necessary in this company because management treat workers fairly (Scored 1=strongly agree to 5=strongly disagree).	4.22	0.9	574
If there was no union in this firm management would take greater advantage of the workforce (Scored 1=strongly disagree to 5=strongly agree.)	4.29	0.87	577
(b) Instrumental solidarity Who represents your interests in the following areas: • PAY ISSUES	0.74	0.44	602
• JOB SECURITY	0.66	0.47	602
• PENSIONS	0.59	0.49	602
• WORKING CONDITIONS (Scored 1=union; 0=other, i.e. management, nobody or the respondent themselves.)	0.64	0.48	602
(c) Offensive wage earner solidarity Improvements in terms and conditions at work will only be achieved through trade union action (Scored 1=strongly disagree to 5=strongly agree.)	3.7	1.08	573
(d) Offensive union solidarity It is only through trade union activity that higher standards of living are achieved (Scored 1=strongly disagree to 5=strongly agree.)	3.52	1.11	579
3. Defensive Political Solidarity Everybody in Irish society is fairly rewarded for the contribution they make.	1.93	1.0	574
The unequal distribution of wealth in Ireland is a fair result given the contribution made by each particular class.	2.28	1.16	571
The poor are largely to blame for their poverty.	1.89	1.04	578
It is very important to reduce the gap between rich and poor. (Scored 1=strongly disagree to 5=strongly agree.) (The last question is scored in reverse.)	1.63	0.85	525

Table 7B: Independent Variables

		Mean	SD
	Workforce Characteristics		
Age	1=15-25 years to 5=56+ years	3.12	1.05
Gender	1=male; 0=female	0.81	0.39
Occupation Level	1=semi-skilled; 2=skilled craft; 3=technician; 4=administrative; 5=supervisory; 6=professional; 7=managerial	2.24	1.71
Manual/Non-Manual divide	1=unskilled/semi-skilled and skilled; 0=routine white collar workers	0.76	0.43
	Organisational Climate		
Organisational Commitment	Commitment is a composite variable combining three questions: (1) I feel myself to be part of this company (2) In my work I like to feel I am making some effort not just for myself but for the company as well (3) The offer of a bit more money with another employer in my locality with similar work would seriously make me think of changing my job: 1=strongly disagree to 5=strongly agree. (Question 3 is reverse scored.)	9.67	2.56
Conflict	Conflict is measured by the frequency of disputes: 1=daily to 8=never	5.11	2.05
	Union/Class		
Union Activism	Union activism is measured using Nicholson et al.'s (1981) five categories of orientation: 1=reluctant members; 2=card carriers; 3=selective activists; 4=apolitical stalwarts; 5=ideological activists	2.98	1.2
Union Position	1=ordinary union member; 2=shop steward in the past; 3=shop steward at present	1.35	0.67
Class Identity	Respondents were asked to select what class they identified with: 1=working class; 0=other (middle class; no class; no opinion)	0.53	0.5

Table 7C: Correlation Matrix of Independent Variables

	1	2	3	4	5	6	7	8	9	10	11	12	13	14	15
1. Age	1.0														
2. Gender	.16**	1.0													
3. Occupation	-.08*	-.03	1.0												
4. Commit	.19**	-.03	.22**	1.0											
5. Initiatives	.08	.09*	-.09*	.16**	1.0										
6. Conflict	.13**	.14**	.14**	.3**	-.07	1.0									
7. Activism	.05	-.004	.06	.14**	.01	.04	1.0								
8. Position	.12**	.09*	.07	.15**	.04	.01	.4**	1.0							
9. Class	.09*	.15**	-.35**	-.16**	-.002	-.13**	-.07	.02	1.0						
10. Man. divide	.05	.09*	-.93**	-.11*	.03	-.16**	-.05	-.03	.23**	1.0					
11. Group sol.	-.02	.02	-.19**	-.39**	-.07	-.3**	.06	-.02	.14**	.1*	1.0				
12. Union sol.	-.1*	.04	-.15**	-.17**	-.02	-.18**	.17**	.1*	.03	.11*	.39**	1.0			
13. Instrum. sol	.09*	.08	-.12**	.17**	.01	.1*	.32**	.15**	.1*	.03	.07	.17**	1.0		
14. Wage sol.	-.01	-.01	-.17**	-.04	.002	-.05	.21**	.14**	.1*	.08	.21**	.26**	.34**	1.0	
15. Political sol.	.04	-.04	.13**	.08	.00	.06	-.13**	-.04	-.02	-.02	-.17**	-.28**	-.1*	-.15**	1.0
16. Off. Union	.15**	.07	.16**	.05	-.01	-.02	.27**	.2**	.13**	.08	.16**	.21**	.39**	.57**	-.07

Significance levels: * < .05   ** < .01

REFERENCES

Bain, G., Coates, D. and Ellis, V. (1973) *Social Stratification and Trade Unionism*. London: Heinemann.

Beck, U. (1987) "Beyond Status and Class: Will There be an Individualised Class Society?" in Meja, V., Misgeld, D. and Stehr, N. (eds) *Modern German Sociology*. New York: Columbia University Press.

Bild,T. and Madsen, M. (1997) "Wage Earner Solidarity – Moribund or Changing?" in D'Art, D. and Turner, T. (eds) *Collectivism and Individualism: Trends and Prospects*. Dublin: Oak Tree Press.

Clark, T. and Lipset, S. (1991) "Are Social Classes Dying?" *International Sociology*, Vol. 4: 297–410.

Clark, T., Lipset, S. and Rempel, M. (1993) "The Declining Political Significance of Class" *International Sociology*, Vol. 3: 293–316.

Clarkson, J. D. (1970) *Labour and Nationalism in Ireland*. New York: AMS Press.

Deery, S. and Walsh, J. (1997) "Collectivist Work Attitudes: Their Causes and Effects on Union Responsibility and Industrial Militancy" in D'Art, D. and Turner, T. (eds) *Collectivism and Individualism: Trends and Prospects*. Dublin: Oak Tree Press.

Dunn, S. (1990) "Root Metaphor in the Old and New Industrial Relations" *British Journal of Industrial Relations*, Vol. 28: 1 March.

Elvander, N. (1974) "In Search of New Relationships: Parties, Unions and Salaried Employees' Associations in Sweden" *Industrial and Labour Relations Review*, Vol. 28, No. 1.

Esping-Anderson, G. (1999) "Politics without Class? Postindustrial Cleavages in Europe and America" in Kitschelt, H., Lange, P., Marks, G. and Stephens, J. (eds) *Continuity and Change in Contemporary Capitalism*. Cambridge: Cambridge University Press.

Fairbrother, P. (1996) "Workplace Trade Unionism in the State Sector" in Ackers, P., Smith, C. and Smith, P. (eds) *The New Workplace and Trade Unionism*. London: Routledge.

Fantasia, R. (1989) *Cultures of Solidarity: Consciousness, Action and Contemporary American Workers*. Berkley: University of California Press

Flood, P., Turner, T. and Willman, P. (1996) "Union Presence, Union Service and the Emergence of Union Activism" *British Journal of Industrial Relations*, Vol. 34, No. 3:415–433.

Fosh, P. and Cohen, S. (1990) *Trade Unions and Their Members: Studies in Union Democracy and Organisation*. London: Macmillan.

Fox, A. (1974). *Man Mismanagement*. London: Hutchinson.

Hartley, J. (1992) "Joining a Trade Union" in Hartley, J. and Stephenson, G. (eds) *Employment Relations*. Oxford: Blackwell

Hoggart, R. (1967) *The Uses of Literacy*. London: Chatto and Windus.

Hyman, R. and Price, R. (1983) (eds) *The New Working Class? White Collar Workers and their Organisations*. London: Macmillan.

Kelly, J. (1996) "Union Militancy and Social Partnership" in Ackers, P., Smith, C. and Smith, P. (eds) *The New Workplace and Trade Unionism*. London: Routledge.

Kelly, K. and Breinlinger, S. (1996) *The Social Psychology of Collective Action*. London: Taylor and Francis.

Lash, S. and Urry, J. (1987) *The End of Organised Capitalism*. Oxford: Polity Press Blackwell.

Lockwood, D. (1966) *The Blackcoated Worker*. London: Allen and Unwin.

Marchington, M. (1982) *Managing Industrial Relations*. London: McGraw Hill.

Nicholson, N., Blydon, P. and Urnell, G. (1981) *The Dynamics of White Collar Trade Unionism*. London: Academic Press.

Poole, M. (1984) *Theories of Trade Unionism*. London: Routledge and Kegan Paul.

Salaman, M. (1998) *Industrial Relations: Theory and Practice*. London: Prentice Hall.

Streek, W. (1993) "The Rise and Decline of Neo-Corporatism" in Ulman, L., Eichangreen, B. and Dickens, W. T. (eds) *Labour and an Integrated Europe*. Washington DC: The Brookings Institution.

Stevenson, J. (1991) "Early Trade Unionism: Radicalism and Respectability" in Pimlott, B. and Cook, C. (eds) *Trade Union in British Politics: The First 250 Years*. London and New York: Longman.

Sverke, M. and Sjoberg, A. (1994) "Dual Commitment to Company and Union in Sweden: An Examination of Predictors and Taxonomic Split Methods" *Economic and Industrial Democracy*, Vol. 15: 531–564.

Taylor, A. J. (1989) *Trade Union and Politics: A Comparative Introduction*. London: Macmillan.

Thompson, E. P. (1967) "Time, Work and Industrial Capitalism" *Past and Present*, Vol. 38: 56–97.

Tilton, T. A. (1979) "A Swedish Road to Socialism: Ernst Wigforss and the Ideological Foundations of Swedish Social Democracy" *American Political Science Review*, Vol. 73.

Valkenburg, B. "Individualization and Soldiarity: The Challenge of Modernization" in Leisink, P., Van Leemput, J. and Vilrokx, J. (eds) *The Challenges to Trade Unions in Europe*. Cheltenham: Edward Elgar.

Visser, J. (1995) "Trade Unions from a Comparative Perspective" in Van Ruysseveldt, J., Huiskamp, R. and van Hoof, J. (eds) *Comparative Industrial and Employment Relations*. London: Sage Publications.

Webb, S. and B. (1894) *The History of Trade Unionism*. London: Longmans.

Zoll, R. (1996) "Modernization, Trade Unions and Solidarity" in Leisink, P., Van Leemput, J. and Vilrokx, J. (eds) *The Challenges to Trade Unions in Europe*. Cheltenham: Edward Elgar.

CHAPTER 8

The Industrial Relations Act 1990: A Critical Review[1]

JOE WALLACE AND MICHELLE O'SULLIVAN

INTRODUCTION

The enactment of the Industrial Relations Act 1990 brought significant changes to both trade disputes law and the institutional provisions for dispute resolution in the State. The changes in trade disputes law were the first major changes since the passage of the Trade Disputes Act 1906 while the institutional changes amended the Industrial Relations Acts 1946 and 1969. This chapter sets out to critically review the Act after over ten years in operation, with the focus being to examine it against the objectives set down when the Act was introduced. While there is limited research available from the workplace on the impact of the changes contained in the 1990 Act, published records of the Labour Relations Commission and the Labour Court do make it possible to reach at least tentative conclusions on the impact and operation of the Act. These findings chiefly revolve around the institutional provisions but in other areas the effects of the Act are still unclear. There is only limited research on the perspectives of union officials and the experiences of shop stewards and ordinary union members is unresearched. Neither is there any extensive empirical research among employers on the use, or non-use, of the trade disputes or institutional provisions in collective bargaining situations and the perceived effects that the Act has had. Accordingly, it is hoped that this chapter will identify areas for further research.

The chapter is divided into three sections and sets out to evaluate the 1990 Act along a number of dimensions. The first section outlines the main changes to trade disputes law and evaluates the operation of these provisions to date. As the trade disputes law has traditionally been the most fraught area of the relationship between trade unions and the law, the main focus in this section is on the implications of the trade disputes provisions for trade unions. The second section addresses the changes to the institutional arrangements

---

1. This is an extended version of a paper that appeared in *Croner's Employee Relations Review* (Wallace, J. and McDonnell, C., 2000). We are grateful for permission to reproduce certain sections of this article. We would also like to acknowledge the research contribution to the chapter of Conor McDonnell, former Teaching Assistant, University of Limerick. The normal disclaimer applies.

and evaluates progress to date against the objectives established at the time the Act was introduced. Finally, the third section examines the overall impact of the Act on strike patterns to see if any effects on strikes are detectable following the introduction of the Act.

SECTION ONE

TRADE DISPUTES AND THE INDUSTRIAL RELATIONS ACT 1990

When introducing the Industrial Relations Act 1990 the Minister for Labour, Bertie Ahern, said he wished "to put in place an improved framework for the conduct of industrial relations and for the resolution of trade disputes [with] the overall aim ... to maintain a stable and orderly industrial relations climate" (Department of Labour, 1991: 1). In so doing, the Minister claimed that he had the objective of keeping the law out of industrial relations. He recognised that a complete consensus "as to what the legislative framework should contain would not be possible" and that he had sought to address the major issues and "devise arrangements which would be workable and which both sides could live with" (Department of Labour, 1991: 5). A general objective of the new Act was to remedy the defects of case law, which, it was claimed, had arisen around the Trade Disputes Act 1906. The Minister for Labour argued that:

> ... the law had become extraordinarily complex and its precise limits were vague and confusing. The usefulness of statute law in providing a guide to conduct had diminished and it was increasingly necessary to look to case law (Department of Labour, 1991: 4).

Thus, the explicit objectives of the trade disputes provisions were: to provide clarity in the law; to keep case law out of industrial relations as far as possible; and to mark off "the boundaries of what is permissible in trade disputes situations" (Department of Labour, 1991: 4). It is against these objectives that the evaluation of the trade disputes provisions of the Act is undertaken.

THE TRADE DISPUTES PROVISIONS

The trade disputes provisions re-enact a number of the original provisions of the Trade Disputes Act 1906, while limiting some immunities and placing certain obligations on trade unions. The following are some of the main provisions:

1. Section 9 withdraws immunities from any form of industrial action in individual disputes which are in breach of agreed procedures contained either in writing or in custom or in practice.

2. Provisions for picketing are both clarified and restricted in Section 11.
   - Picketing is lawful at a place where one works or carries on business or, where this is not practical, at the approaches to the place of work.
   - Limitations are placed on whom workers can picket. Specifically, workers may only "picket their employer".
   - Secondary action will only enjoy immunity if the secondary employer is seeking to frustrate the industrial action by directly assisting the workers' employer.[2] Normal commercial activity would not meet this criterion.

3. Immunities previously available under the Trades Disputes Act 1906 in relation to conspiracy and combination were re-enacted without any amendments.

4. Under Section 13, the former blanket immunity, which trade unions enjoyed from the law of tort under Section 4 of the Trade Disputes Act 1906, was restricted to situations where trade unions were "acting in contemplation or furtherance of a trade dispute" – the golden formula.

5. Under Section 14, trade unions were required to incorporate provisions for a secret ballot into union rulebooks. These require that a secret ballot be conducted in the event of any form of industrial action. Immunities were withdrawn from industrial action where a majority of workers had voted against such action in a secret ballot.

6. The immunities in the Trade Disputes Act 1906 formerly available to disputes between workmen and workmen, that is inter union disputes, were withdrawn.

7. Limitations were placed on the granting of *ex parte* injunctions where a secret ballot in favour of industrial action had been held and where seven days notice of such action had been given to an employer. Interlocutory injunctions were not to be available to an employer where, in addition to the two previous requirements, the union established that it was "acting in contemplation or furtherance of a trade dispute". This was the chief balancing measure in the Act of benefit to the trade unions and was a response to union complaints at the ease with which employers could previously gain injunctions.

The Debate on the Trade Disputes Provisions

The trade disputes provisions have been the most controversial part of the 1990 Act. Prior to its introduction, the Bill was criticised because of the individual disputes provisions. Attention was drawn to the limitations, which

---

2. Secondary action is allowed unlike the situation in the UK, where Section 4 of the Employment Act 1990 withdrew immunity from all secondary action. It is, however, more restricted than it had been under Section 17 of the earlier Employment Act 1980.

Section 9 of the Act placed on the possibility of supporting fellow workers in dismissal cases, especially where shop stewards were involved (Rabbitte and Gilmore, 1990). By requiring that individual disputes be processed through agreed procedures, the probability of such disputes becoming the subject of industrial action is greatly reduced. This is especially so in the case of dismissals where the length of time it would take to exhaust procedures makes the prospect of industrial action, subsequent to a final third party determination, in support of a dismissed worker improbable. In essence, this tends to substitute procedural and legal regulation of issues, such as dismissals, in place of collective solidarity.

While direct evidence is limited, it would seem that the limitation on individual disputes has not been as great a concern in practice as anticipated in the Rabbitte and Gilmore critique. Section 9 has not featured in a major way in the leading cases that have arisen which may be due, in part, to the body of legislation that was in place prior to the 1990 Act and that had already substantially proceduralised individual cases.[3]

A Comparative Perspective on the Trade Disputes Provisions

The provisions of the 1990 Act mirror some of the provisions of the early Thatcher Government legislation in the UK Employments Acts 1980 and 1982. These include limits on secondary action, secondary picketing, picketing in support of a closed shop and requirements for secret ballots. This list shows the similarities with Irish law as embodied in the 1990 Act or, in the case of picketing in support of the closed shop, as previously decided in constitutional cases (see *The Educational Company of Ireland Ltd. and Others v Fitzpatrick and Others* (1961) and *Meskell v CIE* (1973)). In some instances, the 1990 Act went even further than the early UK legislation. Thus, there was not just a requirement for secret ballots but also a requirement that this be incorporated in the trade union rules. This was a departure from the principle laid down in the Trade Union Act 1871 that unions be free to determine their own rules. Also, the provision on secondary action required unions to be able to prove that the secondary employer had sought to directly frustrate the strike, a more restrictive requirement than under Section 17 of the 1980 Employment Act, which was described by Meenan (1991: 10) as establishing "a very high onus" of proof. Subsequently, the UK legislation has been extended well beyond the provisions of the 1990 Act and, as is shown below, the outcome of the appeal

---

3. In effect, the provision in Section 9 of the Act can be seen as a partial adoption of the principle of a distinction between disputes of rights and disputes of interests, a distinction which the Commission of Inquiry on Industrial Relations (1981: 229) had advocated should be adopted in Irish law. Disputes of rights (for instance over a dismissal or equality issue) were, the Commission asserted, in principle arbitrable and the immunities for industrial action should not be available as a result. Disputes of interests (for example disputes over wages) were, on the other hand, held not to be arbitrable, and as such would attract immunities.

in the Nolan Transport case would seem to have limited the possibility of successful actions in tort against Irish unions.

The Trade Disputes Provisions in Action

Post the introduction of the 1990 Act, a number of leading cases have arisen which have seen the law involved in industrial relations in a way not seen since prior to the passage of the Trade Disputes Act 1906.[4] By far the most important case has been that of *Nolan Transport (Oaklands) Limited v Halligan and Others* (1994) and the subsequent appeal of that case to the Supreme Court, on which judgment was delivered in 1998. This case involved the issue of union recognition in a small transport company and the alleged dismissal of two employees.[5] The issue of the operation of procedures did not arise, as there were no procedures in existence and the employer refused to recognise the trade union – the Services Industrial Professional and Technical Union (SIPTU). The key issues in the outcome of the case revolved around the conduct of the ballot for strike action and the question of the existence of a trade dispute. The High Court found that the ballot conducted in the case was fraudulent and that no trade dispute existed, as the real reason for the dispute was an attempt by the union to gain recognition, not the alleged dismissals. SIPTU, Ireland's largest union, was fined IR£600,000 and was also found liable for costs. Taken together, this amounted to some IR£1.3m in 1994 and by the time of an appeal to the Supreme Court in 1998, the costs and damages, including interest charges, were estimated to have reached over IR£2.0m. To many, there were strong parallels with the Taff Vale (1901) case.

Following the 1994 High Court decision in the Nolan Transport case, the 1990 Act was the subject of debate at a number of union conferences. In general, this debate focused around two key points: (1) the belief that political undertakings, given prior to the introduction of the Act, had not been honoured and (2) the attitude of the judiciary to trade unions. The following quotes give a sense of this debate. Jimmy Somers (former General President, SIPTU) at

---

4. Among some of the cases are the following: *McNamara & Co. Ltd v Building & Allied Trades Union* (1991); *Iarnrod Eireann v Darby & O'Connor* (1991); *Westman Holdings Ltd v McCormack and Irish National Union of Vintners, Grocers and Allied Trades Assistants (INUVGATA)* (1991); *River Valley Projects Ltd v Strutt* (1991); *G&T Crampton v BATU and Others* (1997); *Loftus and Bredin v Ulster Bank Limited* (1994-1995).

5. This case initially involved the alleged dismissal of two employees, suggesting that this was a "dispute of rights" type case. However, other issues emerged at trial, including the assertion by the employer that the real purpose of the dispute was an attempt by SIPTU to gain union recognition. While the Commission of Inquiry on Industrial Relations (1981) classified such disputes as "disputes of rights", Prondzynski and McCarthy (1982:231) suggested that there was no clearer example of a "dispute of interest" than a recognition dispute and remarked "it is difficult to see how such disputes are justicable in any substantive way". In essence, the Nolan Transport case illustrates the difficulties that could arise if a full "disputes of rights" and "disputes of interest" distinction were to be introduced into Irish law.

the 1995 ICTU Biennial Delegate Conference noted that the Courts had interpreted and applied the Act in a manner inconsistent with assurances given to Congress [ICTU], which had been repeated in the Dáil and Seanad during the passage of the Bill (ICTU, 1995: 60). He listed the assurances as follows:

1. Only an aggrieved member of a trade union could mount a legal challenge to the outcome of a secret ballot.

2. The availability of the immunities under the Act is not dependent on the holding of a secret ballot.

3. A legal action could not be taken against a trade union arising from its activities in contemplation or furtherance of a trade dispute.

4. *Ex parte* interim injunctions would not be granted in trade dispute cases where a ballot had been held and adequate notice served on the employer.

5. A change in the name or corporate identity of a company could not render unlawful continued picketing in furtherance of a pre-existing dispute.

Brian Anderson of the Manufacturing Science and Finance Union (MSF) laid blame on the judiciary:

> … judges aren't subjected to democratic control. They don't have to consult. They are not up in front of the electorate to justify their office. They are a law unto themselves. They don't have to pay heed to promises made by politicians or governments. They have the power to create law, judges' law. Such laws are invariably in favour of employers and opposed to the needs of workers (ICTU, 1995: 63).

Such comments echo trade union views in the period between 1895 and the enactment of the Trade Disputes Act 1906. For example, trade unions lamented the series of judicial decisions in *Lyons v Wilkins* (1896–1899), complaining that the protection for picketing contained in Section 7 of the Conspiracy and Protection of Property Act 1875 had been nullified by the finding that even peaceful picketing to persuade workers not to work constituted "watching and besetting" (Saville, 1967: 347). Similar points were made following the Taff Vale case, which reversed the previous belief that "since trade unions were not legally constituted corporations they could not be sued for damages" (Saville, 1967: 347). Thus, it can be seen that debates at union conferences tended to coalesce around the issue of the attitude of the judiciary and the failure to deliver on politically-based promises. Less prevalent was a consideration of the reintroduction of elements of the common law which historically regarded trade unions as illegal conspiracies and continues to do so. Any limiting of the immunities in the former Trade Disputes Act 1906 allows for the importation of individualist common-law concepts, which have the potential to be inimical to the collective values of trade unions.

NOLAN TRANSPORT: THE SUPREME COURT JUDGMENT

As early as 1991, Wilkinson (1991: 21) argued that the Industrial Relations Act 1990 had "a restrictive rather than reformative effect" and that it "acted to the detriment of trade unions". Kerr (1991: 256), however, took a different view arguing that the effects of the Act were dependant on the "judiciary's attitude" and interpretation of the balloting provisions and that it was too early to argue that the Act was inimical to the interests of trade unions. The issues highlighted by Kerr were, in fact, to prove crucial in the Supreme Court appeal in the Nolan Transport case. The Court differed with the views of Justice Barron in the High Court case and found that the employees "at the very least, had good grounds for thinking themselves dismissed", that a trade dispute did exist and that the immunities were available to the trade union as it was acting in contemplation or furtherance of a trade dispute. Following the Supreme Court decision, an assertion of a hostile judiciary seems difficult to sustain. Justice O'Flaherty even went so far as to assert that "the whole point of the Industrial Relations Act 1990 was ... to copper fasten the special privileges of trade unions in many respects and to give them additional rights" (p. 3). While it may be difficult to sustain a view of judicial hostility, the assertion in relation to "additional rights" is somewhat mysterious, as the specific rights accorded to trade unions were not enumerated. As noted previously, neither the Conspiracy and Protection of Property Act 1875 nor the Trade Disputes Act 1906 conferred rights on trade unions but granted immunities to actions which would otherwise have been actionable under the law of criminal or civil conspiracy. The Minister for Labour, Ruairí Quinn, had launched proposals for the introduction of a positive-rights approach in 1985, which were further developed in a discussion document in 1986, but these were not proceeded with, largely because of a lukewarm trade union response. With the rejection of the positive-rights approach, the general thrust of the 1990 Act continued the immunities-based approach.

The Nolan Transport Case in Context

While the outcome of the Supreme Court appeal in the Nolan Transport (1998) case was greeted with a sigh of relief by trade unions generally, there has been limited analysis of the residual effect of either the judgment or the overall impact of the Act. This is especially true of the trade union movement which, perhaps understandably, seems now to have lost interest in debating the effects of the trade disputes provisions. Nonetheless, such an evaluation is desirable in order to establish the "rules of engagement" in future disputes and the continuing effect of the Act. It is also important that analysis and debate take place among industrial relations practitioners and not just the legal profession, as to do otherwise risks creeping juridification of industrial relations, something that the 1990 Act was meant to avoid.

It is not clear that the issues highlighted, in relation to the political undertakings outlined above, have been resolved by the Supreme Court decision in a way that would give effect to the promises which it was claimed had been made. The decision does not "prevent the taking of legal action against a trade union arising from its activities in contemplation or furtherance of a trade dispute" but means that if the trade union can establish it had a reasonable belief that it was acting in contemplation or furtherance of a trade dispute, this will provide a defence against such action. If followed in future cases, the Supreme Court decision provides a facilitative interpretation of the requirement on a trade union to establish that it was acting in "contemplation or furtherance of a trade dispute".

While there was agreement in the Supreme Court that the immunities under the Act were not dependant on the holding of a secret ballot, Justice O'Flaherty argued "this irregular ballot led to a lot of trouble ... and many days were spent on it in the High Court. The union cannot avoid blame for that".[6] This led to the possibility "that the union, having won the case, would have to pay costs of £700,000" (O'Keeffe, 1998: 350). In the event, SIPTU decided not to seek its costs and, O'Keeffe (1998: 350) notes, "the Court prudently held that each side should bear its own costs". There are thus at least some potential financial implications hanging over trade unions from a failure to hold a ballot that complies with Section 14 of the 1990 Act.

There are also implications for the protection against injunctions contained in Section 19 of the 1990 Act. While the Supreme Court judgment found that the proper penalty for a trade union which persistently disregarded the outcome of a ballot was the loss of its negotiating license, this is unlikely to have major significance. The prospect of unions persistently failing to comply with balloting requirements seems remote. Much more important is an obligation, following the Nolan Transport decision, to be able to prove that the balloting provisions were complied with in order to be able to enjoy protection in Section 19(2) of the 1990 Act against injunctions. In his judgment, Justice Murphy (p. 38) suggested that "the onus lies on the party resisting an application for an interlocutory injunction to show that a secret ballot as envisaged by Section 14 has been held". Therefore, it is not sufficient for a union to conduct a ballot but it must also be able to prove that it has done so. Justice Murphy (p. 38) went on to argue that the rules of trade unions should be amended not just to ensure that ballots are conducted in accordance with the requirements of Section 14 "but also under professional and independent guidance which will guarantee that all appropriate conditions are complied with and facilitate the union in proving that such was the case". O'Keeffe (1998: 35) argues that such a system is to be hoped for, *"if it would lay to rest the difficulties* [emphasis

---

6. The Supreme Court rejected other grounds of appeal, including one that the Court should reject the findings of fact by Justice Barron, in the High Court, in relation to the credibility of the union witnesses and the conduct of the ballot. While the majority opinion in the case declined to overturn the High Court's finding of fact that the ballot was fraudulent, it is noteworthy that Justice O'Flaherty's comment that the ballot was a "shambles", implies, not a fraudulent ballot, but one badly conducted.

added] which emerged in Nolan and G&T Crampton, and check any such tendencies to accede to employers' requests to scrutinise the ballot in search of irregularities".

In seeking to require that trade unions provide for professional evaluation and inspection of ballots, procedures are being suggested which go beyond the explicit provisions of the 1990 Act. It remains to be seen to what extent trade unions will be prepared, or able in all cases, to comply with the suggestion advanced in the Supreme Court decision. If they do not do so, apart from the restrictions on the granting of *ex parte* injunctions, the effect would be to remove the limitations to granting an injunction and restore the law on injunctions substantially to the position that existed prior to the 1990 Act. The criteria to be applied would be whether the applicant had made a fair case and, if so, where the balance of convenience lay. In *G&T Crampton v Building and Allied Trade Union (BATU)* (1997), these issues arose and the trade union was unable to prevent an injunction because it could not prove that a ballot had been held which complied with the requirements of Section 14 of the 1990 Act. On the other hand, in the Nolan Transport case the trade union involved found itself entrammelled with the law in a way that caused obvious difficulties, but the case was not resolved in favour of the employer.

In the Nolan Transport case, Justice O'Flaherty drew attention to the conduct of both parties, with particular reference to the refusal to use the institutional mechanisms provided by the State. "I am afraid that both employers and striking employees conducted themselves in a manner best calculated to bring about the maximum degree of misunderstanding ... [A]ny form of conciliation, arbitration, or dispute resolution was zealously avoided" (p. 2). While not amounting to an introduction of a mandatory requirement to use the institutions, the comments suggest that the Courts could have regard to the refusal of a party to use the institutions, thus implying the possibility of negative inferences being drawn from the refusal. If developed further, this could have greater implications for employers in approaching disputes in future, as employers, especially in recognition disputes, have been reluctant to use the institutions as they have seen this as conferring *de facto* recognition.

Empirical Evidence on the Operation of the 1990 Act

Preliminary evidence from a pilot survey of union officials at Branch Secretary level or higher, conducted by Wallace and Delany (1997: 114) prior to the Nolan Transport 1998 decision, suggests a strongly negative assessment by those officials of the impact of the trade disputes provisions of the Act (Table 8.1). Seventy three per cent of union officials thought "the 1990 Act was a mistake which should not have been accepted in its current form and which needs major amendment or repeal". The findings indicated the continued importance of injunctions as a further eight indicated they had experienced the initiation of legal action to seek an injunction.

Table 8.1: Attitude of Union Officials to the Industrial Relations Act 1990

	No.	%
The 1990 Act was a necessary development in ensuring responsible trade unionism	1	3
There are minor difficulties with the Act which should be ironed out	5	17
The Act is not perfect but unions should learn to work it properly and live with it	2	7
The 1990 Act was a mistake which should not have been accepted in its current form and which needs major amendment or repeal	22	73

N = 30

Source: Wallace and Delany (1997).

In the Nolan Transport case, Justice O'Flaherty (p. 1) in the Supreme Court saw the balloting provisions as being "designed to strengthen the role of union management against the actions of maverick members ... ".[7] However, further replies to that survey suggest that it is the official trade union structure and not unofficial groups that is the main target of employer attention (Wallace and Delany, 1997: 112). Thus, 57 per cent of union officials reported experience of employers threatening to use the 1990 Act against the trade union itself while 39 per cent experienced the Act being threatened against union officials and 35 per cent against shop stewards or union committee members (Table 8.2). A threat to sue the union under the law of tort had been experienced by 57 per cent of union officials. On many occasions, this threat seems to be used by employers in an attempt to get leverage in negotiations, as only two union officials reported that they had experience of an employer initiating a claim for damages. Thus, just because employers can resort to the law by no means implies that they will do so. They may, as noted in the early days of the UK legislation, just use the law to "reinforce rather than undermine the 'rules of the game' with the union" (Evans, 1985: 134). McIlroy (1991: 95) notes that in the UK "the number of cases provides only a crude measure of the influence of the new laws on industrial relations as it neglects the degree to which an awareness of the legislation, or fear that it would be used or the threat that it would be used, led trade unions and employers to change their behaviour".

---

7. Brown et al. (1997: 75) note that the UK legislation was introduced with the stated intention "to make unions more accountable to their members". They note that instead of this being achieved, "research suggests it strengthened the national leadership of unions" (Brown et al. 1997: 75).

The general effect in Ireland, in the absence of a wide scale survey, is a matter of conjecture. In the UK it is worth noting that the balloting provisions have not led to more moderate outcomes in strike ballots. Brown et al. (1997: 77) note some 92 per cent of ballots for strike action are carried and they suggest that formal ballots may even increase the likelihood of a vote for industrial action. They suggest that ballots may "be used as a cheap substitute for action" with strikes actually occurring in only a minority of cases.

Table 8.2: Groups Against whom the Employer Threatened the use of the 1990 Act

	No.	%*
Ordinary workers	10	44
Unofficial groups	7	30
Shop stewards/union committee members	9	39
Paid union officials	8	35
The trade union itself	13	57

N = 23

*Totals add to more than 100% due to multi-responses.

Source: Wallace and Delany (1997).

These survey results predate the Nolan Transport 1998 decision and the major issue for the future is how the provisions of the 1990 Act will work in the light of that decision. The "demonstration effect" of important cases has been of major significance in the UK (McIlroy, 1991). While the outcome of the Nolan Transport case undoubtedly brought substantial relief to trade unions, a consideration of the judgment suggests that the stated objectives of keeping the law out of industrial relations, and removing case law, are far from having been achieved. Indeed, it is questionable how the latter objective could ever have been attained, given the fact that all legislation is subject to judicial interpretation. The narrow technical basis for the decision in the Nolan Transport case, the unresolved issues of legal interpretation, legal ambiguities and the apparent differences between the judges in their reasoning are illustrative of the continued and even greater importance of case law post the Industrial Relations Act 1990. The recognition in the Nolan Transport Supreme Court decision of the "special place of trade unions" sits uneasily with the hostility to collective organisations of workers, which is at the heart of the common law system, and it remains to be seen how this will work itself out. If unions continue to have to defend themselves in front of the courts this will be costly and will interfere with the effectiveness of industrial action. Alternatively, the courts may wish to avoid becoming embroiled in industrial relations minutiae and the law may recede into the background, leading to a situation not substantially dissimilar to that pertaining under the Trade Disputes Act 1906.

SECTION TWO

THE INDUSTRIAL RELATIONS ACT 1990:
THE NEW INSTITUTIONAL ARRANGEMENTS

The main institutional change was the establishment of the Labour Relations Commission (LRC) and the transfer of a number of functions previously performed by the Labour Court or the Department of Labour to the new body. In summary, the following were the main institutional changes:

- Establishment of the LRC.

- Separation of the Labour Court from the LRC.

- Transfer of the conciliation service and equality service from the Labour Court to the LRC (in 1999 the equality officers and responsibility for provision of an equality service were transferred to the Office of the Director of Equality Investigations).

- Assignment to the LRC of a number of functions:
    - Responsibility for drafting codes of practice
    - Provisions for the conduct or commissioning of research
    - Provisions for monitoring industrial relations (a function previously conducted within the Department of Labour).

- Transfer of the rights commissioners from the Department of Labour to the LRC.

- The establishment of an advisory service within the LRC.

In the round, the structural differences between the arrangements previously in place and those established under the 1990 Act seem in many regards to be minimal and are of an evolutionary nature. The conciliation service was maintained and continues to be staffed by industrial relations officers; rights commissioners continued in operation to hear cases not concerned with pay and conditions of a group of workers; a distinct equality service was retained as was the monitoring service. The most important new initiative was the creation of an advisory service designed to pre-empt disputes and to address long standing industrial relations difficulties within organisations.

The general acceptance of the institutional provisions, and the absence of subsequent controversy attached to them, has meant that they are only now being subject to detailed study. There is a general impression, created by the public pronouncements of politicians and arising from LRC reports, that the new arrangements are working well and achieving their objectives, but an objective evaluation of this impression is necessary. Any starting point for evaluating the institutional provisions must commence, as with the trade disputes provisions, with the objectives that were set down for the 1990 Act when it was being introduced. The key objectives which the new arrangements were meant to achieve were the following:

1. Promote the local settlement of disputes.

2. Restore the Labour Court as a "court of last resort".

Essentially, these objectives involved reducing the reliance of the industrial relations system on institutional intervention and sought to require parties to take greater ownership for the settlement of disputes. In addition to the two objectives above, the LRC has, since its foundation, promoted a greater settlement of disputes at conciliation. Indeed, this objective follows directly from the effort to restore the Labour Court as a court of last resort, although the achievement of a greater level of settlement at conciliation would not, of itself, guarantee a lower case load for the Labour Court.[8] It follows that an examination of the settlement level at conciliation is desirable.

LOCAL LEVEL SETTLEMENTS

In 1991, the first Chief Executive of the LRC, Kieran Mulvey (1991: 5), wrote, "the clear intention of the Act is to change the almost automatic reference to the [Labour] Court". However, this policy was not new. In the 1980s, John Horgan, then Chairman of the Labour Court, noted the failure of one of the original intentions of the Industrial Relations Act 1946, namely that unions and employers would only use the Labour Court in rare instances (Horgan, 1989: 194). Reducing reliance on the Labour Court was a policy pursued by the Court from about 1985 and, as such, predated the Industrial Relations Act 1990. It was noted in the Labour Court Annual Report (1985: 2) that there had been an increase in the conciliation settlement rate, which was seen as "a welcome trend which the Court will encourage wherever possible because it brings home to both management and workers that the primary responsibility over the settlement of disputes lies with the parties themselves". If there were evidence of a major rise in local level settlement of disputes after 1990 this would indicate that one of the major objectives of the 1990 Act had been achieved. Some difficulties exist in testing for such an outcome. Most crucially, data is not collected on the level of local settlements so any test for a greater level of settlement at this level has to rely on indirect proxy measures. A useful proxy for an increase in local settlements is to examine the number of

8. For instance, if there were a larger number of cases being referred to conciliation or if a higher number of cases were being referred directly to the Court (under Section 20.1 of the Industrial Relations Act 1969 or Section 26.5 of the Industrial Relations Act 1990).

cases proceeding to conciliation since the commencement of the operation of the new institutional arrangements in January 1991 and to compare them to the number of cases being referred to conciliation prior to this. When reviewing the statistics it is necessary to have some pre-determined criterion against which to judge any change. It seems reasonable to require that a substantial reduction in cases being referred to conciliation would need to have taken place in order to conclude that the new institutional arrangements have met the objectives for promoting local settlements. Smaller variations would be indicative of only minor changes or could be due to variations caused by other factors, such as the different terms of national agreements.

The annual average number of cases which the LRC reports were referred to conciliation, in the years 1991–2000, was 1,740. While this represents a very slight decrease on the 1980s average of 1,755 cases, disaggregating the figures shows that a decrease had already been evident in the years 1986–1990. The average annual number of disputes in which conciliation conferences were held in the period 1981–1985 was 1,860 while the comparable number for the years 1986–1990 was 1,650 (Table 8.3 and Table 8A).

Unfortunately the figures reported by the LRC from 1991 are not directly comparable with those previously published by the Labour Court. The Labour Court reported figures for "the number of disputes in which conciliation conferences were held" while the LRC figures, in some years, include in addition "cases in which direct contact was made with the conciliation service", for example telephone calls (interview Ray McGee, Head of the LRC conciliation service, 1999). This has the effect of somewhat overstating the extent of the resort to conciliation since 1990 and the comparable figures for referrals to conciliation may be less in some years. This does not, however, affect the general order of magnitude of the usage of conciliation. The number of direct referrals counted in any year seems to have been at most 120 and this may not have applied in all of the ten years covering 1991–2000.[9] In terms of the general order of magnitude, the number of comparable referrals to conciliation, in the years 1991–2000, is on a par with those pertaining in 1986–1990 prior to the transfer of that function to the LRC. The figures in Table 8.3 further show that there has been a major rise in the utilisation of conciliation since the 1960s. Thus, it is possible to conclude that a high degree of utilisation of the conciliation service continues post the new institutional arrangements embodied in the 1990 Act. Furthermore, it is clear that there has been no return to the much lower levels of utilisation that pertained prior to the major jump in usage, which occurred in the 1970s. Taken together these findings provide no support for the hypothesis that the Industrial Relations Act 1990 has promoted any substantially greater settlement of issues at local level.

---

9. It has not been possible to establish the actual number of comparable referrals, excluding the "direct contact" category.

Table 8.3: Disputes at Conciliation: Yearly Averages for Ten Yearly Intervals*

Time Period	Conciliation Cases *Average per annum*
(1946–1950)	146
1951–1960	180
1961–1970	417
1971–1980	1047
1981–1990	1755
(1981–1985)	1860
(1986–1990)	1650
1991–2000	1740

* Five-yearly averages in brackets for certain time periods.

Source: Labour Court and LRC Annual Reports.

SETTLEMENT LEVELS AT CONCILIATION

By contrast with the findings in the previous section, there is evidence of a higher settlement rate at conciliation itself. The average annual percentage settlement rate at conciliation in the years 1971–1980 was 56.5 per cent, rising to an annual average of 62 per cent in the years 1981–1990 and to an annual average settlement level of 76.7 per cent (based on Labour Court data) in the period 1991–2000 (Table 8.4). The LRC figure for settlement at conciliation (78.2 per cent) for the period 1991–2000 is somewhat inflated due to the inclusion in the figures of cases where "direct contact" was made with the LRC and not just cases in which conciliation conferences were held – the protocol previously used by the Labour Court. By definition cases where "direct contact" are made do not proceed to full conciliation hearings and, as such, these cases result in a 100 per cent settlement rate. This has the effect of inflating the settlement rates achieved by the conciliation service, under the LRC, by comparison with the previous Labour Court settlement rates. The extent of the inflation is unlikely to be in excess of two percentage points and may be less than one percentage point, suggesting a settlement rate in excess of 76.2 per cent but less than 78.2 per cent.[10] A further correction needs to be made, as Labour Court figures for the number of referrals from conciliation are higher than the reported LRC figures. The Labour Court figures are preferred because they are consistent with the reporting protocol in place prior to 1991, thus ensuring comparability. The Labour Court figures give an annual average settlement level for the period 1991–2000 of 76.7 per cent. Adjusting this figure to take into account "direct contact" cases by the LRC gives a

---

10. This figure is used imputing a figure of 120 direct contacts per annum.

likely settlement level of greater than 74.7 per cent but less than 76.7 per cent. Even the lower figure is well in excess of the figure of 68.6 per cent attained in the five-year period prior to the 1990 Act (1986–1990) and is even higher than the previous highest annual average of 72.6 per cent for the ten-year period 1961–1970 (Table 8.4). Based on the published data, this greater level of settlement at conciliation is the single-most significant change occurring since the LRC took over responsibility for the conciliation service. It is an improvement that would be most expected on an *a priori* basis as the conciliation service can exercise direct control over efforts to achieve a settlement. If the data is correct, there is a strong case that this improvement is due to the operation of the new institutional arrangements in the 1990 Act, although other possible influences, such as a weaker labour movement and greater social consensus/partnership, cannot be ruled out. However, as the next section shows, the greater settlement level achieved at conciliation has not been followed by an equivalent reduction in the caseload of the Labour Court since 1991.

Table 8.4: Annual Average Conciliation Settlement Levels 1951–2000

Years	Percentage Annual Average Settlement Levels for Period
1951–1960	67.0
1961–1970	72.6
1971–1980	56.6
1981–1990	62.0
1991–2000	76.7* (78.2)

*This statistic is compiled using Labour Court reported figures for referrals to conciliation and is preferred to the LRC reported figures (statistic from those in brackets) as they are directly comparable to the figures prior to 1991.

Source: Derived from Labour Court and LRC Annual Reports.

RETURN OF THE LABOUR COURT TO A "COURT OF LAST RESORT"

The term "court of last resort" can have a number of meanings. A purely technical meaning refers to the Labour Court being the final arbiter in a trade dispute and that cases heard by it should not be the subject of any further hearing by, for example, the LRC.[11] A more fundamental meaning, in terms

---

11. The Labour Court and the LRC have signed a protocol formalising this "court of last resort" aspect of the Industrial Relations Act 1990, to ensure that the Labour Court would be the final arbiter in cases.

of the stated objectives of the Industrial Relations Act 1990, is that there should be a significant reduction in the usage of the Labour Court to resolve industrial disputes and that it should only be used as a last resort. Cases may be referred to the Labour Court from a number of sources, including from the conciliation service of the LRC. There has been a discernible reduction in the number of recommendations (excluding those referred under Irish equality legislation)[12] being issued by the Labour Court since 1985.[13] The levels since 1990 have been around 400 to 600 recommendations per annum by comparison with 900 to 800 in the years 1985–1987. The main reductions, however, occurred in the years 1987–1990 (from 827 to 522 recommendations respectively) and so predate the transfer of functions to the LRC under the terms of the Industrial Relations Act 1990, which only took effect in January 1991. There was even an increase in the number of recommendations issued by the Labour Court in the years 1991–1993 following an unusually low level in 1990. The low 1990 figure was due to technicalities concerned with the transfer of functions from the Labour Court to the LRC, which resulted in a number of cases not being counted by either body.

The current level of recommendations of over 400, although lower than in the 1980s, is high by historical standards and even exceeds the annual average levels for the years 1970–1980, which was 358, and in no way approaches the annual average of 118 for the years 1961–1970. There is no sign of the number of Labour Court recommendations declining to that of the 1960s. Thus, as measured by the usage of the Labour Court, the Irish system of industrial relations continues to be categorised by a high degree of reliance on institutional usage. The limited achievement of the objective of returning the Labour Court to a "court of last resort" is emphasised by the statement by the Chairman of the Labour Court, Finbar Flood, that "the use of the Court as a staging post on the negotiation highway continues to be of concern" (Labour Court, 2000: 6).

---

12. It is, of course, necessary to deduct cases going to the Labour Court under the equality Acts in order to exclude the effects of any increase in the workload of the Labour Court due to that legislation.
13. The figures for conciliation cases and for Labour Court recommendations do not include third party intervention carried out by the private sector (LRC, 1996: 8). As such cases do not show up in the official figures, they underestimate the extent of third party intervention. Any substitution of the State mediation and adjudication services, by private sector services, reduces the extent to which the objective of increased local settlements has been achieved and any reduction in Labour Court cases would be a hollow victory. Referring to the growth in private conciliators, the LRC (1996: 8) states that it is "concerned that this practice might, in the long term, diminish the value and effectiveness of the current dispute-settling process".

THE ADVISORY, DEVELOPMENT AND RESEARCH SERVICE (THE ADVISORY SERVICE)

The introduction of the advisory service of the LRC was an innovative measure and had previously been suggested by a number of reports and industrial relations commentators. It was a much more substantial measure than those contained in the Industrial Relations Act 1969, where the renaming of the conciliation officers to industrial relations officers (IROs) was intended to presage a more proactive role for those officers than they had previously. The reasoning behind the establishment of the advisory service, according to the then Minister for Labour, Bertie Ahern (Dáil Debates, 1990: 372), was that there were some firms using the conciliation service of the Labour Court regularly and it was clear that there were underlying problems which needed to be addressed in a more fundamental manner. There was an initial decline in frequent user referrals from 497 referrals in 1993 to 295 referrals in 1995, indicating an apparent early success for this approach. Since 1995, however, the numbers of these have increased and surpassed the level of 1993 in both 1999 (644 referrals) and 2000 (560 referrals). Looking at frequent user referrals as a percentage of total conciliation referrals, a similar but even more accentuated pattern emerges, with the figure in 2000 (30 per cent) exceeding the 1993 figure of 27 per cent. In addition, there has been a steep rise in the utilisation of the rights commissioner service between 1998 and 2000 (from 233 to 844 referrals) by those designated as frequent users. It is clear from these figures that the objective set down in the 1990 Act in relation to frequent use of third parties has not been fulfilled.

SECTION THREE

The analysis in the previous section was conducted around an examination of the published data on the operation of the changes in the institutional arrangements brought about by the Industrial Relations Act 1990. In general, that analysis did not disclose any substantial transformation to industrial relations nor, with the exception of the greater settlement level at conciliation, did it provide evidence that the objectives set out for the new institutional arrangements had been achieved. Of course, it may be that such an examination, conducted as it is at a micro level around the mechanisms of the institutional arrangements, could miss a transformative effect. In order to detect any such effect, it is necessary to examine the combined effects of both the trade disputes and the institutional provisions of the legislation. The most readily available measures are the published strike statistics, notably the number of strikes and the number of working days lost. While strike statistics are only one of a number of measures of the state of industrial relations, they are the most commonly used. Furthermore, strike levels had been a concern of Irish policy makers since the 1960s and the measures in the Industrial Relations Act 1990 seem to have been targeted at strikes.

The obvious procedure to test for any effect is to examine the Irish strike record both before and after the introduction of the Act. In principle, there are methodological difficulties in conducting such an examination, with the most significant being the potential influence of other variables. Brown et al. (1997: 78) note "that there has been a world-wide decline in strike incidence, suggesting economic and political influences common to many advanced economies". They note that a chief development has been the fragmentation of bargaining systems, leading to a reduction in the "industrial basis of trade union power, tying the interests of union organisations to those of individual employers" (Brown et al., 1997: 69). This, they claim, can be principally attributed to the trend, evident in most industrialised countries, of "the internationalisation of product markets, which diminishes the advantages of national industry based collective bargaining" (Brown et al., 1997: 69; see also Brown and Walsh, 1994). As these changes work to produce similar effects to the intentions for legislation, such as reducing strikes, this creates a difficulty in evaluating the effects of that legislation. In the Irish case the development of the system of consensus industrial relations/social partnership, which has been quite different to the situation in Great Britain, also needs to be taken into account in any evaluation.

Fortunately, the influence of other variables does not cause as many difficulties as might be imagined. The other major variables, such as social partnership and a decline in trade union influence at the workplace (see Gunnigle et al., 1994: 22), can be posited as also causing strikes to decline. The timing of any reduction should point to which variable was most likely responsible for a particular effect. Thus, although it may not be possible to disentangle the effects of any one variable, a significant reduction in strike statistics – post the introduction of the Industrial Relations Act 1990 – could indicate that it had brought about major changes. Finally, by examining the strike record of Ireland and comparing it to other countries, one should be able to detect a greater decline in Irish strike levels than in those countries in which major legislative changes were not introduced.

An examination of the strike statistics pre and post the Industrial Relations Act 1990 disposes of some ill-founded assertions of the impact of the Act. For example, O'Keeffe (1998: 348) notes "that many credit the recent upturn in the economy to the Act … ". Given the limited impact of the institutional changes on dispute processing, evidence for the correctness of such assertions needs to be found elsewhere, with a reduction in strike levels being the most obvious development to look for. While it is certainly correct that Irish strike levels and working days lost have declined dramatically since the 1970s, a cursory examination of strike data shows that the decline in strikes and working days lost predated the introduction of the Industrial Relations Act 1990 (Figures 8.1 and 8.2). The data is so clear as to require little elaboration, although it is worth noting that most of the decline also predated the emergence of the consensus industrial relations associated with the return to centralised bargaining in late 1987.

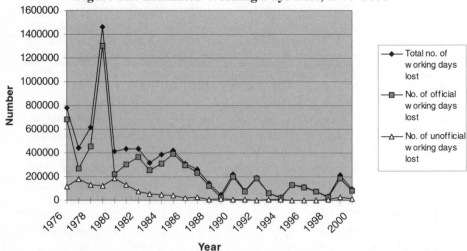

Figure 8.1: Number of Industrial Disputes, 1976–2000[14]

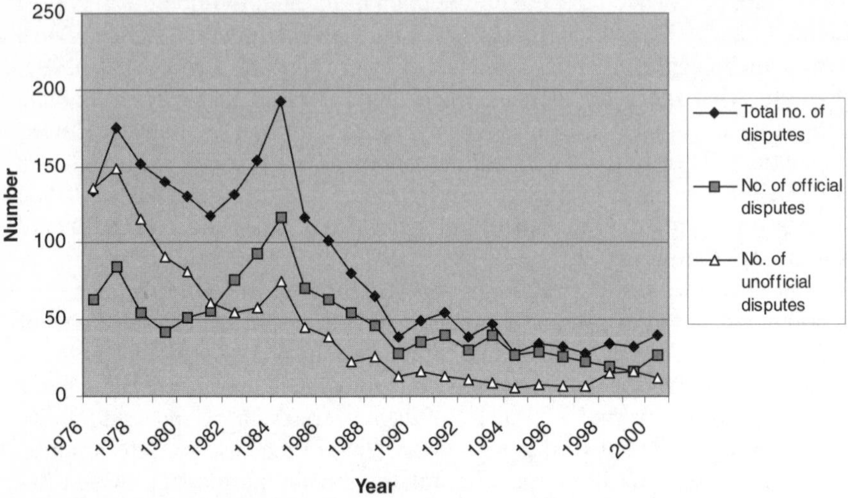

Source: 1975–1981 data from Wallace and O'Shea 1987; 1982–1995 data from Department of Labour Annual Reports; 1996–2000 data from CSO sent directly.

Figure 8.2: Estimated Working Days Lost, 1976–2000[15]

Source: 1975–1981 data from Wallace and O'Shea 1987; 1982–1995 data from Department of Labour Annual Reports; 1996–2000 data from CSO sent directly.

14. There are a number of discrepancies in Fig. 8.1 and Fig. 8.2 due to differences in the figures obtained from the Department of Labour and Central Statistics Office (CSO). This does not affect the general order of magnitude or the conclusions.
15. In Fig. 8.1 and Fig. 8.2, there was one dispute in 2000, which for simplicity, was included as an official dispute but also involved unofficial action. It accounted for 1,250 working days lost.

The decline in unofficial strikes in the period 1984–1989 is especially marked (Figure 8.1), with the decline in working days lost, which commenced in 1980, having already reached extremely low levels by 1986 (Figure 8.2). This was again prior to the first of the current round of centralised agreements – the Programme for National Recovery. Despite the 1990 Act, there has been somewhat of a resurgence of unofficial strikes in the years 1997–2000 inclusive, although the levels are nowhere near those of the 1970s or early 1980s. Working days lost in such strikes have also increased slightly in the years 1997–2000 but they are still well below days lost in official strikes. This represents a continuation, in the 1990s, of the traditional greater contribution which official strikes have made to working days lost due to strikes (Wallace and O'Shea, 1987). In fact, the traditional phenomenon of the vast bulk of working days lost in any one year being due to a small number of official strikes also continued in the 1990s (see Kelly and Brannick, 1983: 69). There were, however, even fewer such large strikes than in the three decades prior to the 1990s.

While there has been a major reduction in strikes and associated working days lost in Ireland since the mid 1980s, it is the change relative to other developed countries which is of special interest, as this could indicate specific factors at work in Ireland. This is the procedure adopted by Brown et al. (1997: 78) for the UK, where they note, "the implications for any distinctive effect of British legislation are ... muted". Table 8.5 contains data on the comparative working days lost per thousand employees in the OECD. This is the best measure for international comparison as it standardises for the number of employees in an economy and is less likely to be affected by inaccuracies in the collection of strike statistics, which tend to miss smaller strikes, and differences in the number of strikes counted.[16] The figures in Table 8.5 chart the decline in Irish working days lost for three five-year periods, commencing in 1981, and for a four-year period 1996–1999. Irish working days lost nearly halved in the period 1986–1990 when compared to the preceding five-year period but Ireland's rank order position only dropped by one place from fifth highest to sixth highest. There was a continued decline in days lost in the five-year period 1991–1995, which was again part of a general international decline. In that period, Ireland's rank order dropped again by one place from sixth to seventh highest. This seventh position was not maintained, however, as Ireland returned to fifth highest position in the OECD in the four-year period 1996–1999. This makes it difficult to sustain a case for any significant effect on working days lost arising from the Industrial Relations Act 1990. What may

16. There are significant differences in data collection across countries, which create difficulties in making international comparisons. An examination of trends over time is less open to difficulties provided the differences in data collection remain constant. However, the US figure is of limited usefulness for comparative purposes as that country only counts working days lost in strikes involving a thousand or more workers (Office for National Statistics, April 2000: 153).

be more surprising is the very limited evidence of any substantial relative decline arising from the consensus industrial relations/social partnership approach.

Table 8.5: International Comparison of Annual Average Working Days Lost per 1000 Employees, 1981–1999

Country	1981–1985	1986–1990	1991–1995	1996–1999
Australia	386	224	130	92
Austria	2	2	6	2
Belgium	n.a.	(48)	32	24
Canada	532	429	159	241
Denmark	306	41	45	357
Finland	326	410	218	37
France	78	111	94	56
Germany	52	5	17	2
Greece	516	6316	1148	29 (1996–1998)
Ireland	474 (5th highest)	242 (6th highest)	109 (7th highest)	95 (5th highest)
Italy	774	315	183	81
Japan	10	5	(3)	2
Netherlands	24	13	33	5
Norway	58	142	62	106
Portugal	176	82	34	23
Spain	584	602	469	157
Sweden	40	134	50	12
Switzerland	n.s.	n.s.	1	3
United Kingdom	440	137	24	22
United States	128	82	42	35

Notes: Brackets indicate averages based on incomplete data; n.a. = not available; n.s. = less than five days lost per thousand. Some figures have been estimated.

Source: 1981–1995 data from Brown et al., 1997: 78, 1996–1999 data from Office for National Statistics, April 2000 and 2001.

CONCLUSION

The foregoing data make it difficult to establish a case that the Industrial Relations Act 1990 has achieved the objectives set down when it was introduced. The evidence is of a country which has a high usage of third parties, something the 1990 Act sought to reduce. This raises the question "why does institutional usage remain high?" The most likely reason is the greater proceduralisation of industrial relations since the 1960s (see Wallace and McDonnell, 1999). Procedure agreements are now widespread (see Murray, 1984) and these procedures invariably contain a "disputes clause" requiring parties to exhaust procedures prior to engaging in any form of industrial action. This development, which has its foundation in one of the principle recommendations of the UK Donovan Commission (1968), is arguably the main workplace development in Irish industrial relations in the last 30 years. The objectives in the Industrial Relations Act 1990, to return the Labour Court to being a "court of last resort" and to encourage greater local settlement of disputes, run directly counter to the proceduralisation of industrial relations. There is strong normative support, from both employer organisations and trade unions, for the requirement that disputes be referred to the Labour Court prior to notice of any form of industrial action being served. Pressure was exerted by the Labour Court for lesser reliance on third parties from about 1985 and this achieved a measure of success, probably in combination with the emerging move to more consensus industrial relations. But the requirement for processing issues through procedures is likely to place some limit on the extent to which a reduction in the usage of third parties is possible. That limit may well have been reached prior to, or around the time of, the introduction of the 1990 Act.

None of this should be taken to imply criticism of the institutions themselves. The available evidence supports an interpretation of an institutional framework that has widespread acceptance and seems to work most of the time for the participants to industrial relations. What is in question is the extent to which the institutional objectives of the Industrial Relations Act 1990 have been realised. Most of the evidence points to trends which were in place prior to the introduction of the Act and which have now levelled out. The most significant effect of the institutional changes associated with the Industrial Relations Act 1990 is the significantly higher settlement level at conciliation, although even this is over-stated by the published LRC figures. This apart, the emerging evidence indicates that the objectives underlying the institutional provisions of the Industrial Relations Act 1990 have not been achieved or, at least, that any improvements cannot be attributed to the Act. The most that might be claimed for the 1990 Act is that it may have cemented the trends which had taken place in the 1980s.

Neither, when rigorously examined, is it possible to sustain a case for any major impact on the incidence of strikes arising from the Act. In the area of trade disputes, the law has again been active in industrial relations in a way not seen since Taff Vale. The Supreme Court decision in the Nolan Transport case has, however, taken the heat out of the controversy which had surrounded the trade disputes provisions from shortly after the 1990 Act was introduced. The technical nature of the decision in that case does not seem to dispose of a number of the complaints made by trade unions of a failure to honour undertakings given to them prior to the introduction of the Act. In the medium term, the outcome of the Nolan Transport case has led to the acceptance of the Act and there is now no discernible campaign for change from either employers or trade unions. In this there is a paradox, as the essence of the decision which has given rise to acceptance lies in the finding that the immunities were available to trade unions. This is, of course, a decision based on the general principle underlying the much-criticised Trade Disputes Act 1906. It remains to be seen, however, if the narrow and technical nature of the interpretation will in the long run be sufficient to keep the law out of industrial relations. To date, at least, case law has not been removed from industrial relations as envisaged in the objectives for the 1990 Act; rather the case law, currently dominated by Nolan Transport, has set a different precedent to that of Taff Vale. Further cases may either reinforce this legal abstentionism or may erode it. General social, political and economic developments may be as important in determining the route which is followed as the assurances given when the Act was introduced or the strict logical interpretation of the text.

APPENDIX

Table 8A: Conciliation Service Case Load and Settlement Levels for the Republic of Ireland from 1946–2000

Year	Number of Disputes in which Conciliation Conferences were held	Number and Percentage of Disputes settled at Conciliation	
1946–47	166	105	63%
1947–48	228	153	67%
1949	135	81	60%
1950	102	66	65%
1951	157	111	71%
1952	169	134	79%
1953	143	94	66%
1954	166	110	66%
1955	188	135	72%
1956	173	116	67%
1957	191	119	62%
1958	226	136	60%
1959	191	125	65%
1960	197	122	62%
1961	211	151	72%
1962	300	214	71%
1963	337	238	71%
1964	388	282	73%
1965	450	289	64%
1966	429	300	70%
1967	532	377	71%
1968	546	408	75%
1969	414	327	79%
1970	564	451	80%
1971	628	429	68%
1972	713	443	62%
1973	855	487	57%
1974	951	646	68%
1975	1108	576	52%
1976	1071	581	54%
1977	1175	638	54%
1978	1288	651	51%
1979	1301	634	49%
1980	1379	693	50%
1981	1582	756	48%
1982	1855	923	50%
1983	2090	1113	53%
1984	1750	1037	59%
1985	2021	1355	67%
1986	1892	1268	67%
1987	1787	1151	64%
1988	1571	1064	68%
1989	1450	1019	70%
1990	1552	1143	74%
1991	1880	1598	85% (85%)[+]
1992	1935	1451	75% (73%)[+]
1993	1884	1338*	71% (69%)[+]
1994	1551	1028	66% (66%)[+]
1995	1692	1184	70% (67%)[+]
1996	1487	1204*	81% (78%)[+]
1997	1588	1318*	83% (82%)[+]
1998	1563	1286*	82% (81%)[+]
1999	1923	1615*	84% (83%)[+]
2000	1899	1614*	85% (83%)[+]

*These figures have been calculated from the rounded percentage figure and as such are approximations. The LRC figures from 1991 for number of disputes settled at conciliation include for some, or all of the years 1991 to 2000, cases settled by direct contact in addition to those settled at conciliation conferences.
[+]Figures in brackets indicate settlement rates using Labour Court reported figures for referrals to conciliation.

Source: Labour Court and LRC Annual Reports.

REFERENCES

Brown, W., Deakin, S. and Ryan, P. (1997) "The Effects of British Industrial Relations Legislation 1979–1997" *National Institute Economic Review*, No. 161: 69–83.

Brown, W. A. and Walsh, J. (1994) "Corporate Pay Policies and the Internationalisation of Markets" in Niland, J., Lansbury, R. and Verevis, C. (eds) *The Future of Industrial Relations*. Thousand Oaks: Sage Publications.

Commission of Inquiry on Industrial Relations (1981) *Report of the Commission of Inquiry on Industrial Relations*. Dublin: Stationery Office.

Department of Labour (1991) *Speech by Minister for Labour at Seminar on the Industrial Relations Act, 1990*, organised by The Irish Society for Labour Law. Dublin: Department of Labour, 13 July.

Department of Labour. *Department of Labour Annual Reports*. Dublin: Stationery Office (various).

Evans, S. (1985) "Research Note: The Use of Injunctions in Industrial Disputes" *British Journal of Industrial Relations*, Vol. 23: 131–137.

Gunnigle, P., Flood, P., Morley, M. and Turner, T. (1994) *Continuity and Change in Irish Employee Relations*. Dublin: Oak Tree Press.

Horgan, J. (1989) "The Future of Collective Bargaining" in *Industrial Relations in Ireland: Contemporary Issues and Developments*. Dublin: University College Dublin.

Ireland (1990) *Dáil Éireann Parliamentary Debates Official Report*. Dublin: Stationery Office, Vol. 397: 15 March, (a).

Irish Congress of Trade Unions (1995) *Proceedings of Biennial Delegate Conference*. Dublin: ICTU.

Kelly, A. and Brannick, T. (1983) "The Pattern of Strike Activity in Ireland, 1960–1979" *Irish Business and Administrative Research*, Vol. 5, No. 1: 65–77.

Kerr, T. (1991) "Irish Industrial Relations Legislation Consensus not Compulsion" *Industrial Law Journal*, Vol. 20, No. 4: 240–257.

Labour Court. *Labour Court Annual Reports*. Dublin: The Labour Court (various).

Labour Relations Commission. *Labour Relations Commission Annual Reports 1991–2000*. Dublin: Labour Relations Commission.

McCarthy, C. and von Prondzynski, F. (1982) "The Reform of Industrial Relations" *Administration*, Vol. 29, No. 3: 220–259.

McIlroy, J. (1991) *The Permanent Revolution? Conservative Law and the Trade Unions*. Nottingham: Spokesman.

Meenan, F. (1991) "Industrial Relations Act, 1990: A Commentary on the Disputes Provisions Part 1" *IR Data Bank*, Vol. 9, No. 208: February.

Mulvey, K. (1991) *The Potential Role of the Labour Relations Commission*. Dublin: Irish Association of Industrial Relations.

Murray, S. (1984) *Employee Relations in Irish Private Sector Manufacturing*

Industry. Dublin: Industrial Development Authority.

O'Keeffe, S. (1998) "Industrial Action Ballots in Ireland: Nolan Transport v Halligan and Others" *Industrial Law Journal*, Vol. 27, No. 4: 347–352.

Office for National Statistics (2000) *Labour Market Trends*. Norwich: The Stationery Office, April.

Office for National Statistics (2001) *Labour Market Trends*. Norwich: The Stationery Office, April.

Rabbitte, P. and Gilmore, E. (1990) *Bertie's Bill*. Dublin: The Workers' Party.

Royal Commission on Trade Unions and Employers' Associations. (1968) *Report of the Royal Commission on Trade Unions and Employers' Associations*. London: HMSO, CMND 3623.

Saville, J. (1967) "Trade Unions and Free Labour: The Background to the Taff Vale Decision" in Briggs, A. and Saville, J. (eds) *Essays in Labour History*. London: Macmillan and Co. Ltd.

Wallace, J. and Delany, B. (1997) "Back to the Future? The Irish Industrial Relations Act, 1990" in Meenan, F. (ed.) *Legal Perspectives: The Juridification of the Employment Relationship*. Dublin: Oak Tree Press.

Wallace, J. and McDonnell, C. (1999) *The Institutional Provisions of the Industrial Relations Act 1990 in Operation*. Paper delivered to the Irish Academy of Management, 9–10 September.

Wallace, J. and McDonnell, C. (2000) "Perception and Reality: The Industrial Relations Act 1990" *Employee Relations Review*, No. 12: 20–28.

Wallace, J. and O'Shea, F. (1987) *A Study of Unofficial Strikes in Ireland*. Dublin: Stationery Office.

Wilkinson, B. (1991) "The Irish Industrial Relations Act 1990: Corporatism and Conflict Control" *Industrial Law Journal*, Vol. 20, No. 1: 21–37.

CASES

Educational Company of Ireland Ltd. and Others v Fitzpatrick and Others (1961) IR 323.

G&T Crampton v BATU and Others (1997) ELR 1.

Iarnrod Éireann v Darby & O'Connor (1991) unreported.

Loftus and Bredin v Ulster Bank Limited (1994–1995) 10 JISLL 47.

Lyons (J.) and Sons v Wilkins (1899) 1 CH.

McNamara & Co. Ltd. v Building & Allied Trades Union (1991) unreported.

Meskell v CIE (1973) IR 121.

Nolan Transport (Oaklands) Limited v Halligan and Others (1998) ELR 177.

Nolan Transport (Oaklands) Limited v Halligan and Others (1994–1995) 10 JISLL.

River Valley Projects Ltd v Strutt (1991) unreported.

Taff Vale Railway Co. v Amalgamated Society of Railway Servants (1901) AC 426 (HL).

Westman Holdings Ltd v McCormack and Irish National Union of Vintners, Grocers and Allied Trades Assistants (INUVGATA) (1991) ILRM 833.

CHAPTER 9

Union Restructuring in a Post-Industrial Society

BRENDAN MACPARTLIN

INTRODUCTION

This chapter focuses on the change in Irish trade union structure that resulted from a wave of trade union mergers that took place between 1987 and 1994. The extent of this merger activity is noteworthy as for 70 years the trade union movement had actively sought, without success, to bring about a restructuring of the movement. Our explanation for this merger wave is that trade union strategy changed in response to the demands of a changed economy. The Irish trade union movement changed in the 1980s from a strategy of adversarial bargaining to one of social partner deliberation because of the environment it encountered. To engage in this latter strategy the movement needed a stronger encompassing trade union centre with an appropriately aligned structure. The word "structure" is used in this context to refer to the pattern of trade unions that make up the trade union movement in the Republic of Ireland.

In the first section of this chapter, the rich and variegated, some would say fragmented and fissiparous, structure of the Irish trade union movement in the middle decades of the 20th century is outlined. The source of this variety is that trade unions established themselves, in the first place, in the job territories laid down by the progress of industrialisation. They survive by clinging to their identities but, in the longer term, this presents a barrier to the structuring and restructuring needed to maintain bargaining effectiveness in the constantly changing terrain of capital formation. The Irish trade union movement had unsuccessfully sought to restructure its organisation for almost 70 years before it came about in the late 1980s. The second section outlines the wave of mergers that restructured the movement in 1987–1994 and discusses the question as to whether this was brought about by the conditions of post-industrialism or as a result of the constant search by the trade union movement for unity and cohesion. Section three identifies the pattern of merger decisions taken by individual trade unions. In the history of British and Irish unions there has been a constant low level of merger activity as patterns of industrialisation and unionisation change. There have also been identifiable bursts of merger activity known as merger waves that can be associated with conducive environmental conditions. Finally, the outcome of all this restructuring activity for the Irish movement is assessed. The primary research on which this chapter is based derives from interviews with national trade union leaders. They were the strategic agents of change. Their viewpoint is a privileged frame of reference in this particular set of events.[1]

THE STRUCTURE OF THE IRISH TRADE UNION MOVEMENT

At the beginning of the 20th century, the Irish trade union movement was made up largely of the British craft unions. General unions and breakaway Irish craft unions began to grow rapidly after 1916. The Trade Union (Amalgamation) Act, 1917, relaxed the requirements of a two thirds majority to a 50 per cent majority in membership balloting for trade union mergers. A wave of mergers in the United Kingdom followed during the period 1917–1924 in which small unions were absorbed by larger ones, giving rise to very large unions such as the Transport and General Workers Union (Buchanan, 1974). In 1919, William O'Brien, General Secretary of the Irish Transport and General Workers' Union (ITGWU), proposed to the Irish Trade Union Congress (ITUC) a design for the Irish trade union movement. It envisaged one big union (OBU) with ten industrial divisions operating at local and national levels. Recognising the inadequacies of their current structure, the

---

[1]

	Table: **TRADE UNION MERGERS 1987–1999.**
1988	AGIBSTU and NUWWM to form BATU AUEW(TASS) and ASTMS to form MSF PA into CMU.
1989	PTWU and CUI to form CWU ICEA into CPSU AIT into UPTCS.
1990	ITGWU and FWUI to form SIPTU ICEU into PSEU
1991	UPTCS and LGPSU to form IMPACT TOU into CWU
1992	ETU and NEETU to form TEEU EEPTU and AEU to form AEEU INPDTU into SIPTU NUTGWU(Irl) into SIPTU IMETU into IMPACT
1993	INUVGATA and IDATU to form MANDATE
1997	NIBCAW into BFATWU CMU into CWU AGEMOU into SIPTU
1998	IALPA into IMPACT
1999	MPGWU into SIPTU IPU into SIPTU

delegates of the 1919 ITUC voted in favour of the proposal. The policy was not implemented partly because of the opposition of British craft unions that wished to retain their individual identity.

The question arose again in the 1930s when Ministers of Trade and Commerce Sean Lemass and Sean McEntee took an interest in trade union rationalisation in the context of industrialisation. The ITUC set up a Commission of Inquiry on Trade Union Organisation in 1936. Its outcome was that O'Brien made a proposal to the Annual Delegate Conference of 1939 that was similar to his OBU proposal of 1919. The Conference split into two camps that ultimately led to a breakaway of the Congress of Irish Unions (CIU) in 1944. The failure to restructure led Sean McEntee to introduce the Trade Union Act, 1941, in an attempt to shape trade union organisation, but with little success. In contrast to countries such as Norway and Sweden, Ireland entered the post-World War II era with an unreformed union structure.

Complexity, fragmentation and dissension were characteristic of the Irish trade union structure. Between 1940 and 1962 there were more than one hundred unions catering for a rapidly growing trade union membership. The membership grew from 148,000 to 358,000 between 1940 and 1965. Ireland is unique in having unions based in another jurisdiction operating in its territory. The presence of parallel Irish- and British-based unions competing in the same job territories complicated structure. There was a drop in the percentage of membership in British unions over the post-World War II decades (see Table 9.1). This may be explained by the withdrawal of unions such as the National Union of Railworkers and the National Union of Boot and Shoe Operatives from Ireland. Parallel British- and Irish-based unions continued to operate in the building, woodwork, fitting, engineering and electrical fields. There were British-based unions in the general and white-collar fields too, although they did not necessarily duplicate services. The category "other manual unions" includes single-industry and occupational unions.

Table 9.1 shows a drop in percentage numbers in the membership of craft unions from 1940 onwards, while there was an increase in general unions. In the 1970s the membership of white-collar unions began to increase rapidly while the craft unions declined further. Table 9.2 reveals a large number of unions with memberships of less than 1,500 and only a few unions with memberships of more than 20,000. In 1966 there were 60 unions with less than 1,500 members. This had reduced to 35 unions in 1983. There was a tendency among other sized unions to increase. In 1983 there were three unions with more than 20,000 members. Of these, the ITGWU in 1981 claimed 178,048 members in the Republic out of a total trade union membership of 531,371 (Hardiman, 1988: 129). The five largest unions accounted for about half of the total membership. Research by ICTU in 1961 showed that there were 123 unions in the Republic and 180 in the whole of the island of Ireland.

Table 9.1: Membership Shares by Union Type, Congress Affiliation and Location of Union Headquarters

Membership Composition of Unions in Ireland by Union Type, Congress Affiliation and Nationality				Percentage of Net Membership	
Year	*General Unions*	*White Collar*	*(Ex-)Craft Unions*	*Congress Affiliation*	*British Unions*
1940	45.5	24.1	16.9	13.5	90.0	22.4
1945	44.3	28.6	15.8	11.3	44.0+45.5	21.4
1950	55.3	21.5	14.1	9.2	38.8+53.4	18.0
1955	57.1	20.7	13.4	8.8	39.0+54.5	14.2
1960	57.2	20.9	13.2	8.7	93.6	13.0
1965	55.8	22.0	13.6	8.7	91.4	14.0
1970	52.9	24.9	13.7	8.5	91.3	14.3
1975	48.6	31.3	11.5	8.6	91.1	15.3
1980	49.4	33.7	11.8	5.1	91.0	14.1
1985	45.0	38.4	11.6	5.0	91.4	14.3
1990	46.9	38.9	12.0	2.2	93.7	13.7
1995	46.3	42.1	10.2	1.4	97.4	11.5

Notes
1. Membership of unions with headquarters in the Irish Republic includes a small percentage of Northern Ireland members (varying around 3%). Hence Congress affiliation will be slightly overestimated and a small margin of error is unavoidable in the case of shares of different union types.
2. Includes one union, the National League of the Blind, whose membership comprises both manual and non-manual employees.
3. Net membership excludes Northern Ireland members of unions based in the Republic.
4. Membership shares for 1945, 1959 and 1955 reflect a split within the Trade Union Congress.

Source: DUES Series adapted from Roche and Ashmore (2000).

In an attempt to tackle this fragmentation ICTU set up the Committee on Trade Union Organisation in 1962. Its terms of reference were to consider and make recommendations on the organisation and structure of the movement and the relationship between unions. During a long interactive process the case for restructuring was established and accepted by the officials of the movement. The individual general secretaries, however, while open to absorptions, were not willing to sacrifice the identities of their own unions in order to achieve what was perceived to be the more general good of the movement. The committee deliberated from 1962–1967 and after five years, 25 Committee meetings and two major seminars became defunct. "The trade union movement's own efforts at reorganisation had failed" (Hillery, 1973: 48).

A further attempt was made through the appointment of a consultant from the International Labour Organisation, Johannes Schregle, in the early 1970s.

Table 9.2: Membership of Trade Unions by Union Size

Union Size	1966 Trade Unions	% all M/Ship	1970 Trade Unions	% all M/Ship	1979 Trade Unions	% all M/Ship	1983 Trade Unions	% all M/Ship
< 1,500	60	7.2	54	6.3	43	4.7	35	3.9
1500–3000	16	9.1	17	9.0	16	6.8	16	7.1
3000–5000	6	6.8	10	10.4	6	4.7	7	5.3
5000–10000	10	18.0	9	15.7	8	11.8	7	10.6
10000–15000	1	3.6	3	11.6	9	24.4	7	17.1
15000–20000	2	8.6					3	9.8
>20,000	2	46.7	2	46.9	2	47.6	3	46.3
Total	97	100	95	100	85	100	78	100

Source: Hardiman (1988: 131).

The Schregle report of 1975, *Restructuring of the Irish Trade Union Movement,* found that "a sincere desire for change and knowledge of the various possibilities was there for a long time but that the implementation was not". The union leadership was aware of the need for rationalisation but the rank and file did not share their awareness or desire. Efficiency was the concern of the union leadership while identity was the concern of the rank and file. Efficiency in achieving the members' interests should be the criterion of structure but the meaning of efficiency was changing with the changing context of collective bargaining which at this point took place at national level. Schregle (1975), therefore, proposed a structure based on industrial unionism headed by a national centre with powers stronger than those of the ICTU. In order to achieve this he recommended the appointment of a change agent who, over time, would stimulate unions towards restructuring. Change should be brought about only from within the trade union movement and not by legislation or state intervention. He also recommended that the two main general unions, the ITGWU and the Workers Union of Ireland (WUI), should continue in their attempts to resolve their schism through amalgamation.

The Trade Union (Amalgamation) Act, 1975, was passed on foot of Schregle's report to encourage trade union amalgamations. Four mergers followed. Two small and struggling unions were absorbed into the ITGWU (the Irish Shoe and Leather Workers Union in 1977 and Irish Actors' Equity Association in 1979). Two smaller unions amalgamated in 1979 to form the Irish Woodworkers' Union. In the same year the WUI amalgamated with the Federation of Rural Workers to form the Federated Workers union of Ireland (FWUI).

BARRIERS TO MERGERS

This period of history shows, on the one hand, a general acceptance of the need to restructure but, on the other, individual trade unions presenting barriers to their own merging. If trade unions have a tendency towards unity and solidarity (Hyman, 1975; Cardiff, 1982: 112) and if amalgamations are one expression of this tendency, then the role of barriers to mergers requires some consideration. The two principal factors affecting union mergers emerging from interviews with trade union respondents were the part played by the general secretary and trade union identity. The latter was expressed in terms of the loyalty to a tradition, the fear of losing identity with change and the special fear of small unions about loss of influence. If barriers are viewed as forces impeding the drive of unions to merge, then, following Chaison (1986), it is logical to look for forces called motivators that overcome barriers. The general secretary of a union has been identified in some cases as the main barrier to a merger and in other cases as the strategic mover of a merger. Similarly, union identity may act as a barrier to merger in some situations or a motivator in others.

In the cases where the general secretary acted as a barrier to merger it was to preserve his union's identity. In many other cases it was the strategic action of the general secretary that brought about mergers. Attitudes to a merger depended on the leadership's perception of the balance of advantages and disadvantages of a merger. Those general secretaries who actively sought the mergers of their own unions also went on to be the main agents in a coalition which made the strategic choice for social partnership as well as for the restructuring of the whole trade union movement. This underlines the role of agency in bringing about change in a system.

Fear of "loss of identity" was frequently mentioned as a reason against initiating a merger search. Related reasons in the same category were "tradition" and "fear of change". Identity is based on the shared perceptions, interests and experiences of people with a common purpose who develop a solidarity of preferences and commitments. When people join already existing unions which cover a wide range of interest groups, the perceived common interests are not always concrete and tangible and, hence, solidarity is based on rational rather than felt identity. Such members have different perceptions as to where their interests lie and are more likely to favour mergers. In many unions they voted by large majorities for mergers. To the extent that members can identify themselves with the core values of unions on a value-rational basis, they gain in freedom for action without fear of loss of identity. Identification based on tradition or sentiment, though tangible and concrete, is less flexible and members are straitjacketed by fear of a sell out of principles.

THE IMPETUS FOR CHANGE

The Working Party on Trade Union Organisation was set up in 1984 (The Working Party was replaced by the Review Group set up by ICTU in 1989) with a view to tackling urgently and vigorously the rationalisation of the trade union movement in order to remain relevant to workers and their needs. Two things were different about this attempt. First, pressures from environmental changes were more acute. Growing trends in contracting out, atypical contracts of employment and competition from human resource techniques threatened to change the structure of trade unionism on their own terms. Secondly, the working party provided a coalition of influential union leaders who had power to act as "persuaders" of union mergers. Coalitions are temporary, means-oriented alliances among individuals or groups which, though differing in their goals, come together to control decision making about future domains in which they have a stake (Gamson, 1961). Thompson (1967: 126, 140) gives an account of how individuals in jobs with high discretion form coalitions to get things done when power is widely distributed. This coalition was the principle agent in the strategic choice to enter social partnership and to follow that up with restructuring.

Change in the Business Environment and Union Restructuring

The circumstances which prompted the impetus for change can only be fully understood in the context of the changing economic and political environment of the 1980s. Writers such as Bernstein (1960) suggest that "structural cycles", crises or periods of "fundamental unrest" stimulate "really critical developments in the morphology of trade unions". The period 1981–1987 witnessed a crisis in the environment that demanded the unfreezing of established trade union patterns of interaction in order to achieve new adaptations. Aspects of the environment that were salient in the minds of trade union leaders were found to be: economic recession and adjustment; management's search for competitiveness; the rise of the political right; the reform of industrial relations; public sector spending and industrial relations; developments in the European Union; decline of trade union membership and a sense of crisis. Trade unionists share with other commentators the view that, in Ireland, the period 1981–1987 was a time of crisis characterised by unprecedented unemployment, emigration and company failures. This was a local manifestation of a more general historical transition that is described as a transition from organised to disorganised capitalism (Lash and Urry, 1987), from mass production to flexible accumulation (Piore and Sabel, 1984; Harvey, 1989), from Fordism and Taylorism to new forms of work organisation (O'Hehir and O'Mahoney, 1993). The regime of New Deal politics and Keynesian economics that reigned in the 1935–1979 period favoured collective bargaining and trade union recognition. The political economy of the 1980s became increasingly intractable to union demands and sometimes overtly hostile. Small unions found it difficult to service their members and survive financially and opted to transfer engagements to larger unions. Large unions decreased in membership as job territories declined and the number of full-time employment contracts decreased. The public service unions found themselves insufficiently co-ordinated to counter moves from their employer. Difficulties encountered in organising protests convinced them of the need to rationalise their movement. Trade union leaders observed how British market liberalism attacked trade unionism. When the opportunity to join in social partnership arose with the new government in 1987 it was a welcome breathing space. It allowed for the formulation of strategy, which included a change in traditional attitudes and practices. Restructuring was called for in order to mobilise the whole movement behind the partnership approach. Significant amalgamations lay at the heart of the restructuring process.

Hardiman (1988) and Breen et al. (1990) have criticised the trade union movement as lacking in capacity for strategy. It was argued that trade unions were dominated by short-term concerns, sectional interests, short-sighted relativities and that the movement lacked the capacity to pursue a course of action based on the systematic, long-term, political exchange necessary for consensus required by agreements such as the National Understandings. This lack of strategic capacity seems also to underlie the situation so far described whereby the unions had a desire to restructure but the implementation was not forthcoming. However, attempts during the 1980s to deal with new forms of technology and work organisation, new industrial relations and social partnership at national level shifted the union movement from a defensive posture to a strategic one.

Strategy in Response to New Forms of Technology and Work Organisation

During the 1980s trade unions dealt with the introduction of new technology on a case-by-case basis as it arose in each workplace. A selection of new technology agreements from that time show that the issues agreed on were: pay; lump sums; hours; redeployment; natural wastage; job security; training; consultation; health and safety; extra holidays; extra staff; implementation; equal opportunity; dispute procedures; rationalisation; and change procedures. Bargaining on these issues was well downstream from the decisions made at top management level on the choice, implementation and effects of the technology. ICTU (1988), however, proposed that employees be involved in decision making about new technology from the earliest stages in the process. It suggested that at the stage of planning for new technology, management would give information and consult with trade unions. Within this framework, joint working parties would carry out the appropriate research and present options and recommendations to management and unions. Management and unions would work out an agreement on the choice of technology and on the organisation of work around it. Through collective bargaining they would then sort out decisions about issues such as training, rewards and the details of work organisation. Subsequently the question of new technology appears to have been subsumed under the broader heading of "managing change" and "new forms of work organisation". In 1992 ICTU commissioned research under these headings in order to take up an informed position on them (see O'Hehir and O'Mahoney, 1993: 10). They identified their options and chose to take a co-operative approach to the introduction of change. They hoped to make gains by seeking information, consultation and some level of participation on the key choices.

A New Model of Industrial Relations

The policy of co-operation required that they move away from an adversarial role in the workplace to one which "will require a new orientation at all levels of union organisation" (O'Hehir and O'Mahoney, 1993). At national level also, ICTU had arrived at the position that the European social market approach contributed more to economic growth and social progress than the conflictual Anglo-Saxon approach. The human resource management school of thought also had its effect in talking up the notion of a "new industrial relations". It prescribed: employee commitment to management goals; recognition, under some conditions, of the resource status of employees; and flexibility rather than classical order. Roche (1992) noted "a new vogue in unitarism and the reassertion of management prerogative at company level". Mooney (1993) pointed to the development of the non-union sector; the use of atypical contracts of employment; increasing organisational and labour-market flexibility; and the weakening of trade union power. What has in fact emerged, admittedly in a relatively small number of enterprises, is enterprise partnership, with some potential for a new paradigm in industrial relations.

Collective Bargaining and Social Partnership

Collective bargaining is an adaptive strategy to the opportunities and threats of the environment. As a system it has to maintain an effective alignment with the changing environment while managing internal order. The "new deal" of Keynesian economics and pluralist industrial relations supported a system of wage rounds and adversarial bargaining. Concertation, social dialogue and globalised competition gave rise to the more consensus-based strategy of social partnership. It is a function of strategy to mobilise resources in its own support. If it is to be involved in social partnership "first, the trade union movement must be able to act strategically and to mobilise its members interests behind a relevant conception of where their interests lie. Second, the trade union movement must possess the capacity, both organisational and ideological, to become involved in political bargaining" (Goldthorpe, 1990).

The submission presented by ICTU for the Programme for National Recovery (PNR) suggested that the way out of the crisis of that time was a medium-term integrated strategy. At the same time participation in the PNR bought time for the union movement that allowed it develop its own position. As one respondent commented "we have secured for ourselves a breathing space to allow us to evaluate our current standing with Irish workers and to take measures to galvanise their support . . . It is prudent, therefore, that we should use this breathing space to concentrate on organisational issues" (Interview, 1990). It was during this time that PTWU amalgamated with CUI to bring about the CWU. The amalgamation of ITGWU with FWUI to form SIPTU took place at the time of agreement of the Programme for Economic and Social Progress (PESP). At the outset of the PESP discussions ICTU was in a position to propose a ten-year strategy. The overall aim of the long-term strategy would be the development of a modern efficient social market economy in Ireland ... with low levels of unemployment and a high level of social protection (ICTU, 1990). Thus, social partnership came as a strategic response to the changed political economy of the 1980s. Restructuring was a strategy of mobilising resources in alignment with the requirements of social partnership.

RESTRUCTURING THROUGH UNION MERGERS

There were about 120 unions in the Republic of Ireland between 1940 and 1961. The rapid change between 1961 and 1966 may be explained by the withdrawal of British-based unions from Ireland and by the integration of many of the 38 civil service associations.

Table 9.3: The Number of Trade Unions for Selected Years 1940–1993

Year of Decade	1940s	1950s	1960s	1970s	1980s	1990s	2000
00	120			95	86	67	46
01			123		86	62	
02					83	59	
03		115			80	59	
04					78	56	
05					77	56	
06			97	89	77	56	
07					76	55	
08					74	47	
09				85	68	46	

Source: Roche and Larragy (1986): ICTU, Annual Reports (unions affiliated to ICTU only); Labour Relations Commission, Annual Report, 1999.

The number of unions in operation has been halved in the past three decades. The processes by which the number of unions decreases is by union "deaths", by the withdrawal of British-based unions from Ireland and by union mergers.

There were few mergers from 1940 until 1964 (see Table 9.4 below). The period 1965–1969 shows a significant increase in merger activity, especially among British trade unions. Buchanan (1974) has identified a wave of mergers in the United Kingdom at that time. In Ireland the merger wave dies down, leaving a residue of activity. A more pronounced wave arises in the period 1985–1994. The majority of the mergers before 1987 were absorptions of small unions by larger unions. From 1987 onwards, amalgamations of large unions become more frequent. Table 9.3 presents absolute numbers and does not relate the number of mergers taking place to the number of trade unions available for merger. Waddington (1988: 22), to give a more satisfactory picture, used the concept of merger intensity. The measure of merger intensity adopted here is the number of unions absorbed in a period of time as a proportion of the average number of unions in existence during that time, multiplied by 100.

Table 9.4: No. of Unions involved in Mergers and Merger Intensity

5 year Periods	No. of Unions in Mergers	Total No. of Unions; Moving Average	Merger Intensity
1940–44	0	120	0.0
1945–49	2	120	1.6
1950–54	3	115	2.6
1955–59	4	115	1.7
1960–64	5	123	3.3
1965–69	12	97	12.4
1970–74	6	93	6.5
1975–79	9	88	10.2
1980–84	9	83	9.6
1985–89	15	74	20.3
1990–94	19	61	27.9
1995–99	5	52	9.6

Column 2: The average number of unions in existence over the five-year period.
Column 3: Merger intensity = (Column 1/Column 2) X 100.

Source: Column 1: Roche and Ashmore (2000); Column 2: as in Table 9.4 above.

Table 9.4 and Table 9.1 indicate that the frequency of union mergers rises 100 per cent above any previous level in the 1985–1989 period and even higher again in the 1990–1994 period. A significant merger wave occurred in the period 1987–1994. This requires explanation. We have argued above that it came about as the implementation of a long-standing aspiration of the movement when internal barriers to mergers were overcome. The threatening environment of the 1980s constrained the trade union movement to unfreeze its old rigidities and search for more effective structures. Whatever the cause, it represents a significant restructuring of the trade union movement especially when it is followed by a further reduction in the number of trade unions over the period 1995–1999.

Figure 9.1: Five Year Moving Average of Merger Intensity

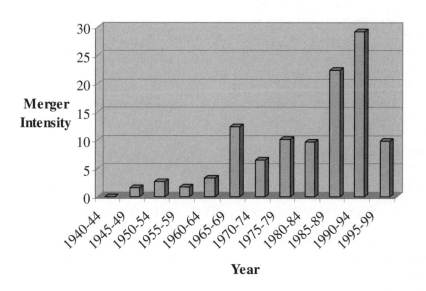

Source: Roche and Ashmore (2000).

Merger Decisions and Merger Patterns

The rationalisation strategy is made up of the many strategies of individual trade unions seeking mergers for their own reasons. We will attempt now to specify the motivations for the merger decisions and the details of merger patterns. Chaison (1986) classified motivations for mergers as consolidatory, complementary and expansionist. Consolidation as a strategy aims to strengthen the cohesion of a union usually in the face of potentially superior forces. It does this by merging unions in adjacent job territories on the premise that increased membership increases the strength of the union. Another premise is that duplication can be eliminated by rationalisation when there are issues of similarity and complementarity between adjacent and overlapping job territories. As a result of consolidation the number of small unions has reduced and the number of medium-sized unions increased in at least five different sectors. A further reason for seeking consolidatory mergers is to develop a union of a suitable size to have influence within the movement itself.

The most notably expansionist union in recent times has been ASTMS under Clive Jenkins. AUEW(TASS) could also be classed as expansionary in the pattern of its mergers. The merging of these two unions to form MSF has placed it as one of the top unions of the United Kingdom. The Irish division of MSF, though not designed for the Irish labour market, competes credibly with SIPTU. SIPTU and its predecessors ITGWU and FWUI themselves had followed an expansionary path as is shown below.

Survival strategies arise in the case of decline in job territory often related to the cycles of specific industries. Such decline may be associated with decline in membership, job losses, financial insecurity, the workload of the general secretary and the cost of running the head office. Buchanan (1974) and Freeman and Brittain (1977) proposed that union willingness to surrender autonomy is in part a function of the business cycle. At times of high inflation followed by depression, unions cannot afford to carry on. This explanation fits with a general rise in the absorption of small unions in the 1980s but it does not appear to account for the continuing integration of unions especially into SIPTU in the late 1990s. Specific reasons can be adduced for specific mergers.

Absorptions of Small Occupational Unions by Large General Unions

From 1977 onwards there are many cases of what Hughes (1967: 36) classifies as the merger of occupational unions with a general union. The motivation of the small unions is survival, as numbers and revenue diminish or as they fail to provide needed services to their members. The motivation of the absorbing unions could probably be classified as expansionist, as they attempt to increase their numbers with an already organised membership or attempt to gain footholds in new territories.

Sixty per cent of unions sought a merger for reasons such as decline in job territory. Small single occupation unions and craft unions are most vulnerable to such decline. Small unions are vulnerable in the case of a strike especially in competition with employers who may be insured against strike for up to eleven weeks. Unions in decline operate on current income, provide a barely satisfactory level of service and progressively fail to cope with the problems coming at them. There is insecurity about the future of the union and for the general secretary about his job. Many of the crafts, and with them their unions, have become extinct. The Coopers' Union of Dublin went out of existence when steel kegs replaced wooden ones. In many situations, a merger can overcome such limitations. Employment in the shoe and leather industry fell from 8,943 to 5,312 between 1971 and 1981 and this was reflected in a decline of membership of its union, ISLU. ISLU transferred its engagements to ITGWU in 1977. The strategy of ITGWU and FWUI in absorbing the following series of small, single occupational unions may be classed as expansionist. The ITGWU absorbed eight small occupational unions since 1977.

Table 9.5: Unions Absorbed by ITGWU since 1975

Unions Absorbed by ITGWU
Irish Shoe and Leather Workers' Union (ISLWU)
The National Union of Gold Silver and Allied Trades (NUGSAT)
Irish Actors' Equity Association, (IAEA)
Irish Federation of Musicians and Allied Professions* (IFMAP)
Society of Irish Playwrights
The Association of Artists in Ireland
The Association of Irish Composers
The Irish Racecourse Bookmakers' Assistants
Racing Board Tote Staff Association

*Merger attempt failed.

The second largest general union in the Republic, the Workers' Union of Ireland (WUI), commenced the merger path in 1979 when it amalgamated with the Federation of Rural Workers (FRW) to create the FWUI.

Table 9.6: Merger with FWUI since 1975

Mergers with FWUI
The Federation of Rural Workers (FRW)
The Irish Women Workers' Union (IWWU)
The Irish Agricultural Advisers' Organisation (IAAO)
The United Stationary Engine Drivers Firemen Cranemen Motormen and Machineman's Trade Union (USEDU)
The National Association of Transport Employees (NATE)
The Meat Federation
Racing Staffs Association
Medical Laboratories Technologists Association*

* MLTA was federated to FWUI.

The Irish Women Workers Union (IWWU) found itself increasingly in a diminishing situation and finally transferred its engagements to FWUI in 1984. NATE, a single occupational union, the Irish successor of the NUR, transferred its engagements to the FWUI in 1987. It retained its identity as a division of

FWUI. Its special position attenuated under SIPTU. SIPTU was subsequently not as effective in recognising the identity of its train driver members who attempted to form a breakaway union ILDA. Other small unions to transfer to FWUI were USEDU, IAAO, the Meat Federation and the Racing Staffs Association. MLTA is an example of a union that went into federation with FWUI and has retained that status. This means that it holds its negotiation licence because of the federation but is autonomous in every other way.

Following the amalgamation of ITGWU and FWUI, the resultant union, SIPTU, continued the pattern of absorbing other trade unions.

Table 9.7: Absorption by SIPTU

Absorptions by SIPTU		Year
Irish National Decorators and Painters Trade Union	INDPTU	1991
National Union of Tailors Garment Workers Union	NUTGWU	1991
Automobile General Engineering Mechanical Operatives Union	AGEMOU	1997
The Irish Print Union	IPU	1999
The Marine Port and General Workers Union	MPGWU	1999

Each of these absorbed unions has become a "trade group" within SIPTU. They enable SIPTU to gain footholds in new sectors. The gain in membership through absorptions appears to be offsetting a trend of diminishing membership in SIPTU and enabling SIPTU to hold its membership at around 200,000. There appears to be little progress in recruitment in hitherto unorganised job territories, including those where employment is expanding.

Whether planned or emergent, there is a consistent pattern in the stream of decision making about absorptions by ITGWU, FWUI and SIPTU. Such a pattern can credibly be called a strategy and in this case an expansionary strategy.

SIPTU: The Key Merger

Schregle (1975) had encouraged the healing of the schism between the ITGWU and WUI as the key to change. The effect would be to create a union with such services as to attract smaller unions. Schregle's view appears to be validated by the trend of absorptions into SIPTU.

The SIPTU amalgamation consolidated job territories where both constituent unions had competed for membership. They also had complementary footholds in rural and urban settings; in the public and private sector; and in the railways of Northern Ireland. As a result SIPTU, with a membership of 191,000 in 1999 and a centralised authority structure, is now spread across a wide range of geographical and industrial areas. Some job territories, such as those in health and local authorities, commercial semi-states, culture, education, the railways, painting and decorating, are organised on a nationwide basis in a horizontal form of organisation. Vertical forms of organisation work along the lines of regions and branches. The complex of vertical and horizontal organisation maximises the union's capacity for participation and effectiveness and counteracts the ancient fear of a huge bureaucracy "dominating, not directing the union' (Greaves, 1982). The strength and tenacity of unions comes from combination around common interests and identifications based on job territory rather than in class organisation uniting all those who work for a living (Hyman, 1975).

Mergers of Craft Unions

The history of craft unions is one of mergers between closed, single-craft unions to form multi-craft unions. More recent mergers are between multi-craft or open unions and single-craft unions (see Hughes, 1967: 63). Examples of the former are to be found in the amalgamations of unions for tilers, slaters and plasterers to form multi-craft unions, as happened throughout the post-war period culminating in the Operative Plasterers and Allied Trades Society of Ireland (OPATSI). The key merger in construction in the present phase of development has been the amalgamation of AGIBSTU and NUWWM to form the Building and Allied Trades Union (BATU) in 1988. A key merger in the electrical and engineering sector was the merging of the two principal unions, ETU, with 10,000 members, and NEETU, with 6,000 members, to form the 22,000-strong Technical, Engineering and Electrical Trade Union (TEEU).

An example of a merger with an open union within the same sector was the amalgamation between IDATU and INUVGATA to form MANDATE in 1994. It was a major consolidation of representation in the distributive sector of the economy. Other unions in the distributive sector were MPGWU and SMAUI, both of which organised commercial travellers. MPGWU transferred its engagements to SIPTU.

The Public Sector Unions

A similar process began among the public service unions. In 1987 there were eighteen public service unions not including four telecommunications unions. In 2000 there are twelve public service unions and two telecommunications unions. Most of the mergers involved the absorption of small and very small unions by larger ones. The one big amalgamation in this sector resulted in the formation of IMPACT.

Table 9.8: Mergers of Public Sector Unions

Merger	Year
CSSOA into CPSSA	1975
PNA affiliates with LGPSU	1975
Landing Officers Association (Comhaltas Cainne) into CSEU	1980
CEWA into FUGE	1985
ITOU into UPTCS	1989
AIT into UPTCS	1989
ICEU into PSEU	1989
ICEA into CPSU	1990
IMETU into LGPSU	1990
UPTCS and LGPSU to form IMPACT	1990

The tax unions AIT and ITOU merged to become branches, first of UPTCS and then, when it merged, of IMPACT. UPTCS grew through absorbing a series of staff associations such as the Ordinance Surveyors' Association and ITOU in 1987. Absorption of the AIT in 1989 enabled the formation of a taxation branch. The culmination of the mergers in the civil and public service unions was the amalgamation of LGPSU and UPTCS to form IMPACT in 1990. A summary of the amalgamations at the core of the merger wave are shown in Table 9.9 for the years 1986 to 1994. Beginning in 1988 and in each succeeding year, a significant amalgamation took place in each industrial sector.

Table 9.9: Amalgamations at the Core of the Merger Wave

Sector	Amalgamation	Year
Construction	AGIBTSU + NUWWM => BATU	1988
Finance	AUEW(TASS) + ASTMS => MSF	1988
Telecommunications	PTWU + CUI => CWU	1989
General	ITGWU + FWUI => SIPTU	1990
Public Service	UPTCS + LGPSU => IMPACT	1991
Electric & Engineering	NEETU + ETU => TEEU	1992
Distribution	IDATU + INUVGATA => MANDATE	1994

OUTCOMES AND EMERGING PATTERNS

The merger wave of 1987 to 1994 has resulted in a more simplified and consolidated trade union structure. The number of unions in the Republic affiliated to ICTU stands at 46 in the year 2000. The ten largest unions, each with a membership above 15,000, represent 81 per cent per cent of the total membership. This figure stood at 56 per cent in 1979.

Table 9.10: Membership of Trade Unions by Union Size

Union Size	1987 Trade Unions	%all M/Ship	1993 Trade Unions	%all M/Ship	2000 Trade Unions	%all M/Ship
< 1,500	31	3.7	23	2.6	22	2.0
1500–3000	15	6.9	9	4.0	3	1.4
3000–5000	8	6.3	5	4.0	4	2.9
5000–10000	6	9.7	5	8.4	3	4.5
10000–15000	7	17.8	3	8.0	4	9.0
15000–20000	3	10.5	3	12.0	3	11.0
>20,000	3	45.1	5	61.0	7	70.0
Total	73	100	53	100	46	100

Source: ICTU Information 1987; ICTU Information 1993; ICTU, Congress Affiliated Membership, 2000.

Twenty-two of the smallest unions represent 2 per cent of the membership (see Table 9.10). The number of small unions (under 3,000 members) has decreased from 59 in 1979 to 25 in 2000 (see Tables 9.2 and 9.10).

SIPTU's size puts it in a category apart from any other union. Six unions are in the membership range of 20-30,000 members. There is an opinion that this is the size required if a union is to mount the standard and scale of services required today. There is a middle ground of medium-sized unions from 3–15,000 that is populated by eleven unions. By focusing on the larger unions a picture of a coherent structure of sectoral unions emerges.

**Table 9.11: Trade Union Membership Classified by Broad Categories
2000**

Category of Union	Number of Unions	Members	Biggest Unions
General	2	212,682	SIPTU; ATGWU
Public Service	8	63,116	IMPACT; CPSU
Teachers	4	49,890	INTO; ASTI; TUI
Telecommunications	2	19,608	CWU
Electrical, Engineering	2	36,514	TEEU
Construction	4	23,911	UCATT; BATU
Distribution & Transport	6	40,068	MANDATE
Professional/White collar	11	71,361	
Medical			INO
Banking, Finance			IBOA; MSF
Miscellaneous	7	6,474	
Total	46	523,624	

Source: Adapted from ICTU, Congress Affiliated Membership, 2000.

The dominant size of SIPTU, with almost half of the membership of the total movement, is an issue for many unions and part of the reason for the formation of sectoral unions. Unions such as IMPACT are in direct competition with SIPTU in some job territories. The image of the "One Big Union" has not gone away. The incorporation of a large majority of Irish unions into SIPTU could arguably lead to a consolidation of the various industrial sectors covered by SIPTU as well as an overall command by the peak of the SIPTU organisation. SIPTU and ICTU would then occupy nearly similar roles as peak organisations. ICTU's co-ordinating role would be performed by the peak organisation at the head of a group of sectoral unions; SIPTU's commanding role would be performed by the peak organisation of an OBU.

There is a decline in the membership and in the number of British-based unions. Many of those that remain are strong and parallel similar Irish unions in the same job territories. Most notable is the competition and overlap between SIPTU and ATGWU, and between SIPTU and MSF. Similar parallels occur in printing, construction and engineering. The British-based unions tend to be stronger in Northern Ireland, while the Irish-based unions are stronger in the Republic. This pattern of organisation can, with appropriate co-ordination, maintain the trade union movement as an all-Ireland institution. Blocs of the trade union movement that diverge on issues such as wage determination are held together by the co-ordinating role of ICTU. The capacity of ICTU to hold its position in a social partnership agreement is tested by changing market conditions and the demands they provoke in sections of the organised workforce.

Despite the trend towards larger blocs, individual occupations and job territories are the basic unit of trade union organisation. Inadequate representation of the interests of sectional groups gave rise to breakaways in the past. This is manifested in the histories of unions such as the Busmen's Union (NBRU), the Psychiatric Nurses' Association (PNAI), the Motor Mechanics' Union (UMTTIE) and the train drivers' association (ILDA). Hence the importance of the role of the peak organisation, ICTU.

It has been a deliberate policy of ICTU to strengthen its role as the peak co-ordinator of the movement. One tactic has been to strengthen its command over the whole trade union movement by encouraging unions to affiliate. In 1987, ten unions were not affiliated to ICTU. In 1993, only NBRU, PNA and UMTTIE with a combined membership of probably less than 2,000 were not affiliated. In the year 2000, these three were joined by two others, but probably only temporarily. Law precludes the police and army associations from affiliation. With 55 per cent of employees unionised ICTU is relatively encompassing. The fragmentation of previous decades was reversed by ICTU in the second half of the 20th century. It can plausibly be argued that the criticisms of trade union structure on the grounds that it is chaotic and lacks a capacity for strategy are no longer valid.

OUTCOMES IN TERMS OF TRADE UNION FUNCTIONS

The major purpose of trade unionism is to represent the members' interests. Restructuring has been a major response to fulfilling this task in post-industrial society. To what extent has the representation of members' interests been improved? To answer this question, we assess changes in bargaining effectiveness, bargaining structures, membership service, structures, organisation and recruitment, and capacity for strategy. It appears that the trade union respondents interviewed believed that an overall effect of the mergers has been to enhance their unions *bargaining effectiveness*, that is, their representational capacity, bargaining power and negotiating influence. Respondents interviewed used the terms "clout" or "voice" as meaning bargaining power or the capacity of actors to achieve desired or intended outcomes. For example, the phasing out of departmental grades in the civil service and the absorption of smaller unions gave IMPACT a greater ability to influence the reorganisation of grades. Other gains reported have been in their capacity for representation, for mounting a strike and for servicing members.

Many unions claim *improved service* to the members as the major consequence of their mergers. In many cases, this was a purpose of the merger and, in others, a side effect of economies made through rationalisation.

Economies of scale also facilitated new services such as information services, research, training and education. From their earliest days, trade unions performed welfare functions providing individual benefits for members. After merger, more sophisticated benefits are possible through the increased size of memberships. Ability to deal with members' inquiries to the head office is perceived as a major advantage of reorganised head offices.

Bargaining strength is an asset that enables the union to shape outcomes. This in turn is dependent on ability to fund a strike. Many small unions do not have the capacity to fund a strike and it is commonly believed among trade unions that only very large unions can afford to strike. It can be argued that the merging of medium-sized unions into larger units increased their capacity to sustain prolonged industrial action. Larger units can be more strategic in their use of the strike weapon. In terms of *union recruitment*, smaller unions mostly reported that mergers gave them a capacity whereby they could dedicate one or more of their full-time officials to recruitment. In many cases, whatever the reason, membership is growing.

Capacity for Strategy

The so-called fragmented structure of the trade union movement was arguably a rational adaptation to the requirements of free collective bargaining in a liberal economy. The complexity of its structure, its lack of unity and centralisation, the predominance of sectional and short-term interests and the absence of workers' participation at enterprise level, while effective in a *laissez-faire* system is nevertheless not well adapted to centralised bargaining. The centralised national wage bargaining of Ireland of the 1970s required a more coherently articulated and centralised trade union structure. Such arrangements require that the key level of union organisation should match the centralised level of collective bargaining. The purpose of the restructuring in the late 1980s was to develop a "capacity for strategy" for social partnership. Social partnership was a strategy devised in an attempt to cope with the political economy of the 1980s. Strategic management by a dominant coalition of union leaders persuaded mergers in the direction of a restructuring of the whole trade union movement in order to gain capacity for strategy. A strengthening of the authority and coverage of the peak organisation and a rationalisation of the affiliated unions has increased that capacity.

Weil (1994) found that successful trade unions adjust to their environment, respond to their members, identify their strategic values and build supportive structures. It is the aspect of building supportive structures for the whole trade union movement that has been the focus of this chapter. However, the restructuring has been chiefly driven by the union leadership with the consequent danger that the process appears as managerialist in style. Heery and Kelly (1994) identify "managerial unionism" as a process that draws on the perspectives and techniques of strategic management. They suggest that the attributes of the union are then realigned in the direction of top-level leadership. The members are approached as satisficing customers. Hence, the move to accentuate the aspect of membership service and the growth of new forms based on market calculation. Knights and Morgan (1990) point out that strategy reproduces unequal social relations within an organisation. It becomes the means whereby professional officers can access organisational resources and legitimise their view of reality. To deal with the external environment the strategic manager needs to increase the power of the organisation that he/she leads. Mergers are a way to increase the size of membership and thereby gain access to high-level committees and networks. Competition among trade unions calls for a strategic appraisal of one's power position within the system. One such channel has been involvement with national-level bargaining, which increased the role and status of the general secretary by bringing him into contact with a wider range of influences. At the same time it has also removed him from immediate contact with his membership. The merger is a way of increasing the power of the union as an organisation and fostering the strategic position of the leadership.

CONCLUSION

Until 1987 there was a low level of merger frequency in the Irish trade union movement. However, the period of social partnership and the merger wave of 1987–1994 has brought a significant change to the structure of the Irish trade union movement. This change was determined not solely by environmental factors but also by the strategic action of a coalition of leaders. It changed the character of the movement by giving it a greater capacity for strategy at the national level. The characteristics of post-industrial society as they emerged in the 1980s created the conditions for change. Trade union structure, previously adapted to adversarial bargaining, now adapted to social dialogue. The long-desired goal of restructuring was reached, not through a direct attempt to change structures but through taking on new strategies that brought in their wake an adjustment of structures. Strategic leadership was required to bring it about. Such an approach carries the real danger of increasing the distancing between the leadership and the rank and file. This restructuring of the union movement has, however, increased its capacity for strategic action.

ABBREVIATIONS

AEEU	Amalgamated Engineering & Electrical Union
AEU	Amalgamated Engineering Union
AGEMOU	Automobile General Engineering and Mechanical Operatives
AGIBSTU	Ancient Guild of Incorporated Brick and Stonelayers Trade Union
AIT	Association of Inspectors of Taxes
ASTI	Association of Secondary Teachers, Ireland

ASTMS	Association of Scientific, Technical and Managerial Staff
ASW	Amalgamated Society of Woodworkers
ATGWU	Amalgamated Transport & General Workers' Union
AUEW (TASS)	Amalgamated Union of Engineering Workers
BATU	Building and Allied Trades Union
BFWAU	Bakery and Food Workers Amalgamated Union
CEWA	Custom and Excise Watchers' Associations
CIU	Congress of Irish Unions
CMU	Communications Managers' Union
CPSSA	Civil and Public Service Staff Association
CPSU	Civil and Public Service Union
CSEU	Civil Service Executive Union
CSSOA	Civil Service Staff Officials' Association
CUI	Communications Union of Ireland
CWU	Communications Workers' Union
EEPTU	Electrical, Engineering, Plumbers' Trade Union
ETU	Electrical Trade Union
FRW	Federation of Rural Workers
FUGE	Federated Union of Government Employees
FWUI	Federated Workers' Union of Ireland
GPMU	Graphical, Paper and Media Union
GPOPOA	General Post Offices and Postal Officials' Association
IAAO	Irish Agricultural Advisers' Organisation
IAEA	Irish Actors Equity Association
IALPA	Irish Airline Pilots' Association
IBOA	Irish Bank Officials' Association
ICEA	Irish Customs and Excise Association
ICEU	Irish Customs and Excise Union
IDATU	Irish Distributive and Administrative Trade Union
IEETU	Irish Engineering and Electrical Trade Union
IEIETU	Irish Engineering, Industrial and Electrical Trade Union
IFMAP	Irish Federation of Musicians and Associated Professions
IMETU	Irish Municipal Employee's Trade Union
IMPACT	Irish Municipal, Public And Civil Trade Union
INO	Irish Nurses' Organisation
INPDTU	Irish National Painters and Decorators' Trade Union
INTO	Irish National Teachers' Organisation
INUVGATA	Irish National Union of Vintners, Grocers and Allied Trades
INUW	Irish National Union of Woodworkers
IPU	Irish Print Union
ISLWU	Irish Shoe and Leather Workers Union
ITGWU	Irish Transport and General Workers' Union
ITOU	Irish Tax Officials Union
LGPSU	Local Government Public Services Union
MPGWU	Marine Port and General Workers Union
MSF	Manufacturing, Science Finance
NEETU	National Engineering and Electrical Trade Union
NGA	National Graphical Association
NUGMW	National Union Goldsmiths and Metal Workers

NUGSAT	National Union of Gold, Silver and Allied Trades
NUR	National Union of Railwaymen
NUSMWI	National Union of Sheet Metal Workers of Ireland
PA	Postmasters' Association
PNAI	Psychiatric Nurses' Association of Ireland
POWU	Post Office Workers' Union
PSEU	Public Service Executive Union
PTWU	Post and Telecommunications Workers' Union
SMAUI	Sales Marketing and Administrative Union of Ireland
SOGAT	Society of Graphical and Allied Trades
TEEU	Technical Engineering and Electrical Union
TOU	Telecommunication Officials Union
TUI	Teachers' Union of Ireland
UCATT	Union of Construction, Allied Trades and Technicians
UMTTIE	Union of Motor Trade, Technical and Industrial Employees
UPTCS	Union of Public, Technical Civil Servants
WUI	Workers' Union of Ireland

REFERENCES

ACTU (1987) *Australia Reconstructed*. Report.

Bernstein, I. (1960) "Union Growth and Structural Cycles" in Galenson Walter and Lipset, S. M. *Labour and Trade Unionism*. New York: John Wiley.

Breen, R. D., Hannan, F., Rottman, D. and Whelan, C. (1990) *Understanding Contemporary Ireland: State Class and Development in the Republic of Ireland*. London: Macmillan.

Buchanan, R. T. (1974) "Merger Waves in British Unionism" *Industrial Relations Journal*, Vol. 5, No. 2: Summer, 37–44.

Buchanan, R. T. (1981) "Mergers in British Trade Unions, (1949–1979)" *Industrial Relations Journal*, Vol. 12, No. 3: May/June, 40–49.

Cardiff, P. (1982) "Reform – What Needs to be Done?" in Pollock, H. *Reform of Industrial Relations*. Dublin: The O'Brien Press.

Cassells, P. (1987) "The Organisation of Trade Unions" *Industrial Relations in Ireland: Contemporary Issues and Developments*. Dublin: University College Dublin.

Chaison, G. N. (1986) *When Unions Merge*. Indianapolis: Lexington Books.

Chaison, G. N. (1996) *Union Mergers in Hard Times: The View from Five Countries*. Ithaca, NY: Cornell University Press.

Chandler, A. (1962) *Strategy and Structure: Chapters in the History of the Industrial Enterprise*. Cambridge, Massachusetts: The MIT Press.

Clark, J., Modgil, C. and Modgil, S. (1990) (eds) *John H. Goldthorpe: Consensus and Controversy*. London: Falmer Press.

Freeman, J. and Brittain, J. (1977) "Union Merger Process and Industrial Environment" *Industrial Relations*, Vol. 16, No. 2: 173–185.

Gamson, W. A. (1961) "A Theory of Coalition Formation" *American*

Sociological Review, Vol. 26: 565–73 cited by Kelly, J. (1969) *Organisational Behaviour*. Illinois: Irwin-Dorsey.

Goldthorpe, J. H. (1990) "A Response" in Clarke, J. et al. (eds) *John H. Goldthorpe: Consensus and Controversy*. London: Falmer Press.

Greaves, C. D. (1982) *The Irish Transport and General Workers Union*. Dublin: Gill and Macmillan.

Hardiman, N. (1988) *Pay, Politics and Economic Performance in Ireland (1970–87)* Oxford: Clarendon Press.

Harvey, D. (1989) *The Condition of Postmodernity*. Oxford: Basil Blackwell.

Heery, E. and Kelly, J. (1994) "Professional, Participative and Managerial Unionism: An Interpretation of Change in Trade Unions" *Work, Employment and Society*, Vol. 8: March, 1–21.

Hillery, B. (1974) *The Committee on Trade Union Organisation 1962–1967*. UCD: Unpublished PhD Thesis.

Hughes, J. (1967) *Trade Union Structure and Government*. Research Paper 5 (1), *Royal Commission on Trade Unions and Employers' Associations*. London: HMSO.

Hyman, R. (1975) *Industrial Relations: A Marxist Introduction*. London: Macmillan.

ICTU. (1988) "Technology: Who Decides?" ICTU Pamphlet.

ICTU. (1989) *Trade Unions and Change: Shaping the Future*. Dublin: ICTU.

ICTU. (1990) *Ireland 1990–2000: A Decade of Development, Reform and Growth*. A Position Paper.

Knights, D. and Morgan. G. (1990) "The Concept of Strategy in Sociology: A Note of Dissent" *Sociology*, 24 August, 475–483.

Lash, S. and Ury, J. (1987) *The End of Organised Capitalism*. Cambridge: Polity Press.

McCarthy, C. (1977) *Trade Unions in Ireland 1894–1960*. Dublin: IPA.

Mooney, P. (1993) "Changing Patterns in Irish Industrial Relations" *Irish Industrial Relations Review*, May, 20–34.

O'Hehir J. and O'Mahony. F. (1993) *New Forms of Work Organisation: Options for Unions*. Dublin: ICTU.

Olson, M. (1965) *The Logic of Collective Action: Public Goods and the Theory of Groups*. Cambridge, Mass.: Harvard University Press.

Piore, M. and Sabel. C. (1984) *The Second Industrial Divide: Possibilities for Prosperity*. USA: Basic Books.

Roche, W. K. (1989) "State Strategies and the Politics of Industrial Relations in Ireland Since 1945" in Murphy, T. (ed.) (1987–89) *Industrial Relations in Ireland: Contemporary Trends and Developments*. Dublin: Department of Industrial Relations, University College Dublin.

Roche, W. K. (1992) "Modelling Trade Union Growth and Decline in the Republic of Ireland" *Irish Business and Administrative Research*, Vol. 13: 87–103.

Roche, W. K. (1994) "The Trend in Unionisation" in Murphy, T. V. and Roche, W. K., *Irish Industrial Relations in Practice*. Dublin: Oak Tree Press.

Roche, W. K. and Ashmore, J. (2000) "Irish Unions in the 1990s: Testing the Limits of Social Partnership" in Griffin, G. (ed.) *Changing Patterns of Trade Unionism*. Sydney: Mansell.

Roche, W. K. and Larragy, J (1990) "Cyclical and Institutional Determinants of Annual Trade Union Growth and Decline in Ireland: Evidence from the DUES Data Series" *European Sociological Review*, Vol. 6, No.1, 49–72.

Roche, W. K. and Larragy, J. (1986) "Pattern of Merger and Dissolution of Trade Unions in Ireland since 1940" *Industrial Relations News Review*, Vol. 38, 9 October.

Schregle, J. (1975) *The Restructuring of the Irish Trade Union Movement*. Geneva: ILO.

Silverman, D. (1970) *The Theory of Organisations*. London: Heinemann.

Thompson, J. (1967) *Organisations in Action*. New York: McGraw Hill.

Waddington, J. (1988) "Trade Union Mergers: A Study of Trade Union Structural Dynamics" *British Journal of Industrial Relations*, Vol. 26, No. 3: November.

Weil, D. (1994) *Turning the Tide: Strategic Planning for Labor Unions*. New York: Lexington Books.

CHAPTER 10

Organised Labour in the New Economy: Trade Unions and Public Policy in the Republic of Ireland

PATRICK GUNNIGLE, MICHELLE O'SULLIVAN AND MICHAEL KINSELLA[1]

INTRODUCTION

The past two decades have witnessed the fashioning of a wide-ranging debate with respect to the nature of the employment relationship in almost all market economies. The basis for this debate is that the nature of work, business and organisations has experienced a number of very significant changes largely stimulated by increased competitiveness and turbulence in product, labour and capital markets. From an industrial relations perspective, some of the most pertinent and significant developments include a decline in trade union density and legitimacy, an increase in managerial autonomy, a decline in employment security and growth in atypical employment, growth in the extent and pace of organisation re-structuring and an arguable increase in the pace and intensity of work for many employees (see Kochan et al., 1986; Sparrow and Hiltrop, 1994). As a result of these stimuli, there is little doubt that industrial relations in the developed world has undergone dramatic change over the past two decades. The nub of such change stems from a diminution of the role of collective bargaining and trade unions and a growth in non-union approaches. This trend has been particularly marked in the US, where we have witnessed the progressive dilution of the "New Deal" industrial relations system and a huge decline in trade union membership and influence (Kochan et al., 1996). However, industrial relations in European countries has also undergone significant change, notably in regard to the role of organised labour during the 1980s whereby, as Sparrow and Hiltrop (1994: 135) observe, Western Europe experienced "a perceptible decline in the legitimacy and representativeness of trade unions".

In Ireland, however, the conventional wisdom is that the prevalence of

1. Patrick Gunnigle and Michelle O'Sullivan work in the Department of Personnel and Employment Relations, University of Limerick. Michael Kinsella is a Human Resource Executive with Shannon Aerospace Limited. The authors would like to thank Adrian Twomey, A. and L. Goodbody, Joe Wallace, University of Limerick and Richard Block, Michigan State University, for their comments on initial drafts of this chapter.

centralised agreements since the mid 1980s has maintained a prominent role for trade unions and collective bargaining at enterprise and national level with the consequence that the position of organised labour in Irish society is significant and enduring. The Irish experience is thus seen as contrasting that of the UK and US where the election of conservative governments with strong anti-labour agendas meant that the eighties and much of the nineties were characterised by a hostile political climate. Indeed, an anti-union public policy agenda in the UK and US was seen as an important factor contributing to the decline in trade union membership and influence, and in the coverage and significance of collective bargaining during the period (Kochan et al., 1986; Beaumont, 1992; Beaumont and Harris, 1994; Sparrow and Hiltrop, 1994; Wood and Goddard, 1999). Clearly public policy in Ireland followed a very different and apparently more benign route. The most widely touted explanation for Irish "exceptionalism" relates to the Irish socio-political environment, which, it is argued, remains conducive to a strong collectivist orientation in industrial relations. This explanation is most aptly captured by Roche and Turner who point to Ireland's tradition in acknowledging the legitimacy of organised labour in society and the absence of an anti-union agenda among any of our political parties:

> The long established legitimacy of trade unions in Irish economic, political and cultural life has yet to be seriously or trenchantly challenged by any Irish Government, political party or any strong body of employer opinion ... In the absence of a strong anti-union ideology in Irish politics and business, trade unions still hold a relatively high – if probably declining – degree of legitimacy in the eyes of employees ... This pattern, combined with the high profile of leading union officials nationally, "normalises" unions and union membership in the eyes of employees to an appreciably greater degree than in the United States or even in the United Kingdom ... (Roche and Turner, 1994: 745).

Nevertheless, trade unions in Ireland have also come under increasing pressure over recent decades, particularly in regard to a decline in trade union density (Roche, 1997b), increased employer resistance to trade union recognition (McGovern, 1989; Gunnigle, 1995) and the diffusion of "union substitution" practices at enterprise level (Gunnigle, 1998). Such evidence of employer resistance to conventional pluralist industrial relations appears decidedly at odds with the national industrial relations system characterised by a government-led consensus approach. This chapter considers this apparent contradiction by firstly reviewing three key aspects of the interaction between public policy, trade unions and industrial relations in Ireland. Secondly, recent research evidence is reviewed in the areas of trade union density and trade union recognition. Based on this analysis, we conclude that despite almost fourteen years of national level "partnership" agreements between government, employers and organised labour, there is evidence of extensive employer resistance to trade unions. These findings, we argue, raise important paradoxes between espoused government policy, which appears to support a strong trade union role in society, and actual practice, which encourages the attraction of start-up industries which actively avoid trade union recognition. Some of the reasons for this phenomenon are also explored.

INDUSTRIAL RELATIONS AND PUBLIC POLICY

As many commentators have noted, industrial relations in Ireland has traditionally been associated with a strong pluralist orientation (see Gunnigle and Morley, 1993; Hillery, 1994; Roche, 1997a). Indeed, despite Ireland's relatively recent industrialisation, organised labour has long played a prominent role in Irish history, with trade unions well established in many industries by the early 1900s (Boyd, 1972). Thus, pluralist industrial relations traditions are well ingrained in our national psyche and manifest in comparatively high levels of union density and recognition, a reliance on adversarial collective bargaining and industrial relations as the key human resource (HR) priority in most medium and larger organisations. Turning to the issue of public policy and industrial relations, we can identify three aspects of particular significance:

1. Government support for trade unions and collective bargaining and the related promotion of centralised "social partnership" agreements.

2. A strong public policy focus on attracting foreign direct investment (FDI).

3. Constitutional support for freedom of association.

As noted in our introduction, Irish governments have, over recent decades, supported the principle of collective bargaining and accepted the legitimacy and role of trade unions at enterprise and national level. Traditionally, government approaches to industrial relations were grounded in the voluntarist tradition, essentially characterised by a "hands off" approach with a minimal legislative and procedural framework to underpin collective bargaining. This approach was largely an historical legacy of the British voluntarist tradition. However, in the early 1980s, the industrial relations trajectories of the British and Irish governments took markedly contrasting routes. In the UK, Conservative governments during the 1980s embarked on a series of initiatives, both legislative and otherwise, to reduce union power and influence, lessen the coverage of collective bargaining and ensure that wage levels and other industrial relations outcomes were determined, to the greatest degree possible, by market forces. In Ireland, the voluntarist tradition has also become diluted over recent decades. In contrast to the UK, however, this change has taken the form of greater centralisation of industrial relations. Recent governments have been strong advocates of centralised agreements on pay and other aspects of economic and social policy involving negotiations between the "social partners". Since 1987, Ireland has had five centralised agreements, with the current PPF (Programme for Prosperity and Fairness) agreement scheduled to expire in 2003. As we know, these agreements deal not only with pay but also with a range of economic and social issues such as welfare provision, employment creation and tax reform. Thus, at a macro level, the Irish industrial relations system provides for significant trade union influence in shaping economic and social policy. Turning to enterprise level, we find that both the most recent centralised agreements (Partnership 2000 and the PPF) explicitly promoted partnership-based industrial relations arrangements at enterprise level with the first of these agreements providing for the establishment of a National Centre for Partnership[2] with a mandate to advance partnership at enterprise level in both the private and public sector.

Another important aspect of the impact of public policy on industrial relations relates the strategy of successive governments of attracting foreign direct investment (FDI) through incentives to multinational corporations (MNCs) to establish facilities here. There are now over 1,200 overseas firms operating in Ireland which employ approximately 130,000 people with a particular focus on electronics, pharmaceuticals, software and internationally traded services. The main sources of FDI in Ireland are the US (almost 50 per cent), the UK and Germany. The period since the 1980s has seen significant growth of FDI into Ireland. OECD data indicate a threefold increase in FDI inflows to Ireland since 1990, with the US now accounting for almost 85 per cent of all such inflows (OECD, 1999). The significance of US FDI in Ireland was also highlighted in the *Economist*'s (1997) finding that almost a quarter of US manufacturing investment in Europe located in Ireland, while over the period 1980–1997 some 40 per cent of all new US inward investment in the electronics sector went to Ireland. Clearly the Irish economy has reaped some significant benefits from multinational investment, most notably in their contribution to employment creation, economic growth, modernisation of the Irish industrial base and increased national productivity (see Tansey, 1998; Gunnigle and McGuire, 2001). In the industrial relations sphere, multinational firms have been associated with innovation in areas such as the diffusion of so called high-performance work systems (Mooney, 1989), performance-related pay (Gunnigle et al., this volume, Chapter 4) and with enhancing the status of the specialist personnel/HR function (Gunnigle, 1998). However, the picture is not all positive. There is a considerable body of international evidence which indicates that MNCs can undermine pluralist industrial relations traditions, most commonly through opposing trade union recognition and refusing to engage in collective bargaining (Gennard and Steuer, 1971; Bomers and Peterson, 1977; Ferner, 1997). Even where collective bargaining is acceded to, MNCs can adopt strategies which trade unions may find difficult, if not

---

2. The PPF agreement provides for the establishment of the National Centre for Partnership and Performance. This new body, to be headed by Peter Cassells, represents a variation on the original National Centre for Partnership.

impossible, to counter. Key strategies here include the capacity of MNCs to switch the locus of production to plants outside of the host country and the use of threats to close plants or reduce production in negotiations with trade unions. The issue of union avoidance is probably the most notable and brings us to our final important plank of public policy and industrial relations in Ireland, namely the Irish Constitution's provision in regard to freedom of association.

In the Irish Constitution (1937), the State guarantees liberty for the exercise of the "right of citizens to form associations or unions". This amounts to an effective Constitutional guarantee of freedom of association, as embodied in Article 40.6.1.iii of the Irish Constitution, and confers the right on workers to form or join associations or unions. The Constitution guarantees this right subject to "public order and morality" and goes on to provide that laws may be enacted for the "regulation and control in the public interest" of the exercise of this right. However, beyond this Constitutional guarantee of freedom of association there is no statutory provision to govern the process of trade union recognition. Where disputes over trade union recognition arise, these may be referred to the Labour Court which may ultimately issue a recommendation. However, these recommendations are generally not binding on the parties involved. More recently, there have been some initiatives to provide stronger supports in the area of trade union recognition and we review the import of these moves later in this chapter. However, we begin by considering the available evidence on the role of trade unions in the Irish economy.

TRENDS IN TRADE UNION MEMBERSHIP

The Republic of Ireland has traditionally been characterised by relatively high levels of trade union membership. In Figure 10.1, we present a summary of trends in trade union membership in Ireland from 1925 to 1999. Here we see that trade union membership increased, more or less progressively, from the 1930s right up to 1980.[3] We then witnessed a significant decline in union membership from 1980 to the end of the decade. This decline in union membership in the eighties is principally attributed to macro-economic factors, particularly economic depression, increased unemployment and changes in employment structure involving decline/stagnation of employment in traditionally highly unionised sectors (such as areas of the public sector and "traditional" manufacturing) and growth in sectors traditionally more union averse, such as private services and areas of "high technology" manufacturing (see Roche and Larragy, 1989; Roche, 1992, 1997b; Roche and Ashmore, 2000). In addition to these factors, it is also likely that developments at enterprise level also contributed to this decline, most notably changes in

---

3. For a detailed review of trends in trade union membership in Ireland see Roche, 1997b; Roche and Ashmore, 2000.

management approaches to industrial relations. Of particular significance in this respect was the growth in union avoidance strategies on the part of employers and the increased adoption of so-called "human resource management" (HRM) practices (see McGovern, 1989; Roche and Larragy, 1989; Gunnigle, 1995; Gunnigle, Morley and Turner, 1997).

Figure 10.1: Trade Union Membership in Ireland 1925–1999

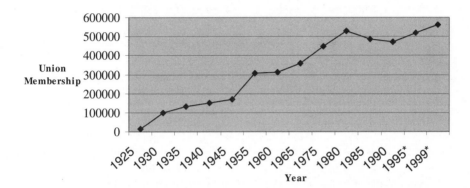

* Figures for 1995 and 1999 are estimates derived from the annual affiliated membership of the Irish Congress of Trade Unions and also from the Department of Enterprise and Employment.

Source: Figures for 1925–1990 are derived from the UCD DUES Data Series (see Roche 1992; Roche 1997b, Roche and Ashmore 2000).

Looking at more recent trends we find that union membership has risen from 475,000 in 1990 to over 560,000 in 1999 (Roche and Ashmore, 2000). This increase in membership clearly reflects the progressive and significant increase in employment levels over this period.

Probably the most robust measure of trade union penetration in a country is trade union density. This provides a measure of the proportion of the unionisable workers currently in membership of trade unions and is normally based on two measures: workforce density and employment density. *Workforce density* measures the percentage of the total civilian workforce (i.e. including those employed and those seeking employment) who are trade union members while *employment density* measures the percentage of civilian employees in the labour force (excluding the self-employed, security forces and assisting relatives) who are trade union members. When we look at the data on trends in union density the picture is not so sanguine for trade unions. Using the most recent available statistics our calculations indicate that in 1999 employment density was 44.5 per cent and workforce density 38.5 per cent (see Table 10.1). This represents a fall in employment density of almost 10 per cent since 1994, in a period when the numbers at work in Ireland increased

Table 10.1: Trends in Trade Union Density in Ireland

Year	Total Union Membership	Total Employed	Total Labour Force	Employment Density	Workforce Density
1994	499.7	1221	1432	54.3%	41.7%
1995	518.7	1282	1459	53.2%	41.5%
1996	539.1	1329	1508	52.4%	41.1%
1997	538.4	1380	1539	50.2%	40.6%
1998	545.3	1494	1621	46.5%	38.9%
1999	561.8	1591	1688	44.5%	38.5%

Source: Economist Intelligence Unit Quarterly Reports, Ireland (data derived from CSO [Labour Force Surveys/National Household Surveys]); Union membership figures are estimates based on annual trade union returns to the Department of Enterprise, Trade and Employment.

by a third. Historically, employment growth has positively impacted on trade union density. Clearly this has not been the case in the boom years of the 1990s and represents a very worrying trend in regard to trade union density in Ireland. Taking a longer-term perspective, these figures for employment density represent a fall of a staggering 17 per cent since the high point of 1980, when employment density reached 62 per cent.

Trade Union Membership at Organisation Level

While national statistics provide us with an overall picture of trade union density, it is necessary to look at union membership levels at organisation level to gain insights into the operational role and impact of trade unions. The Cranfield-University of Limerick (CUL) Study conducted in 1992, 1995 and 1999 investigated human resource management (HRM) and industrial relations practices in large and medium-sized Irish organisations.[4] In this study,

---

4. The Cranfield-University of Limerick (CUL) Study of Human Resource Management in Ireland forms part of the Cranfield Network (*Cranet*) on International HRM, first established in 1989 and currently involving 26 participating countries. The Irish node of this study is located at the *Employment Relations Research Unit*, University of Limerick and directed by Michael Morley, Patrick Gunnigle and Tom Turner. For a summary of data emanating from the international study see Brewster, C. and Hegewisch, A. (1994), *Policy and Practice in European Human Resource Management: The Price Waterhouse Cranfield Survey*, London: Routledge. For review of the 1992 Irish data see Gunnigle, P., Flood, P., Morley, M. and Turner, T. (1994), *Continuity and Change in Irish Employee Relations*, Dublin: Oak Tree Press, and for the 1995 data, see Gunnigle, P., Morley, M., Clifford, N. and Turner, T. (1997), *Human Resource Management in Irish Organisations: Practice in Perspective*, Dublin: Oak Tree Press. Information from the most recent survey (1999) is available from the University of Limerick.

respondents were asked to indicate the proportion of the workforce in their organisation that was in membership of a trade union. These findings are summarised in Figure 10.2. If we take a point in time perspective, one might argue that these data indicate that union density levels among larger organisations in Ireland are reasonably high: in 1999 over half the organisations reported that 50 per cent or more of their employees were trade union members.[5] However, if we look at the trend in regard to union density we find a pattern of progressive decline. In the first survey (1992), two thirds of organisations reported that 50 per cent or more of their workforce were trade union members; by 1999 this had fallen by some 13 per cent.

Figure 10.2: Proportion of Workers in Membership of a Trade Union

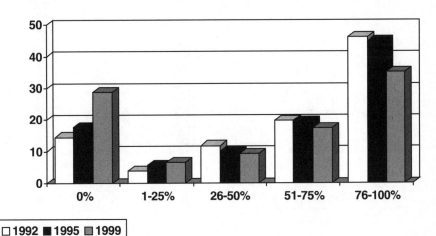

Source: Cranfield-University of Limerick 1992, 1995, 1999.

As in the previous phases of the CUL survey, the 1999 data reveal that levels of union density remain particularly high in the public sector. The difference in union density is clearly outlined in Figure 10.3, which compares union membership levels in private and state/semi-state organisations. While only a small fraction of state or semi-state organisations report low or zero levels of union membership, some 40 per cent of private companies report no union

---

5. It should also be noted that the CUL study covers organisations employing 50 or more employees and thus provides insight on industrial relations and HRM among larger organisations in Ireland. However, much of Ireland's business activity takes place among firms employing less than 50 workers. It is well established in the literature that union penetration is lower in smaller organisations (see Gunnigle, 1989; Gunnigle and Brady, 1984; Goss, 1991; Stanworth, 1991; McMahon, 1996). Consequently, union density levels in the small firm sector are likely to be well below those indicated in the CUL study.

members with a further 20 per cent reporting membership levels of 50 per cent or less. In contrast, state or semi-state companies account for by far the greatest proportion of highly unionised organisations. Eight in ten public sector companies reported union membership levels of between 76 and 100 per cent; the equivalent private sector figure was just two in ten. These findings are in line with other studies: for example, Hourihan (1996) estimated that union density in the public service was approximately 80 per cent but only around 36 per cent in the private sector.[6]

Figure 10.3: Proportion of Workers in Membership of a Trade Union: Private v State Sector

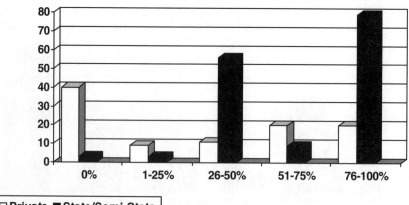

TRADE UNION RECOGNITION: A CRITICAL BATTLEGROUND FOR IRISH UNIONS?

In our introduction we noted that a number of international commentators have pointed to changes in the extent and nature of collective employee representation as a critical dimension of a shift in industrial relations practice (see Kochan et al., 1986). In particular, we pointed to the widespread trend of decline in trade union density, legitimacy and representativeness among developed economies (Sparrow and Hiltrop, 1994). Of especial significance is the trend in regard to trade union recognition and, consequently, the coverage of collective bargaining. Collectivism in industrial relations incorporates the extent to which management acknowledges the right of employees to collective representation and the involvement of the collective in influencing management

---

6. Indeed, in a recent *Industrial Relations News* report, industrial relations consultant Tom Hayes suggested that union membership in the private sector is set to drop below 20 per cent in the near future (Industrial Relations News, 2000a).

decision making (Purcell, 1987; Gunnigle, 1995). Trade union recognition represents a critical barometer of "collectivism" in industrial relations. This is particularly the case in Ireland which has no mandatory legal procedure for dealing with union recognition claims. Thus, the granting of recognition remains largely an issue to be worked out voluntarily between employers and trade unions and ultimately depends on whether or not employers agree to recognise and bargain with a trade union representing all or a proportion of its workforce. We noted earlier that while the Irish Constitution supports the right of workers to join trade unions, there is no legal obligation on employers to recognise or bargain with such unions.

The concession of union recognition by employers represents a critical phase in establishing the foundations for pluralist industrial relations interactions between employers and organised labour. Salamon (1998: 175) defines trade union recognition as "the process by which management formally accepts one or more trade unions as the representative(s) of all, or a group of, its employees for the purpose of jointly determining terms and conditions of employment on a collective basis" and describes it as "... perhaps the most important stage in the development of an organisation's industrial relations system . . . it confers legitimacy and determines the scope of the trade union's role". By securing recognition, an employer acknowledges the right of a trade union to represent and protect their members' interests in the workplace and to become jointly involved in regulating key aspects of the employment relationship. As Torrington and Hall (1995: 492) specifically comment, trade union recognition represents ". . . an almost irrevocable movement away from unilateral decision making by management". In addition to data on trade union density, trends in relation to union recognition thus provide another important indication of trade union penetration in an economy. We now consider Irish evidence in this area.

Trade Union Recognition in Larger Organisations

Turning to empirical evidence in regard to trade union recognition, data from the 1999 Cranfield-University of Limerick (CUL) study find what first appears as a reasonably healthy picture of trade union recognition in Ireland. In the 1999 survey, some 69 per cent of participating organisations recognised trade unions for collective bargaining purposes. However, when we look at the trend in regard to trade union recognition, we find that the proportion of organisations which recognise trade unions fell from 83 per cent in the first survey (1992) to the current level of 69 per cent, a fall of 14 per cent over a seven-year period. As noted earlier, the CUL study focuses only on larger organisations, excluding those with less than 50 employees. However, as we know, trade union penetration is significantly higher in larger rather than among smaller firms: thus, levels of trade union recognition in small firms are likely to be considerably less than the CUL figures presented in Table 10.2 (see Gunnigle, 1989; McMahon, 1996).

**Table 10.2: Trade Union Recognition in Larger Organisations
1992–1999**

Trade Union Recognition	1992	1995	1999
Yes	83% (186)	80% (205)	69.2% (296)
No	17% (38)	20% (50)	30.8% (132)

Source: Cranfield-University of Limerick 1992, 1995, 1999 (actual numbers in parentheses).

Overall, the national statistics and data from the CUL study present a mixed picture on trade union penetration in Ireland. Looking at trends in regard to aggregate levels of trade union density we find a picture of steady decline since 1980. A similar picture emerges from our review of trade union membership levels within organisations. However, while there is some decline in the numbers of workers in membership at organisational level, the data indicate that most of Ireland's larger organisations are characterised by reasonably high levels of union penetration: in the 1999 CUL study, seven in ten organisations recognised trade unions for collective bargaining purposes while over one third reported that 75 per cent or more of their workforce were trade union members. Thus, whilst the evidence indicates decline in union penetration, the case remains that reasonably high levels of trade union recognition and density characterise most of Ireland's larger organisations.

At face value, this evidence might lead one to conclude that there is a high level of congruity between public policy – seen as supporting the institutions of trade unions and collective bargaining – and actual practice, whereby the Irish trade union movement plays a key role in both national-level and enterprise-level industrial relations. However, to better inform our understanding of trade union penetration in Irish industry, it is necessary to look to additional sources of data. In this chapter, we consider two such sources, namely data on trade union recognition in new greenfield firms and analysis of trade union recognition claims referred to the Labour Court over recent years. We first consider evidence on union recognition and avoidance in greenfield sites.

THE GREENFIELD SITE EVIDENCE REVIEWED

It is well established that trade union penetration in Ireland is strongest in the public service and particular industrial sectors such as "traditional" manufacturing (see Gunnigle et al., 1994; Gunnigle, Morley, Clifford and Turner, 1997; Roche, 1997b; Roche and Ashmore, 2000). It is, therefore, appropriate that we should look beyond these sectors for additional indicators of the changing role of trade unions in Ireland. One area where we have a body of research is that of new "greenfield site" firms. Looking first at the international literature, we find that a significant aspect of the debate on change in enterprise-level industrial relations has focused on developments in greenfield sites (Beaumont, 1985, 1992; Beaumont and Townley, 1985; Newell, 1993; Guest and Hoque, 1996; Leopold and Hallier, 1997). Two particular facets of this debate are noteworthy. First, we find that a recurrent theme in analyses of industrial relations in greenfield sites is the suggestion that employers and management have assumed a dominant role in establishing the parameters of industrial relations practice at firm level (Beaumont and Harris, 1994; Gunnigle, 1995). Secondly, we have the contention that the decision of many corporations to establish at, or re-locate to, greenfield sites has led to increased union avoidance (Foulkes, 1980; Kochan et al., 1986; Beaumont and Harris, 1994).

In reviewing developments in Ireland, we can draw on survey and interview data from a representative sample of firms in the manufacturing and internationally traded services sectors which established at greenfield sites over a ten year period 1987–1997.[7] The data set was gathered in two distinct phases. Phase one covered all qualifying greenfield-site firms established in the manufacturing and internationally traded services sectors over the period 1987–1992 (see Gunnigle, 1995; Gunnigle, Morley and Turner, 1997). This phase covered a study population of 53 firms. The second phase relied on the same definitions and methodology but focused on a sample of 23 (33 per cent) from a total of 70 qualifying firms (see Gunnigle, MacCurtain and Morley, 2001). Altogether, the greenfield-site data set draws on information from 76 greenfield firms (62 per cent of qualifying firms over the total period, 1987–1997). Of the total, 44 (58 per cent) were US owned with the remainder comprising of thirteen Irish (17 per cent), ten European (13 per cent), and nine (12 per cent) other foreign owned firms. These 76 firms employed some 22,900 workers at the time of investigation. As one might expect, there was a concentration of firms in "high technology" sectors, with the largest numbers in office/data processing equipment manufacture and in software.

Given the profile of the greenfield site population and, particularly, the prevalence of both US and "high technology" firms, one would anticipate a high incidence of non-union firms. As can be seen from Figure 10.4, this was certainly the case with over two thirds (65 per cent) of firms not recognising trade unions. This evidence is indicative of significant growth in union avoidance among large greenfield start-ups in Ireland. Given that the incidence of non-union approaches was significantly higher in the latter (second) phase of the study than in the first, the findings also reflect the progressive diminution of union penetration in greenfield firms over the ten year period studied (91

---

7. The study excluded firms with less than 100 employees and used qualitative semi-structured interviews with senior managers and statistical analysis of a questionnaire-based survey completed by the senior manager responsible for industrial relations.

per cent of firms were non-union in the second phase while the corresponding figure for the first phase was 53 per cent). Non-unionism is clearly most prevalent amongst multi-nationals of US origin in high-technology industries, a factor commonly attributed to both the prevalence of a unitarist managerial ideology among US owned companies and also to the competitive nature of the technology sector and the consequent managerial preference for maintaining high levels of numerical and functional flexibility (see Toner, 1987; Roche and Gunnigle, 1997).

Figure 10.4: Trade Union Recognition in Greenfield Sites by Ownership 1987–1997

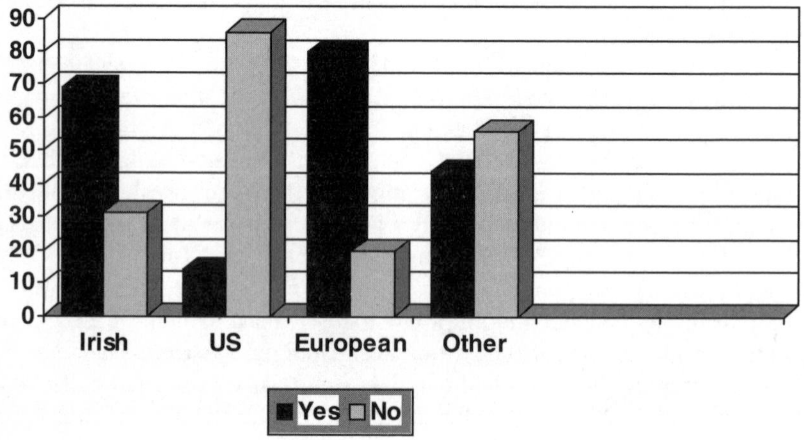

An *Industrial Relations News* analysis of union recognition trends among overseas firms found a similar pattern in regard to union avoidance. This survey examined foreign-owned firms which announced at least 100 new jobs over the 23 month period, January 1994 to November 1995 (Hourihan, 1996). Out of a total study population of 50 firms, only twelve (24 per cent) recognised trade unions (see Table 10.3). When the population is disaggregated into "new" (32) and "expanding" (18) firms, an even starker picture emerges. Of the twelve firms that recognised trade unions, ten were expanding companies. Thus, only two (6 per cent) of the 32 new companies recognised trade unions. These findings confirm a significant trend of union avoidance in new firms.

If we look more generally at the longitudinal pattern of union recognition in large greenfield sites, we find that non-union approaches began to take off in the early 1980s, became significantly more commonplace as the decade progressed and are now characteristic of the great majority of greenfield site firms in the manufacturing and internationally traded services sectors (see Murray, 1984; McGovern, 1989; Gunnigle, 1995; Gunnigle, MacCurtain and Morley, 2001). While the early non-union firms were predominantly US owned and located primarily among "high-tech" firms (mostly electronics, software

Table 10.3: Overseas Companies and Union Recognition by Country of Ownership: 1994–1995

Ownership	Union Recognition in "New" Companies (N = 32)	
	Yes	*No*
USA	0	20
UK	1	5
Other EU	1	2
Other	0	3
	Union Recognition in "Expanding" Companies (N = 18)	
	Yes	*No*
USA	7	7
Other EU	1	0
Other	2	1

N = 50

Source: Hourihan 1996.

and internationally traded services), our more recent evidence from the 1990s points to the broader diffusion of union avoidance to embrace both Irish and other foreign-owned firms, and a broader range of industrial sectors. It is all the more revealing that this decline in union penetration in new firms has occurred during an era when the trade union movement has exerted significant influence in shaping economic and social policy and when economic growth and employment creation have been exceptionally high.

THE LABOUR COURT AND UNION RECOGNITION

The Labour Court and Labour Relations Commission are Ireland's principal institutions for the consideration of industrial disputes. Where a union recognition dispute arises, this has traditionally been resolved by a trial of strength or by referral to the Labour Court. However, the "Court" title is somewhat of a misnomer: its recommendations are generally non-binding on the parties involved. Whether to accept the Court's recommendation or not is left as a matter for the management and unions to decide. The continuing demand for the Labour Court since its creation suggests it has achieved acceptability from trade unions and management, a factor which is generally considered the most important condition for any third party intervention (see Wallace, 1992).

To examine the role of the Labour Court in union recognition disputes, we have analysed the cases that have reached the Court in which a union was

Table 10.4: Labour Court Trade Union Recognition Cases 1990–1999

Year	1990	1991	1992	1993	1994	1995	1996	1997	1998	1999	Total
Total no. cases in previously non-union firms	4	17	10	10	10	8	6	6	4	6	**81**
Union recognition recommended	3 (75%)	17 (100%)	10 (100%)	10 (100%)	9 (90%)	7 (88%)	6 (100%)	5 (83%)	3 (75%)	5 (83%)	**75 (93%)**

seeking recognition from an employer for the first time. Cases involving previously unionised companies have not been scrutinised given our specific focus on union penetration in hitherto non-union firms. Between 1 January 1990 and 31 December 1999 the Court heard 81 recognition dispute cases, involving previously non-union companies (Table 10.4). The Court recommended in favour of outright union recognition in 75 of these cases (or 93 per cent). This indicates a clear tendency for the Court to support claims by workers for union representation in their dealings with employers at enterprise level. This is in line with the provisions of the 1946 Industrial Relations Act which seek to promote collective bargaining. For example, a high profile case involving the retail chain Dunnes Stores and the union MANDATE arose in the Labour Court in 1995 over job conditions associated with atypical employment. The union was seeking, among other things, more full-time jobs. In its recommendation, the Labour Court stated that it accepted the trade union's need to protect its members (LCR 14816).

To examine the level of compliance with the recommendations of the Court it was necessary to establish whether recognition was subsequently conceded in the 75 cases where the Court's recommendation favoured such recognition. To this end an attempt was made to contact each of the 75 firms involved. Definitive responses were obtained in 30 of the 75 companies (40 per cent).[8] Out of the 30 companies, only nine had actually recognised a union. This compliance rate (30 per cent) is significantly lower than that for the Labour Court in general: on average, over three-quarters of the Labour Court recommendations are accepted by both parties (Gunnigle et al., 1999: 83). This low compliance rate in cases of union recognition, though based on a small sample, supports earlier research dealing with the period 1985–1991

---

8. An examination of all Labour Court recommendations on union recognition in the relevant period was undertaken, followed by a categorisation of recommendations according to case number, company name, union, location, outcome of recommendation, etc. Where the recommendation favoured union recognition (75 cases) an attempt was made to contact the company and/or union involved to establish whether recognition was in fact conceded. Definitive responses on this matter were obtained in 30 of the 75 companies (40 per cent). The main reasons for non-response were either companies being non-contactable, had ceased operations, were trading under a different name or were unwilling to respond.

which found that while the Labour Court recommendations favoured union recognition in almost 90 per cent of cases, union recognition was subsequently conceded in less than a third (27 per cent) of companies involved (Gunnigle, 2000). Thus, the overall picture points to a significantly lower compliance rate amongst employers in relation to recommendations dealing with union recognition as compared to the general pattern of compliance with Labour Court recommendations.

In previous research, it has been noted that the existence or otherwise of unions in a company may be associated with the origin of the company (see McGovern, 1989; Gunnigle, 1995; Roche and Ashmore, 2000). In particular, research has highlighted the tendency of MNCs of US origin to avoid union recognition. In the 30 companies followed up, 21 were Irish owned and 9 were MNCs. Union recognition had been granted in seven (33 per cent) of the Irish companies and in two (22 per cent) of the MNCs. This albeit limited evidence suggests that resistance to unions is prominent not only in MNCs but also among indigenous Irish firms (see Gunnigle and Brady, 1984; McGovern, 1989). The majority (7), of the MNCs that refused to concede union recognition were of US origin, confirming the preference for US firms here to opt for non-union status (McGovern, 1989; Gunnigle et al., 1997a; Roche and Ashmore, 2000).

Overall, our analysis indicates that while the Labour Court has supported union recognition in its decisions, the majority of employers have chosen to ignore this recommendation. In general, the figures point to a failure in the Labour Court's ability to effect union recognition. Thus, we find that a State-provided body, in an attempt to resolve industrial disputes, has encouraged the recognition of, and negotiation with, trade unions by employers. Up to now, it has done so in the tradition of voluntarism with generally non-binding recommendations. In practice, however, many employers have resisted this support for pluralist industrial relations. This represents another facet of the contradiction between public policy and practice in enterprise-level industrial relations. More recently we have seen moves to alter and enhance the role of the Labour Court in the area of union recognition disputes. These changes have occurred within the backdrop of significant public policy changes in the UK, which has led to the introduction of mandatory union recognition procedures there. In the next section, we examine the union recognition provisions in operation in the US and UK. This review provides a useful backdrop to our subsequent analysis of the recent debate and legislation introduced on union recognition in Ireland.

International Provisions on Trade Union Recognition

The decline in union penetration in Ireland, manifested in falling union density and the non-adherence of Labour Court recommendations in union recognition cases, is clearly a matter of some concern to both individual unions and to the Irish Congress of Trade Unions (ICTU). One commonly discussed response to arrest this decline is the possibility of mandatory trade union recognition. In this scenario, an employer may be forced to recognise and negotiate with a trade union through legislative measures. This does not mean that trade unions can use such mandatory or compulsory recognition provisions against reluctant employers in all instances. In countries where statutory recognition procedures are in operation, such as the US or the UK, a union is required to exhibit a high level of support from employees for representation.

An example of one country where mandatory or statutory union recognition has long been in operation is the US. The American model is, for the most part, a result of the National Labour Relations Act 1935, known as the "Wagner Act". Under the Act, employees have the right to bargain collectively with their employer through representatives of their own choosing and employers are required to bargain in good faith, when requested to do so (Carrell and Heavrin, 1985: 19). To bargain in good faith involves three criteria as set by the National Labour Relations Board: (1) active participation in deliberations with the intention to find a basis for agreement; (2) a sincere effort to reach a common ground; and (3) binding agreements on mutually acceptable grounds. In the area of trade union recognition, independent labour relations boards enforce the law. According to Wood and Goddard (1999), the required level of support is clearly defined as demonstrated majority support for what is known as a bargaining unit. This may be defined as a group of employees with common employment interests which form a cohesive group for the purposes of collective bargaining. It then becomes a decision of the bargaining unit whether to unionise or not. A secret ballot is required in all cases except for those where a voluntary agreement has been made and collective agreements have the status of legal documents.

The American system of mandatory recognition has been criticised on a number of grounds. First, while the Wagner Act was seen as a major stepping-stone towards worker collectivism, it excluded temporary, domestic, agricultural and managerial/supervisory employees. Secondly, statutory recognition provisions have not arrested the steep decline in union penetration and union density remains low (figures for 2000 were 13.5 per cent for all employees and 9 per cent for private (non-agricultural) employees) (Bureau of Labor Statistics, 2001). This may partly be due to employer practices such as "union busting", which tries to prevent employee support for union recognition despite the fact that these are considered unfair labour practices and are illegal under the Wagner Act (D'Art, this volume, Chapter 2). Thirdly, where recognition has been achieved, effective employee representation has not always followed because some unions have been unable to develop a bargaining relationship with the employer who refuses to bargain in good faith (Wood and Goddard, 1999). Finally, it has also been argued that should employees support mandatory union recognition it may heighten employer opposition towards unions (Adams, 1993: 8).

Statutory union recognition, however, has not historically been a part of the Anglo-Irish tradition. Rather, when trade unions in the UK and Ireland have achieved recognition, it has been through voluntarist methods. Up to the 1980s, voluntarism was a feature of both UK and Irish industrial relations. Since the 1980s, voluntarism has remained a feature of Irish industrial relations while the UK system has become far more regulated. As mentioned earlier, under a voluntarist system, trade unions and management have the freedom to determine the content and nature of their relationship and the State provides only a minimal legal framework (Salamon, 1998: 58). Therefore, the issue of union recognition has traditionally been left as a matter for negotiation at enterprise level and not imposed by legislation. Furthermore, should a collective agreement be negotiated between an employer and union(s), this does not have legal status, as in the US. The only State involvement in Ireland in the area of trade union recognition, up to the early 1980s, was through industrial promotions bodies, which generally encouraged incoming MNCs to recognise trade unions, and through the provision of dispute resolution bodies such as the Labour Court. According to Wood and Goddard (1999), trade union membership and density in the UK have been in decline since the 1980s. In more recent years, the proportion of organisations with union recognition has fallen from 53 per cent in 1990 to 42 per cent in 1998 (Gall, 2000: 26). Similarly, as noted earlier, union recognition also appears to be increasingly difficult in Ireland. However, there have been a number of recent developments in the UK and Ireland to help counteract some of the difficulties which trade unions face in attempting to gain recognition. These have consisted of moves away from voluntarism towards greater legislative intervention. In the UK the Employment Relations Act 1999 provides a provision for mandatory recognition of a trade union. This Act emphasises the use of voluntary agreements but, more importantly, incorporates a statutory recognition procedure where employers are obliged to recognise a union in certain circumstances (see Wood and Goddard, 1999). Under the Act, union recognition can now be achieved through various routes: through the voluntary route, the ballot-based route or the automatic route. Under the voluntary route, a union may request representation rights from an employer and both sides negotiate union recognition voluntarily. If a solution is not achieved at this stage, and if the union can meet the specific requirements of the Central Arbitration Committee (CAC), a ballot may be held. If a majority of those voting and at least 40 per cent of those eligible to vote support union recognition, then it is granted by the CAC (Wood and Goddard, 1999). The automatic route comes into play whereby recognition is granted automatically, without the need for a ballot, if it can be shown that more than half of the workforce are members of a trade union. According to Wood and Goddard (1999), emphasis lies on the primacy of the voluntary path and the statutory recognition procedure is seen as a last resort. While the long-term effects of the Act are as yet uncertain, Wood and Goddard (1999) have considered its potential consequences. One possible effect is that employer opposition to unions may increase, thus having a limited impact on union growth if the partnership approach to union recognition, as envisaged, is not realised. There is also the possibility of inter-union competition to secure recognition or the growth of employer techniques such as company councils or suppression to avoid unions (see Gall, 2000: 29). Suppression in the form of "union busting" seminars have already taken place in the UK by American anti-union consultants (see Walsh, 2000: 8).

Recent Union Recognition Debate and Legislation in Ireland

Unlike the UK, where no written constitution exists, the Irish Constitution provides for the right of freedom of association, that is workers have the right to form or join unions. As a result of a number of legal cases that have arisen, the courts have taken this right to confer an implied right of disassociation, that is the right not to join a union (see *Educational Company of Ireland v Fitzpatrick and others*). They have also concluded, however, that this right does not imply the imposition on employers to recognise or negotiate with a trade union (see *Abbott and Whelan v The Southern Health Board*). As the State does not impose mandatory union recognition on employers, trade union recognition disputes can arise between unions and management. For example, in the case of Pat the Baker and SIPTU (*Pat the Baker Ltd v SIPTU, 1991*), the company refused to recognise the trade union SIPTU to the point where they closed their manufacturing facility. In 1994, a union recognition case was taken to the High Court involving Nolan Transport and SIPTU *(Nolan Transport (Oaklands) Ltd v Halligan and Others/SIPTU, 1998)*. The ruling was significant for unions seeking recognition as it was suggested that the union had "rigged" a ballot on industrial action. Costs and damages were awarded against the union. However, this decision was later overturned (only partly in relation to costs), on appeal to the Supreme Court in 1998, when it was found that SIPTU had retained the immunities afforded to it under the Industrial Relations Act 1990 because a legitimate trade dispute had existed.

Historically, it can be argued that the lack of a statutory mechanism for facilitating trade union recognition was not problematic, since most of the larger employers tended to recognise and conclude collective agreements with trade unions. The willingness to deal with unions has been attributed to a tradition of trade union recognition and reliance on collective bargaining in Ireland (Roche, 1989; Roche and Turner, 1994). However, it is equally clear that the decline in union density since the early 1980s and the increased incidence of union avoidance among employers has made trade union recognition a much more significant issue in Irish industrial relations (Gunnigle and Brady, 1984; McGovern, 1989; Gunnigle, 1995). Indeed, the Irish Congress of Trade Unions has sought ways to increase union influence, legitimacy and representativeness at both enterprise and national level (see ICTU, 1993, 1995). Against this background of growing concern, a "High-Level Group" was established under the Partnership 2000 agreement, to examine the issue of trade union recognition. This working group comprised a broad membership representative of government departments, Irish Congress of Trade Unions

(ICTU), Irish Business and Employers Confederation (IBEC) and the Industrial Development Authority (IDA). The first report of the High-Level Group was issued in 1997 and recommended the use of voluntary rather than mandatory procedures. However, the report was effectively de-railed after a dispute between SIPTU and Ryanair in 1998. This involved the refusal by Ryanair to concede to a union recognition attempt by 30 baggage handlers and led to the closure of Dublin Airport. One result of the dispute was that unions were no longer willing to accept the initial High-Level Group report which had made no provisions for mandatory union recognition. Amendments were subsequently made and a final report was put forward by the Group in March 1999. The Government has since approved proposals arising from the report culminating in the Code of Practice on Voluntary Dispute Resolution and the Industrial Relations (Amendment) Act 2001.

This Act does not impose mandatory union recognition but provides for a voluntary process to be followed in the event of a trade union recognition dispute (see Code of Practice). Where bargaining arrangements fail or are non-existent, a voluntary procedure "kicks in" (see Figure 10.5 and Appendix). The parties can seek the assistance of the Labour Relations Commission, a State-provided dispute resolution body, on disputes over pay and conditions. If unresolved at this level, the Labour Court may issue a non-binding recommendation (*Irish Relations News*, 2000b: 21–23).

Figure 10.5: Procedures on Recognition of Unions

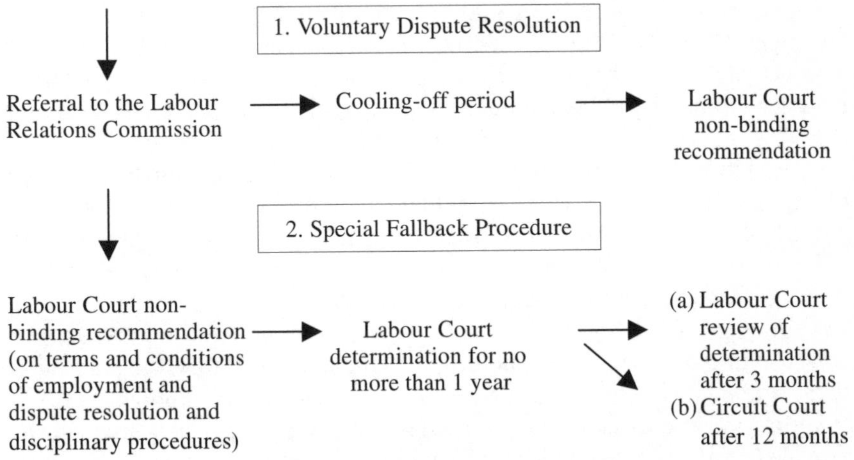

Source: Code of Practice on Voluntary Dispute Resolution; Industrial Relations (Amendment) Act, 2001. For a detailed outline of the steps involved see Appendix.

A special fallback procedure is in place whereby a trade union or accepted body may request a further investigation by the Labour Court. In this instance, the Court must be satisfied that (1) an employer did not follow the voluntary process, (2) appropriate procedures have not resolved the issue and (3) there has been no industrial action during the process (*Industrial Relations News*, 1999: 20). If the dispute remains unresolved after the Labour Court recommendation in this instance, the Court shall have the power to issue a determination, which would be binding for one year in respect of pay and conditions and dispute resolution and disciplinary procedures. After this stage a union may take one of two routes. Twelve months after the determination has been issued, the union can apply to the Circuit Court for an enforcement order. Alternatively, it can apply to the Labour Court for a review of the determination (Figure 10.5) (Higgins, 2001: 14). The original Industrial Relations (Amendment) Bill had set a twelve-month waiting period before such a review could be applied for. This has since been changed during the legislative process so that a review can be sought three months after the determination. The Labour Court can then vacate, affirm or vary the determination (Higgins 2001: 14). If an employer does not comply with the reviewed determination within six weeks, the union can then seek an enforcement from the Circuit Court. While it was reported that the Labour Party was in favour of legislative and constitutional amendments to provide for union recognition, many union leaders and employers from the Irish Business and Employers Confederation opted for a voluntarist solution (Sheehan, 1998a: 17 and *Industrial Relations News*, 2000b: 21–23). The Code of Practice and Industrial Relations (Amendment) Act achieve this aim.

The High-Level Group report also recognised the policy of non-recognition that can be found in the multinational sector (Sheehan, 1998b: 4) and which previous commentators have noted and analysed (see McGovern, 1989; Gunnigle, 1995). The original Industrial Relations (Amendment) Bill included a provision that the Labour Court, in the course of an investigation, shall have regard to the entirety of labour relations practices in the employment concerned (see Appendix). The report, on which the Bill was based, stated that in the case of MNCs, the policy of non-recognition was associated with the existence of strong HRM policies. It was concluded that, due to the "generally good" terms and conditions offered by such companies, "employees generally do not seek to join unions to protect their interests" (Sheehan, 1998b: 4). In the Irish context, there is some empirical evidence both in support and against this argument. Toner's (1987) findings in the electronics sector pointed to the presence of good terms and conditions of employment among the non-union firms studied (also see Flood and Toner, 1997). However, Gunnigle's (1995) study of greenfield firms does not support the thesis that non-union firms provide pay and benefits which are above either the regional or sectoral norms or better than those provided by similar unionised firms. Despite these contrasting findings, it has been suggested that the predominantly non-union status of American high-technology companies will remain unchallenged by the provisions of the Act (Dobbins et al., 1999: 7–8). The Bill was amended, however, so that the Labour Court will not only have regard to the entirety of labour relations practices in the employment concerned but will also include "labour relations practices engaged in by the employer or an associated employer in another employment, including an employment outside the State". The Labour Party, believing that a union's case would be strengthened if the same employer recognised unions in another country, had apparently sought this amendment (Higgins, 2001: 14). On the other hand, it has been suggested by Higgins (2001: 14) that the amended provision could be a "double-edged sword" in that a union's case could be weakened if the same employer had a global policy of not recognising trade unions. It is important to bear in mind that one of the key results of the High-Level Group report, and subsequent Act, is that the mandatory recognition sought by unions will not be imposed (Sheehan, 1998b: 3–4). The process outlined relates only to claims regarding the terms and conditions of employment, dispute resolution and disciplinary procedures. It is likely that the IDA, as members of the High-Level Group, would have articulated the implications of mandatory union recognition as a significant disadvantage in their efforts in selling Ireland as a site for foreign direct investment (see Gunnigle, 1995; Gunnigle and McGuire, 2001). Given that IBEC's membership comprises a number of non-union firms, it is unlikely that their representatives would agree to any legally binding system of dealing with trade union recognition disputes.

An Effective Recognition Procedure?

We have seen that data from the Labour Court have indicated its endorsement for the collective representation of workers at enterprise level. The data also illustrate the Court's inability to gain acceptance of its recommendations by a majority of employers in union recognition cases. This is indicative of the union avoidance strategies used by employers and of declining trade union penetration despite growing employment. The Labour Court, as mentioned, has traditionally operated within a voluntarist system. This contrasts with the US where mandatory union recognition has been in place since the 1930s yet this has not resulted in high union density levels. Much debate on union recognition has also taken place in the UK leading to the introduction of the Employment Relations Act, 1999. It is much too early to tell what the effects of the legislation will be.

On the face of it, employers and the government in Ireland appear to have recognised the concerns of unions regarding union penetration, given the lack of acceptance of Labour Court recommendations, the number of high profile disputes and declining trade union density levels. The experiences of other systems, such as the US and UK, illustrated the options that were open to the parties in Ireland – mandatory recognition involving a high degree of legalism or a voluntary approach with a "last resort" provision for mandatory recognition. The option taken by the parties in Ireland is neither of the above. The Industrial Relations (Amendment) Act represents a somewhat unique measure to address the issue of union recognition within a voluntarist framework. Legal intervention is kept to a minimum, with the provision for binding recommendations on pay and conditions presumably being designed to encourage the parties to reach agreement short of such a measure. It remains to be seen how this innovative measure will work. At a glance there are several possible defects. Twomey (2001: 10) suggests that the Act "side-steps the issue" of union recognition. The provisions are also somewhat complex and may well prove quite tortuous in practice (although perhaps somewhat less so since, as already outlined, the waiting period for a Labour Court review of the determination was significantly reduced from twelve months to three months: also see Appendix). However, the general disincentives to industrial action contained in the Bill, could delimit one of the historically most effective measures of gaining union recognition. The legislation avoids the possibility that employers may provide inducements to employees not to join a union, an act which could be defined as an "unfair labour practice" under the Wagner Act in the US. Arguably, however, the Act may not have a significant impact on much of the non-union sector where unions are unable to achieve penetration not only because of employer failure to implement Labour Court recommendations on recognition but also because unions appear unable to even gain a foothold which would allow them to process a case for recognition.

DISCUSSION

In our introduction we indicated that Ireland presents a somewhat distinctive context for examining the relationship between public policy, industrial relations and trade unions. We noted, in particular, the contrast with developments in the UK and US from the early 1980s where trade unions had to face a quite hostile public policy environment. The most explicit manifestations of this contrast include the widely accepted legitimacy of trade unions in Irish society, the absence of a strong anti-union ideology among any of the leading political parties and the immense influence which the union movement has exercised as party to the series of centralised agreements since 1986. Indeed, the trade union movement appears to have become an increasingly important actor in shaping economic and social policy in its role as social partner. By and large, the combination of these factors is widely seen as contributing to a social, political and economic context considered conducive to the sustenance of both a strong trade union role in society and pluralist industrial relations traditions. However, this has demonstrably not been the case. Since 1980, there has been a progressive and serious decline in union density (Roche and Ashmore, 2000; also see Roche, 1997b). Even over the past decade, when we have seen a huge upsurge in the numbers employed, the take-up of union membership has clearly not kept pace with employment creation. Consequently, union density continued to decline throughout the nineties. This is a particularly worrying phenomenon for unions since it has traditionally been the case that an economic boom and employment growth have positively impacted on trade union penetration (Roche, 1992).

Thus, in spite of an apparently supportive public policy context, the evidence presented in this chapter clearly indicates that trade unions and collective bargaining are facing particular challenges in our new "celtic tiger" economy. This evidence points to some inconsistency between the apparently high level of public policy support for trade union organisation on the one hand and the evidence on the ground of considerable erosion of trade union penetration on the other. This inconsistency is manifest in a number of areas, notably the decline in trade union density, increased employer resistance to union recognition, the tendency for employers to ignore Labour Court recommendations favouring trade union recognition and our industrial policy focus on sectors and corporations likely to resist union penetration.

Looking first at the issue of trade union density, we find a picture of steady and ongoing decline since the turn of the eighties. In regard to trade union recognition, there is conclusive evidence of extensive union avoidance among newer manufacturing and internationally traded service companies. A significant proportion of these companies are US owned and located in high-technology sectors. It is likely that this trend will be accentuated by the increasing numbers and visibility of firms successfully pursuing the non-union route which, in turn, provides useful models for new organisations considering establishing on a non-union basis (Gunnigle, Morley and Turner, 1997). This development reinforces the paradox between public policy support for trade unions and a State-sponsored pattern of industrial development which is significantly union averse. The encouragement of foreign direct investment is a critical aspect of Irish public (industrial) policy. Our economy is significantly more reliant on multinational investment than any other EU nation. Employment in foreign-owned multinational corporations (MNCs) now accounts for roughly one third of the industrial workforce. These foreign-owned companies account for 55 per cent of manufactured output and some 70 per cent of industrial exports (Tansey, 1998). US owned firms have a particularly strong presence in Ireland – a result of our overwhelming success in attracting US multinational investment. As noted earlier, a report in the *Economist* (1997) found that Ireland attracts close to a quarter of all available US manufacturing investments in Europe, and some 14 per cent of all foreign direct investment locating in Europe. These are remarkable statistics given that Ireland accounts for just one per cent of the EU's population.

Turning specifically to the role of trade unions, it is clear that the work of Ireland's industrial promotions agencies vested with responsibility for wooing foreign investment incorporates a significant industrial relations dimension. Until the early 1980s, these bodies promoted trade union recognition among inward-investing firms, specifically by recommending the conclusion of pre-production union recognition agreements and arranging introductions to trade union representatives. However, since the 1980s, it is clear that these bodies have shifted from this pro-union stance and adopted a more neutral position, indicating to inward-investing firms that they have the freedom to go the union or non-union route (see McGovern, 1989; Gunnigle et al., 1997). This change was accentuated by increased competition for mobile foreign investment and, particularly, as a result of competition from the Welsh and Scottish development agencies. In the "Thatcher era" of market-driven economic policies, these agencies appeared to target the attractions of non-union status to US inward-investing companies. In dealing with such competition, the Irish industrial promotions bodies altered their traditional collectivist orientation. Instead, they adopted a position whereby new companies were informed of their capacity to adopt whatever combination of human resource/industrial relations practices best suited their particular business needs (also see Gunnigle and McGuire, 2001). This stance is accurately captured in the following quote from Richard Bruton, former Minister for Enterprise and Employment, on the role of Ireland's largest industrial promotions agency, the IDA (Industrial Development Authority):

> The IDA is there to encourage the establishment of new companies. It is not there to press one particular way of dealing with industrial relations. I don't see that as part of the IDA agenda . . . Some companies have an approach to personnel relations which doesn't involve [trade] unions. But, fine, we have to be realistic and recognise that that is the approach they have taken. We can't set preconditions ... (Richard Bruton, TD: 1996 [see Hourihan, 1996]).

While this change has attracted adverse commentaries from sections of the trade union movement, it points to a reality that the industrial promotions agencies also operate in an increasingly competitive market (for mobile foreign investment) and are continually adapting their polices in the light of market needs (such as a desire to go non-union).

It also seems that the locus of much recent industrial development has been in sectors that are quite hostile to trade unions, particularly the computer/electronics sector. Many of these firms prioritise numerical and functional flexibility as means of responding quickly to fluctuations in demand (see Roche and Gunnigle, 1997). The perception that union recognition would inhibit their capacity to adjust their operating systems and employment patterns is an important factor encouraging such firms to go non-union. The following quote from the HR director of one of Ireland's fastest growing manufacturing companies illustrates this point:

> We are tremendously demanding on employees...The non-union issue is pretty strong. We need to be tremendously flexible – our products change every two years – and this is a reason for preferring our non-union status (HR director: US firm).

Thus, despite widespread political support for trade unions and their integration into centralised agreements, it seems that Ireland's industrial policy focus is contributing to a major diminution in trade union penetration in industry. More generally, our analysis of trade union membership patterns in Ireland suggests that, since the turn of the 1980s, trade union density has been in steady decline. Of equal significance has been increased employer opposition to trade union recognition, most evident among new firms in manufacturing industry and the internationally traded services sectors. On the industrial policy front, we have already seen above that the sectors targeted by the industrial development bodies, especially the computer, software and "back-office" sectors, tend to be quite hostile towards trade unions.

It is useful to briefly reflect on these developments, particularly the diminution in union penetration among new firms in the manufacturing and international services sectors. Why is union recognition so low in these sectors, particularly in an era of unprecedented economic growth? These issues have been addressed extensively by a number of commentators (see McGovern, 1989; Roche, 1997B, 2001; and Turner, 1994; Gunnigle et al., 1997; Roche and Ashmore, 2000) and only some summary observations are offered here.[9]

At enterprise level it is clear that the adoption of particular human resource management (HRM) practices have helped a number of firms establish and maintain non-union status. This is evident from the international literature which cites the use of "individualist" HRM practices as an important factor contributing to the diminution of trade union penetration at enterprise level (see Storey, 1992; Bacon and Storey, 1993; Storey and Bacon, 1993). The logic of this argument is that by facilitating employee involvement, providing satisfactory remuneration and promoting a benign "corporate culture", these policies help to remove traditional triggers to union organisation (for example, dissatisfaction with pay and conditions) and thus inhibit or prevent union penetration in such firms (Toner, 1987; Flood and Toner, 1997). Analysis of greenfield-site firms in Ireland pointed to a high take-up of individualist HRM practices, particularly in the areas of performance-related pay and direct communications. Gunnigle, Morley and Turner (1997) found that the adoption of such practices negatively impacts on union penetration in new firms. While the adoption of such practices was initially confined to US "high-tech" firms, the greenfield study suggests that such approaches are also being adopted in other companies and industrial sectors. Nevertheless, our evidence also indicates that the use of a combination of HR practices to establish and sustain non-union status is most common in high-technology manufacturing and service sectors.

Firm-based explanations only provide a partial explanation of decline in union penetration. Indeed, it is likely that HRM policies alone may exert only a limited influence in restricting union penetration. As Roche and Turner (1994)

---

9. Bill Roche, in several papers (see, for example, Roche, 1997b; Roche, 2001) provides a comprehensive review of the main influences on trade union growth and decline in Ireland. More recent insights and data are also available in his later piece, co-authored with Jacq Ashmore (Roche and Ashmore, 2000).

observe, one must consider developments in the broader economic and social environment to identify sources of change. Despite recent growth, it is important to remember that the Irish economy experienced quite a deep recession for much of the 1980s. This was a period of considerable rationalisation, "downsizing" and unemployment. Of particular note were changes in employment structure involving a decline in many areas of high unionisation, such as traditional indigenous manufacturing and areas of the public sector (particularly healthcare), and employment growth in sectors which have proved difficult for unions to penetrate (such as private services and "high-tech" manufacturing). Particular sectors of the economy present greater union penetration obstacles. In 1975, the services sector accounted for 46 per cent of all civilian employment but this rose to 62 per cent in 1997. Wallace et al. (2001) note the substantial employment growth in personal services (that is domestic servants and cleaners and other service workers), a category characterised by low union density. They also highlight the increase in professional and associated occupations, which, in the private sector, are substantially non-union. Overall, the services sector presents many barriers to unionisation given the high number of female, temporary and part-time employees (the services sector accounted for 84 per cent of total part-time jobs in 1997) (see Wallace et al., 2001). Over broadly the same period, we have also seen a considerable intensification in product market competition. In confronting these competitive challenges, many employers sought to re-structure their industrial relations approaches in such a way as to reduce operating costs and improve performance, quality and service. For many new firms in particular, the adoption of non-union strategies became an important perceived means of achieving required levels of flexibility and "agility". Thus, economic depression and unemployment contributed to an environment whereby new firms could adopt union avoidance policies and encounter very little opposition, either in terms of public policy impediments or, indeed, from trade unions themselves.

A third related and considerably more contentious factor which may have contributed to the decline in union penetration, particularly in newer firms, is the changing education and skill profile of the workforce. By EU standards the Republic of Ireland has a very young workforce. However, education levels have increased considerably since the 1960s. We have also seen change in the labour profile required by employers. In particular sectors, it is clear that employers demand better educated and more highly trained workers. From an industrial relations perspective, it is argued that labour market changes, particularly the growth of white-collar employment, and expansion in the service sector (see above) make for a workforce profile which appears less likely to take up union membership (see Kochan et al., 1986). In the US, for example, Farber (1985) estimated that 40 per cent of the decline in unionisation levels between the mid 1950s and the late 1970s was explained by structural changes in the US labour market, with the growth of white-collar and service-sector employment being particularly significant. However, this may be an over estimation (see D'Art, this volume, Chapter 2). In Ireland, we often find that large non-union employers commonly use the argument that white-collar/professional employees, especially technical graduates, have little interest in union membership (Toner, 1987; Flood and Toner, 1997; also see Foulkes, 1980). This perspective is captured in the following quote from a senior manager, with experience in two different US companies:

> While there was undoubtedly an overall corporate anti-union bias...one of the most interesting developments which I found was that Irish employees, particularly graduate software engineers, quickly embraced the individual performance evaluation approach of their peer group colleagues in the parent company. Many of them, who were recognised and rewarded financially by the company as "individual contributors", preferred to represent themselves rather than get tied up in a union-imposed grading system with the accompanying incremental wage scales based on years of service, not only for salary increases, but also for promotion (CEO: US "high-tech" manufacturing company).

However, the aggregate data on union membership does not categorically support the above position. For instance, the 1996 Labour Force Survey estimated that some 53 per cent of professional and technical workers were trade union members, the highest figure for any of the occupational categories surveyed, as highlighted in Table 10.5. A problem with this data is that it is not disaggregated into public and private sector groupings. It is well established,

Table 10.5: Unionisation, Occupational and Educational Level in Ireland, 1996

Unionisation and Occupational Level				
	Operatives, Labourers, Transport & Communications	Clerical Workers	Service Workers	Professional and Technical Workers
Union Density	46%	45%	20%	53%
Unionisation and Education Level				
	Primary Education	Junior Certificate	Leaving Certificate	Third Level
Union Density	28%	35%	39%	43%

Source: Labour Force Survey 1996 (Union density is calculated as the number of respondents who indicate membership of a union as a proportion of the estimated number of people at work by industry, occupation and educational level. The overall number of people at work according to the 1996 survey was 1.285 million).

for example, that some of the most highly unionised workers are professional categories in the public sector, such as teachers. It would be interesting to review trends in the private sector, particularly in relation to professional and technical grades given the suggestion above that such workers may have a lower propensity to unionise. A critical consideration in this regard is the issue of "union supply" (Hartley, 1992). As we have already seen, there are a number of sectors of the Irish economy where unions have made little or no inroads and where union density is extremely low. What is unclear is whether professional/technical workers in these sectors would join unions if the choice were available to them. Thus, the conundrum of whether such workers do not unionise because of a lower propensity to do so, or simply because union membership is not available to them, remains unclear.

CONCLUSION

These findings raise important paradoxes between espoused public policy, which supports a strong trade union role in industry, and actual practice, which contributes to an ongoing diminution in the role of organised labour. The reasons for this change stem less from any ideological change but rather from Ireland's vulnerable position as a very open, export-oriented economy which is heavily reliant on foreign direct investment (FDI). In an increasingly competitive market for the attraction and retention of FDI, Irish industrial policy has adopted the practice of portraying Ireland as a "union neutral" environment. This public policy stance emanates largely from a desire for Ireland to be characterised as a "new" economy: pro-business and enterprise and attractive to foreign direct investment. Indeed, it appears that FDI has become a critical factor impacting on public policy decisions in the sphere of industry and industrial relations. Our current public policy approach in the industrial relations arena seems largely determined by pragmatism and dependence on FDI. Thus, trade unions in Ireland, while playing an influential role at national level, appear to face much the same challenges at enterprise level as unions in other developed countries, some of which have experienced an overtly more hostile public policy position *vis-á-vis* trade unions. In Ireland, it appears that public policy has done little to promote union penetration but rather has overseen a progressive decline in union influence and Ireland's succession to a neo-liberal economy. This is very much in line with Hyman's (1999: 93) more general observation on the international scene that "after two decades in which the superior performance of such institutionalised economies as Germany and Japan was widely recognised, the conventional wisdom of the 1990s has been that dense social regulation involves rigidities requiring a shift to market liberalism". Trade unions are often seen, most particularly by US firms, as key contributors to excessive labour market "rigidities". Ireland has been to the fore in promoting an economic context in which firms – particularly US owned firms – can conduct their business free from such "rigidities". This has been a key factor in contributing to the decline in trade union density, recognition and influence at enterprise level in Ireland.

It remains to be seen if trade unions can arrest this decline in penetration. In commenting on recent union membership statistics, Sheehan (2001) found that while the data confirm union difficulties in increasing employment density, some unions have been successful in targeting particular groups. He notes in particular the cases of Mandate and SIPTU. The former has had considerable success in organising retail workers over recent years while SIPTU used three specialist recruiters to help organise construction workers over the past year and has also been very successful in this regard. Clearly, unions themselves can play an important role in arresting the decline in union penetration. More generally we must also await the impact – if any – of the new Industrial Relations (Amendment) Act on trade union penetration in Ireland.

APPENDIX: PROCEDURES ON RECOGNITION OF UNIONS

Procedures of the Code of Practice on Voluntary Dispute Resolution (Extracts)

Where negotiating arrangements are not in place and where collective bargaining fails to take place, the following process should be put in place with which management and unions should fully co-operate in seeking to resolve the issues in dispute effectively and expeditiously:

1. In the first instance, the matter should be referred to the Labour Relations Commission who will appoint an Officer from its Advisory Service to assess the issues in dispute.

2. The Labour Relations Commission Officer will work with the parties in an attempt to resolve the issues in dispute.

3. In the event that the issues in dispute are not capable of early resolution by the Labour Relations Commission intervention, an agreed cooling off period shall be put in place.

   During the cooling-off period, the Labour Relations Commission Advisory Service will continue to work with the parties in an attempt to resolve any outstanding issues. The Commission may engage expert assistance, including the involvement of ICTU and IBEC, should that prove helpful to the resolution of any differences.

4. If after the cooling-off period all issues have been resolved, the Labour Relations Commission will disengage. Before disengaging, the Commission may make proposals to the parties for the peaceful resolution of any further grievances or disputes.

5. In the event of issues remaining unresolved after the cooling-off period, the Labour Relations Commission shall make a written report to the Labour Court on the situation. The Labour Court shall consider the position of the employer and the union and shall issue recommendations on outstanding matters.

Where the voluntary process has not been followed: Industrial Relations (Amendment) Act, 2001 (Extracts)

2. (1) Notwithstanding anything contained in the Industrial Relations Acts, 1946 to 1990, at the request of a trade union or excepted body the Court may investigate a trade dispute where the Court is satisfied that:

    (a) it is not the practice of the employer to engage in collective bargaining negotiations and the internal dispute resolution procedures (if any) normally used by the parties concerned have failed to resolve the dispute,

    (b) the employer has failed to observe a provision of the Code of Practice on Voluntary Dispute Resolution under section 42 of the Industrial Relations Act, 1990 (or any code of practice amending or replacing that code), or has failed to observe such a provision in good faith,

    (c) the trade union or the excepted body or the employees, as the case may be, have not acted in a manner which, in the opinion of the Court, has frustrated the employer in observing a provision of such code of practice, and

    (d) the trade union or the excepted body or the employees, as the case may be, have not had recourse to industrial action after the dispute in question was referred to the Commission in accordance with the provisions of such code of practice.

  (2) In the course of an investigation under subsection (1), the Court shall have regard to the entirety of labour relations practices in the employment concerned including labour relations practices engaged in by the employer or an associated employer in another employment including an employment outside the State.

3. On receipt of a request under section 2, the Court may hold a preliminary hearing to determine whether or not the requirements specified in that section have been met.

5. (1) The Court, having investigated a trade dispute under section 2, may make a recommendation giving its opinion in the matter and, where appropriate, its view to the action that should be taken having regard to terms and conditions of employment, and to dispute resolution and disciplinary procedures, in the employment concerned.

  (2) A recommendation under subsection (1) shall not provide for arrangements for collective bargaining.

6. (1) Where, in the opinion of the Court, a dispute that is the subject of a recommendation under section 5 has not been resolved, the Court may, at the request of a trade union or excepted body and following a review of all relevant matters, make a determination.

  (2) A determination under subsection (1) may have regard to terms and conditions of employment, and to dispute resolution and disciplinary procedures, in the employment concerned but shall not provide for arrangements for collective bargaining.

  (3) A determination under subsection (1) shall be in the same terms as a recommendation under section 5 except where:

    (a) the Court has agreed a variation with the parties, or

(b) the Court has decided that the recommendation concerned or a part of that recommendation was grounded on unsound or incomplete information.

8. (1) Subject to subsection (2), the Court shall cease its investigation or review under section 6 and withdraw any recommendation where, either at the request of the employer or on its own initiative, the Court has satisfied itself that industrial action in relation to the dispute that is the subject of an investigation has taken place.

(2) If, having regard to all the circumstances, the Court is satisfied by a trade union or excepted body that it is reasonable to proceed with its investigation or review under section 6, it shall so proceed.

(3) Subsection (1) shall not apply where the procedures provided for by sections 2, 5 and 6 have been exhausted.

9. After a period of three months but not later than one year from the date of a determination under section 6, the Court may, on the application of either party to a dispute, review such determination, and

(a) vacate the determination and the order giving effect to the determination where, in the opinion of the Court, the dispute has been resolved,

(b) affirm the determination and the order giving effect to the determination where, in the opinion of the Court, the dispute has not been resolved, or

(c) vary the terms of the determination and the order giving effect to the determination where

(i) the Court has agreed a variation with the parties, or

(ii) the Court is satisfied that the determination or a part of the determination was grounded on unsound or incomplete information.

10. Where an employer fails to comply with:

(a) the terms of a determination under section 6 within one year from the date on which the determination is communicated to the parties, or

(b) the findings of a review of a determination under section 9 within 6 weeks from the date on which such findings are communicated to the parties,

on the application of a trade union or excepted body, the Circuit Court shall, without hearing the employer or any evidence (other than in relation to the matters aforesaid) make an order directing the employer to carry out the determination or review in accordance with its terms or findings, as appropriate.

11. Where a determination is made by the Court under section 6, either party to the dispute may appeal to the High Court on a point of law.

Source: Code of Practice on Voluntary Dispute Resolution; Industrial Relations (Amendment) Act, 2001.

REFERENCES

Abbott and Whelan v The Southern Health Board (1982) 1 J.I.S.L.L. 56.

Adams, R. (1993) "The North American Model of Employee Representational Participation: 'A Hollow Mockery'" *Comparative Labor Law Journal*, Vol. 15, No. 4: 4–14.

Bacon, N. and Storey, J. (1993) "Individualization of the Employment Relationship and the Implications for Trade Unions" *Employee Relations*, Vol. 15, No. 1: 5–17.

Beaumont, P. B. (1985) "New Plant Work Practices" *Personnel Review*, Vol. 14, No. 5: 15–19.

Beaumont, P. B. (1991) "Trade Unions and HRM" *Industrial Relations Journal*, Vol. 22, No. 4: 300–308.

Beaumont, P. B. (1992) "The US Human Resource Management Literature: A Review" in Salaman, G. (ed.) *Human Resource Strategies*. London: Open University/Sage Publications.

Beaumont, P. B. and Harris, R. I. D. (1994) "Opposition to Unions in the Non-Union Sector in Britain" *International Journal of Human Resource Management*, Vol. 5, No. 2: 457–471.

Beaumont, P. B. and Townley, B. (1985) "Greenfield Sites, New Plants and Work Practices" in Hammond, V. (ed.) *Current Research in Management*. London: Frances Pinter.

Blyton, P. and Turnbull, P. (1992) *Reassessing Human Resource Management*. London: Sage Publications.

Bomers, G. and Peterson, R. (1977) "Multinational Corporations and Industrial Relations: The Case of West Germany and the Netherlands" *British Journal of Industrial Relations*, Vol. 15, No. 1: 45–62.

Boyd, A. (1972) *The Rise of Irish Trade Unions: 1729–1970*. Tralee: Anvil.

Brewster, C. and Hegewisch, A. (1994) *Policy and Practice in European Human Resource Management: The Price Waterhouse Cranfield Survey*. London: Routledge.

Bureau of Labor Statistics (2001) *Labor Force Statistics from the Current Population Survey*, http://stats.bls.gov/release/union2.nr0.htm

Carrell, M. and Heavrin, C. (1985) *Collective Bargaining and Labor Relations, Cases, Practice and Law*. Columbus: Charles E. Merrill Publishing Company.

Dobbins, T., Geary, J. and Sheehan, B. (1999) "Breakthrough on Trade Union Recognition" *Eiro Observer*, 21 March, 7–8.

Economist (1997) "Green is Good: Advantages of Ireland as a Host for F.D.I." *Economist*, Vol. 343, No. 8017: 21–24.

Educational Company of Ireland v Fitzpatrick and Others (1961) IR323.

Farber, H. S. (1985), "The Extent of Unionisation in the United States" in Kochan, T. A. (ed.) *Challenges and Choices Facing American Labor*. Cambridge: Mass.: MIT Press.

Ferner, A. (1997) "Country of Origin Effects and HRM in Multinational

Companies" *Human Resource Management Journal*, Vol. 7, No. 1: 19–36.

Flood, P. C. and Toner, B. (1997) "How do Large Non-Unions Companies Avoid a Catch 22?" *British Journal of Industrial Relations*, Vol. 35, No. 2: 257–277.

Foulkes, F. (1980) *Personnel Policies in Large Non-Union Companies*. Englewood Cliffs N. J.: Prentice-Hall.

Gall, G. (2000) "In Place of Strife?" *People Management*, 14 September, 26–30.

Gennard, J. and Steuer, M. D. (1971) "The Industrial Relations of Foreign-Owned Subsidiaries in the United Kingdom" *British Journal of Industrial Relations*, Vol. 9: 143–159.

Goss, D. 1991. *Small Business and Society*, London: Routledge.

Gray, A. W. (1997) (ed.) *International Perspectives on the Irish Economy*. Dublin: Indecon Economic Consultants.

Guest, D. and Hoque, K. (1996) "Human Resource Management and the New Industrial Relations" in Beardwell, I. J. (ed.) *Contemporary Industrial Relations: A Critical Analysis*. Oxford: Oxford University Press.

Gunnigle, P. (1989) "Management Approaches to Industrial Relations in the Small Firm in University College Dublin" in *Industrial Relations in Ireland: Contemporary Issues and Developments*. Dublin: Department of Industrial Relations, University College Dublin.

Gunnigle, P. (1995) "Collectivism and the Management of Industrial Relations in Greenfield Sites" *Human Resource Management Journal*, Vol. 5, No. 3: 24–40.

Gunnigle, P. (1998) "Human Resource Management and the Personnel Function" in Roche, W. K., Monks, K. and Walsh, J. (eds) *Human Resource Management Strategies: Policy and Practice in Ireland*. Dublin: Oak Tree Press.

Gunnigle, P. (2000) "Paradox in Policy and Practice: Trade Unions and Public Policy in the Republic of Ireland" *Irish Business and Administrative Research*, Vol. 21, No. 2: 39–54.

Gunnigle, P. and Brady, T., (1984) "The Management of Industrial Relations in the Small Firm" *Employee Relations*, Vol. 6, No. 5: 21–24.

Gunnigle, P. and McGuire, D. (2001) "Why Ireland? A Qualitative Review of the Factors Influencing the Location of US Multinationals in Ireland with Particular Reference to the Impact of Labour Issues" *Economic and Social Review*, Vol. 32, No. 1 (forthcoming).

Gunnigle, P. and Morley, M. (1993) "Something Old, Something New: A Perspective on Industrial Relations in the Republic of Ireland" *Review of Employment Topics*, Vol. 1, No. 1: 114–142.

Gunnigle, P., Flood, P., Morley, M. and Turner, T. (1994) *Continuity and Change in Irish Employee Relations*. Dublin: Oak Tree Press.

Gunnigle, P., MacCurtain, S. and Morley, M. (2001) "Dismantling Pluralism:

Industrial Relations in Irish Greenfield Sites" *Personnel Review* Vol. 30, No. 3 (forthcoming).

Gunnigle, P., Morley, M. and Turner, T. (1997) "Challenging Collectivist Traditions: Individualism and the Management of Industrial Relations in Greenfield Sites" *Economic and Social Review*, Vol. 28, No. 2: 105–134.

Gunnigle, P., Morley, M., Clifford, N. and Turner, T. (1997) *Human Resource Management in Irish Organisations: Practice in Perspective*. Dublin: Oak Tree Press.

Hartley, J. (1992) "Joining a Trade Union" in Hartley, J. and Stephenson, G. (eds) *Employment Relations: The Psychology of Influence and Control at Work*. Oxford: Blackwell.

Higgins, C. (2001) "Fast Track Measures in Amended Union Recognition Bill" *Industrial Relations News*, No. 19: 14.

Hillery, B. (1994) "The Institutions of Industrial Relations" in Murphy, T. V. and Roche, W. K. (eds) *Irish Industrial Relations in Practice*. Dublin: Oak Tree Press.

Hourihan, F. (1996) "Non-Union Policies on the Increase Among New Overseas Firms" *Industrial Relations News*, No. 4, 25 January, 17–23.

Hyman, R. (1999) "National Industrial Relations Systems and Transnational Challenges: An Essay in Review" *European Journal of Industrial Relations*, Vol. 5, No. 1: 89–110.

Industrial Relations News (1998) "Union Recognition Formula Points to Limit of Partnership Approach" *Industrial Relations News*, No. 3: 16–17.

Industrial Relations News (1999) "High Level Group on Recognition of Unions and the Right to Bargain (Final Agreed Text)" *Industrial Relations News*, No. 11: 20–21.

Industrial Relations News (2000a) "Union Membership Set to Drop to 20% in the Private Sector" *Industrial Relations News*, No. 39: 18–19.

Industrial Relations News (2000b) "Union Recognition – New Dispute Settling Power for the Labour Court Based on ICTU/IBEC Formula" *Industrial Relations News*, No. 5: 21–23.

Irish Congress of Trade Unions (ICTU) (1993) *New Forms of Work Organisation: Options for Unions*. Dublin: ICTU.

Irish Congress of Trade Unions (ICTU) (1995) *Managing Change*. Dublin: ICTU.

Kochan, T. A., Katz, H. C. and McKersie, R. B. (1986) *The Transformation of American Industrial Relations*. New York: Basic Books.

Leopold, J. W. and Hallier, J. P. (1997) "Start Up and Ageing in Greenfield Sites" *Human Resource Management Journal*, Vol. 7, No. 2: 72–88.

McGovern, P. (1989) "Union Recognition and Union Avoidance in the 1980's" *Industrial Relations in Ireland: Contemporary Issues and Developments*. Dublin: University College Dublin.

McMahon, J. (1996) "Employee Relations in Small Firms in Ireland: An Exploratory Study of Small Manufacturing Firms" *Employee Relations*, Vol. 5, No. 5: 66–80.

Mooney, P. (1989) *From Industrial Relations to Employee Relations in Ireland*, Unpublished PhD Dissertation. Dublin: University of Dublin.

Murray, S. (1984) *Employee Relations in Irish Private Sector Manufacturing Industry*. Dublin: Industrial Development Authority.

Newell, H. (1993) *Field of Dreams: Evidence of "New" Employee Relations in Greenfield Sites*, D.Phil Thesis. Oxford: Oxford University.

Nolan Transport (Oaklands) Ltd. v Halligan and Others and SIPTU (1998) 9 E.L.R. 177.

Organisation for Economic Co-operation and Development (1999) *OECD Economic Survey: Ireland*. Paris: OECD.

Pat the Baker Limited v SIPTU (1991) LCR13305.

Purcell, J. (1987) "Mapping Management Styles in Employee Relations" *Journal of Management Studies*, Vol. 24, No. 5: 533–548.

Roche, W. K. (1992) "Modelling Trade Union Growth and Decline in the Republic of Ireland' *Irish Business and Administrative Research*, Vol. 13, No. 1: 86–102.

Roche, W. K. (1997a) "Pay Determination, the State and the Politics of Industrial Relations" in Murphy, T. V. and Roche, W. K. (eds) *Irish Industrial Relations in Practice: Revised and Expanded Edition*. Dublin: Oak Tree Press.

Roche, W. K. (1997b) "The Trend of Unionisation" in Murphy, T. V. and Roche, W. K. (eds) *Irish Industrial Relations in Practice: Revised and Expanded Edition*. Dublin: Oak Tree Press.

Roche, W. K. (2001) "Accounting for the Trend in Trade Union Recognition" *Industrial Relations Journal*, Vol. 32, No. 1: 37–55.

Roche, W. K. and Ashmore, J. S. (2000) "Irish Unions in the 1990s: Testing the Limits of Social Partnership" in Griffin, G. (ed.) *Changing Patterns of Trade Unionism: Comparisons between English-speaking Countries*. London: Mansell (in press).

Roche, W. K. and Gunnigle, P. (1997) "Competition and the New Industrial Relations Agenda" in Murphy, T. V. and Roche, W. K. (eds) *Irish Industrial Relations in Practice: Revised and Expanded Edition*. Dublin: Oak Tree Press.

Roche, W. K. and Larragy, J. (1989) "The Trend of Unionisation in the Irish Republic" *Industrial Relations in Ireland: Contemporary Issues and Developments*, Dublin: Department of Industrial Relations, University College Dublin.

Roche, W. K. and Turner, T. (1994) "Testing Alternative Models of Human Resource Policy Effects on Trade Union Recognition in the Republic of Ireland" *International Journal of Human Resource Management*, Vol. 5, No. 3: 721–753.

Salamon, M. (1998) *Industrial Relations: Theory and Practice*. London: Prentice-Hall.

Sheehan, B. (1998a) "Union Recognition Formula Points to Limit of Partnership Approach" *Industrial Relations News*, No. 3: 16–17.

Sheehan, B. (1998b) "Draft Proposals on Union Recognition Likely to Face Trenchant Opposition" *Industrial Relations News*, No. 1/2: 3–5.

Sheehan, B. (2001) "UK Union Recognition Law Having Major Impact" *Industrial Relations Journal*, No. 28: 18.

Sparrow, P. and Hiltrop, J. M. (1994) *European Human Resource Management in Transition*. Hemel Hempstead: Prentice Hall.

Stanworth, J. (1991) *Bolton 20 Years On: The Small Firm in the 1990s*. London: Paul Chapman.

Storey, J. (1992) *Developments in the Management of Human Resources*. Oxford: Blackwell.

Storey, J. and Bacon, N. (1993) "Individualism and Collectivism: Into the 1990s" *International Journal of Human Resource Management*, Vol. 4, No. 3: 665–683.

Tansey, P. (1998) *Ireland at Work: Economic Growth and the Labour Market 1987–1997*. Dublin: Oak Tree Press.

Toner, B. (1987) *Union or Non-Union Employee Relations Strategies in the Republic of Ireland*. Unpublished PhD thesis. London: London School of Economics.

Torrington, D. and Hall, L. (1995) *Personnel Management: Human Resource Management in Action*. London: Prentice Hall.

Twomey, A. F. (2001) *The Industrial Relations (Amendment) Bill, 2000: Birth of a Boom-Breaker?* Paper delivered at the CIPD Annual Strategic Law Conference, 14 March.

United States Bureau of Labor Statistics (2001) *United States Unionisation and NRLB Election Data and Computations, 1998–2000*. Washington: Bureau of Labor Statistics.

Wallace, J. (1992) *The Industrial Relations Act 1990 and other Developments in Labour Law*. Paper delivered to the Institute of Personnel Management.

Wallace, J., Dineen, D. A. and O'Sullivan, M. (2001) "The Contribution of the Services Sector to the Irish Employment Miracle" in Dølvik, J. E. (ed.) *At your Service: Comparative Perspectives on Employment and Labour Relations in the European Private Services Sector*. Brussels: P. I. E. Peter Lang European University Press.

Walsh, J. (2000) "Avoid 'Economic Heart Attack' by Busting Unions, says Lawyer" *People Management*, 25 May, 8.

Wood, S. and Goddard, J. (1999) "The Statutory Union Recognition Procedure in the Employment Relations Bill: A Comparative Analysis" *British Journal of Industrial Relations*, Vol. 37, No. 2: 203–245.

CHAPTER 11

Corporatism In Ireland: A View From Below

DARYL D'ART AND THOMAS TURNER

INTRODUCTION

After 1945 many European governments adopted a Keynesian approach to economic management and the promotion or maintenance of full employment. The resultant increase in union bargaining power and the consequent threat of inflation encouraged many governments to embrace income policies or bargained corporatism. While the form of corporatist arrangements varies considerably across European countries, a number of characteristic features of the model can be identified. First, the centralised agreements negotiated between the social partners go beyond purely industrial relations matters to include broader socio-economic goals. Secondly, the agreement is a negotiated exchange between the parties. Trade unions agree to co-operate with government and employers to restrict union members to agreed pay norms. In return, unions and employers may gain a measure of influence over public policy in areas of critical concern to their constituents such as employment, social welfare and taxation (Maier, 1984; Roche, 1994). By the 1970s, there appeared to be a convergence among Western European societies on a bargained corporatist pattern of industrial relations (Crouch, 1992). Within a decade, under the impact of recession, intensifying international competition, the abandonment of Keynesianism and a political shift to the right, bargained corporatism was at a discount. In many European countries, centralised bargaining was either gradually or immediately replaced by bargaining at firm or industry level. Even in Austria, where corporatist bargaining survived, more was demanded from the labour movement in terms of flexibility and restraint (see Traxler, 1995). It was, according to Traxler (1995), a shift from demand-side corporatism geared to Keynesian economic policies to supply side corporatism, emphasising competitiveness, worker flexibility and restraint.

The case of bargained corporatism or social partnership in Ireland appears to be an exception to this general trend. Since 1987, social partnership-type agreements between trade unions, employers and government have been the dominant feature of collective bargaining in Ireland. Such agreements also occurred in an earlier period form 1970 to 1980 but were less comprehensive in scope and proved more unstable than present agreements (O'Brien, 1981;

Hardiman, 1992). Indeed, on a cumulative scale of corporatism, Irish social partnership-type arrangements of this period would register as a medium model (Lehmbruch, 1984: 66). Since 1987, the revival and development of centralised bargaining in Ireland may apparently represent a shift towards a stronger model of corporatism. This has taken place in the context of a booming economy, the achievement of near full employment and the demand for labour outstripping supply in some sectors of the economy. All this is reminiscent of the halcyon days of European corporatism. While these arrangements brought many benefits, they presented the participating union movements with problems that proved difficult to resolve. The Swedish model is an exemplar of the tensions and contradictions for union movements involved in these arrangements.

According to Teague (1995), there is a widely held perception among Irish trade union officials that the centralised agreements negotiated since 1987 represent a new departure. These agreements are perceived as indicating a move towards the Swedish model of corporatism. While Swedish corporatism has produced many beneficial social and economic outcomes, it also had a number of unintended consequences that were to prove problematic for labour and trade unions. First, a substantial concentration of wealth towards employers and, secondly, a rank-and-file revolt of union members challenging the outcomes of centralised agreements. Swedish union members were not opposed in principle to centralised bargaining but to its apparent inability to redress the unequal distribution of wealth and union weakness at plant level.

All corporatist arrangements have the common objective of establishing a virtuous circle of wage restraint, investment and growth (Maier, 1984: 57). The weakest link in this chain is generally considered to be the workers whose wages are to be regulated. Whatever the systemic benefits of regulated wages, the primary point of instability and breakdown is at the micro level, that is, in the willingness of workers to sacrifice short-term wage gains in the pursuit of the general welfare (Lange, 1984: 98). Indeed, it was a rank-and-file revolt of Swedish workers discontented with union weakness at plant level and increasing inequality in the distribution of wealth that forced the labour movement to adopt a programme of industrial and economic democracy. Once accepted by the social democrats, the embodiment of industrial democracy in labour legislation was remarkably rapid. The laws enacted in the previous 60 years governing relations in the labour market were almost entirely replaced between 1972 and 1978.[1] While industrial democracy reforms may have been a solution for problems encountered at enterprise level, other difficulties confronted the labour movement on a macro level. How could centralised bargaining be maintained without exacerbating the unequal distribution of wealth and the concentration of economic power and how could employee

---

1. Board Representation of employees, 1973; Act on Shop Stewards, 1974; Work Safety Law, 1974; Security of Employment Act, 1974; Act on Employee Participation and Decision Making Act, 1977.

influence be increased over the economic process (Meidner, 1978)? The proposed solution was that 20 per cent of pre-tax profits in certain firms would be annually transferred in the forms of shares to a central employee wage-earner fund controlled and administered by the trade union movement. Wage restraint could now be pursued free of its maldistributive aspects, for the greater a firm's profit the faster would wage earner shares accumulate in the fund. Thus, wage restraint by workers in the most profitable companies would not benefit private owners (Meidner, 1978). Yet these attempts to modify the existing corporatist arrangement in favour of increased equity and democracy ultimately threatened its continuance (Aberg, 1984; Schwerin, 1984; D'Art, 1992: 152–166; Kjellberg, 1992; Visser, 1996).

Are the strains and problems experienced by the Swedish labour movement common to all developed forms of corporatism? Certainly, during the early 1970s, the operation of incomes policies in Denmark produced similar problems for the Danish labour movement and called forth a solution that anticipated the Meidner plan (D'Art, 1992: 204–208). Furthermore, the potential destablising effect of inequitable outcomes on incomes policy was a concern felt beyond Scandinavia. A resolution of the European Parliament insisted that "an incomes policy cannot be effective unless it is accompanied by a policy whereby large sections of the population are favoured in asset formation and whereby would be avoided an excessive concentration of assets in the hands of a few" (E.C., 1979). Consequently, it seems plausible to argue that the Irish labour movement will not escape the difficulties encountered by its Scandinavian and European counterparts (see Wallace et al., 1998). These are the issues addressed in this chapter. Indeed, it is a particularly apposite time to consider these problems after more than ten years of social partnership and on the threshold of a new agreement. If the Irish case follows a similar pattern to the Scandinavian models, we can expect, first, to see greater returns to capital than labour and a resulting scepticism among the rank and file concerning the outcomes of these agreements and, secondly, a weakening of the effectiveness of union organisation at plant level.

SURVEY DATA

The data in this chapter are based on a survey of members of the Amalgamated, Transport and General Workers Union (ATGWU) in Ireland carried out in 1998.[2] A total of 2,080 members in 43 companies were surveyed. Union members were randomly selected using the membership list for each company provided by the trade union. The questionnaires were addressed to the selected members and distributed to the companies either directly by the authors or through relevant union officers. Each questionnaire included an envelope

---

2. Support for the project was provided by the union and the Department of Personnel and Employment Relations, University of Limerick.

addressed to the authors for the completed questionnaire. A total of 605 completed questionnaires were returned. This represents 29 per cent of the sample surveyed. Such a return rate is acceptable for a postal survey. The majority of respondents, 64 per cent, worked in the private sector and the remainder, 34 per cent, in the public sector. In all, 78 per cent worked in the manufacturing sector and 22 per cent in services.

TRENDS IN ECONOMIC PERFORMANCE 1987–1996

The period since 1987, and particularly after 1994, has been one of continuous and rapid growth in the Irish economy. The economic crisis that acted as a catalyst for the emergence of centralised agreements has vanished. Real national income increased by 54 per cent between 1987 and 1996 compared to an increase of 7 per cent between 1980 and 1987. In 1996 alone national income grew by 8 per cent (Table 11.1).

Table 11.1: Economic Indicators 1987–1998*

Year	National Income	Average Earnings**	Company Profits	Number Employed	Unemploy-ment***
	% change	% change	% change	% change	% change
1987–1998	+ 54.2 (1987–1996)	+ 17.5	+ 77.7 (1987–1996)	+ 41.7	– 27

*All prices standardised using the consumer price index: base year 1968.
** Refers to average industrial earnings before taxation deductions.
*** Seasonally adjusted standardised unemployment rates from the live register.

Source: Central Statistics Office: Labour Force Survey and National Income and Expenditure Reports.

While unemployment increased from 7.3 per cent of the labour force in 1980 to 17.5 per cent in 1987, it subsequently decreased to 6.2 per cent by September 1999. This sharp fall in unemployment has been accompanied by a substantial rise in the number of people at work, the employed labour force increased from 1,090,000 in 1987 to 1,544,700 by November 1998, an increase of 41.7 per cent. A similar trend is evident in the growth of real wages since 1987. Between 1980 and 1987, there was no real increase in the gross average industrial wage, whereas gross average earnings of industrial workers increased by 17.5 per cent between 1987 and 1998. Indeed, it is estimated that real average *disposable* income actually fell by between 8 and 10 per cent between 1980 and 1987, while real *disposable* income is estimated to have increased by about 27 per cent between 1987 and 1998 partly as a result of changes in taxation (see Leddin and Walsh, 1997: 8). However, company profits increased at a more rapid rate than average wages, 78 per cent from 1987 to 1996. A recent paper has examined the movement of profit and wage shares in the nine-year period between 1987 and 1996. There has been a dramatic shift in income share from labour to capital with the profit share rising from 25.1 per cent in 1987 to 34.8 per cent by 1996 and a corresponding decline in the wage share from 74.9 per cent to 65.2 per cent. In short, there has been a radical income shift away from labour and towards capital during this period (Lane, 1998).

In summary, like the Swedish experience, the centralised agreements negotiated since 1987 have been associated with, in the main, beneficial outcomes for the social partners in terms of real wages, profits and decreasing unemployment. In an increasingly buoyant economy it would be surprising if all parties did not experience some gains. A more appropriate question in this regard is the extent to which the agreements have promoted equity and fairness in the distribution of wealth. The reverse seems to be the case as the chief beneficiaries have been the employers. As Allen observes, instead of a "trickle down effect there is a trickle up" effect (Allen, 1999: 41).

UNION MEMBERS PERCEPTIONS OF OUTCOMES

Members of a general union were surveyed to assess their opinion regarding the effect of national wage agreements in two areas: the distributive effects of the agreements on various social groupings in Irish society and the impact of the agreements on their specific pay and conditions. As Table 11.2 indicates, wage earners, the unemployed and low income groups were perceived to have benefited considerably less than employers, the self-employed and the

Table 11.2: Perceptions of which Groups Benefited from the National Wage Agreements

	No Benefit	A little Benefit	Benefit Greatly	N
Wage earners	31%	67%	2%	100% (581)
Unemployed	48%	42%	10%	100% (555)
Low income groups	46%	49%	5%	100% (561)
Employers	6%	24%	70%	100% (557)
Self-employed	23%	36%	41%	100% (538)
Government	2%	11%	87%	100% (553)

Source: Union member survey.

government. Indeed, respondents felt that government and, particularly, employers have benefited greatly from the agreements. A majority of the respondents reported that wage earners, the unemployed and low-income groups had received some benefits. Yet almost half the respondents believed that the unemployed and low-income groups had experienced no benefit from the agreements.

A majority of respondents (69 per cent) believe that national wage agreements have not been effective in giving workers a fairer share of the national cake (Table 11.3).

Table 11.3: National Wage Agreements since 1987 have given a Fairer Share to Workers*

	Percentage
Strongly Disagree	25
Disagree	44
Agree	28
Strongly Agree	3
N	100% (536)

* Respondents with no opinion are excluded.

Source: Union member survey.

Turning to the impact of national wage agreements on member's own pay and working conditions, Table 11.4 indicates that only a minority believed that national wage agreements had a detrimental effect on pay, pensions, job security

Table 11.4: The Impact of National Wage Agreements on Respondents' Pay and Conditions of Employment

	Pay	Pensions	Job Security	Hours Reduction
Much Worse	5%	3%	8%	2%
Slightly Worse	5%	4%	7%	4%
No Change	20%	66%	73%	79%
Minor Improvement	68%	25%	10%	14
Major Improvement	2%	2%	2%	1%
N	100% (596)	100% (559)	100% (582)	100% (588)

Source: Union member survey.

and working hours. However, aside from changes in pay, a majority felt that either there had been no change or a deterioration in pensions (73 per cent), job security (88 per cent) and hours worked (85 per cent). A majority of respondents (68 per cent) believed there had been minor improvements in pay.

The above results indicate that a large proportion of union members believe that the government and employers have benefited most from national wage agreements, while the unemployed and low-income groups have benefited least. Furthermore, the agreements are perceived to have been ineffective in redistributing a fairer share of national income to workers. More specifically, apart from a minor improvement in pay, the areas of pensions, job security and hours worked are perceived to have either remained unchanged or deteriorated.

EFFECTIVENESS OF UNIONS

We address the question of union effectiveness at two levels: the influence of trade unions in Irish industrial relations and the wider economy and the effectiveness of members' own union at workplace level. Almost 50 per cent of members surveyed indicated that the capacity of the Irish Congress of Trade Unions to promote social policies which reduce unemployment and reform taxation policy had not changed. Those who perceived a change were more likely to believe that ICTU influence in the areas of unemployment and taxation had increased rather than decreased. However, a total of 37 per cent of respondents believed that the ability of unions to win recognition from employers had decreased, while 16 per cent believed it had increased, with 47 per cent perceiving no change in this area (Table 11.5).

Regarding respondents' own union, 57 per cent believed that the effectiveness of their union had decreased in negotiations, while 12 per cent indicated it had increased. This probably reflects the inevitable loss of autonomy for individual unions when national wage agreements are negotiated. More significantly, 49 per cent of respondents believed that the ability of their union to get things done at the workplace had decreased, compared to 14 per cent who felt that it had increased. Taken together, the effectiveness of the union and its capacity at the workplace, the results indicate that more union members perceive a decrease rather than an increase in the effectiveness of their union. Conversely, a greater proportion of respondents believed that the influence of ICTU had increased rather than decreased in the areas of unemployment and taxation but the ability of trade unions generally to gain recognition from employers had decreased.

Almost 50 per cent of respondents indicated no change in the union's capacity to negotiate over changes in work practices, productivity deals and the introduction of new technology (Table 11.6). Yet more members believe that the union's capacity to negotiate in these areas had decreased compared

Table 11.5: National Wage Agreements and their Impact on Trade Union Effectiveness

	Ability of ICTU* to promote social policies which reduce unemployment	Effectiveness of ICTU in reforming government taxation policy	Capacity of union to gain recognition from employers	Effectiveness of ATGWU in negotiations	Ability of your union to get things done in your workplace
Decreased	19%	20%	37%	57%	49%
No change	51%	48%	47%	31%	37%
Increased	30%	32%	16%	12%	14%
N	100% (587)	100% (589)	100% (588)	100% (595)	100% (595)

* Irish Congress of Trade Unions.

Source: Union member survey.

to those who perceived increased union influence. More respondents perceived their union's ability to ensure management honour negotiated agreements and prevent the dismissal of workers had increased rather than decreased.

The evidence from the above tables suggests that respondents perceive an overall reduction in their unions influence at national level and a reduction in their effectiveness at firm level during the period of national wage agreements.

Table 11.6: Changing Influence of Respondents' Unions at their Workplaces*

	To Negotiate Changes in Work Practices	To Negotiate Introduction of New Technology	To Negotiate Over Productivity	To Ensure Management Keep to Agreements Negotiated	To Prevent the Dismissal of Workers
Decreased	32%	32%	31%	26%	13%
No Change	48%	48%	47%	44%	60%
Increased	20%	20%	22%	30%	26%
N	100% (579)	100% (569)	100% (570)	100% (577)	100% (574)

*The question asked was: In recent times has the ability of the union in your company to get things done *changed* in the following areas?

Source: Union member survey.

WORKPLACE INITIATIVES AND PARTNERSHIP AT FIRM LEVEL

The Irish Congress of Trade Unions has encouraged the development of social partnership between unions, employees and management at firm level to complement agreement at national level. The present national wage agreement, Partnership 2000, includes a more comprehensive reference to social partnership at firm level than previous agreements. Both the Irish Business Employers Confederation (IBEC) and ICTU have agreed to the development of appropriate initiatives at enterprise level. However, the agreement did not attempt to "impose any single structure or model of partnership" and recognised the need to "tailor the approach to fit different employment settings" [Partnership 2000, 1996]. The agreement lists a number of topics appropriate for discussion, which range from employee co-operation with change, including new forms of work organisation, to forms of financial involvement. While there may be some differences regarding the detail of their application, there is a remarkable level of consensus among the peak organisations as to the nature of these initiatives. This consensus is mainly due to the ICTU's shift in emphasis from representative participation (for example worker directors) to task-based schemes of employee involvement (see FIE/ICTU Joint Declaration on Employee Involvement, 1991). Accordingly, schemes of employee involvement such as team working, quality circles or profit sharing schemes at the level of the individual firm all come under the rubric of appropriate initiatives.

In this section we focus on the extent to which new workplace initiatives have been introduced in the companies surveyed and on union members' perceptions of their effect in fostering partnership with management. It should be noted that what is being measured here is members' perceptions of particular initiatives have been introduced in recent years. It may well be the case that many members are unaware of the existence of new initiatives in their companies. However, our purpose here is not to document such initiatives but to examine members' experiences.

An implicit premise of the trade union position is that such developments will have beneficial outcomes both for individual union members in their daily jobs, encourage greater partnership between employees and management, strengthen local union organisation and give workers a fairer share of a company's economic success. Table 11.7 addresses these issues and evaluates member perceptions of the outcomes of new workplace initiatives.

While 60 per cent of respondents believed that the influence they had over how to do their job remained unchanged, 24 per cent felt it had actually decreased, with 16 per cent indicating it had increased. However, 65 per cent of respondents believed that the amount of work to be done had increased, 32 per cent indicated no change and only 3 per cent stated that it had decreased. Clearly, employees felt that they were working harder but had not, in most cases, experienced any increased influence over their day-to-day task activities. In terms of partnership between management and employees, the development

Table 11.7: New Initiatives and Organisational Outcomes*

	Job Related Outcomes		Institutional Outcomes		Rewards
	Influence in Deciding how your Job is Done	*Amount of Work you have to do*	*Feelings of a "them and us" Divide*	*Influence your Trade Union has in your workplace*	*Fairer Share of Profits to Workers in your Firm*
Decreased	24%	3%	17%	38%	22%
No Change	60%	32%	53%	47%	63%
Increased	16%	65%	30%	15%	15%
N	100% (470)	100% (469)	100% (473)	100% (476)	100% (459)

*The question asked: If you have experienced any new workplace initiatives have they achieved any of the following? (See items in table above.)

of new workplace initiatives does not appear to have fostered an increased sense of partnership. A total of 30 per cent of respondents indicated an increase in the sense of a "them and us" divide between management and employees, while 53 per cent indicated no change and 19 per cent reported that the divide had decreased. A substantial proportion of members (38 per cent) believed that the influence of their union in the workplace had decreased compared to 15 per cent who felt it had increased, while 47 per cent indicated no change in the union's influence. Lastly, a greater number of members surveyed (22 per cent) believed that the share of profits going to workers in their firm had decreased while 15 per cent indicated an increase and 63 per cent no change in the situation. The evidence here appears to show that new workplace initiatives have been largely perceived to have either no impact or a negative outcome for workers. In particular, local union influence is perceived to have decreased. Although it may be the case that this perceived decline in union influence is unrelated to the workplace initiatives, it raises questions about the efficacy of such initiatives for improving or developing local union organisation. On a general note, it is plausible to conclude that the development of a genuine sense of partnership at firm level has not occurred to any significant degree in the companies surveyed here. As Table 11.8 indicates, responses to the general question about the emergence of social partnership at firm level reveal that the majority of respondents either believe that co-operation has declined (37 per cent) or has remained unchanged (40 per cent). These perceptions find some support in recent studies, which suggest that the extent and depth of collaborative production in Ireland may be exaggerated (Gunnigle, 1997; D'Art and Turner, 1999; Roche and Geary, 1999).

One caveat should be entered before proceeding as to the generalisability of our findings. The objection might be raised that the views of ATGWU union members are unrepresentative of the generality of Irish trade union

Table 11.8: Social Partnership and Co-operation Between Management and Workers at Firm Level*

Co-operation between management has declined to a great extent	14%
There is less co-operation in this workplace than before	23%
Nothing has changed here	40%
Co-operation has increased to some extent	22%
Co-operation has increased greatly	1%
Total	100% (587)

*The ICTU have promoted the idea of social partnership and co-operation between management and workers at firm level. What is your experience of this in your firm?

opinion, given that the ATGWU union leadership has been publicly sceptical of previous national wage agreements. However, only a minority, 20 per cent of the members we surveyed, were completely opposed to any new wage agreement.[3] Furthermore, beyond the confines of the ATGWU there has been a growth in opposition to acceptance of the latest wage agreement, the Programme for Prosperity and Fairness. Therefore, the attitudes of ATGWU members cannot be considered to be wholly unrepresentative of Irish rank-and-file opinion.

CONCLUSION

The perception among some Irish trade unionists that the centralised agreements negotiated since 1987 represent a shift towards the Swedish model of corporatism may be somewhat fanciful or overstated. After all, by the end of the 1960s the Swedish model represented the most developed form of a labour capital compromise or bargained corporatism in Europe and a high point of social democratic achievement. Nevertheless, the Swedish experience illustrates some of the problematic aspects of bargained corporatism for all trade unions involved in such arrangements. First, wage restraint for some rank-and-file members may appear contrary to the *raison d'être* of trade unions. Of course, the strength of this perception will likely vary with the nature of the particular labour movement and, more importantly, with the extent to which

---

3. Attitudes towards a new national wage agreement:
Definitely Yes	21% (124)
No Alternative	10% (59)
No Opinion	3% (20)
Depends on what is Offered	46% (271)
Definitely Not	19% (110)
Total	**100% (585)**

it can be concretely demonstrated that the outcome of wage restraint benefits in roughly equal measure labour as well as capital. Evidence of an unequal distribution of benefits may well encourage disenchantment with an incomes policy. Indeed, in the Swedish case when it became apparent that capital had inordinately benefited from wage restraint it was the necessity for remedial action that contributed to the long-run destabilisation of the model.

Similar difficulties appear to be occurring in the Irish case. As we have seen, since 1987 there has been a radical income shift from labour towards capital, with the chief beneficiaries being employers. Yet, of possibly greater significance for the long-term stability of centralised agreements, this was also the perception of the rank-and-file union members.

Wage earners, the unemployed and low-income groups were perceived by union members surveyed to have benefited considerably less than employers, the self-employed and the government. Indeed, a majority of union members believed that the national wage agreements have not been effective in giving workers a fairer share of the national cake. Aware of this defect, the Irish Congress of Trade Unions advocated profit sharing at the level of the individual firm as a way of securing a more equitable outcome to wage restraint. Unfortunately, such a stratagem may be potentially productive of new disparities in income and division among the general membership. The Irish Business and Employers' Confederation is opposed to any legal obligation on their members to introduce such schemes. Consequently, the inevitable haphazard and piecemeal application of profit sharing/employee shareholding will exclude many from its benefits in the private sector along with workers such as teachers and nurses in the public sector. This could become a source of discontent and add to the difficulties in operating an income policy.

A second difficulty with bargained corporatism or income policy is the tendency, evident in the Swedish case, for power or influence to shift from the shop floor and national union towards the union centre. With pay bargaining largely conducted at national level the role of national unions and local shop steward organisation may appear redundant, encouraging a perception among rank-and-file members of declining influence. In the Irish case there appears to be a perception, at least among the union members we surveyed, of a power shift towards the union centre. A majority of respondents believed that the influence of the ICTU at national level had increased in the areas of unemployment and taxation, but that the ability of trade unions generally to gain recognition from employers had decreased. Regarding their own trade union, members perceived an overall reduction in the union's capacity nationally and, in particular, a reduction in its effectiveness at firm level. Congress has attempted to pre-empt such a development by encouraging the development of social partnership between unions, employees and management at firm level as a way to complement agreement at national level. This strategy of partnership and new workplace initiatives could potentially have negative as well as positive outcomes for employees. While such task-based participation may address the lack of involvement or alienation among shop-floor workers, it could also result in work intensification. Among the union members we surveyed, the new workplace initiatives were largely perceived to have either no impact or, in some cases, involve a negative outcome for workers. The development of a genuine sense of partnership at firm level does not seem to have occurred to any significant extent in the companies surveyed.

Our survey has pointed out some of the unintended consequences of bargained corporatism as presently operating in Ireland. These are the increasingly skewed distribution of wealth and the concentration of decision-making power at the union centre with the potential for rank-and-file alienation. Yet, these outcomes and the problems they pose for trade unions are not unique to the Scandinavian or Irish versions of bargained corporatism. Similar problems with income policies were experienced in Europe and Britain during the late 1970s. Crouch sketched out the requirements for a policy that would increase the acceptance and integration of trade unions in such arrangements (Crouch, 1978: 233). The more workers' representatives are involved in controlling economic variables, he argued, the more willing they will be to pursue wage restraint. This would include, he suggested, measures of co-determination, involvement in effective national planning instruments and participation in control of occupational pension funds and collective profit sharing funds such as the Meidner plan – schemes for which he noted had already been advanced in the Netherlands, Sweden, Britain and West Germany (Crouch, 1978: 234).

Such a policy of co-determination at firm level and collective profit sharing at national level is a solution to the problems posed for the labour movement by corporatism. Furthermore, it is a solution that can be defended on the grounds that it promotes a greater measure of both equity and democracy. With the benefit of hindsight, the obvious weakness of such a policy is its transcendence of the existing capital-labour relationship, which inevitably calls into play powerful forces of resistance. There is no evidence that the Irish trade union movement has effectively addressed these questions. Indeed, over time, the Irish Congress of Trade Unions has moved away from demands for co-determination and collective profit sharing.[4] In the present and future partnership arrangements it seems the Irish trade union movement is fated to occupy the status of a junior partner. Even this modest position may be less than secure. During the 1980s and 1990s Irish unions have found it increasingly difficult to gain recognition (McGovern, 1989). Admittedly, between 1987 and 1998 there has been an increase in union membership but this has not kept pace with the growth in employment. Union density as a percentage of the employed workforce has fallen from 56.2 per cent in 1987 to 42 per cent

---

4. Up to the early 1980s, the Irish Congress of Trade Unions favoured schemes of collective capital formation in preference to schemes of financial participation based at the level of the individual firm (D'Art, 1992). This position has largely been abandoned as can be seen from ICTU's present advocacy of profit sharing/employee shareholding (ICTU, 1999).

in 1998.[5] This represents the lowest figure for union density since 1950 (see Roche and Larragy, 1989: 22). That this decline is occurring in political and economic circumstances that would normally be expected to favour union growth raises questions about the long-term prospects of the Irish union movement and the continuance of bargained corporatist arrangements. A prerequisite for the initiation and continuance of bargained corporatism is that unions possess and exercise power in the labour market, which in large measure will depend on the level of unionisation among the employed workforce. The Irish trade union movement may become one of those sleeping partners that can easily be dispensed with.

REFERENCES

Aberg, R. (1984) "Market-Independent Income Distribution: Efficiency and Legitimacy" in Goldthorpe, J. (ed.) *Order and Conflict in Contemporary Capitalism*. Oxford: Clarendon Press.

Allen, K. (1999) "The Celtic Tiger, Inequality and Social Partnership" *Administration*, Vol. 47, No. 2: 31–55.

Bulletin of the European Communities (1979) *Employee Participation in Asset Formation Memorandum from the Commission*. Supplement 6/79.

Crouch, C. (1978) "Inflation and the Political Organisation of Economic Interests" in Hirsch, F. and Goldthorpe, J. (eds) *The Political Economy of Inflation*. London: Martin Robertson.

Crouch, C. (1992) "The Fate of Articulated Industrial Relations Systems: A Stocktaking after the 'Neo-Liberal' Decade" in Regini, M. (ed.) *The Future of Labour Movements*. London: Sage Publications.

D'Art, D. and Turner, T. (1999) "An Attitudinal Revolution in Irish Industrial Relations: The End of Them and Us?" *British Journal of Industrial Relations*, Vol. 37, No.1: 101–116.

D'Art, D. (1992) *Economic Democracy and Financial Participation: A Comparative Study*. London: Routledge.

Federation of Irish Employers (FIE) and Irish Congress of Trade Unions (ICTU) (1991) *FIE/ICTU Joint Declaration on Employee Involvement in the Private Sector*. Dublin, June.

Gunnigle, P. (1997) "More Rhetoric than Reality: Enterprise Level Industrial

---

5. Membership figures for 1987 are from Roche, (1994); Union membership figures for 1998 are based on the affiliated membership of ICTU; employment figures are based on the Labour Force Survey. The total affiliated union membership of ICTU for 1998 (December) is 521,036. According to Congress, their affiliated membership accounts for approximately 97–98 per cent of all union members. However, Congress's figures may be an overestimate as they contain members who are retired or lapsed. Union density is calculated by dividing the number of union members by the number reported at work from the Labour Force Survey.

Relations Partnerships in Ireland" *Economic and Social Review*, Vol. 28, No. 4: 179–200.

Hardiman, N. (1992) "The State and Economic Interests: Ireland in Comparative Perspective" in Goldthorpe, J. and Whelan, C. (eds) *The Development of Industrial Society in Ireland.* Oxford: University Press.

Irish Congress of Trade Unions (ICTU) (1999) *Sharing the Gains – Supporting Partnership, Guideline for Unions on Gainsharing, Profit Sharing and Employee Share Ownership Plans.* Dublin.

Kjellberg, A. (1992) "Sweden: Can the Model Survive?" in Ferner, A. and Hyman, R. *Industrial Relations in the New Europe.* Oxford: Blackwell.

Lane, P. (1998) "Profits and Wages in Ireland, 1987–1996" *Trinity Economic Papers Series*, Technical No. 14, Dublin, May.

Lange, P. (1984) "Unions, Workers and Wage Regulation: The Rational Bases of Consent" in Goldthorpe, J. (ed.) *Order and Conflict in Contemporary Capitalism.* Oxford.

Leddin, A. and Walsh, B. (1997) "Economic Stabilisation, Recovery and Growth: Ireland 1979–1996" *Irish Banking Review*, summer: 2–18.

Lehmbruch, G. (1984) "Concertation and the Structure of Corporatist Networks" in Goldthorpe, J. (ed.) *Order and Conflict in Contemporary Capitalism.* Oxford: Clarendon Press.

Maier, C. (1984) "Preconditions for Corporatism" in Goldthorpe, J. (ed.) *Order and Conflict in Contemporary Capitalism.* Oxford: Clarendon Press.

McGovern, P. (1989) "Union Recognition and Union Avoidance in the 1980s" in *Industrial Relations in Ireland: Contemporary Issues and Developments*. Department of Industrial Relations, University College Dublin.

Meidner, R. (1978) *Employee Investment Funds: An Approach to Collective Capital Formation.* London: Allen and Unwin.

O'Brien, J. (1981) *A Study of National Wage Agreements in Ireland.* Dublin: Economic and Social Research Institute.

Partnership 2000 for Inclusion, Employment and Competitiveness (1996) Government Publications Office, Dublin, December.

Roche, W. (1994) "Pay Determination, the State and the Politics of Industrial Relations" in Murphy, T. and Roche, W. *Irish Industrial Relations in Practice.* Dublin: Oak Tree Press.

Roche, W. and Geary, F. (2000) "Collaborative Production and the Irish Boom: Work, Organisation, Partnership and Direct Involvement in Irish Workplaces" *The Economic and Social Review*, Vol. 31, No. 1: 1–36.

Roche, W. and Larragy, J. (1989) "The Trend of Unionisation in the Irish Republic" in Industrial Relations in Ireland: Contemporary Issues and Developments. Department of Industrial Relations, University College Dublin.

Schwerin, D. (1984) "Historic Compromise and Pluralist Decline? Profits and Capital in the Nordic Countries" in Goldthorpe, J. (ed.) *Order and Conflict in Contemporary Capitalism.* Oxford.

Teague, P. (1995) "Pay Determination in the Republic of Ireland: Towards Social Corporatism" *British Journal of Industrial Relations*, Vol. 33, No. 2: 253–268.

Traxler, F. (1995) "From Demand-Side to Supply-Side Corporatism? Austria's Labour Relations and Public Policy" in Crouch, C. and Traxler, F. (eds) *Organised Industrial Relations in Europe: What Future?* Avebury, England.

Van Ruysseveldt, J. and Visser, J. (1996) (eds) *Industrial Relations in Europe: Traditions and Transitions*. London: Sage Publications.

Visser, J. (1996) "Corporatism Beyond Repair? Industrial Relations in Sweden" in Van Ruysseveldt, J. and Visser, J. (eds) *Industrial Relations in Europe: Traditions and Transitions*. London: Sage Publications.

Wallace, J., Turner, T. and McCarty, A. (1998) "Entry to the EMU and Irish Industrial Relations" in Kaupinen, T. (ed.) *The Impact of EMU on Industrial Relations in the European Union*. Helsinki: Finnish Industrial Relations Association.

CHAPTER 12

Corporatism in Ireland: A Comparative Perspective

THOMAS TURNER

INTRODUCTION

One of the notable, if not outstanding, industrial relations features of most European countries after World War II was the kind of institutional arrangements that developed between capital and labour, with governments as both partner and broker to these arrangements. Indeed, by the 1970s there appeared to be a convergence among Western European societies towards what was termed a bargained corporatist pattern of industrial relations (Crouch, 1977: 262). A number of characteristic features of corporatism can be identified. Principally, the agreements negotiated went beyond purely industrial relations matters to include broader economic and social goals. The agreements were a negotiated exchange between the parties in which trade unions agreed to exercise wage restraint in co-operation with government and employers in exchange for political intervention and influence in public policy areas of critical concern to their constituents such as employment and social welfare policy (Maier, 1984; Roche, 1994). Surprisingly, there have been few attempts to locate the type of corporatist arrangements existing in Ireland since 1987 in a comparative European context (see Teague, 1995).

The aim of this chapter is to provide an assessment of the present era of social partnership in Ireland in the context of the European corporatist tradition. First, there is a brief discussion of the measures used to rank corporatist arrangements and its outcomes. Secondly, using these measures and outcomes, the nature of Irish corporatism is assessed. Thirdly, we compare the outcomes of social partnership in Ireland with other European countries. The basic argument articulated here is that while there has been some development of institutional support structures for corporatist arrangements, the outcomes in terms of reducing inequalities between social classes still lags far behind the strongly corporatist Nordic countries. Indeed, it appears that inequality has actually increased during the present period of social partnership in Ireland.

CORPORATIST ARRANGEMENTS: MEASUREMENT AND OUTCOMES

Studies of corporatism, particularly by economists, tend to stress the wage bargaining or income policy side of corporatism, the level of centralised bargaining and union strength, while political scientists and sociologists tend to stress the political exchange side (see Henley and Tsakalotos, 1993: 87). Studies on corporatism vary in the weight given to either the level of centralisation or political exchange as a means of defining the level of corporatist arrangements in a country. However, this does not present a major definitional problem since there tends to be a relatively high correlation between the level of centralisation and measures of political exchange or corporatism (see for example, Dell'Aringa and Lodovici, 1990; Teulings and Hartog, 1998: 27). Although it can be expected that a country's ranking may change over time, nevertheless, more recent rankings have not altered earlier rankings to any great extent (see for example, Henley and Tzakalotos, 1993; Teulings and Hartog, 1998). Thus, we begin with a description of the measures of centralisation and political exchange. An important feature of corporatist arrangements is the institutional supporting structure linking organised interests and the state and, below this level, the structures that integrate lower organisational levels into corporatist arrangements. These institutional supports are described with particular reference to the Nordic countries. Finally, two main types of corporatism with different outcomes are identified.

Measures of Centralisation and Political Exchange

Centralisation is a measure of the level at which bargaining takes place. An index of centralisation includes the level of bargaining – whether local or national – and the number of labour and employer peak organisations and the extent of co-operation within each group respectively. One of the most widely reported studies by Calmsfor and Driffill (1988) on the relationship between corporatism and economic performance uses a centralisation index based on these two measures. In addition, Visser (1990) also refers to the strength of the union movement, that is, the level of union density as well as the degree of cohesion and unity between trade unions. There is, of course, a considerable level of subjectivity in the interpretation of the above measures when ranking a country. Nevertheless, there is a high correlation in the rankings of centralisation by different authors (see Calmsfor and Driffill, 1988: 18).

Political exchange, according to Lehmbruch (1984), can be viewed as a continuum from weak to strong arrangements. Corporatism, at the weak end of the continuum, involves merely a type of indicative planning or exchange of information on wages, profits, investment and employment. There is no explicit quid pro quo between the parties but rather the creation of consensus on the needs of the economy and the appropriate policy responses to achieve those needs. At the strong end of the continuum, which Lehmbruch labels as "generalised exchange",[1] the concertation process involves a much wider policy agenda and greater stability and durability than that entailed in traditional incomes policies.

The Institutional Context of Corporatism

Traditionally, concern with the institutions supporting corporatism has focused on the industrial relations system. There has been particular emphasis on peak level organisational structures, modes of participation below this level and the role of the state. Strong corporatist institutions, according to Henley and Tzakalotos (1993: 97–98), require not only a wide policy agenda but also a consensus about macro-economic objectives and stable long-term relations between the social partners. Such a consensus implies that the state and social partners have shared objectives and a common understanding of how the economy works. Thus, an important element in the existence of corporatist arrangements is the extent of government support. Socialist or social democratic parties, particularly where they have been in power for a considerable period of time as in the Nordic countries, are associated with strong corporatism. This *political dimension* is predicated on the granting to the peak interest organisations of labour and capital privileged access to government and the growth of institutionalised linkages to facilitate this (Lehmbruch, 1984: 61). In Austria, for example, the majority of parliamentarians came from the peak labour and capital organisations and, indeed, at one time the president of the Austrian National Assembly was also the acting president of the Austrian trade union confederation (Marin, 1985). The "vertical interlocks" between socialist parties and unions are especially widespread and close in strong corporatist countries (Lehmbruch, 1984: 75). In Sweden, for example, during the 1970s many of the union leaders were also members of parliament and co-operation between them at local and regional level was so close that it was difficult to distinguish between trade union and political elements (Elvander, 1974: 61).

Aside from the political dimension, the linking structures between the state and interest groups constitute one of the crucial tenets of corporatism in Austria (Marin, 1985) and the Nordic countries (Johansen and Kristensen, 1982: 189). As Crouch (1985: 79) notes, it is the increasing "density of the network of relations" that characterises bargained corporatism and distinguishes it from pluralist or liberal market economies. Lehmbruch (1984) distinguished between two dimensions of corporatist institutional structures: first, a *horizontal dimension* which relates to the pattern of concertation or set of arrangements through which peak organisations meet with government in order to co-ordinate

---

1. However, for Martin (1979) the strongest form of corporatism occurs when political exchange begets the need to ensure sufficient investment and growth to underpin the commitment to welfare provision and active labour market intervention. This level of corporatism was attempted in Sweden in the form of the Meidner wage earner fund but was abandoned because of employer opposition.

and negotiate policies and agreements; secondly, a *vertical dimension* composed of linking structures below the peak level of the main organised interests.

The horizontal dimension has tended to be informal in character. For example, in Norway, the "contact committee" established in 1962 was understood as an informal "bargaining table" but without any authority to determine policy, while in Sweden the "Economic Planning Council", which included members of government and the peak organisations, was described as "merely a deliberating body, as a discussion and information centre where no decisions were taken" (Lehmbruch, 1984: 69–70). Such loose informality was possible because of the comprehensive vertical structures existing in the Nordic countries.[2] The vertical dimension refers to the structures or pattern of participation of individual peak and lower organisational levels and is characterised by the importance of public committees (the "Remiss" system) in Norway, Sweden and Denmark (Johansen and Kristensen, 1982: 196).[3] Indeed, the interest groups themselves rank these committees as the principal means of influencing policy making when compared with other means such as parliament and political parties.

Another notable feature of corporatist institutional structures is the support for workplace-level organisation. In addition to public committees, there are statutory works councils that allow a measure of industrial democracy on the shopfloor. The works council system in Austria provides a statutory representational system at firm level that gives trade unions a legal status and role in workplace organisations (Marin, 1985: 106). In Sweden, for example, industrial democracy was expanded after 1972 to include board representation of employees, protection for shop stewards and generally employee rights to participate in certain workplace decisions (D'Art, 1992).

---

2. Marin (1981: 33) describes the Austrian system as a "pyramid of institutionalisation with a highly formalised institutional infrastructure supporting the trapeze act of the top organisational leaders to negotiate and co-operate without explicit norms, written contracts and other securities" (quoted in Lehmbruch, 1984: 70).
3. Johansen and Kristensen's (1982) study of the committee system in Denmark gives some sense of the extensiveness of the system in the strong corporatist countries. By 1975 there were 667 public committees covering a wide range of economic, social and environmental issues and the peak organisations labour and capital had representation on 55 per cent of the committees (Johansen and Kristensen, 1982: 202). Apart from the wide range of policy areas covered it also appears that interest organisations participated in all phases of policy making. Johansen and Kristensen, (1982: Table 3, 209) categorise the committees into those primarily engaged in the preparation of legislation and those primarily involved with the administration or implementation of some policy or law. In 1975, 303 committees were engaged in the preparation of legislation with 49 per cent having peak organisation representation. A total of 313 committees were engaged in the administering or implementation of policies and legislative acts with 62 per cent having peak representation.

Different Forms of Corporatism and their Outcomes

Although the centralisation and cohesion of interest organisations and the existence of particular institutional arrangements are a prerequisite for corporatism, different forms of corporatism can be identified. These have been divided into two main categories: social corporatism and liberal corporatism (Pekkarinen et al., 1992; Rowthorn, 1992; Therborn, 1992).

Social corporatism is based on a political and ideological analysis. It perceives conflict as endemic to capital labour relations and the resultant compromise arises from a position where the power of labour and capital are roughly balanced.[4] Corporatism acts to institutionalise conflict as part of a democratic class struggle (Korpi, 1983). The acknowledgement of class conflict as the basis for compromise has fostered the mobilisation of labour and its emphasis on inclusiveness and egalitarianism. Labour and capital are organised from below according to the principles of democracy and regarded as labour market parties whose autonomy and conflict rights are respected. Pekkarinen et al. (1992) identify this approach as a form of social corporatism. No social group is excluded from the labour market and there is a high degree of equality in both sharing the benefits of increasing economic welfare or the miseries of recession and the burden of economic adjustment. Consequently, a high degree of labour and social solidarity is its comcomitant (Pekkarinen et al., 1992). The Nordic countries have probably achieved the most developed form of social corporatism. They have historically opted for social security systems with a wide and egalitarian coverage and a solidaristic wage policy, particularly in Sweden, aimed at reducing wage dispersion in the labour market.

Liberal corporatism, by contrast, is based on an understanding of an essential commonality of interests between capital and labour. Over time there is a gradual institutionalisation of a consensus, particularly between leaders rather than members. The process tends to be exclusive with the gains going to insiders, that is, outcomes mirror the relative power of peak organisations and their members. The management of economic adjustment and the sharing of burdens and rewards are controlled by the élites at the top of hierarchies of interest organisations. This type of corporatism tends to result in the preservation of existing disparities in wealth and life chances. Examples of this liberal corporatist approach are, according to Pekkarinen et al. (1992), Austria and the Netherlands.

From Liberal to Competitive Corporatism

By the end of the 1970s it appeared that social corporatism as a specific political and economic approach to economic management had declined in many European countries (for a discussion of the causes see Rhodes, 1996; Golden et al., 1999: 194–198; Hall, 1999; Kitschelt et al., 1999). However, liberal corporatism,

---

4. As the social democratic minister for finance in Sweden in 1938 observed in a talk to stockbrokers and industrialists, "neither the labour movement nor private capitalists could hope to suppress the other altogether" (quoted in D'Art, 1992: 149).

albeit under the label of "competitive corporatism", has proved a great deal more resilient. Since the early 1990s, social concertation in Europe "has undergone an astonishingly lively and broad-based revival" but in a different form (Pochet and Fajertag, 2000: 9; see also Fajertag and Pochet, 2000; Rhodes and Meny, 1998). The concept of "competitive corporatism" has been used to describe the social pacts emerging or re-emerging in many European countries in the 1990s (Rhodes, 1998; Pochet and Fajertag, 2000). The emergence of competitive corporatism can be traced to the crisis in employment and competitiveness in the European union in the 1990s (see for example, Rhodes, 1998; Visser, 1998; Bispinck and Schulten, 2000). Competitive corporatism has been viewed as an alternative or "third way" by both social democratic parties and trade unions to the neo-liberal prescription of deregulated labour markets and reduced welfare systems (Rhodes, 1998: 200; Bispinck and Schulten, 2000: 194). As such, it is an attempt to meet the economic demands for efficiency while promoting equity or, at least, defending existing social protection systems (see Rhodes, 1998: 179).

Like liberal corporatism, the outcomes tend to preserve the status quo both in terms of preserving the essential social protection of the old welfare systems and also preserving or indeed increasing existing income inequalities. In both liberal and competitive corporatism there is an absence or weak commitment to egalitarianism. Competitive corporatism involves agreements between the social partners based on increased flexibility in the labour market which in turn means greater wage flexibility and wage dispersion. It also involves, where necessary, greater flexibility in the design of social security systems and the tailoring of social intervention more closely with the demands of competition in a market economy. Reducing unemployment and increasing employment is promoted by means of labour market reforms through flexibility of employment contracts and wages, work organisation and working time rather than through government-created demand (Goetschy, 2000).[5]

AN EVALUATION OF CORPORATIST ARRANGEMENTS IN IRELAND

Based on the measures of centralisation used by Calmsfor and Driffill (1988), social partnership in Ireland can be rated high on both the level of wage co-ordination and the number of existing central union and employer confederations. Wages have been set at the national level since 1987 and there is only one peak organisation, the Irish Congress of Trade Unions (ICTU),[6] and one main

---

5. An example is the alliance for jobs pact pursued in Germany. This rests on three pillars: the creation of a subsidised low-wage sector to encourage employment growth; increased training to make companies more competitive; and lower personal taxation for employees and lower corporate tax's on company profits to attract more international direct investment (Bispinck and Schulten, 2000).
6. A monopoly or near monopoly as the sole union confederation which has no competitor

employer organisation, the Irish Business Confederation of Employers (IBEC). It is more difficult to assess the degree of cohesion and unity in ICTU. Analysis of the problems of a previous period of national wage agreements (1970 to 1981) suggested that the ability of ICTU to develop a collective unified strategy was undermined by organisational weaknesses resulting chiefly from a multiplicity of unions and Congress's lack of authoritative command over affiliates (Hardiman, 1987; Breen et al., 1990). It is difficult, however, to establish the significance of these factors. Certainly, the period since 1970 has been one of union consolidation as the number of trade unions declined from 93 in 1970 to 52 by 1999 (MacPartlin, this volume, Chapter 9). Indeed, the amalgamation of the two largest general unions into SIPTU in 1990 has created an increasingly encompassing general union. SIPTU's membership accounted for 40 per cent of ICTU membership in 1995. This was the largest proportion of membership accounted for by a single union in any of the peak organisations in the European union (Ebbinghaus and Visser, 2000: 66).

However, there has been no change in the authoritative relationship between ICTU and its affiliated members. Congress has no additional formal powers to control affiliates apart from a moral authority (Roche and Ashmore, 2000). Yet, as the single peak organisation, the participation in national wage agreements has possibly enhanced its strategic capacity for policy formulation (see MacPartlin, this volume, Chapter 9). Thus, taking into account the consolidation and weakening of inter-union rivalry, it seems plausible to rate the degree of cohesion among unions and peak organisations in Ireland as moderate. In summary, corporatism in Ireland ranks as, at least, moderate to high with regard to the measures of wage co-ordination, centralisation and cohesion, and probably can be ranked just behind the Nordic countries, who are generally taken as examples of strong corporatist arrangements.

Political Exchange Bargain

Both of the recent agreements, Partnership 2000 and the Partnership for Prosperity and Fairness, have included a wider range of policy agenda than the previous three agreements. Policy objectives in Partnership 2000 included a commitment to economic and social solidarity with an action program for social inclusion and equality involving an expenditure of £525 million, tax reductions of £1 billion particularly targeted at those on low but taxable incomes,[7] the adoption of a National Anti-Poverty Strategy, the reduction of long-term unemployment and the orientation of education policy to give priority in the allocation of resources to those in greatest need. This is not an exhaustive list.[8]

---

exists in Austria, the German DGB, the Irish Congress of Trade Unions and the British Trade Unions Congress (Ebbinghaus and Visser, 2000).

7. Supposed to be aimed at the low paid but in practice went to the better off.
8. The range of agreed policies in the PPF include commitment to a national minimum wage, social welfare reform (real increases in rates of social welfare), improvements in health care, expansion of local authority housing and monitoring developments in relation

Yet, apart from the items listed above with a clear expenditure allocation, many of the other policies have no clear measurable targets. In both agreements there is an explicit quid pro quo regarding employment, taxation and social inclusion measures.

An important feature of Lehmbruch's strong form of corporatism is the existence of a consensus between the state and social partners about macro-economic objectives and a common understanding of how the economy works (Lehmbruch, 1984). The earlier period of national wage agreements (1970 to 1981) apparently lacked such a consensus, with considerable differences of opinion regarding the problems of the economy between the trade unions and that of the government or employers (see Hardiman, 1987: 164). A notable feature of the present agreements is the development of a high level of consensus between the social partners concerning the evolution of a coherent agreed policy framework (see O'Donnell, 1998: 136 and also NESF, 1997: 3–5). Thus, in terms of the scope of agenda covered in both of these agreements, the nature of the ongoing resolution of issues within the partnership framework and the high degree of consensus regarding policy objectives, it seems reasonable to categorise social partnership in Ireland as a strong form of concertation or generalised exchange.

Political Dimension and Institutional Structures

Governments in strongly corporatist countries have for long periods been dominated by social democratic parties closely linked to a strong union movement and sharing an agreed ideological project. Such close ideological and political linkages with dominant political parties is largely absent in the Irish case. However, according to Hardiman (1987: 161) close association with a political party of the left is not essential or decisive for corporatism. More important is the willingness of government to undertake necessary policy commitments, that is to engage with peak organisations, and a capacity to deliver on the commitments. While O'Donnell and Thomas (1998: 126) note that, traditionally, peak organisations in Ireland have had a relatively high degree of access to the political arena, they argue that the present era of social partnership has resulted in a "more institutionalised and regularised mode of participation", giving increased involvement in public policy formulation, monitoring and implementation. In practice, there is a high degree of "personalised interaction", between the principle participants and there are "close working relationships" between the trade union leadership and senior civil servants (O'Donnell and Thomas, 1998: 126). Indeed, according to O'Donnell and Thomas (1998: 134) "the political institutionalisation of partnership since 1987" has ensured that it

---

to the supply and affordability of housing, policies to support child care and family life, legislation to eliminate discrimination in employment and in services, life long educational measures, improvements in the coverage of occupational pension schemes, and the establishment and deepening of the partnership process at enterprise level.

has effectively evolved into a "functional sub-polity of the formal representation system" and they go on to draw a favourable comparison with these developments and the relationship between corporatist institutions and parliament in Austria. Unlike the previous era of national wage agreements when Breen et al. (1990: 176) observed that "neo-corporatist sentiments abounded, but neo-corporatist institutions did not", it would appear that vertical structures have emerged with strong linkages between the trade union movement and the political arena. However, not all commentators would accept that social partnership is as "securely anchored in the political process" (see Hardiman, 2000: 304) or that such a tendency is a positive development (O'Cinneide, Winter 1998/99). Hardiman (2000: 304) suggests that the trade union movements access to the political process is dependent on their continued capacity to deliver on pay moderation, competitiveness and productivity.

An increase in the formality of the horizontal set of arrangements through which peak organisations meet with government to negotiate and monitor agreements has occurred in recent agreements. The three national wage agreements from 1987 to 1997 contained a provision for a central review committee, with representatives from government and the social partners, to monitor the achievement of the targets and objectives in each programme. There was no set timetable and the committee met in response to particular issues and requests for a meeting from one of the social partners. In the two recent agreements, Partnership 2000 and the Programme for Prosperity and Fairness (PPF), there has been a notable increase in the formality of the monitoring structures agreed compared to the earlier agreements. The programme provides for annual plenary meetings of the social partners in place of the previous central review committee. This committee acts as a central review mechanism, representing what is called the four pillars in the partnership process (trade unions; employers; farming organisations; and community and voluntary organisations), whose function is to oversee the implementation of the programme, to assess progress and ensure the effective implementation of the programme (PPF: 130). To achieve this there are quarterly meetings of the members of the four pillars, under the auspices of government, to review and monitor the operation of the programme. Despite the increase in formality, the horizontal top-level structures discussed here have no legal or enduring status and have emerged out of each national wage agreement. Nevertheless, they appear to be quite comprehensive compared to structures in the Nordic countries.

Regarding interest group participation below the leadership level, the vertical dimension, it is useful to distinguish between those structures emerging from the actual agreement process and more established structures. Since Partnership 2000, a considerable number of working groups have been established with representation from the four pillars. These groups are set up to tackle issues that arise out of the agenda negotiated between the social partners. Reports from these groups are acted on in plenary sessions/quarterly meetings of the four pillars. As there is little research in this area it is difficult to evaluate the importance of these working-group reports but they do appear to carry some weight. The working groups exist to tackle a particular issue and would rarely go beyond the lifetime of the national wage agreement. It is probably true to say that the working groups provide a solution to the problems of grappling with a more extensive and complex range of issues, such as childcare facilities, which can be settled outside of the main negotiation arena.[9] Two more formalised bodies exist to support the partnership process: the National Economic and Social Forum and the National Economic and Social Council.[10] Both of these bodies are central to partnership as the reports they produce provide the framework for the national negotiations, though neither has a legal status.[11]

At the workplace level in Ireland, there is no statutory representational system at firm level comparable to the works council system in many European countries. Although trade unions have a legal right to represent workers there is no statutory support or recognition for union workplace organisation, particularly the shop steward system of worker representation. Workplace initiatives advocated by Partnership 2000 and the PPF are voluntary in nature and amount to a list of suggestions rather than any firm agreements (see for example Partnership 2000: 63–64). Yet, the PPF (p. 130) document claims that under Partnership 2000 "there has been significant progress in social partnership at national, local and enterprise/organisational levels". However, the evidence from research on partnership at firm level provides little support for this claim (see Roche and Geary, this volume, Chapter 3; Gunnigle, 1998). Roche and Geary's comprehensive survey of Irish workplaces indicates that partnership at firm level remains relatively weak.

In this section, the aim was to evaluate the institutional strength of corporatism in Ireland in a comparative European context. On a number of the indices used – centralisation, scope of political agenda, political linkages, horizontal and vertical institutional dimensions – it is a plausible argument that the framework of partnership in Ireland is developing towards the strong type

---

9. Under Partnership 2000, fifteen working groups were set up and 23 working groups have been established under the PPF, covering a range of issues which include a consultative committee on gain sharing, the public service bench marking body, the housing forum and the task force on lifelong learning.
10. The National Economic and Social Council was established in 1973 to report to the Government on the development of the national economy and the achievement of social justice. The major interest organisations have representation on the council. NESC has produced over 100 published reports on a variety of economic and social topics. Funding comes from government and is in the order of 0.5 million pounds per year. The NESF was established in 1993 with similar interest representation. The role of NESF is to develop economic and social initiatives and to contribute to the formation of a national consensus on economic and social matters.
11. For example, in negotiations for Partnership 2000 participants were given the opportunity to present position papers in the context of the NESF document *Post PCW Negotiations – A New Deal?* and the NESC report *Strategy into the 21st Century* (O'Donnell and Thomas, 1998). In negotiations for the PPF the framework adopted for addressing poverty and social inclusion was based on the NESC (1999) Report *Opportunities, Challenges and Capacities for Choice.*

of corporatism associated with the Nordic or Austrian model of corporatism. However, a weakness was noted regarding institutional structures at firm level. Compared to the Nordic countries, the vertical structures in Irish partnership are relatively new. While the development of vertical structures in the Irish context has been rapid and relatively extensive, it has a somewhat *ad hoc* nature (see O'Donnell and Thomas, 1998: 129). In addition, the structures operate at the top hierarchical levels in the peak organisations with the possibility that only élites are engaged with attendant oligarchic dangers, particularly in the labour movement. Finally, aside from NESC, the structures have no formal status beyond the lifetime of each agreement, unlike the public committee system in the Nordic countries, and are thus temporary and contingent.

OBJECTIVES AND OUTCOMES: RHETORIC AND REALITY

While the institutional context is important, it is the form of corporatism, whether of the liberal/competitive or social democratic variant, which has fundamental consequences for the labour movement. In this section we focus first on ICTU's (as the sole representative of the labour movement) objectives and strategy for social partnership, that is, the rhetoric of partnership. Secondly, the economic and social outcomes are examined, that is, the reality of partnership. Given the paucity of independent trade union documentation regarding the union movement's strategic aims in social partnership,[12] the approach adopted here is to focus on the principal aims as articulated in recent agreements. These aims are based on NESC and NESF reports and subsequent discussions of the reports and, ultimately, negotiations at the plenary sessions of the social partners. The key objectives of Partnership 2000 were: (1) the "continued development of an efficient modern economy capable of high and sustainable economic and employment growth"; (2) "ensuring that Irish society becomes more inclusive"; and (3) that "the benefits of growth are more equally distributed" (Partnership 2000: 5). Somewhat similar overall aims are expressed in the PPF. The core objective of the program, the agreement states, "is to build a fair, inclusive society in Ireland" (PPF: 3).

Undoubtedly, these aims reflect an inclusive, solidaristic project. Indeed, the ICTU have traditionally identified with welfare and employment issues as they affected working class people but, as Hardiman (1987: 164) noted, this collective identity was not linked with a strategy of political exchange in the previous period of national agreements. According to Hardiman (1987: 172), the trade unions lacked faith in any political exchanges being delivered on and it was difficult for governments to deliver, given the poor state of the economy at

---

12. As far as the author can ascertain, the ICTU produces no prior or position documents either before negotiation agreements or generally. Congress base their negotiation strategy on the reports from NESC and NESF, except for the pay bargaining elements of the agreements. More generally, there are some publications which refer at some point to the strategic approach of ICTU (see ICTU, 1989 and 1993).

the time. Obviously, these economic conditions have changed and governments have delivered on a number of areas such as taxation, employment and welfare.

Important measures of social corporatism are the universality of the welfare system, the extent of income inequality and social mobility. In the Irish case, the negotiation of the social partnership agreements was initially limited to the main peak organisations, the trade unions and employers with other minority groups, such as community groups and the unemployed, having a minimal input to the negotiations (see NESC, 1996 and NESF, 1996). However, these marginalised groups were given full social partnership status and participated in the negotiation and ratification of Partnership 2000 and the recent PPF. Some difficulties, though, were acknowledged in the attempt to include a disparate range of groups from the voluntary and community sector (NESF, 1997), a sector in any case difficult to define and limit (O'Cinneide, 1999: 49). Nevertheless, O'Donnell and Thomas (1998: 137) argue that the "conceptualisation of social partnership concertation as a model of tripartite functional economic interdependence is increasingly insufficient" and suggest that there is a "nascent corporate pluralism emerging in which there is regularised, compart-mentalised and structured co-option into the public policy process for a diverse network of interest groups". Such a process, with its emphasis on a harmonisation of diverse interest groups, is characteristic of a liberal model of corporatism. Certainly, the very basis of corporatism, a class compromise between labour and capital, appears less central and a logical result of corporate pluralism would be a struggle between civic groups for scarce resources rather than between contending classes. In any case, an evaluation of partnership in Ireland in terms of the liberal versus social distinction identified earlier cannot rely only on the articulation of aspirations and objectives expressed in the partnership agreements. Below we address the economic and social outcomes of the agreements.

CORPORATISM AND ECONOMIC PERFORMANCE

In general, there are a considerable number of empirical studies all indicating a positive relationship between the degree of corporatism and economic performance during the 1970s (see Calmsfor and Driffill, 1988; Dell'Aringa and Lodovici, 1990; Henley and Tzakalotos, 1993: Chapter 3; Teulings and Hartog, 1998: Chapter 1). There is some debate, however, as to the performance of corporatist economies during the 1980s. Many commentators believed that in a changed political and economic climate the conditions were no longer propitious for corporatist-type arrangements (Rhodes, 1996). Both Dell'Aringa and Lodovici (1990) and Crepaz (1992) examined this altered effectiveness thesis of corporatism by comparing the relationship between corporatism and economic performance for the 1970s and the 1980s. While Dell'Aringa and Lodovici (1990) argued that their results cast some doubt on the efficacy of the corporatist model in the 1980s, Crepaz (1992) found that the measure of corporatism had no significant impact, either positive or negative, on economic growth. Moreover, he argued that his results provided "strong evidence that corporatism did not lose its redistributive capacity in the 1980's" (Crepaz, 1992: 155).

There can be little disagreement concerning the performance of the Irish economy. On all the measures of economic performance, employment growth, unemployment, gross domestic product (GDP) growth, rates inflation levels, debt reduction and current revenue surpluses, the trend has been positive (for reviews see Bradley, 2000; Fitzgerald, 2000). The period since 1987, and particularly after 1994, has been one of continuous and rapid growth in the Irish economy. There was a sharp fall in unemployment and a substantial rise in the number of people at work (see D'Art and Turner, this volume, Chapter 11). A similar trend is evident in the growth of real wages since 1987. The gross average real earnings of industrial workers increased by about 27 per cent between 1987 and 1998. However, company profits increased at a more rapid rate than average wages (see Lane, 1998). The evidence indicates that social partnership in Ireland has been beneficial for all the parties involved: the numbers in employment have increased substantially, unemployment has decreased, the economy has expanded, workers have experienced real increases in earnings after tax and governments now have substantial surpluses of revenue over current expenditure. However, in relative terms, the gains appear to be greater for employers, shareholders and the self-employed than for wage earners, with profits increasing at a more rapid rate than wages. To what extent the improvement in economic welfare since 1987 can be attributed to social partnership is difficult to definitively establish. Hardiman (2000: 292), for example, takes a relatively positive view of its impact, while Teague (1995) and Allen (2000) take a negative view. Undoubtedly, the performance of the Irish economy in creating jobs and reducing unemployment in this period far surpasses even the performance of the strongly corporatist Nordic countries.

CORPORATISM AND SOCIAL OUTCOMES

To evaluate the political and social outcomes of partnership since 1987 it is useful to consider the distinction between liberal and social corporatism. As noted above, liberal and competitive forms of corporatism tend to preserve the existing social and economic status quo of society while, in contrast, social corporatism is solidaristic with an emphasis on egalitarian goals. The indicators used to examine this question are the trends in wage dispersion or the degree of solidaristic wages, the universality of the welfare system, the level of social expenditure, income inequality, social mobility and trends in poverty.

Solidaristic Wages

A solidarity wage policy is closely associated with the Swedish trade union movement. In 1951, the Swedish Trade Union Confederation (LO) adopted the "Rehn Model" of which the solidaristic wage policy formed part of the strategic measures designed to reduce economic inequality and contribute to the labour movement's long-run egalitarian goals (D'Art, 1992: 150–151). Although the policy of solidaristic wages weakened in Sweden during the 1980s and 1990s, wage dispersion in Sweden and, indeed, in the other strong corporatist systems remain among the lowest in OECD countries. Sweden, Denmark and Norway were among the countries with the lowest levels of wage inequality in 1990 and wage dispersion had remained relatively stable between the years 1979 and 1990 (see Freeman and Katz, 1995: Table 2, p. 11). In contrast, the most recent evidence on trends in wage dispersion in Ireland indicates an increase in earnings inequality since 1987 (Barrett et al., 1999; Turner, 1999). Using data from two large-scale household surveys carried out by the ESRI in 1987 and 1994, Barrett et al. (1999: 77) found a "surprising large growth in wages dispersion". Indeed, in a comparison with other OECD countries for 1994, only Canada and the US have greater earnings inequality than Ireland (Barrett et al., 1999: 83). Furthermore, between 1987 and 1994, the increase in earnings dispersion in Ireland is among the highest in the OECD countries (Barrett et al., 1999: 84).

In addition to the high wage dispersion, Ireland has a high proportion of low-paid workers relative to other OECD countries. The definition of low pay used by the OECD is the number of full-time workers who earn less than two thirds of median earnings for all full-time workers (OECD, 1994; OECD 1996). According to Barrett et al. (1999: 84), the proportion of low paid workers increased from 18 per cent in 1987 to 21 per cent by 1994, making Ireland second only to the US in terms of low pay. Turner (1999: 41) suggests an even higher proportion of low pay with 24 per cent below two thirds of the median wage in 1987 compared to 27 per cent by 1995. The introduction of the national minimum wage in April 2000, combined with the recent dramatic fall in unemployment and a general tightening of the labour market, may have pushed up wage levels reducing the proportion below two thirds of the median wage. On the other hand, the tightening labour market may have increased the earnings of higher paid workers more than lower paid, thus increasing wage dispersion.[13]

Universality of the Welfare System

The common benchmark used to compare European welfare systems of social provision is the Scandinavian universal welfare model (see Kennelly and O'Shea, 1998). The emphasis is on social rights, with the State the primary agency for ensuring citizenship. Benefits are available to all citizens regardless of their participation in the workforce. What are considered public goods, such as health and education, are not considered to be "products" available for com-mercialisation. The welfare system in Ireland is generally perceived to conform to the liberal Anglo-Saxon model (Kennelly and O'Shea, 1998: 201). In this

---

13. In addition the effect of recent taxation changes may have increased the dispersion of after tax earnings.

model the welfare state is a compensator of last resort and need (for example unemployed and low paid) is the principle on which the state intervenes on a discretionary basis. The welfare system only becomes involved in order to guarantee a minimum level of social participation by recipients. The Irish welfare state has been described as a pay-related welfare system which provides a basic minimal level of security. However, it allows wealthier citizens to gain advantages through, for example, extra spending on health and education (O'Connell and Rottman, 1992). According to O'Riain and O'Connell (2000: 326) "the Irish experience of welfare state expansion stands in stark contrast to the development of the Scandinavian pattern" where universalistic entitlements created a solidarity between social classes and a commitment to reduced inequalities pervaded all areas of social policy. However, the recent period of unparalleled economic growth and social partnership may possibly have shifted Ireland closer to the Scandinavian welfare model. We turn to an examination of this possibility.

Levels of Social Expenditure

In terms of the proportion of GDP spent on welfare in 1995, i.e. total social protection expenditure, Ireland was ranked last in a comparison of European union countries (Table 12.1). Between 1990 and 1996 expenditure on social protection decreased from 19.1 per cent to 18.9 per cent of GDP. Focusing only on health expenditure as a percentage of GDP, Ireland was again ranked lower than all the other European countries in the OECD report in the proportion spent on health, and this proportion declined by 9 per cent between 1987 and 1997 (OECD, *Health Data 99*, OECD, Paris, 1999).

Income Inequality

Income inequality is commonly based on the household rather than the individual as the income unit. While in studies of wage dispersion the focus is on the employee's gross wage, the measure used in studies of income inequality is actual disposable income and includes direct wage earnings from the market, less income tax and employees' social security contributions plus all social welfare payments (see Nolan and Maitre, 2000: 148–149). Nolan and Maitre (2000) report the findings of a number of surveys carried out in 1987, 1994 and 1997. The general approach is to divide households into ten groups and report the percentage of all disposable income going to each group or decile. Between 1987 and 1994 the results from the household budget survey show a shift in income from the bottom to the top groups and an increase in the Gini coefficient which is a single overall measure of income inequality. However, using the more comprehensive ESRI surveys, the Gini coefficient shows a slight decline in overall inequality (Nolan and Maitre, 2000: 153).

Between 1994 and 1997 the distribution of the share of disposable income among the ten groups or deciles remained generally stable, although the share

Table 12.1: Corporatism and Social Trends*

Corporatist Rankings (Based on Calmsfor and Driffill (1988)	(1) Wage Dispersion: Ratio of Top to Bottom Decile for 1997	(2) Low Pay	(3) Total Expenditure on Social Protection as % of GDP for 1995	(4) Public Health Expenditure as % of GDP for 1997	(5) Income Inequality, Gini Coefficient for Mid 1990s	(6) % of Persons Below 50% of Mean Income for 1993
Austria	X**	7	6	11	4	X
Norway	X	X	10	9	6	X
Sweden	1	1	1	3	3	X
Denmark	X	X	2	5	1	1
Finland	2	2	3	13	2	X
Germany	X	8	8	1	10	5
Netherlands	X	4	4	10	5	2
Belgium	X	3	7	6	8	3
Australia	4	10	X	14	12	X
France	5	9	5	4	9	4
UK	6	11	9	12	13	7
Italy	3	5	11	15	16	6
Switzerland	X	6	X	2	7	X
US	8	13	X	7	15	X
Canada	X	X	X	8	11	X
Ireland	7	12	12	16	14	8
Trend in Ireland since 1987	Wage Disperson Increased by 7%	% Low Paid Increased by 17% up to 1994	Expenditure Decreased from 19.1% in 1990 to 18.9% of GDP in 1996	Expenditure Decreased by 9%	A Modest Decrease in Income Inequality up to Mid 1990s	Relative Income Poverty Rates Increased up to 1997

*Countries are ranked in ascending order from 1=most egalitarian/ highest % spent on social protection to the least egalitarian.
** An X denotes no data available for this country.

Sources
1. Barrett et al., 2000: 132.
2. OECD, 1996: 72; Barrett et al., 1999. Data refer to median earnings for years 1993,1994 and 1995. Low pay is defined as two-thirds of the median gross wage.
3. Eurostat Yearbook 1998/99, *A Statistical Eye on Europe 1987–1997*, edition: 264. Social protection encompasses all action by public or private bodies to relieve households/ individuals of a defined set of risks or needs associated with old age, sickness, childbearing, disability, unemployment etc. Expenditure on education is excluded.
4. OECD, *Health Data 99*, OECD, Paris, 1999.
5. Forester, 2000: 75, Table 2.2.
6. Layte et al., 2000: figures for 1987 to 1997, Table 9.1, p. 165. Comparative figures for 1993: Table 9.3, p. 169.

of the bottom decile did decline slightly. Nevertheless, the Gini coefficient was marginally lower. Thus, over the period 1987 to 1997, the evidence would appear to indicate a marginal decline in income inequality. While there are no data on income distribution after 1997, Nolan and Maitre (2000: 155) speculate that the tax and welfare changes since 1997 may well have favoured the higher income groups. Comparing income inequality in Ireland with other OECD countries provides a sharper picture of the trends. Out of sixteen countries, income inequality in Ireland was ranked third highest with only the US and Italy having higher levels of inequality (Table 12.1). However, the mean trend in income inequality in these countries as a whole showed a modest decrease in income inequality from the mid 1980s to the mid 1990s (Forester, 2000: 74, Table 2.1).

Trends in Poverty

Layte et al. (2000) provide a comprehensive survey of the most recent evidence on trends in poverty in Ireland. Between 1987 and 1997, relative income poverty rates increased. The proportion of households and the percentage of persons in those households below 40 per cent, 50 per cent or 60 per cent of mean equivalent household income all increased (Layte et al., 2000: Table 9.1, p. 165). In comparative terms, the proportion of persons below 50 per cent or 60 per cent of median income was higher in Ireland in 1987 than most other European countries (see Atkinson et al., 1995: 168). There appears to have been little change by 1993 when Ireland was ranked last out of eight European countries in the number of persons below 50 per cent and 60 per cent of mean income (see Table 12.1). However, the negative trends are reversed when other non-monetary indicators of deprivation (for example not being able to afford heating, new rather than second-hand clothes, not falling into debt for everyday household expenses, low levels of saving) are used in combination with relative income poverty. The percentage reporting basic deprivation fell from 33 per cent in 1987 to 25 per cent in 1994 and even more rapidly to 15 per cent by 1997 (Layte et al., 2000: 171). When the measures for deprivation and relative income are combined (i.e. those below mean income levels also reporting deprivation), it also shows a decrease over time. In 1987, there were 10 per cent of persons below the 50 per cent relative income poverty line who were also experiencing basic deprivation. By 1997, this had fallen to 7 per cent. Thus, there is a substantial fall in poverty between 1987 and 1997 using the combined measure of income and deprivation.

Given the acceleration of economic growth during the 1990s it is not surprising that mean household income increased significantly in real terms. In absolute terms, the number defined as poor has decreased. While 20 per cent of persons were below 50 per cent of mean household income in 1987, by 1997, if that mean household income for 1987 was index-linked to general price rises then only 7 per cent of persons would be below that indexed income level (Layte et al., 2000: 166).

Generally, it appears that absolute levels of poverty are declining, mean household income is growing and a combined measure of relative income and deprivation shows a decline, particularly since 1994. However, using only the measure of relative income differences, there is little change between 1987 and 1997 and, in comparative terms, Ireland is ranked as one of the most unequal. Paradoxically, although absolute poverty levels are disappearing, Ireland is becoming a more unequal society.

This trend in inequality tends to conform to what Layte and Whelan (2000: 105) describe as "maximally maintained inequality where any change is a consequence of expansion in opportunities rather than their distribution". Thus, in the period between 1973 and 1994, as opportunities expanded, there were increased levels of absolute class mobility in Ireland. However, Layte and Whelan (2000: 105) found little evidence of greater equality of opportunity or the emergence of a more meritocratic society and "no diminution in the impact of class origins on educational level" over time. In an analysis of the relationship between social class and education from 1980 to 1997, Smyth and Hannan (2000: 125) observe that there has been "a remarkable persistence of social class inequalities in educational outcomes".

SOCIAL OR LIBERAL CORPORATISM?

One of the significant outcomes of the period of partnership from 1987, and particularly since 1994, is the reduction in poverty in absolute terms and a decrease in the numbers experiencing relative deprivation. However, although all have gained, income inequality has increased. In comparative European terms, Ireland has one of the lowest levels of social protection expenditure but the highest levels of income inequality, wage dispersion and proportion of relatively low-paid workers. Thus, the Irish case, so far, can be seen to conform more closely to liberal corporatism, which emphasises the alleviation of poverty and a guaranteed minimum standard for everyone. The status quo, that is the existing distribution of resources or share out between the social classes, tends to remain stable. Where social mobility has occurred it is a result of the expansion of new job opportunities (for example in the managerial and professional/technical area) rather than any redistribution of opportunities between social classes. There appears, at least up to 1997, to be no evidence of any significant move towards more equality in the distribution of society's rewards. Indeed, as Table 12.1 indicates, in most cases the trend since 1987 is actually towards greater inequality.

CONCLUSION

In terms of the formal measures of centralisation and the development of horizontal and vertical structures, it would appear that social partnership in Ireland is moving towards a strong form of corporatism in the Nordic mould. The present period of social partnership agreements has created or coincided with an era of unparalleled success in the Irish economy. Since 1994 the economy has grown faster than any other European country, the labour force has expanded by over 40 per cent, unemployment has fallen and real average earnings have increased substantially. These achievements are by any measure substantial. Yet these economic achievements, while benefiting all sections of Irish society, have not yet been spread equitably across all social classes. The recent two agreements, Partnership 2000 and the Programme for Prosperity and Fairness, have as a core principle the reduction of inequality in Irish society. However, compared to many other European countries Ireland remains a more unequal society. To what extent the inequalities in Irish society can be challenged from within social partnership agreements remains an open question. For example, Hardiman (2000: 306) argues that the real process of policy development in such areas as taxation and social spending are mainly decided "outside the parameters of social partnership".

Social partnership in Ireland conforms most closely to a form of liberal or competitive corporatism. In the context of the debate on social pacts in the 1990s it can be described as an "experiment in competitive corporatism" to use its more contemporary usage (see Hardiman, 2000: 287). As already noted, competitive corporatism is an attempt to meet the economic demands for efficiency and defending existing social protection systems. However, competitive corporatism also has its critics. One consequence of competitive corporatism, according to Bispinck and Schulten, (2000: 210–211), is to transfer the micro economic logic of competition between companies to a macro-level and leads to competition between states. The agenda of the social pacts in the 1990s focus mainly on cost cutting strategies that allow a reduction in taxation levels, wages and social security contributions. As a niche strategy, they argue, it might work well for smaller countries but not if all European states enter into a race of "best" bad practices. From a European perspective, competitive corporatism is based on a "beggar-thy-neighbour" policy which is aimed at national benefits at the expense of other countries. For example, reductions in corporate tax rates directs foreign investment to the countries with the lowest rates of taxation. Indeed, competition between European states has already begun that has "led to a permanent fall in the wage share of national income with a massive redistribution from labour to profit income" (Bispinck and Schulten, 2000: 211). There are also negative consequences for social solidarity as national communities seek to defend their solidarity through competitive and productive measures rather than through the traditional policies of protection and redistribution. In a competitive corporatist regime, a society's ability to act in a solidaristic manner is likely to become totally dependent on its competitive success (Bispinck and Schulten, 2000: 213). Nevertheless, many commentators argue that competitive corporatism represents the best means, or at least the "least bad" solutions by all partners in hard times, of adjusting economies to the new demands of the global era while preserving social welfare systems intact, albeit at a reduced level (Rhodes, 1998: 195; Visser, 1998;[14] Goetschy, 2000; Negrelli, 2000).

---

14. For example, competitive corporatism has been seen as successful in the Netherlands as

To what extent the efficiency elements of this form of corporatism differ from the classical corporatism of the 1960s and 1970s remains in question.[15] It does, however, appear to "down play the equity function of more traditional social democratic forms of corporatism" (Rhodes, 1998: 200). For some, the social pacts of the 1990s represent an entirely new and different adjustment made between economy and society "aimed at overcoming the inefficiencies and rigidities of the past" (Negrelli, 2000: 109; see also Goetschy, 2000). Social partnership in Ireland, it has even been argued, "might possibly assist the formulation of a new concept of post-corporatist concertation, as it is emerging in many European countries" (O'Donnell and O'Reardon, 2000: 252). In this new scenario, O'Donnell and O'Reardon (2000) claim that information is the key resource influencing policy development and outcomes rather than the "traditional" power resources mobilised by organised interests. Unlike social corporatism where egalitarianism is central to the labour–capital class compromise, post-corporatist concertation appears to be based on the liberal pluralist view of society as composed of a series of competing interest groups. The bargaining effectiveness of a social partner depends on their ability to organise and solve problems with others rather than through representational power blocs such as the trade unions (O'Donnell and O'Reardon, 2000: 251). Although disagreements over distribution can occur, the implication of this post-corporatist thesis is that the conflicts are not simply reducible to inequalities between social classes and are best articulated by issue-specific organisations (for example combat poverty, the women's council, the unemployed and so on). However, as our earlier discussion indicated, it may be premature to assume the end of class as a social and economic reality. While issue-specific organisations have a valuable role to play, it is unlikely that an inclusive egalitarian agenda could be effectively pushed without strongly organised interest groups. Indeed, as Pochet and Fajertag (2000: 14) note, the inability of the Irish case to respond to the challenges of relative poverty and inequality "has prevented this otherwise successful experience from becoming a 'model' for other countries".

Leaving aside these criticisms, competitive corporatism can be evaluated in terms of its market logic that gives priority to efficiency and competitiveness over equity. It supersedes the social democratic corporatist notion of a labour–capital compromise based on a balance between efficiency and equity. The logic of this model directs effort and resources towards policies that result in positive economic outcomes such as increased investment and profits which are in turn related to economic growth and job creation. In the social or welfare arena, policies which are directly or indirectly beneficial for the economy are

---

it increased employer profits and improved their position in international markets. For unions it created more jobs and members as well maintaining vital aspects of the welfare state in spite of retrenchment (Visser, 1998).

15. As Moen and Wallerstein (1999: 234) note, "the Nordic variety of corporatism was associated not with protectionism and monopolistic pricing, but with free trade and the subsequent need to remain competitive".

encouraged, such as changes in personal taxation, welfare and investment in the educational infrastructure. It is important, however, to distinguish between policies in the social arena that have a neutral or negligible impact on economic efficiency and competitiveness but have a positive impact on matters of equity. In the Irish case, for example, a number of "competitively neutral" areas can be identified, such as inclusive housing, inclusive health care and inclusive education. The evidence of trends in these areas is not encouraging. The broad reliance on market mechanisms to control house prices has not proved successful.[16] Health care in Ireland has increasingly become a two-tier private and public system (Nolan and Wiley, 2000) and access to education is still heavily dependent on membership of a particular social class. Despite the market logic of competitive corporatism, there is no imperative that prevents these social areas from being comprehensively addressed.

REFERENCES

Allen, K. (2000). *The Celtic Tiger: The Myth of Social Partnership in Ireland.* Manchester University Press.

Atkinson, A., Rainwater, L. and Smeeding, T. (1995) *Income Distribution in OECD Countries: Evidence from the Luxembourg Income Study.* Paris: OECD.

Barrett, A., Callan, T. and Nolan, B. (1999) "Rising Wage Inequality, Returns to Education and Labour Market Institutions: Evidence from Ireland" *British Journal of Industrial Relations,* Vol. 37, No.1: 77–100.

Barrett, A., Fitzgerald, J. and Nolan, B. (2000) "Earnings Inequality, Returns to Education and Low Pay" in Nolan, B., O'Connell, J. and Whelan, C. (eds) *Bust to Boom? The Irish Experience of Growth and Inequality.* Dublin Institute of Public Administration.

Bispinck, R. and Schulten, T. (2000) "Alliance for Jobs – is Germany Following the Path of Competitive Corporatism?" in Fajertag, G. and Pochet, P. (eds) *Social Pacts in Europe – New Dynamics.* Brussels: European Trade Union Institute.

Bradley, J. (2000) "The Irish Economy in Comparative Perspective" in Nolan, B., O'Connell, J. and Whelan, C. (eds) *Bust to Boom? The Irish Experience of Growth and Inequality.* Dublin Institute of Public Administration.

Breen, R., Hannan, D., Rottman, D. and Whelan, C. (1990) *Understanding Contemporary Ireland: State, Class and Development in the Republic of Ireland.* London: Macmillan.

Bruno, M. and Sachs, J. (1985) *The Economics of Worldwide Stagflation.* Cambridge: Harvard University Press.

---

16. The numbers on the social housing list in Ireland increased from 23, 242 in 1991 to 39,176 in 1999, an increase of 69 per cent (source: Department of the Environment).

Calmsfor, L. and Driffill, J. (1988) "Centralisation of Wage Policy" *Economic Policy*, 6, April: 13–61.

Crepaz, M. (1992) "Corporatism in Decline? An Empirical Analysis of the Impact of Corporatism on Macroeconomic Performance and Industrial Disputes in 18 Industrialised Democracies" *Comparative Political Studies*, Vol. 25, No. 2: 139–168.

Crouch, C. (1977) *Class Conflict and the Industrial Relations Crisis*. London: Heinemann.

Crouch, C. (1985) "Corporatism in Industrial Relations: A Formal Model" in Grant, W. (ed.) *The Political Economy of Corporatism*. London: Macmillan.

Crouch, C. (1992) "The Fate of Articulated Industrial Relations Systems: A Stocktaking after the 'Neo-Liberal' Decade" in Regini, M. (ed.) *The Future of Labour Movements*. London: Sage Publications.

D'Art, D. (1992) *Economic Democracy and Financial Participation: A Comparative Study*. London: Routledge.

Dell'Aringa, C. and Lodovici, M. (1990) "Industrial Relations and Economic Performance" in Brunetta, R. and Dell'Aringa, C. (eds) *Labour Relations and Economic Performance*. London: Macmillan.

Ebbinghaus, B. and Visser, J. (2000) *Trade Unions in Western Europe Since 1945*. London: Macmillan.

Edwards, P. (1992) "Industrial Conflict: Themes and Issues in Recent Research" *British Journal of Industrial Relations*, Vol. 30: 361–404.

Elvander, N. (1974) "In Search of New Relationships: Parties, Unions and Salaried Employees Associations in Sweden" *Industrial and Labour Relations Review*, Vol. 28, No. 1: 60–74.

Fajertag, G. and Pochet, P. (2000) (eds) *Social Pacts in Europe – New Dynamics*. Brussels: European Trade Union Institute.

Ferner, A. and Hyman, R. (1998) (eds) *Changing Industrial Relations in Europe*. Oxford: Blackwell.

Fitzgerald, J. (2000) "The Story of Ireland's Failure and Belated Success" in Nolan, B., O'Connell, J. and Whelan, C. (eds) *Bust to Boom? The Irish Experience of Growth and Inequality*. Dublin Institute of Public Administration.

Forester, M. (2000) *Trends and Driving Factors in Income Distribution and Poverty in the OECD Area, Labour Market and Social Policy*. Occasional Paper, No. 42, Paris: OECD.

Freeman, R. and Katz, L. (1995) (eds) *Differences and Changes in Wage Structures*. Chicago: University of Chicago Press.

Goetschy, J. (2000) "The European Union and National Social Pacts: Employment and Social Protection Put to the Test of Joint Regulation" in Fajertag, G. and Pochet, P. (eds) *Social Pacts in Europe – New Dynamics*. Brussels: European Trade Union Institute.

Golden, M., Wallerstein, M. and Lange, P. (1999) "Postwar Trade-Union Organisation and Industrial Relations in Twelve Countries" in Kitschelt, H., Lange, P., Marks, G. and Stephens, J. (eds) *Continuity and Change in*

Contemporary Capitalism. Cambridge: Cambridge University Press.

Gunnigle, P. (1998) "More Rhetoric than Reality: Enterprise Level Industrial Relations Partnerships in Ireland" *Economic and Social Review*, Vol. 28, No. 4: 179–200.

Hall, P. (1999) "The Political Economy of Europe in an Era of Interdependence" in Kitschelt, H., Lange, P., Marks, G. and Stephens, J. (eds) *Continuity and Change in Contemporary Capitalism.* Cambridge: Cambridge University Press.

Hardiman, N. (1987) "Consensual Politics? Public Goods and Collective Action in Ireland" in Scholten, L. (ed.) *Political Stability and Neo-Corporatism: Corporatist Integration and Societal Cleavages in Western Europe.* London: Sage Publications.

Hardiman, N. (2000) "Social Partnership, Wage Bargaining, and Growth" in Nolan, B., O'Connell, J. and Whelan, C. (eds) *Bust to Boom? The Irish Experience of Growth and Inequality.* Dublin Institute of Public Administration.

Healy, S. and Reynolds, B. (1998) (eds) *Social Policy in Ireland: Principles, Practices and Problems.* Dublin: Oak Tree Press.

Henley, A. and Tsakalotos, E. (1993) *Corporatism and Economic Performance: A Comparative Analysis of Market Economies.* Aldershot: Edward Elgar.

ICTU (1989) *Trade Unions and Change: Shaping the Future.* Dublin: ICTU.

ICTU (1993) *New Forms of Work Organisation: Options for Unions.* Dublin.

Johansen, L. and Kristensen, O. (1982) "Corporatist Traits in Denmark, 1946–1976" in Lehmbruch, G. and Schmitter, P. (eds) *Patterns of Corporatist Policy Making.* London: Sage Publications.

Kennelly, B. and O'Shea, E. (1998) "The Welfare State in Ireland: A European Perspective" in Healy, S. and Reynolds, B. (eds) *Social Policy in Ireland: Principles, Practice and Problems.* Dublin: Oak Tree Press.

Kitschelt, H., Lange, P., Marks, G. and Stephens, J. (1999) (eds) *Continuity and Change in Contemporary Capitalism.* Cambridge: Cambridge University Press.

Kitschelt, H., Lange, P., Marks, G. and Stephens, J. (1999) "Introduction" in Kitschelt, H., Lange, P., Marks, G. and Stephens, J. (eds) *Continuity and Change in Contemporary Capitalism.* Cambridge: Cambridge University Press.

Korpi, W. (1983) *The Democratic Class Struggle.* London: Routledge and Kegan Paul.

Lane, P. (1998) "Profits and Wages in Ireland, 1987–1996" *Trinity Economic Papers Series*, Technical Paper No. 14, May.

Layte, R. and Whelan, C. (2000) "The Rising Tide and Equality of Opportunity: The Changing Class Structure" in Nolan, B., O'Connell, J. and Whelan, C. (eds) *Bust to Boom? The Irish Experience of Growth and Inequality.* Dublin Institute of Public Administration.

Layte, R., Nolan, B. and Whelan, C. (2000) "Trends in Poverty" in Nolan, B., O'Connell, J. and Whelan, C. (eds) *Bust to Boom? The Irish Experience of Growth and Inequality*. Dublin Institute of Public Administration.

Leddin, A. and Walsh, B. (1997) "Economic Stabilisation, Recovery and Growth: Ireland 1979–1996" *Irish Banking Review*, summer: 2–18.

Lehmbruch, G. (1984) "Concertation and the Structure of Corporatist Networks" in Goldthorpe, J. (ed.) *Order and Conflict in Contemporary Capitalism*. Oxford: Clarendon Press.

Maier, C. (1984) "The Preconditions for Corporatism" in Goldthorpe, J. (ed.) *Order and Conflict in Contemporary Capitalism*. Oxford: Clarendon Press.

Marin, B. (1985) "Austria – The Paradigm Case of Liberal Corporatism?" in Grant, W. (ed.) *The Political Economy of Corporatism*. London: Macmillan.

Martin, A. (1979) "The Dynamics of Change in a Keynesian Political Economy: The Swedish Case and its Implications" in Crouch, C. (ed.) *State and Economy in Contemporary Capitalism*. London: Croom Helm.

Moene, K. and Wallerstein, M. (1999) "Social Democratic Labour Market Institutions: A Retrospective Analysis" in Kitschelt, H., Lange, P., Marks, G. and Stephens, J. (eds) *Continuity and Change in Contemporary Capitalism*. Cambridge: Cambridge University Press.

Negrelli, S. (2000) "Social Pacts in Italy and Europe: Similar Strategies and Structures; Different Models and National Stories" in Fajertag, G. and Pochet, P. (eds) *Social Pacts in Europe – New Dynamics*. Brussels: European Trade Union Institute.

NESC (1996) *Strategy into the 21st Century*. Report No. 99, Dublin: National Economic and Social Council.

NESF (1996) *Post PCW-Negotiations – A New Deal*. Opinion No. 4, Dublin: National Economic and Social Forum.

NESF (1997) *A Framework for Partnership – Enriching Strategic Consensus through Participation*. Forum Report No. 16, Dublin: National Economic and Social Forum.

Nolan, B. and Maitre, B. (2000) "Income Inequality" in Nolan, B., O'Connell, J. and Whelan, C. (eds) *Bust to Boom? The Irish Experience of Growth and Inequality*. Dublin: Institute of Public Administration.

Nolan, B. and Wiley, M. (2000) *Private Practices in Irish Hospitals*. Economic and Social Research Institute, Dublin.

Nolan, B., O'Connell, J. and Whelan, C. (2000) (eds) *Bust to Boom? The Irish Experience of Growth and Inequality*. Dublin: Institute of Public Administration.

O'Brien, J. (1981) *A Study of National Wage Agreements in Ireland*. Dublin: Economic and Social Research Institute.

O'Cinneide, S. (Winter 1998/99) "Democracy and the Constitution" *Administration*, Vol. 46, No. 4: 41–58.

O'Connell, P. and Rottman, D. (1992) "The Irish Welfare State in Comparative Perspective" in Goldthorpe, J. and Whelan, C. (eds) *The Development of Industrial Society in Ireland*. The British Academy and Oxford University Press.

O'Donnell, R. and O'Reardon, C. (2000) "Social Partnership in Ireland's

Economic Transformation" in Fajertag, G. and Pochet, P. (eds) *Social Pacts in Europe – New Dynamics*. Brussels: European Trade Union Institute.

O'Donnell, R. and Thomas, D. (1998) "Partnership and Policy Making" in Healy, S. and Reynolds, B. (eds) *Social Policy in Ireland: Principles, Practices and Problems*. Dublin: Oak Tree Press.

O'Riain, S. and O'Connell, P. (2000) "The Role of the State in Growth and Welfare" in Nolan, B., O'Connell, J. and Whelan, C. (eds) *Bust to Boom? The Irish Experience of Growth and Inequality*. Dublin: Institute of Public Administration.

Pekkarinen, J., Pohjola, M. and Rowthorn, B. (1992) "Social Corporatism and Economic Performance: Introduction and Conclusions" in Pekkarinen, J., Pohjola, M. and Rowthorn, B. (eds) *Social Corporatism: A Superior Economic System*. Oxford: Clarendon Press.

Partnership 2000 for Inclusion, Employment and Competitiveness (1996) Dublin: Government Publications Office.

Pekkarinen, J., Pohjola, M. and Rowthorn, B. (1992) (eds) *Social Corporatism: A Superior Economic System*. Oxford: Clarendon Press.

Pochet, P. and Fajertag, G. (2000) "A New Era for Social Pacts in Europe" in Fajertag, G. and Pochet, P. (eds) *Social Pacts in Europe – New Dynamics*. Brussels: European Trade Union Institute.

Programme for Prosperity and Fairness (1999) Dublin: Government Publications Office.

Rhodes, M. (1996) "Globalisation and Western European Welfare States: A Critical Review of Recent Debates" *Journal of European Social Policy*, Vol. 6, No. 4: 305–27.

Rhodes, M. (1998) "Globalisation, Labour Markets and Welfare States: A Future of Competitive Corporatism" in Rhodes, M. and Meny, Y. (eds) *The Future of European Welfare: A New Social Contract*. London: Macmillan.

Rhodes, M. and Meny, Y. (1998) *The Future of European Welfare: A New Social Contract*? London: Macmillan.

Roche, W. (1994) "Pay Determination, the State and the Politics of Industrial Relations" in Murphy, M. and Roche, W. *Irish Industrial Relations in Practice*. Oak Tree Press.

Roche, W. K. and Ashmore, J. (2001) "Irish Unions in the 1990s: Testing the Limits of Social Partnership" in Griffin, G. (ed.) *Changing Patterns of Trade Unionism*. Sydney: Mansell.

Rowthorn, B. (1992) "Corporatism and Labour Market Performance" in Pekkarinen, J., Pohjola, M. and Rowthorn, B. (eds) *Social Corporatism: A Superior Economic System*. Oxford: Clarendon Press.

Smyth, E. and Hannan, D. (2000) "Education and Inequality" in Nolan, B., O'Connell, J. and Whelan, C. (eds) *Bust to Boom? The Irish Experience of Growth and Inequality*. Dublin: Institute of Public Administration.

Teague, P. (1995) "Pay Determination in the Republic of Ireland: Towards Social Corporatism?" *British Journal of Industrial Relations*, Vol. 33, No. 2: 253–73.

Teulings, C. and Hartog, J. (1998) *Corporatism or Competition? Labour Contracts, Institutions and Wage Structures in International Comparison.* Cambridge University Press.

Therborn, G. (1992) "Lessons from Corporatist Theorisations" in Pekkarinen, J., Pohjola, M. and Rowthorn, B. (eds) *Social Corporatism: A Superior Economic System.* Oxford: Clarendon Press.

Turner, T. (1999) "Income Equality in the Irish Labour Market: Changes in Earnings and Taxation Levels, 1987 to 1995" *Irish Business and Administrative Research*, Vol. 19/20, No. 1: 36–46.

Visser, J. (1990) "In Search of Inclusive Unionism" Bulletin of Comparative Labour Relations, No. 18. Devener: Kluwer Law and Taxation Publishers.

Visser, J. (1998) "Two Cheers for Corporatism, One for the Market: Industrial Relations, Wage Moderation and Job Growth in the Netherlands" *British Journal of Industrial Relations*, Vol. 36, No. 2: 269–292.

Williamson, P. (1989) *Corporatism in Perspective: An Introductory Guide to Corporatist Theory.* London: Sage Publications.

CHAPTER 13

The Transformation of Irish Employment Relations?

DARYL D'ART AND THOMAS TURNER

In March 1998 Dublin Airport was closed for the first time in its history. Thousands of SIPTU members took unofficial action in sympathy with fewer than 50 baggage handlers who were fighting for trade union recognition in Ryanair, one of Irelands' most profitable companies. The revival of the "sympathetic strike" on such a scale seemed an appalling anachronism in a society feeling increasingly at home with "social partnership".

Padraig Yeates, *Lockout: Dublin 1913*

INTRODUCTION

During the 1990s, Ireland underwent a period of rapid economic development. Furthermore, the decade was characterised by a high degree of social partnership that was far more comprehensive in scope than previous arrangements. In this context, it would seem plausible to argue that Irish employee relations underwent a fundamental transformation. According to the *Oxford English Dictionary*, transformation involves a change in which a previous state is "altered out of recognition". However, to measure the extent of change or transformation, it is necessary to use those criteria or concepts perceived to be central to defining or, at least, capturing the essence of employment relations. Such concepts should ideally form part of a theoretical tradition combining "a set of intellectual assumptions, key questions and fundamental concepts which generate a common set of reference points for social analysis over an extended period of time" (Holton, 1992: 50). The central concepts and concerns of employment relations include: individualism and collectivism; conflict and co-operation; control and participation; and the influence of political economy on work organisation and social class. Consequently, a transformation in Irish employment relations would involve a fundamental alteration in these areas. For example, a pronounced shift from traditional collectivism to an individualisation of the employment relationship, adversaralism to co-operation and control to participation would establish a new equilibrium. The various chapters in this book have examined the extent to which change in these areas have occurred.

THE POST-INDUSTRIAL THESIS AND THE ABSENCE OF POWER AND POLITICS

Three perspectives on post-industrial society were outlined in Chapter 1. One perspective emphasises the centrality of knowledge and information in the emergence of a new economy. A second perspective emphasises the end of hierarchical Fordist-type production of goods and services. In the post-Fordist analysis, information technology and the search for profitability apparently combine to create new forms of work organisation and relations in the workplace. A third perspective focuses on the political and ideological shifts in the advanced industrial societies since the 1970s, emphasising the emergence of the new right and the end of collective solidarities and social classes. These perspectives, it was argued, have featured prominently in contemporary analyses of change in industrial organisations and society. In general, these perspectives, particularly the information society and post-Fordist scenarios, suggest benign outcomes, both in work and society, emerging from the post-industrial order. For example, information society theorists argue that these trends connote the rise of a new class of knowledge workers whose work is characterised by high levels of technical skill and theoretical knowledge that require long periods of education and training. Advocates of post-Fordism associate the new economy with a combination of improved pay, employee participation, greater discretion in work and harmonious industrial relations. The developments associated with the emergence of the new post-industrial socio-economic order have been seen by many as signalling a break-up of the traditionally homogenous and collective experience of employment.

As a result, the salience of class and trade unions appear increasingly redundant. However, the claims of these theorists to a total transformation of industrial society, we argued, must be treated with some caution, particularly as their accounts appear to ignore considerations of power and politics.

Power and conflict are characteristic features of economic markets. Markets are structures in which certain economic agents are able, because of their power position, to reap special benefits in and through the market mechanism (Littler, 1993). Thus, the mobilisation of power resources is related to market outcomes. In the case of the outcomes for labour, this will depend on the influence labour brings to bear on capital. Consequently, the extent of power that workers can collectively mobilise defines the nature of the capital labour compromise and the resultant benefits for the parties.

At firm level, contests for control, conflict and co-operation at work have been intermittent but recurring features of all industrial relations systems since the 19th. century. Governments and management have continually attempted to regulate and minimise these conflicts or, alternatively, to encourage a shift towards co-operation at work. This may sometimes be complemented by corporatist arrangements at a political level. While these approaches have had varying levels of success in establishing an equilibrium, some indeed for a considerable period of time, they remained open to conflict and instability.

The root of this instability is to be found in the continually shifting and contending forces of conflict and co-operation that characterise the employment relationship in a market system. Consequently, fundamental change in Irish employee relations, or any system of industrial relations, would seem to require a transcendence of these traditional characteristics.

TRANSFORMATION OF THE EMPLOYMENT RELATIONSHIP?

It was argued in Chapter 2 that a paradigm shift in the nature of the employment relationship has not taken place. Despite the increased professionalisation of occupations, the decline of blue-collar work and the expansion of the service sector, the employment relationship remains characterised by the old contradictions and conflicts. The effective management of that relationship still seems to require a recognition and engagement with its complexities. Trade union recognition and collective bargaining, it was suggested, remained the most effective and flexible method of negotiating and renegotiating the maintenance of order and co-operation. Forms of non-unionism represent an attempt to escape these complexities and constraints. However, as shown in Chapter 2, the promised freedoms of non-unionism, in either its benign or coercive forms were rarely realised. This is hardly surprising given that the employment relationship remains rooted in a capitalist market context. As Weber (1958: 17) observes, "capitalism is identical with the pursuit of profit, and forever renewed profit, by means of continuous, rational, capitalistic enterprise". Given the primacy of profit making it is inevitable that employee interests or needs will be of secondary importance.

Despite the changed economic and industrial context, the traditional features that have characterised employment relations in a market system remain. For example, both Chapter 6 and Chapter 11 show that, despite the supposed shift from adversarialism to co-operation, surveys of employee attitudes indicated that there was no diminution in the "them and us" divide. Failure to bring about attitudinal change was attributed to four causes: employees' lack of choice over participating in the initiative; a lack of trust between workers and management; an inequality of status and outcomes; and lack of institutional support from top management. However, it appeared that firms with a cohesive and functioning union organisation had a greater potential to address these problems. There is considerable evidence to show that unions are more effective than individual employees in seeking improvements and safeguards for their members' working conditions and ensure that management are aware of the preferences of their members when new work arrangements are introduced (for example Cully et al., 1999). These findings support the argument in Chapter 2 for the utility and continuing relevance of trade unions and collective bargaining, both in representing employee interests and assisting in the management of the employment relationship.

Partnership at Work

As already noted, during the 1990s many commentators hailed the advent of "new industrial relations". Co-operative relations or partnership at work had seemingly replaced the "old" adversarialism. Such a dichotomy appears to suggest that conflict and co-operation are mutually exclusive. However, it is more accurate to regard both as integral to any system of industrial or employee relations. For instance, recent social partnership initiatives at firm level do not seem to have eradicated the traditional conflicts and tensions around the sharing of control in the workplace. An extensive survey of Irish companies reported in Chapter 3 seems to confirm the above perceptions. This chapter questioned the degree to which new modes of collaborative production have gained ground in Ireland during the 1990s. While there was some evidence of collaborative production, exclusionary forms of decision making were shown to dominate. The authors reject any suggestion of transformation. These findings are similar to the study reported in Chapter 1, which examined the extent of worker autonomy and participation in decision making. In the seven countries studied, there was little evidence that participative organisational practices had made significant incursions into traditional managerial prerogatives in the workplace. The survey of union members reported in Chapter 11 on new workplace initiatives, indicated that these initiatives were largely perceived to have either no impact or, in some cases, involved a negative outcome for workers. The development of a genuine sense of partnership at firm level does not seem to have occurred to any significant extent in the companies surveyed. Despite the rhetoric of empowerment, the old conflicts centred on control and managerial prerogative apparently persist. Nevertheless, the Irish Congress of Trade Unions considers the development of social partnership at firm level as a central objective of recent agreements. Indeed, the Deputy General Secretary of ICTU "saw Partnership 2000 as the last window of opportunity to deepen the national partnership process onto a genuine partnership at the level of the workplace". For congress it would "determine whether social partnership developed or died" (O'Donovon, 1999: 118).

Partnership at National Level

In Chapter 12 it was argued that social partnership in Ireland conforms most closely to a form of liberal or competitive corporatism. Competitive corporatism is an attempt to meet the economic demands for efficiency and defending existing social protection systems. However, it appears to diminish the equity function of more traditional social democratic forms of corporatism. There is an implicit assumption in the literature on competitive corporatism of the end of class as a social and economic reality. In this model the bargaining effectiveness of a social partner depends on their ability to organise and solve problems with others rather than through representational power blocs such as the trade unions (O'Donnell and O'Reardon, 2000: 251). There can be little doubt that co-operation between trade unions, employers and government in social partnership at national level has occurred in a period of dramatic economic growth. While the contribution of social partnership to this prosperity is arguable, nevertheless, during this period trade unions have exercised considerable wage restraint. Yet, these economic achievements, while benefiting all sections of Irish society, have not yet been spread equitably across all social classes. Indeed, as Chapters 11 and 12 show, the outcomes in terms of solidaristic wages, income inequality, social expenditure and the universality of the social welfare system have been disappointing compared with similar arrangements in many European countries. It may be that achievements in these areas are of secondary importance. Indeed, it could be argued that union participation in national level partnership was not an offensive but a survival strategy designed to cope with an increasingly hostile environment. Hardiman (1992: 347) suggests that the reason for the trade unions' initial entry into partnership agreements in 1987 was to avoid the fate of their counterparts in the UK. There, government hostility and legislative instruments aimed at curbing union behaviour led to falling union membership and steep reductions in the unionised proportion of the workforce. It is questionable if the partnership strategy adopted by the Irish trade union movement has entirely avoided such an outcome.

National Partnership and Union Outcomes

Chapters 10 and 11 noted the existence of propitious political and economic circumstances that would normally be expected to favour union growth. Instead, union density levels have continued to fall and there is increasing employer resistance to trade unions. In Chapter 10 it is argued that espoused government policy appears to support a strong trade union role in industrial relations, but does little to encourage new companies to recognise trade unions. The trade union movement's response to this problem was to seek formal procedures that would oblige employers to recognise a trade union where employees wished for such representation. In the Irish case, the proposed procedures fall short of mandatory union recognition and compare unfavourably with the more direct process established in the UK. Furthermore, as Chapter 10 notes, the general disincentives to industrial action contained in the proposed Bill could delimit one of the historically most effective measures of gaining union recognition. Despite the participation of trade unions in drawing up the procedures, there appears to be a high level of ambivalence as to the desirability of a mandatory process. This may be due to the traditional attachment to voluntarism in Irish industrial relations. In this context, a mandatory union recognition process may be associated with coercive or oppressive state interference in the business enterprise. However, such a position fails to acknowledge the potentially complementary nature of such a process to any democratic pluralist society. As we have seen in a number of chapters, conflicts of interest and disparity of power between the employer and employees are permanent characteristics of relations at work in a market economy. Consequently, the freedom of employees to exercise choice in joining a union may be severely circumscribed or overridden by employer preference and superior power. Indeed, as reported in Chapter 10, few of the Labour Court recommendations supporting the recognition of a trade union tend to be accepted by employers. An essential aspect of pluralist democratic values is a recognition of the right of interest groups to combine and have an effective voice in their own destiny. From this perspective, part of the state's function is to ensure the freedom of combination and also check the dominance and power of strong interests who might suppress the exercise of choice and distort interest group competition. Thus, mandatory union recognition merely creates the conditions in which a democratic choice can be exercised free from interference or coercion by superior power. It is at once both a manifestation and a concrete realisation of democratic pluralism. The Irish constitution guarantees employees the right to join or not to join a trade union. Legislation on union recognition would enable employees to fully exercise these rights free from overt or covert interference by the more powerful. As presently constituted, the Bill on union recognition falls far short of this basic requirement and, it has been suggested, avoids the issue. In our view, a simple and effective union recognition process is a necessity if trade unions are to play a continuing role in the new economy.

THE FUTURE OF COLLECTIVE BARGAINING AND TRADE UNIONS

A primary purpose of this book was to assess the extent of a transformation in Irish employee relations under the impact of international political and economic developments since the 1980s. Predictions by post-Fordist and information society theorists of a fundamentally benign and liberatory change in the nature of relations at work do not seem to have been borne out. Indeed, the generality of employees in the European Union appear to be working harder and in more stressful conditions than ever before (Merllie and Paoli, 2001). Such an outcome is not surprising when the contextual factors of power and politics in which these changes have taken place are considered. These changes must be seen against a political backdrop of the increasing dominance of so-called new right ideology. Though to call it new may be a misnomer, as this ideology is firmly rooted in early 19th century economic doctrine of classical liberalism with its espousal of individualism, unrestricted free-play of market forces and the pursuit of profit. The operation of this ideology was one of the factors that brought trade unions and social democratic parties into being in the first instance.

An underlying assumption of many post-industrial theories is that global competition, information technology, industrial restructuring, social and economic change are the result of inexorable natural forces. In particular, the pressures from international markets creates an economic and political paradigm which assumes that the regulation of employment and the employment relationship is best left to the unrestricted free-play of market forces. Collective bargaining becomes increasingly irrelevant, either as a mechanism for regulating wages and conditions at firm level or for articulating the interests of labour as an organised group or class at national level. In these scenarios, the role of human agency and the scope to mediate or control these changes through social democratic or trade union action is either absent or understated. Yet, contrary to this technological or economic determinist view of social and organisational change, historical and comparative research suggests scope for choice (Visser, 1996).

While there are competitive constraints in an international market for a small open economy, there is also a wide range of choices available to unions, employers and the government in the development of economic and social policies. Market signals do not, in any case, provide solutions; rather markets pose economic problems and challenges that require management and interpretation. As noted in Chapter 12, the logic of the liberal or competitive model of corporatism directs effort and resources towards policies that increase economic efficiency while encouraging social policies which are directly or indirectly beneficial for the economy. It was argued that even within the parameters of this model it is possible to distinguish between policies in the social arena that have a neutral or negligible impact on economic efficiency but have a positive impact on matters of equity and democracy. However, there is little evidence of more equitable outcomes in the areas of health, housing, education and wealth distribution as a result of national partnership. These disappointing results may be explained by the Irish Congress of Trade Union's lack of a strong social democratic political arm. Although recent agreements have emphasised social inclusion and a more equitable distribution of wealth, the political power necessary to implement these aspirations appears to be absent. Given the prevailing balance of political forces these are undoubtedly difficult areas for the union movement to effect progress. Yet, even the modest goals of trade union growth or consolidation do not appear to have been realised. Participation in national bargaining has not halted union decline or consolidated union organisation at firm level. A prerequisite for the initiation and continuance of bargained corporatism, Chapter 11 points out, is that unions possess and exercise power in the labour market. This, in large measure, will depend on the level of unionisation among the employed workforce (see Traxler et al., 2001: Chapter 7).

If trade unions and collective bargaining are to remain the principal method of determining wages and working conditions, we would argue that additional supportive mechanisms are necessary. In particular, two initiatives would help maintain the continuance of collective bargaining. First, that employees can exercise a free choice with regard to union representation. Many studies have shown that a much greater proportion of employees would avail of trade union representation if a union were available at their workplace (Hartley, 1992: 166. Green, 1990). Unfortunately, the proposed procedures for union recognition seem unlikely to provide this choice. Secondly, there is a need for enabling legislation to support union organisation and employee participation at firm level. An example of such legislation is the extensive labour laws designed to legitimise and strengthen workplace trade unionism in Sweden.[1] These issues are central not only for trade unions but also for the continuance of corporatist arrangements.

A critical stance towards social partnership agreements does not necessarily imply opposition to such agreements. Indeed, the positive outcomes from corporatist arrangements throughout Europe have been substantial not only for trade unions and their members but for society generally. Corporatist arrangements have been associated with higher levels of social welfare and more universal systems, lower levels of inequality, lower levels of wage dispersion, higher levels of union density and state support for union organisation at workplace level. Corporatism as an institutional mechanism can modify the unequal outcomes of a free market in terms of wealth, education and life chances generally. These arrangements have the potential to construct a workable compromise between the demands of the market and humanistic democratic values.

A critical feature of any compromise is its conditional nature which is open to various destabilising influences. Consequently, its maintenance requires continual negotiation and adjustment. The contemporary ideological climate renders the restatement of these obvious truisms a necessity. As noted in Chapter 12, some commentators appear to suggest that conflict between capital and labour has been largely superseded by national partnership. A recent resurgence of industrial conflict, threatening the continuance of partnership, questions such a claim. Strikes, those supposedly "appalling anachronisms", seem to be displaying a capacity for vigorous endurance. Post-Fordist, post industrialists and information society theorists might characterise this recurrence as merely a dying echo "of old unhappy far off things and battles long ago". Their millenarian expectations of the imminent dawn of a new harmonious order, this book would suggest, seems a long way from being realised.

REFERENCES

Cully, M., Woodland, S., O'Reilly, A. and Dix, G. (1999) *Britain at Work As Depicted by the 1998 Workplace Employee Relations Survey.* London: Routledge.

Green, F. (1990) "Trade Union Availability and Trade Union Membership in Britain" *Manchester School of Economic and Social Studies*, Vol. 58: 378–94.

---

1. These laws include: Board Representation of employees, 1973; Act on Shop Stewards, 1974; Work Safety Law, 1974; Security of Employment Act, 1974; Act on Employee Participation and Decision Making Act, 1977.

Hardiman, N. (1992) "The State and Economic Interests: Ireland in Comparative Perspective" in Goldthorpe, J. and Whelan, C. (eds) *The Development of Industrial Society in Ireland*. Oxford University Press.

Hartley, J. (1992) "Joining a Trade Union" in Hartley, J. and Stephenson, G. (eds) *Employment Relations: The Psychology of Influence and Control at Work*. Blackwell Oxford.

Holton, R. (1992) *Economy and Society*. London: Routledge.

Littler, C. (1993) "Industrial Relations Theory: A Political Economy Perspective" in Adam, R. and Metz, N. (eds) *Industrial Relations Theory*. New Jersey: Scarecrow Press.

Merllie, D. and Paoli, P. (2001) *Ten Years of Working Conditions in the European Union – Summary*. European Foundation for the Improvement of Living and Working Conditions: Dublin.

O'Donnell, R. and O'Reardon, C. (2000) "Social Partnership in Ireland's Economic Transformation" in Fajertag, G. and Pochet, P. (eds) *Social Pacts in Europe: New Dynamics*. Brussels: European Trade Union Institute.

O'Donovan, P. (1999) "Social Partnership: A Trade Union Perspective" in Reynolds, B. and Healy, S. (eds) *Social Partnership in a New Century*. Dublin: Cori Justice Commission.

Traxler, F., Sabine Blaschke, S. and Kittel, B. (2001) *National Labour Relations in Internationalised Markets: A Comparative Study of Institutions, Change, and Performance*. Oxford: Oxford University Press.

Visser, J. (1996) "Traditions and Transitions in Industrial Relations: A European View" in Van Ruysseveldt, J. and Visser, J. (eds) *Industrial Relations in Europe Traditions and Transitions*. London: Sage Publications.

Weber, M. (1958) *The Protestant Ethic and the Spirit of Capitalism*. New York: Charles Scribner and Sons.

Yeates, P. (2001) *Lockout: Dublin 1913*. Dublin: Gill and Macmillan.

Index

adversarialism, 36, 73, 128-9, 139, 304
Ahern, Bertie, 170, 186
alienation, 270, 271
Amalgamated Transport and General Workers' Union (ATGWU)
  militant stance, 162
  survey, **154-66**, 214, 261-2, **263-9**
  see also solidarity
Amalgamated Union of Engineering Workers (AUEW (TASS)), 208
American Federation of Labor and the Congress of Industrial Organisation (AFL/CIO)
  survey, 41
analysis
  emic, 109-10
  etic, 109, 110
Ancient Guild of Incorporated Brick and Stonelayers' Trade Union (AGIBSTU), 211
Anderson, Brian
  and Industrial Relations Act, 1990, 174
Association of Inspectors of Taxes (AIT), 212
Association of Scientific, Technical and Managerial Staffs (ASTMS), 208
Australia, 162
Austria, 259
  National Assembly, 277
  works council system, 278
autonomy, 10

Barron, Justice, 175, 176n
behavioural commitment, 130-1
Bennetton, 9-10
Boreham, P., 10-11
British Journal of Industrial Relations, 93n, 127n

Britain, 162 *see also* United Kingdom
brownfield companies, 99-102
Bruton, Richard, 246
Building and Allied Trades Union (BATU), 211
bureaucracy, 120-1
Burton group, 10
Bush, George, (Snr), administration, 40

Canada, 38
capital, 3, 5, 279
capitalism, 1, 2, 3, 12, 14, 32, 148, 303
capitalist democracy, 37
Celtic Tiger, 58, 73, 85, 245
Central Arbitration Committee (UK), 239
Central Review Committee, 283
Central Statistics Office, 188n
Chartists, 148
Chicago school of economists, 13, 37
Circuit Court, 242
class, 21
  and collective solidarity, 14
  and educational attainment, 14
  end of, **12-14**, 147, 294
  fragmentation, 162, 163
  identity, 160
  politics, 147
  and stratification, 130
  struggle, 279
Code of Practice on Voluntary Dispute Resolution, 241, 242
  procedures, 251
co-determination, 271
collaborative production, 15, 268, 304
  and bargaining arrangements, 88
  and change, 81-2, 84-5
  importance of, 89-90